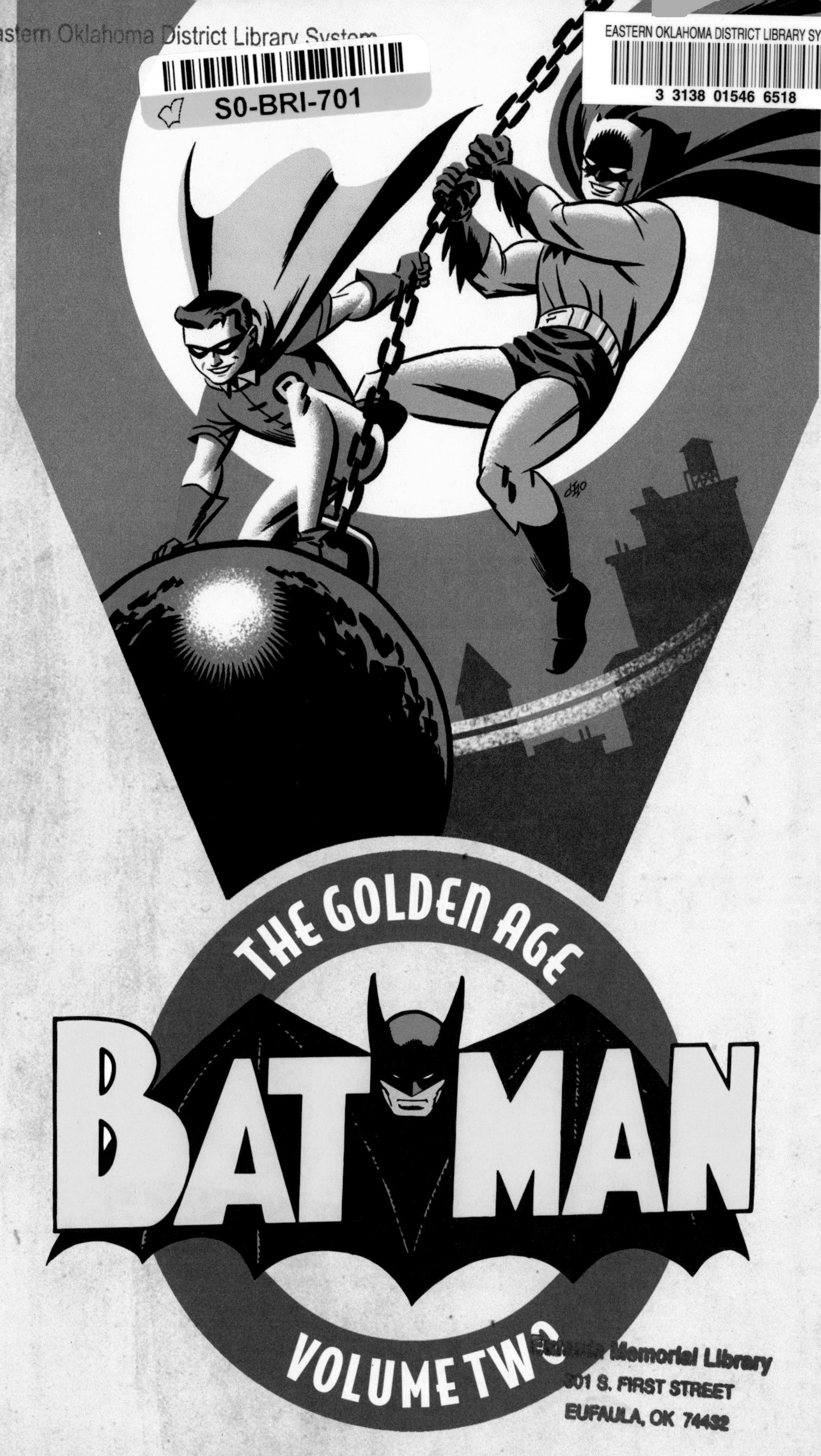
THE GOLDEN AGE
BATMAN
VOLUME TWO

BILL FINGER
WRITER

BOB KANE
ARTIST
WITH **JERRY ROBINSON** AND **GEORGE ROUSSOS**

MICHAEL CHO
COVER ARTIST

BATMAN created by **BOB KANE** with **BILL FINGER**.

THE GOLDEN AGE

BATMAN

VOLUME TWO

WHITNEY ELLSWORTH Editor – Original Series **JEB WOODARD** Group Editor – Collected Editions
STEVE COOK Design Director – Books **LOUIS PRANDI** Publication Design

BOB HARRAS Senior VP – Editor-in-Chief, DC Comics

President **DIANE NELSON**
Publisher **DAN DiDIO**
Publisher **JIM LEE**
President & Chief Creative Officer **GEOFF JOHNS**
Executive VP – Business & Marketing Strategy, Direct to Consumer & Global Franchise Management **AMIT DESAI**
Senior VP – Direct to Consumer **SAM ADES**
VP – Talent Development **BOBBIE CHASE**
Senior VP – Art, Design & Collected Editions **MARK CHIARELLO**
Senior VP – Sales & Trade Marketing **JOHN CUNNINGHAM**
Senior VP – Business Strategy, Finance & Administration **ANNE DePIES**
VP – Manufacturing Operations **DON FALLETTI**

LAWRENCE GANEM VP – Editorial Administration & Talent Relations
ALISON GILL Senior VP – Manufacturing & Operations
HANK KANALZ Senior VP – Editorial Strategy & Administration
JAY KOGAN VP – Legal Affairs
THOMAS LOFTUS VP – Business Affairs
JACK MAHAN VP – Business Affairs
NICK NAPOLITANO VP – Manufacturing Administration
EDDIE SCANNELL VP – Consumer Marketing
COURTNEY SIMMONS Senior VP – Publicity & Communications
JIM (SKI) SOKOLOWSKI VP – Comic Book Specialty Sales & Trade Marketing
NANCY SPEARS VP – Mass, Book, Digital Sales & Trade Marketing

BATMAN: THE GOLDEN AGE VOLUME 2

DC Comics, 2900 West Alameda Ave., Burbank, CA 91505
Printed by LSC Communications, Salem, VA, USA. 1/13/17. First Printing.
ISBN: 978-1-4012-6808-4

Library of Congress Cataloging-in-Publication Data is Available.

All stories by **BILL FINGER** and all art by **BOB KANE** except where noted.

*These titles were originally untitled and are titled here for reader convenience.

Until the 1970s, it was not common practice in the comic book industry to credit all stories. In the preparation of this collection, we have used our best efforts to review any surviving records and consult any available databases and knowledgeable parties. We regret the innate limitations of this process and any missing or misassigned attributions that may occur.

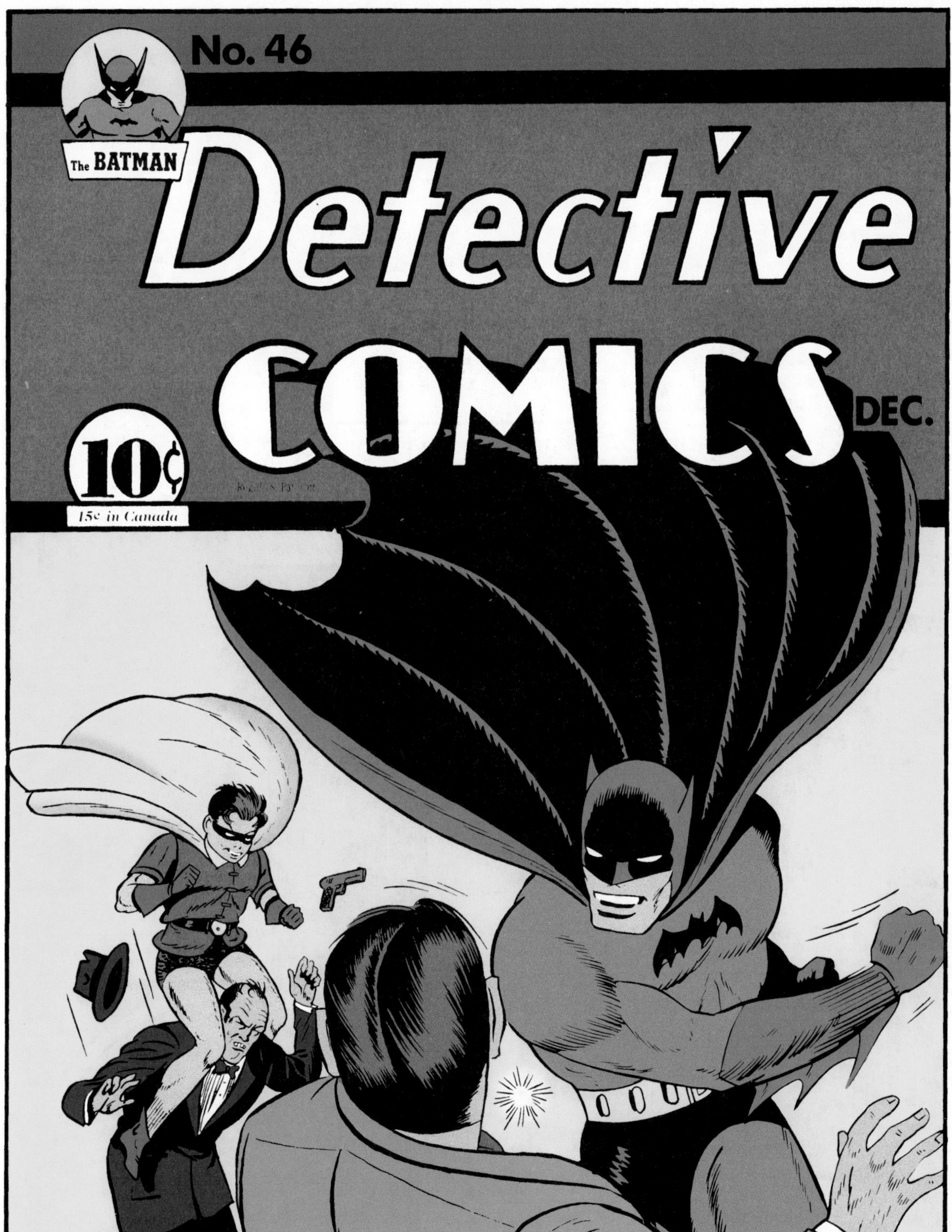
No. 46
The BATMAN
Detective
COMICS
DEC.
10¢
15¢ in Canada

BATMAN
WITH Robin
-THE BOY WONDER-
BY- BOB KANE
ONCE AGAIN CRIME REARS ITS UGLY HEAD TO PREY UPON SOCIETY..... AND ONCE AGAIN EMERGES THAT SUPER-FOE OF CRIME — THE BATMAN! GARBED IN THE HUES OF NIGHT ITSELF, HE HOVERS ABOVE THE HORDES OF EVIL LIKE IMPENDING DOOM.... AND ALWAYS AT HIS SIDE, LIKE A STRONG RIGHT ARM, IS GRINNING, RECKLESS ROBIN, THE BOY WONDER, WHO IS SOMETHING OF A CRIME-BUSTER IN HIS OWN RIGHT!
LETCHER SILVER Co.
AS THE THIEVES BEGIN TO LOOT A WAREHOUSE, SUDDENLY A BAT-CLOAKED SHAPE SWINGS OVER THEIR HEADS..
...TO PLUMMET DOWN LIGHTLY ATOP THE WAREHOUSE STEPS!

3 UNDAUNTED BY OVERWHELMING ODDS, THE BATMAN STANDS HIS GROUND!

As the thugs shakily pick themselves up!...
Ow! My head!
What hit me?
'Musta been a hurricane passing by!
.... The Batman catapults forward... and down they go again!
Zorn's Candy Shop
Moving easily, deceptively swift as a striking snake, the Batman weaves about the men, his fists inducing quick sleep!
Okay.... You can relax now!
As his hand closes about a surviving hoodlum....
D..Don't hit me! Please don't hit me!
Wha th'...! A kid... a kid no more than seventeen at most!
Okay, kid, I won't hit you-but you're going to jail like the rest of your pals!
Jail! Don't send me to jail! It would kill my mother! She doesn't know about this!
I should think she wouldn't, but just the same, I...
Don't send me to jail!... Please! I'll do anything! I'll even tell you about something, something big!
"Something big!" What are you talking about? Spill it!
You gotta promise to protect me! If they ever knew, my life wouldn't be worth two pins!

THESE MEN CAN'T HEAR A THING! THEY'RE BLISSFULLY UNCONSCIOUS OF EVERYTHING! TALK!
WELL.... CARSTAIRS, THE RACKETEER, IS PLANNING SOMETHING, CAUSE HE GOT A BIG GANG TOGETHER LAST NIGHT!... HE SAYS WE'RE GONNA BE MILLIONAIRES IF WE STRING ALONG WITH HIM!

HE SAYS THE PEOPLE AND THE COPS WON'T PUT UP ANY FIGHT WHEN WE DO OUR JOBS! HE'S WORKING WITH SOME PROFESSOR THAT PLANNED THE WHOLE THING!

ALL OF US GOT A VIAL OF THESE PILLS. THEY'RE SUPPOSED TO MAKE US IMMUNE TO THE PROFESSOR'S STUFF IF WE SWALLOW ONE!
IN THAT CASE, I'LL TAKE A FEW PILLS WITH ME. THEY MIGHT COME IN HANDY AT THE RIGHT MOMENT! NOW... WHEN IS THE NEXT MEETING OF CARSTAIRS' MEN?

ER SILVE CO.
WE'RE SUPPOSED TO GO TO ONE TONIGHT!.... BUT IT LOOKS LIKE THESE GUYS WON'T BE ABLE TO GO.... IF YOU'RE GONNA TURN 'EM IN!
BOTH YOU AND THESE MEN WILL GO! IT WILL BE WORTH IT IF I CAN FIND OUT A WAY TO COMBAT THE PROFESSOR'S MENACE TO THE PEOPLE.

YOU'RE GOING TO THAT MEETING TONIGHT! I'LL MEET YOU HERE TOMORROW NIGHT AT TWELVE SHARP! YOU'RE TO TELL ME ALL THAT WENT ON! UNDERSTAND?
(GULP!) OKAY, IF YOU SAY SO!

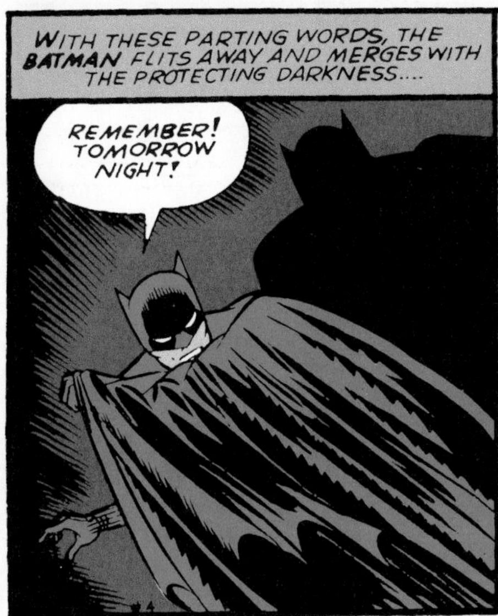
WITH THESE PARTING WORDS, THE BATMAN FLITS AWAY AND MERGES WITH THE PROTECTING DARKNESS....
REMEMBER! TOMORROW NIGHT!

GONE! ...IT'S... IT'S AS IF HE DISAPPEARED IN THE SHADOWS -- LIKE - LIKE A GHOST!

SOMETIME LATER THE HOODLUMS AWAKEN, AND RISE ON SHAKY LEGS.....
GOSH! ME JAW FEELS AS IF IT'S BROKE!
THE BATMAN! HE AIN'T HERE! WADAYA SUPPOSE HAPPENED?
IT'S A BREAK FER US, ANYWAY! C'MON, LET'S GET GOIN' T'THAT MEETIN'! --- BUT QUICK!

INTO THE ROOM WALKS A MAN ONCE THOUGHT DEAD-- THE CRAFTY, DIABOLICAL, ARCH-CRIMINAL, PROFESSOR HUGO STRANGE!

I WILL GIVE YOU YOUR INSTRUCTIONS NOW. FOR TOMORROW WE STRIKE! TOMORROW AT NOON-TIME! NOW, LISTEN CAREFULLY...

THE BANK LOOTED, THE THUGS RACE OUTSIDE TO MEET POLICEMEN WHO WERE ATTRACTED BY THE TELLER'S SHOUT....

TREMBLING WITH FEAR, THE POLICE QUAIL BEFORE THE BANDITS... ICY TERROR CLUTCHES THEIR HEARTS.....
D-DON'T HIT ME!
HAW, HAW! LOOK AT HIM!... SCARED STIFF! HAW HAW!
FIRST TIME I EVER SAW A POLICEMAN SCARED BEFORE! SURE IS A NOVELTY!
FEAR!!! FEAR! FEAR!
AND ALL OVER THE CITY IT IS THE SAME! BANDITS LOOT BANKS, WARE-HOUSES, STORES, AS A STRANGE MALADY SEIZES THE PEOPLE... FEAR... FEAR HAS BECOME MASTER OF THE CITY!
AND LATER THAT DAY, WHEN THE BANDITS BRING THEIR PLUNDER, THAT MASTER OF VILLAINY, PROFESSOR STRANGE, IS JUBILANT!
THAT STUFF OF YOURS IS A SUCCESS, PROFESSOR! AND WHAT A SUCCESS! THERE'S THE PROOF ON THE TABLE!
I KNEW MY "FEAR" DUST WOULD BE! AND I HAVE A BIGGER PLAN FOR IT! AT TONIGHT'S MEETING I'LL TELL YOU ALL ABOUT IT!
AS THE MEN PREPARE TO LEAVE, PROFESSOR STRANGE'S SHREWD EYES GROW HARD...
AT LAST NIGHT'S MEETING THAT BOY THERE LOOKED NERVOUS, STRAINED! I'VE A FEELING HE'S UP TO SOMETHING.
YEAH... HE DOES AT THAT! I'LL HAVE A FEW OF THE BOYS TAIL HIM!
THAT NIGHT, AS A COWLED FIGURE DARTS ACROSS SHADOWY STREETS, THE CLOCK TOLLS MIDNIGHT HOUR.... IS THIS TOLLING THE DEATH-KNELL OF THE BATMAN? DOES THE BATMAN KEEP A RENDEZVOUS WITH DEATH?
QUICK! TELL ME! IS THE PROFESSOR RESPONSIBLE FOR WHAT HAPPENED THIS AFTERNOON?
I THOUGHT YOU'D NEVER GET HERE!
BUT THE BATMAN IS NEVER TO HEAR THE ANSWER TO THAT QUESTION, FOR AT THAT MOMENT A CRUSHING BLOW RENDERS HIM SENSELESS!
... AND WHEN THE BATMAN AWAKENS, HE SEES BEFORE HIM A FACE HE HAD HOPED NEVER TO SEE AGAIN....
PROFESSOR STRANGE! YOU-YOU'RE THE PROFESSOR! I SHOULD HAVE KNOWN IT WOULD BE YOU!
GREETINGS, BATMAN,.... IT SEEMS THAT FATE HAS SEEN TO IT THAT WE SHOULD MEET AGAIN! FATE HAS BEEN UNKIND THIS TIME... TO YOU!

OLD ENEMIES, CRIMINAL AND CRIME-SMASHER STAND BEFORE EACH OTHER!
I SAY UNKIND BECAUSE THIS TIME I SHALL VENT MY FULL HATRED UPON YOU! YOU SHALL FEEL IT SLOWLY. SLOWLY BUT SURELY!
DO YOUR WORST! YOU DON'T SCARE ME WITH YOUR MELODRAMATIC THREATS!
AT A SIGNAL FROM THE MADMAN, THE BATMAN'S ARMS ARE SUDDENLY PINIONED TO HIS SIDES AND A HULKING THUG SPRINGS FORWARD!
NOW GO TO IT!
AS THE BATMAN SAGS UNDER THE EFFECT OF THE CRUEL FOUL BLOW. THE OTHER THUGS IN THE ROOM SPRING FORWARD AND DIRECT BLOWS AT HIM AS HE VALIANTLY TRIES TO FIGHT AGAINST OVERWHELMING ODDS!
THIS IS FOR WHAT HE DID TO ME ON THE PIER!
GIVE IT TO HIM! KILL HIM!
AS THEIR NEMESIS SLUMPS HELPLESSLY BEFORE THEM, THE COWARDLY THUGS SUBJECT HIM TO A TERRIBLE BEATING!
..UNTIL FINALLY HIS SENSES SWIM AND HE IS DROWNED IN WELCOME OBLIVION!
BOY, CAN HE TAKE IT!
YEAH! I THOUGHT HE WOULD NEVER DROP!
TAKE HIM IN TO THE NEXT ROOM!
TIME CREEPS BY, AND UNDER THE BLESSED SLEEP, THE BATMAN'S BODY SLOWLY GAINS REST AND RECOUPS ITS STRENGTH
GOT TO GET UP!... MUST! AH. THAT'S BETTER!... I ACHE ALL OVER! HEAR A VOICE!
..AND WITH MY "FEAR" DUST WE CAN TAKE OVER THE COUNTRY! IF WE SPRAY IT OVER THE CITY, THE COUNTRY, EVEN THE CAPITOL ITSELF, WHO WILL OPPOSE US?
ALL THE HIGH MEN IN PUBLIC OFFICE WILL BE AFRAID OF US! THEY WILL LET ME TAKE OVER THE REINS OF THE GOVERNMENT! I CAN BE DICTATOR OF AMERICA! UNDER THE INFLUENCE OF MY "FEAR DUST" THE WORLD WILL BOW!

FIRST WE MUST PUT "FEAR" DUST INTO THE PEOPLE. THEY MUST BE AFRAID TO BUY, BE AFRAID OF INVASION,.... SO AFRAID THAT ALL WILL BE CHAOS! THEN IS THE TIME TO STRIKE!
HERE ARE PAPERS GIVING YOU ALL INSTRUCTIONS WHERE TO SPRAY THE "FEAR" DUST! I MYSELF WILL GET MY PLANE AND DISCHARGE DUST OVER THE CITY!
CAN'T TRUST MYSELF TO RUSH THEM YET, TILL I GET MY FULL STRENGTH BACK! MUST WAIT!
SOMETIME LATER THE THREE MEN LEFT AS GUARDS SUDDENLY SEE THE DOOR OPEN AND A SLUMPING FIGURE STAND WEAKLY ON THE THRESHOLD!
OH.... STILL HERE!... I...... THOUGHT...
WELL-WELL! LOOK WHO'S UP!
C'MON- LET'S GET TO WORK ON HIM AGAIN AND PUT HIM BACK TO SLEEP.
SUDDENLY THE SLUMPING FORM STRAIGHTENS, SMOOTH MUSCLES RIPPLE, SUGGESTING HIDDEN STRENGTH, AS THE GIGANTIC FRAME OF THE BATMAN STANDS TOWERING IN THE LIGHT!
SO YOU THINK IT'S FUNNY, EH?....
ULP!
HUH!
.....WELL, THIS OUGHT TO PUT YOU IN STITCHES!
YEARS OF RIGOROUS ATHLETIC TRAINING HAVE ENABLED THE BATMAN NOT ONLY TO RESIST BUT TO RECOVER FROM THE BRUTAL BEATING THAT WOULD HAVE MORTALLY INJURED MOST MEN!
WHY DON'T YOU KICK ME NOW, YOU BRAVE MAN!
RIFLING THE PROFESSOR'S PAPERS, THE BATMAN FINDS THE LIST OF INSTRUCTIONS AND THEN HASTILY CONTACTS HIS YOUNG AIDE, ROBIN, THE BOY WONDER!
OH, IT'S YOU, BATMAN! WHERE HAVE YOU BEEN THE WHOLE NIGHT? I'VE BEEN WANDERING ALL AROUND TOWN LOOKING FOR YOU!
CAN'T STOP TO EXPLAIN NOW, BUT TAKE ONE OF THOSE PILLS I GAVE YOU LAST NIGHT AND LISTEN CAREFULLY! COPY THIS DOWN.

AT BREAKNECK SPEED, THE BATMAN STREAKS OUT INTO THE NIGHT.......
IT'S STILL POSSIBLE FOR ROBIN AND ME TO STOP STRANGE'S THUGS. FIRST STOP.... FORTY-SECOND STREET STATION!

IN THE SUBWAY A THUG IS ABOUT TO RELEASE THE "FEAR" SPRAY, WHEN A FIGURE HURTLES OVER THE TURNSTILE..
NOW ALL I HAVE TO DO IS SPRAY THE DUST IN TO THE CROWDED TRAIN! WHA...?

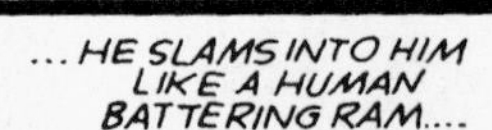
... HE SLAMS INTO HIM LIKE A HUMAN BATTERING RAM....

... AND SENDS HIM SAILING WITH A WELL-PLACED BLOW!
GUM

THE BATMAN!
HE'S GONE.... QUICK AS HE CAME!
SAID TO TURN THIS GUY OVER TO THE POLICE!

WHILE AT THAT MOMENT ROBIN, THE BOY WONDER, IS BUSILY ENGAGED IN CLIMBING A TELEGRAPH POLE NEAR THE CITY RESERVOIR....
I SEE THOSE MEN THE BATMAN TOLD ME WERE GOING TO EMPTY "FEAR" SPRAY INTO THE RESERVOIR!

GOOD THING I DID THIS SORT OF THING WHEN I WORKED WITH MOTHER AND DAD IN THE CIRCUS!

....REACHING HIS QUARRY HE DIVES IN A SUICIDE PLUNGE....

...TO LAND WITH AMAZING RESULTS!

THE THUGS QUICKLY DRAW THEIR SPRAY GUNS AND THROW "FEAR" DUST AT THE BOY WONDER.

...ROLL OUT THE BARREL

THAT'S THAT ROBIN KID!

THE "FEAR" DUST DOESN'T EVEN AFFECT HIM!

WOULD THEY BE SURPRISED TO KNOW I SWALLOWED AN ANTIDOTE PILL JUST AS THEY DID!

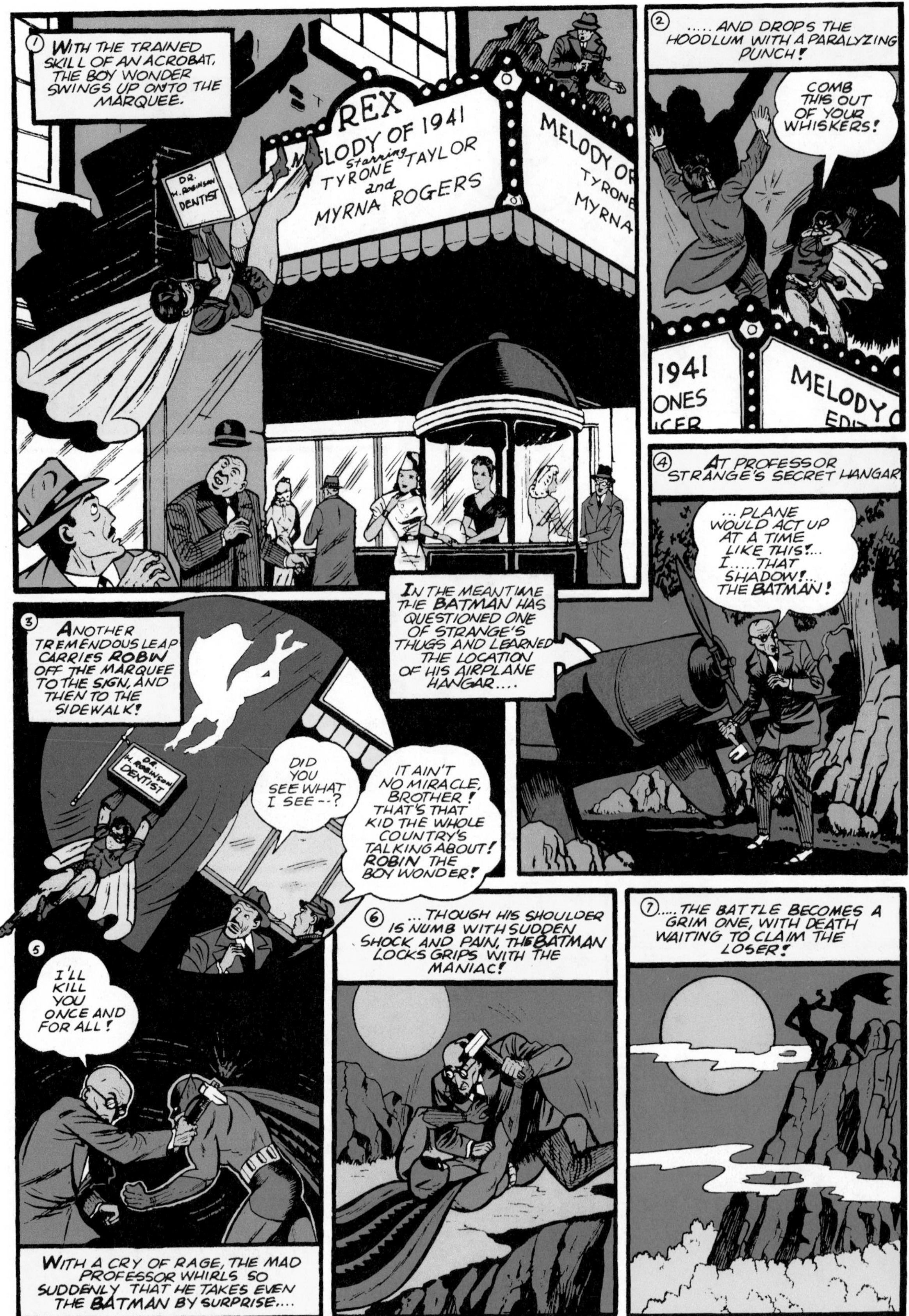
1
WITH THE TRAINED SKILL OF AN ACROBAT, THE BOY WONDER SWINGS UP ONTO THE MARQUEE.
REX
MELODY OF 1941
starring TYRONE TAYLOR and MYRNA ROGERS
DR. M. ROBINSON DENTIST
2
.....AND DROPS THE HOODLUM WITH A PARALYZING PUNCH!
COMB THIS OUT OF YOUR WHISKERS!
3
ANOTHER TREMENDOUS LEAP CARRIES ROBIN OFF THE MARQUEE TO THE SIGN, AND THEN TO THE SIDEWALK!
DID YOU SEE WHAT I SEE--?
IT AIN'T NO MIRACLE, BROTHER! THAT'S THAT KID THE WHOLE COUNTRY'S TALKING ABOUT! ROBIN THE BOY WONDER!
IN THE MEANTIME THE BATMAN HAS QUESTIONED ONE OF STRANGE'S THUGS AND LEARNED THE LOCATION OF HIS AIRPLANE HANGAR....
4
AT PROFESSOR STRANGE'S SECRET HANGAR
...PLANE WOULD ACT UP AT A TIME LIKE THIS!... I.....THAT SHADOW!... THE BATMAN!
5
I'LL KILL YOU ONCE AND FOR ALL!
WITH A CRY OF RAGE, THE MAD PROFESSOR WHIRLS SO SUDDENLY THAT HE TAKES EVEN THE BATMAN BY SURPRISE....
6
...THOUGH HIS SHOULDER IS NUMB WITH SUDDEN SHOCK AND PAIN, THE BATMAN LOCKS GRIPS WITH THE MANIAC!
7
.....THE BATTLE BECOMES A GRIM ONE, WITH DEATH WAITING TO CLAIM THE LOSER!

ABRUPTLY, THE ARCH-CRIMINAL MANAGES TO LOOSEN HIS HAND, AND LASHES OUT AT THE BATMAN....
BLAST YOU!
MISSED! TSK, TSK!

....BUT THE NIMBLE BATMAN IS NOT TO BE CAUGHT NAPPING A SECOND TIME. THERE IS A CRACK LIKE THAT OF A RIFLE SHOT AS HIS FISTS LAND ON THE CRIMINAL'S CHIN......
BUT I WON'T!

...FOR A MOMENT HE TEETERS ON THE EDGE, CLAWING FOR BALANCE, AND THEN WITH A TRAILING SHRIEK TOPPLES TO HIS DOOM!
WELL....THIS TIME IT REALLY LOOKS AS IF IT IS THE END OF THE EVIL CAREER OF PROFESSOR HUGO STRANGE!
YAAAAAA......

THAT NIGHT, AS THE MOON SHEDS ITS LIGHT OVER A NOW PEACEFUL CITY, TWO FIGURES STAND ON A LONELY ROAD....
WELL...I GUESS WE CLEANED OUT THE "FEAR" GANG! NOW WHAT DO WE DO?
NOTHING MUCH LEFT TO DO BUT TO SET FREE THE KID THAT HELPED ME BREAK THIS CASE. HE'S TIED UP IN STRANGE'S HOUSE!

YOU KNOW... IT MUST HAVE BEEN A PECULIAR SIGHT TO SEE POLICEMEN AFRAID FOR THE FIRST TIME....
THEY COULDN'T HELP BEING AFRAID UNDER THE INFLUENCE OF THAT "FEAR" DUST ANYMORE THAN YOU COULD HELP CATCHING A COLD!

WHAT ABOUT THE PEOPLE THE "FEAR" DUST AFFECTED? WHAT CAN BE DONE ABOUT THEM!
I'LL GIVE THE PILLS TO A RESEARCH LABORATORY. THEY'LL FIND OUT WHAT THEY'RE MADE OF AND MAKE ENOUGH ANTIDOTE FOR THOSE POOR UNFORTUNATES!

THANKS FOR BEING WITH US AGAIN THIS MONTH! ROBIN AND I LOOK FORWARD TO THESE LITTLE GET-TOGETHERS WITH ALL YOU READERS EVERY MONTH IN DETECTIVE COMICS! LET'S MAKE IT A STANDING DATE!
BOB KANE

No. 47
A DC PUBLICATION
The BATMAN
Detective
JAN.
COMICS
10¢
Reg. U.S. Pat. Off.
BOB KANE

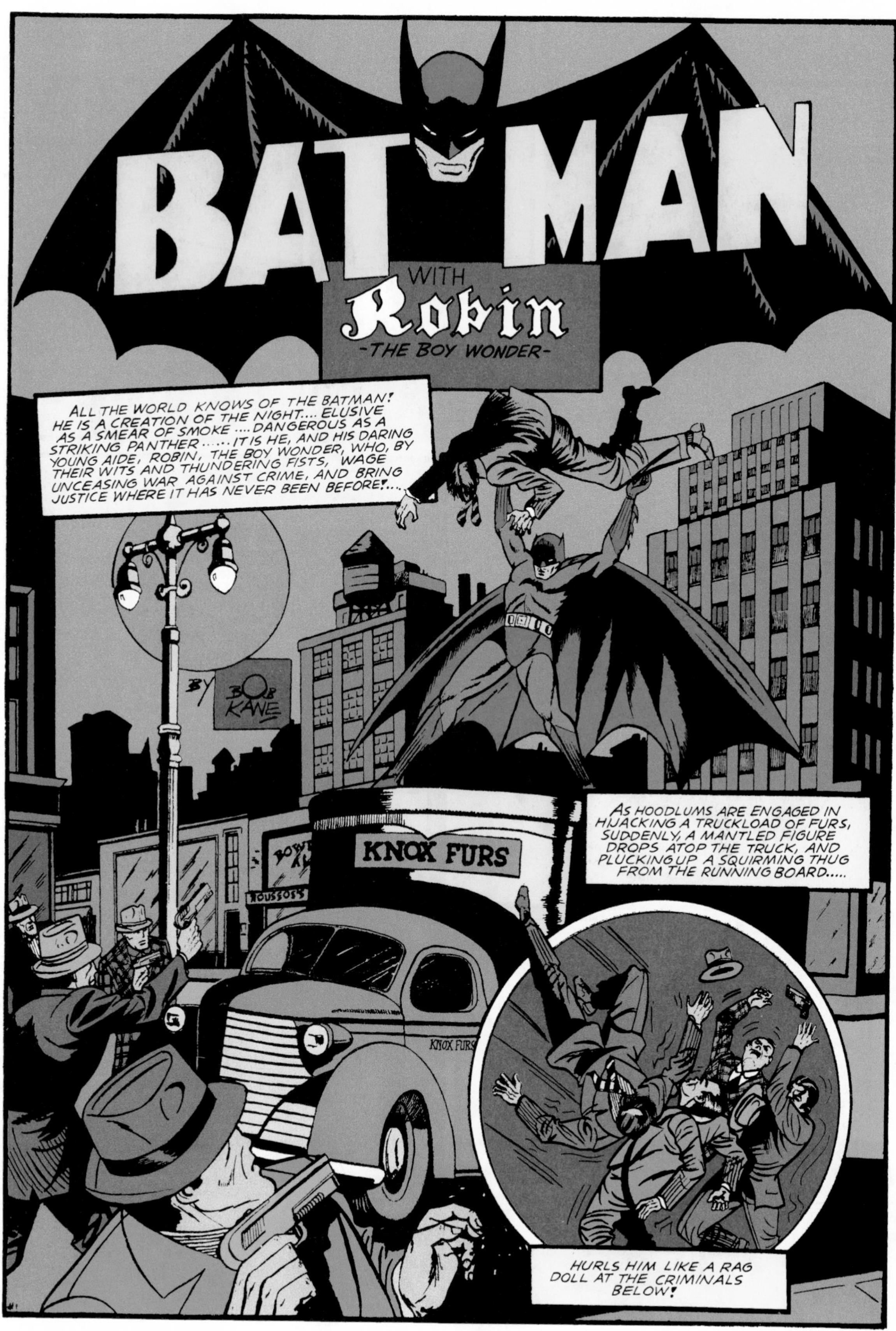
BAT MAN
WITH
Robin
-THE BOY WONDER-
ALL THE WORLD KNOWS OF THE BATMAN! HE IS A CREATION OF THE NIGHT.... ELUSIVE AS A SMEAR OF SMOKE .... DANGEROUS AS A STRIKING PANTHER ...... IT IS HE, AND HIS DARING YOUNG AIDE, ROBIN, THE BOY WONDER, WHO, BY THEIR WITS AND THUNDERING FISTS, WAGE UNCEASING WAR AGAINST CRIME, AND BRING JUSTICE WHERE IT HAS NEVER BEEN BEFORE!...
BY BOB KANE
AS HOODLUMS ARE ENGAGED IN HIJACKING A TRUCKLOAD OF FURS, SUDDENLY, A MANTLED FIGURE DROPS ATOP THE TRUCK, AND PLUCKING UP A SQUIRMING THUG FROM THE RUNNING BOARD.....
KNOX FURS
KNOX FURS
HURLS HIM LIKE A RAG DOLL AT THE CRIMINALS BELOW!

CRIME FIGHTER...... SUPERFOE OF EVIL.... THE BATMAN HAS STRUCK AGAIN!
AU REVOIR, GENTLEMEN.... I TRUST I'VE NOT INTRUDED!

SUDDENLY, THE BLAST OF A POLICE WHISTLE CUTS THROUGH THE AIR..... THERE IS THE SOUND OF EXCITED VOICES.....
THE SHOT CAME FROM AROUND THE CORNER!
POLICE! —MY EXIT CUE!

WHEELING ABOUT SWIFTLY, THE DARK KNIGHT SPRINGS OFF THE TRUCK.....
COME TO PAPA!

...HIS OUTSTRETCHED HANDS CLOSE VISE-LIKE AROUND THE LOWER RUNG OF A NEARBY FIRE-ESCAPE LADDER....
JONES Cafe

PERPLEXED POLICE ARRIVE ON THE SCENE....
WHA..? THESE GUYS LOOK LIKE THEY WERE STRUCK BY A HURRICANE!
THEY CERTAINLY WEREN'T FIGHTING THEMSELVES! I WONDER WHAT HIT THEM?

....AND UNOBSERVED, IS THE ANSWER TO THAT QUESTION.... THAT MYSTERIOUS PERSONALITY...DUBBED BATMAN!

UP OVER THE ROOFTOPS HE FLITS...... DIZZY HEIGHTS HOLD NO TERROR FOR THE BATMAN!

SOMETIME LATER, HE ENTERS WHAT SEEMS TO BE A DESERTED BARN ON A BARREN FIELD.....

UPON PRESSING A BUTTON, A SECTION OF THE BARN'S FLOOR SLIDES AWAY, REVEALING A FLIGHT OF STEPS...

....HE PADS SILENTLY THROUGH THE TUNNEL BELOW.....

...HE ASCENDS ANOTHER FLIGHT OF STEPS AT THE END OF THE LONG TUNNEL.....

....AND STEPS THROUGH ANOTHER PANEL INTO A LUXURIOUSLY FURNISHED ROOM!
H'YA DICKEY, M'LAD!
THE SECRET LABYRINTH HAS LED TO THE LAIR OF THE BATMAN!

...JUST A MINOR SKIRMISH WITH THE CRIMINAL ELEMENT! ANYONE PHONE WHILE I WAS GONE?
YOUR BANKER, HARVEY MIDAS, SAID TO CALL IN THE MORNING FOR THE ANNUAL REPORT ON YOUR HOLDINGS!

..IN THE MORNING, HE STEPS FROM THE DOORWAY OF HIS PRIVATE HOME,... NOT AS THE EERIE BATMAN.... BUT AS THE SPENDTHRIFT, PLEASURE-LOVING SOCIETY PLAY BOY..... BRUCE WAYNE!
HMM! NICE DAY FOR A BIT OF POLO!

LATER, HE ENTERS THE SUMPTUOUS OFFICE OF HARVEY MIDAS, MULTI-MILLIONAIRE BANKER.
HELLO MIDAS! HOW'S THE MARKET BEEN TREATING YOU LATELY?
ARRUMPH! NOT BAD, BRUCE...NOT BAD! NOW LET'S GET DOWN TO BUSINESS! CAN ONLY SPARE A MOMENT OR TWO! PRESSED FOR TIME, YOU KNOW!

SUDDENLY, THE DOOR BURSTS OPEN....
HI, BRUCE! HELLO, DAD! ARE YOU ALL SET TO GO TO THE OPENING FOOTBALL GAME WITH ME?
ROGER MY BOY.... I'M SORRY, BUT, I CAN'T MAKE IT-TOO BUSY!

ARRUMPH! AFTER ALL, ROGER, IF I DIDN'T ATTEND TO MY BUSINESS, YOU WOULDN'T BE ABLE TO POSSESS ALL THE MONEY YOU HAVE NOW!
(BLAST THE MONEY!)

I THOUGHT I HEARD YOU SAY SOMETHING, ROGER?
NOTHING IMPORTANT.... JUST TALKING TO MYSELF.
BUT, ONE PERSON DID HEAR! BRUCE'S KEEN EARS HAVE CAUGHT THOSE WORDS!

WHEN ROGER GOES.....
WISH I COULD BE MORE OF A COMPANION TO THE BOY, BUT, AFTER ALL.... BUSINESS BEFORE PLEASURE!
PERHAPS, BUT I WOULDN'T LET IT INTERFERE WITH THE COMRADE-SHIP OF MY OWN SON!

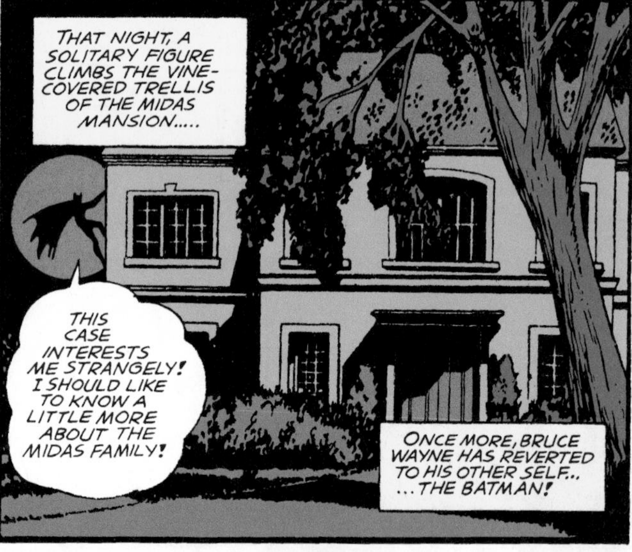
THAT NIGHT, A SOLITARY FIGURE CLIMBS THE VINE-COVERED TRELLIS OF THE MIDAS MANSION.....
THIS CASE INTERESTS ME STRANGELY! I SHOULD LIKE TO KNOW A LITTLE MORE ABOUT THE MIDAS FAMILY!
ONCE MORE, BRUCE WAYNE HAS REVERTED TO HIS OTHER SELF.. ...THE BATMAN!

HE PEERS INTO A LIGHTED ROOM...
MOTHER, SOME OF THE GIRLS FROM SCHOOL ARE HAVING A LITTLE TEA PARTY TOMORROW AFTERNOON. THEY'RE BRINGING THEIR MOTHERS! WILL YOU COME TOO?
YOU KNOW I CAN'T! WE'RE HAVING OUR CLUB LUNCHEON TOMORROW! NOW, PLEASE DON'T BOTHER ME! I'VE GOT THESE INVITATIONS TO GET OUT!

MR. BROWN ON THE TELEPHONE, MISS DIANE!
IT'S JOHNNY! I'LL TAKE IT, JUPKINS.
JOHNNY BROWN AGAIN! DIANE, I THOUGHT I TOLD YOU NOT TO SEE HIM!

WHY? WHAT'S THE MATTER WITH JOHNNY? JUST BECAUSE HE'S NOT RICH AND...
I WILL NOT HAVE MY DAUGHTER GOING OUT WITH A MERE CLERK IN HER FATHER'S BANK! YOUR FATHER WILL HEAR OF THIS! AFTER ALL, YOU MUST THINK OF YOUR SOCIAL POSITION, MY DEAR!

IN THE ENSUING DAYS, BRUCE WAYNE IS SEEN IN MANY NIGHT SPOTS.....
I SEE BRUCE WAYNE IS OUT AGAIN TONIGHT. DOESN'T HE EVER GO HOME?
THAT FELLOW'S CHIEF OCCUPATION SEEMS TO BE JUST RUNNING AROUND THE NIGHTCLUBS!

BUT THEY ARE WRONG, FOR BRUCE WAYNE'S CHIEF OCCUPATION AT THE MOMENT IS KEEPING A WATCHFUL EYE ON YOUNG ROGER MIDAS!

THAT KID HAS BEEN HITTING IT UP QUITE A BIT THESE NIGHTS!

YOUNG ROGER IS SEEN AT THE GAMBLING TABLES, NIGHT AFTER NIGHT....BUT, ALWAYS LURKING IN THE BACKGROUND, IS BRUCE WAYNE!
BETS, PLEASE!
100 ON 18 RED.

ONE NIGHT, BRUCE IS SURPRISED WHEN ROGER PICKS UP A CLARINET FROM ONE OF THE MEN OF THE NIGHTCLUB BAND AND PLAYS ALONG WITH THEM...
...SAY-THAT BOY'S GOOD!

...AND WHEN BRUCE CALLS ROGER TO HIS TABLE AND ASKS HIM ABOUT IT...
SAY, ROG..... YOU CAN REALLY PLAY THAT THING, CAN'T YOU?
YOU NEVER KNEW I WANTED TO LEAD MY OWN ORCHESTRA, DID YOU? FATHER WOULDN'T HEAR OF IT!..SAID IT WOULD NEVER DO FOR THE SON OF HARVEY MIDAS TO BE A MERE ORCHESTRA LEADER!

IT IS NOT SO LONG AFTER, THAT DIANE MIDAS MAKES HER DEBUT INTO SOCIETY..... AND WHAT A DEBUT IT IS......
Society
by Jerry Robinson
DIANE MIDAS MAKES DEBUT
DEB'S COMING OUT PARTY COSTS $50,000
MOST LAVISH OF ALL DEBUTS

...AND UNDER THE STRONG INFLUENCE OF HER SOCIAL-MINDED FATHER AND MOTHER MARRIES NOT JOHNNY BROWN, BUT A DEFUNCT EUROPEAN COUNT!
DARLING! NOW, YOU ARE MINE!
YES, AND SO'S MY MONEY!

AND AT HIS HOME, BRUCE WAYNE PONDERS...
FATHER AND MOTHER MIDAS HAVE CERTAINLY MADE A WRECK OF THEIR CHILDREN'S LIVES! IF THERE WERE ONLY SOMETHING I COULD DO.....IF ONLY SOMETHING WOULD HAPPEN....
BUT, SOMETHING WILL HAPPEN..... EVENTS HAVE ALREADY SHAPED THEMSELVES SO THAT BRUCE WAYNE MAY DISCARD THE ROLE OF IDLE PLAYBOY, AND BECOME THE EERIE BATMAN.

IN THE ENSUING MONTHS, ROGER IS SEEN CONSTANTLY WITH EVIL COMPANIONS...ONE NIGHT AS GAMBLERS AND HE PREPARE FOR A GALA EVENING....
C'MON, ROGER... LET'S GO DOWN TO AL'S PLACE!
SURE... AL'S PLACE! YIPPEE! HIC!

AS IF OUT OF THE EMPTY SKY, A WEIRD FIGURE PLUMMETS DOWN!

STRANGE COMPANY YOU KEEP, ROGER -TIN HORN GAMBLERS!
THE BATMAN!
GET THIS CAR GOIN'! GET OUTTA HERE!

AS THE CAR DARTS FORWARD, THE TIPSY BOY IS UNABLE TO CONTROL THE WHEEL, AND IT CAREENS MADLY..
HEY.... TAKE IT EASY! LOOK OUT... THE NEWSBOY!
Q714

LIKE A JUGGERNAUT, THE CAR HURTLES TOWARD THE HELPLESS BOY.
THE NEXT DAY SHOCKING NEWS HEADLINES THE PAPERS...
DAILY BUGLE
NEWSBOY CRIPPLED BY SPEEDING CAR
"HIT AND RUN" DRIVER SPEEDS FROM SCENE OF CRIME...
THE COWARDLY DRIVER OF THE CAR THAT CRIPPLED POOR DANNY MOORE, A NEWSBOY, OUGHT TO BE

...THE CAR SPEEDS AWAY, LEAVING BEHIND A STILL FORM SPRAWLED IN THE GUTTER!
I-I HIT HIM! I OUGHT TO TAKE HIM TO A HOSPITAL!
KEEP GOIN', YOU FOOL! DO YOU WANT TO GET ARRESTED?
YOU FELLOWS WON'T TELL ANYBODY ABOUT THIS, WILL YOU? MY FATHER WOULDN'T LIKE IT!
YEAH! I GUESS HE WOULDN'T WANT IT KNOWN THAT HIS SON WAS A HIT AND RUN DRIVER!
SURE! THAT WOULDN'T BE SO NICE FOR THE SON OF HARVEY MIDAS!

....AND THAT VERY NIGHT,....IN THE MIDAS HOME.....
...AND YOU MEAN TO SAY THESE MEN WANT $5000 FROM ME TO KEEP THEM QUIET ABOUT THIS UNFORTUNATE ACCIDENT...OR ELSE THEY WILL TELL THE NEWSPAPERS?
YES! THEY SAID YOU WOULD PAY ANYTHING TO KEEP SOME MUD FROM SMEARING THE FAMILY NAME! WHAT CAN WE DO?

ABRUPTLY.....
-DO NOTHING AND TAKE YOUR PUNISHMENT! DO YOU THINK THAT ONE PAYMENT WILL STOP THESE MEN? THEY'LL BLACKMAIL YOU ALL YOUR LIFE!
HUH?
WHA? WHO ARE YOU?
THE BATMAN— AT YOUR SERVICE...AND GIVING YOU SOME SOUND ADVICE. DO NOT GIVE IN TO THE BLACKMAILERS' DEMANDS!
BATMAN, EH? WELL, MR. BATMAN, I'LL DO AS I SEE FIT. PLEASE MIND YOUR OWN BUSINESS AND GET OUT OF MY HOUSE!

MIDAS, YOU THINK YOUR MONEY CAN BUY ANYTHING? ONE THING IT CAN'T BUY IS YOUR SON'S SELF-RESPECT!
GET OUT! ...GET OUT!

...AND ON THE FLOOR BELOW, IS ANOTHER COSTUMED FIGURE....ROBIN, THE BOY WONDER!
I'M SORRY, ALEXIS. I DON'T LOVE YOU! I ONLY MARRIED YOU BECAUSE OF MOTHER AND DAD! I'M LEAVING FOR RENO IN THE MORNING!
YOU CAN'T DIVORCE ME....YOU CAN'T!

IF SHE DIVORCES ME, I WON'T HAVE ANY INCOME TO LIVE ON! HM! THINK I'LL HAVE TO DO AS I DID WITH MY FIRST WIFE!
SLAM

AS ALEXIS LEAVES AND SPEEDS AWAY IN HIS CAR, A SMALL FIGURE IS SEEN CLINGING TO THE TIRE-RACK....IT IS THE BOY WONDER, ROBIN!
GOOD THING THE BATMAN TOLD ME TO KEEP AN EYE ON THIS BIRD! HE'S UP TO NO GOOD!

ALEXIS QUICKLY CONTACTS TWO HOODLUMS. AS THEY PLOT, THEY ARE UNAWARE THAT THEIR TALK IS HEARD BY THE WONDER BOY!
THE SAME JOB WE DID FOR YA ONCE BEFORE, EH?
YES! I WILL LEAVE THE SIDE DOOR OPEN. WHEN YOU ENTER I WILL TELL YOU WHERE THE FAMILY JEWEL SAFE IS!
PRETTY SMOOTH. WE SPLIT FIFTY-FIFTY AND THE FAMILY DOESN'T EVER KNOW YOU'RE IN ON THE JOB! SMOOTH!

LATER, ... ROBIN REPORTS...
...AND THE COUNT IS OPENING THE DOOR TOMORROW NIGHT AT EXACTLY EIGHT O'CLOCK!
HMMM....AND MIDAS IS PAYING OFF THE BLACKMAILERS AT TEN O'CLOCK! LOOKS LIKE WE'RE GOING TO BE QUITE BUSY TOMORROW!

THE NEXT NIGHT... AT A FEW MOMENTS BEFORE EIGHT O'CLOCK!

U-UUHH! THAT SHADOW... WHO?...

GREETINGS FROM THE BATMAN, MY DEAR COUNT!

LOOKS LIKE THE COUNT IS DOWN FOR THE COUNT!
HIST! THEY'RE COMING! BETTER HIDE!

A MOMENT LATER... A BANDIT CAUTIOUSLY POKES HIS HEAD INTO THE HOUSE..
HEY-WHERE ARE YOU?

RIGHT HERE, SWEETHEART!
AWK!

THE BATMAN'S FIST SHOOTS OUT JUST ONCE MORE AND THAT'S QUITE SUFFICIENT!

THE B-BATMAN! THIS IS NO PLACE FOR ME!

LATER THAT EVENING, MIDAS' CAR DRAWS UP TO THE APPOINTED DWELLING DESIGNATED BY THE BLACKMAILERS....
SURE THIS IS THE PLACE, ROGER?
YES, THAT'S THE NUMBER, ALL RIGHT!

AS MIDAS AND ROGER ENTER THE DWELLING, TWO MANTLED FIGURES LEAP OFF THE CAR-ROOF....THEY ARE THE BATMAN AND ROBIN!
WHETHER MIDAS LIKES IT OR NOT, WE'RE GOING TO STOP THOSE DIRTY BLACKMAILERS!

GOT THE FIVE GRAND, MIDAS?
YES, IN FIVES AND TENS, AS YOU REQUESTED.

SUDDENLY, THERE IS THE SOUND OF SPLINTERING WOOD-AND A PAIR OF BROAD SHOULDERS CRASHES THROUGH THE DOOR.....
SORRY-BUT I DON'T THINK I'LL BOTHER TO KNOCK!
OH, MAMA! IT'S THE BATMAN!.

GUNPLAY ALWAYS DID BOTHER ME!
O-OH!

PHFFT!
HOW'S THAT FOR USING MY HEAD!

PANIC-STRICKEN, THE REMAINING BLACKMAILERS RETREAT......
C'MON, WE'LL SPLIT UP! I'LL GO UP THE FIRE-ESCAPE AND YOU GO DOWN!
BE WITH YOU IN A SEC! I WANNA DO SOMETHIN' FIRST!

SIC THE BATMAN ON US, WILLYA... TAKE THIS!
ROGER! LOOK OUT!

ROGER -SHOT!
ROBIN - YOU TAKE THE RAT GOING TO THE ROOF! I'LL GET THE ONE THAT FIRED THE SHOT!

WELL-KNOWING HIS DANGER, THE BOY WONDER DOESN'T EVEN HESITATE, BUT SCRAMBLES UP THE FIRE-ESCAPE AFTER THE FLEEING BLACKMAILER!

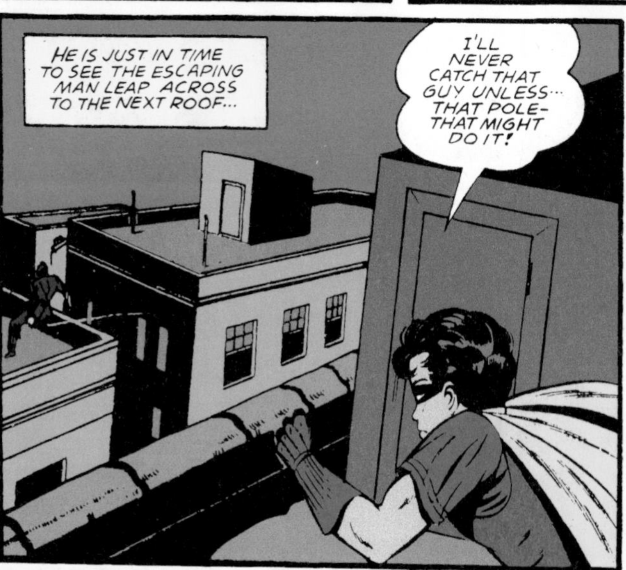
HE IS JUST IN TIME TO SEE THE ESCAPING MAN LEAP ACROSS TO THE NEXT ROOF...
I'LL NEVER CATCH THAT GUY UNLESS... THAT POLE-THAT MIGHT DO IT!

BRINGING FORTH HIS SILKEN ROPE, ROBIN TWIRLS IT ABOUT HIS HEAD A DEFT THROW.. AND IT CATCHES HOLD....
THAT DOES IT!

..TAKING A SHORT RUN, THE BOY WONDER SPRINGS.. HIS BODY SWINGS LIKE A PENDULUM OVER SHEER AND DIZZY HEIGHTS...

....IT SWINGS OVER TO THE NEXT ROOF.... AND AS THE BOY LETS GO OF THE ROPE, DROPS WITH STUNNING FORCE ONTO THE BLACKMAILER!!
SURPRISE!

HE MEANS BUSINESS!
MEANWHILE, THE BATMAN HAS BEEN HAVING QUITE A TIME PURSUING HIS CHOSEN MAN.... A BULLET FANS HIS CHEEK...

AS THE MAN LEAPS INTO HIS OPEN CAR, THE BATMAN DECIDES TO STAKE ALL ON A RISKY TRY....

...A DEATH-DEFYING LEAP INTO SPACE....
HERE GOES NOTHING!

....AND THE BATMAN'S PLUNGING BODY DROPS INTO THE REAR SEAT OF THE CAR!
I COULD SHAKE THE MEASLES EASIER THAN THIS GUY!
MADE IT! WHEW!

BROTHER.... YOUR RIDE IS OVER RIGHT NOW!

WITH NO-ONE TO HOLD THE WHEEL, THE CAR VEERS INTO A POLE, JUST AS THE BATMAN LEAPS IN THE NICK OF TIME!...

THE BLACKMAILERS QUICKLY TRUSSED, THE BATMAN AND ROBIN TURN TO THE BUSINESS AT HAND....
WH-WHAT ARE YOU DOING?
HE'LL BLEED TO DEATH HERE! I'M TAKING HIM TO YOUR DOCTOR. THERE MAY BE STILL A CHANCE!

THE BATMAN SPEEDS THE WOUNDED BOY TO THE DOCTOR IN RECORD TIME....
YOU'VE GOT TO SAVE HIM!—YOU'VE GOT TO! I'LL PAY YOU ANYTHING!
MONEY WON'T HELP, NOW! HIS LIFE IS IN THE HANDS OF A GREATER POWER THAN MINE!

THE FRANTIC FATHER AND THE BATMAN STEP INTO THE NEXT ROOM!...
MIDAS, I KNOW THIS IS CRUEL—BUT THERE YOU STAND WITH A SATCHEL FULL OF MONEY AND YOU'RE POWERLESS TO SAVE YOUR SON!
NOW, I KNOW WHAT YOU MEANT WHEN YOU SAID MONEY CAN'T CURE EVERYTHING! WHAT A FOOL I'VE BEEN!

TO THE ANXIOUS PAIR, MINUTES SEEM TO CLING LIKE FLYPAPER.....THEN, AT LONG LAST, THE DOOR SWINGS OPEN...
DOCTOR, WILL HE...?
IT'S A MIRACLE, BUT HE'LL PULL THROUGH! HE WILL LIVE!
THANK HEAVENS!

A MONTH LATER, ROGER MIDAS AND THE PARENTS OF THE INJURED NEWSBOY STAND BEFORE A JUDGE...
YOU WISH TO DROP THE CHARGES AGAINST THIS YOUNG MAN. ! WHY?
HE HIRED SPECIALISTS TO OPERATE ON MY BOY, SO THAT HE MAY WALK AGAIN!
HE HAS ALSO PUT ASIDE A TRUST FUND SO MY BOY CAN GO TO COLLEGE -- AND HAS GIVEN ME A JOB. HE HAS BEEN VERY KIND, AND VERY HUMBLE!

I KNOW THAT MY MONEY CAN'T ATONE FOR MY CRIME! I'M READY TO STAND TRIAL AND TAKE MY PUNISHMENT!
YOUNG MAN-- YOU'VE MADE RESTITUTION... BUT, WHAT'S MORE IMPORTANT IS THAT YOU'VE LEARNED YOUR LESSON! CASE IS DISMISSED!

LATER THAT DAY..... BRUCE WAYNE VISITS THE MIDAS HOME....
JUST CAME FROM YOUR OFFICE, MIDAS! THOSE STATEMENTS ON MY HOLDINGS...
SORRY, BRUCE! YOUR BUSINESS WILL HAVE TO WAIT! I'M GOING TO A FOOTBALL GAME WITH MY SON!
INCIDENTALLY, BRUCE, LISTEN TO ME ON THE AIR TONIGHT.... "ROGER MIDAS AND HIS MELODEERS".

HURRY, DIANE.... WE CAN'T KEEP JOHNNY BROWN WAITING ALL DAY!
WILL WONDERS NEVER CEASE?
COMING, MOTHER DEAR!

LATER... THE WAYNE HOME..
LOOKS LIKE MRS. MIDAS HAS FORGOTTEN HER SOCIAL PREJUDICES, EH?
YES... AND MR. MIDAS HAS DECIDED TO TAKE A LITTLE TIME OFF FROM BUSINESS AND BECOME A REAL PAL TO HIS SON! OTHER PARENTS CAN TAKE A TIP FROM THIS CASE! IT'S WELL WORTH THINKING ABOUT!

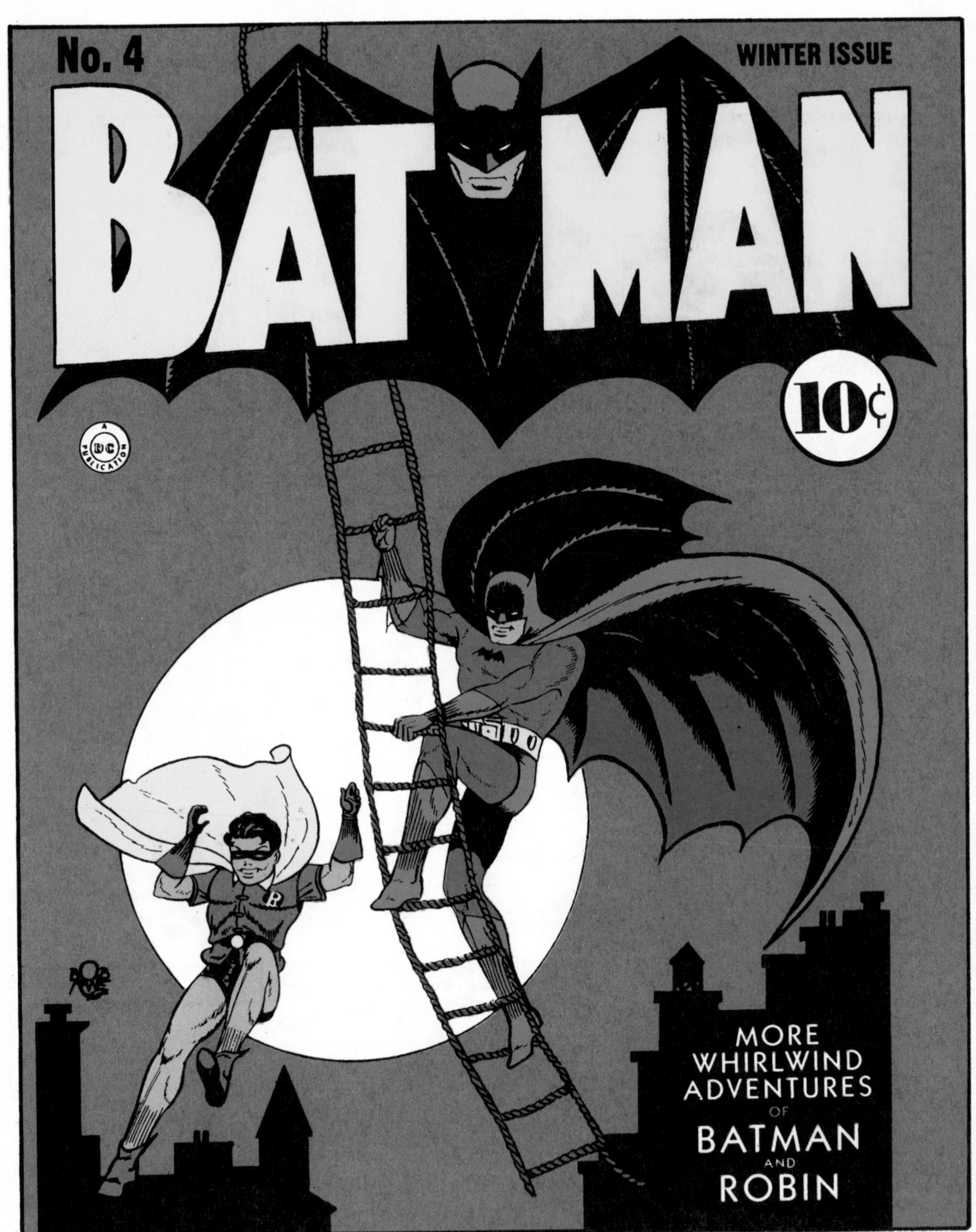
No. 4
WINTER ISSUE
BATMAN
10¢
A DC PUBLICATION
MORE
WHIRLWIND
ADVENTURES
OF
BATMAN
AND
ROBIN

BATMAN
with Robin
THE BOY WONDER
BY BOB KANE
THE BATMAN AND ROBIN
AMERICA'S FASTEST-GROWING
ADVENTURE TEAM
Z-I-N-G!

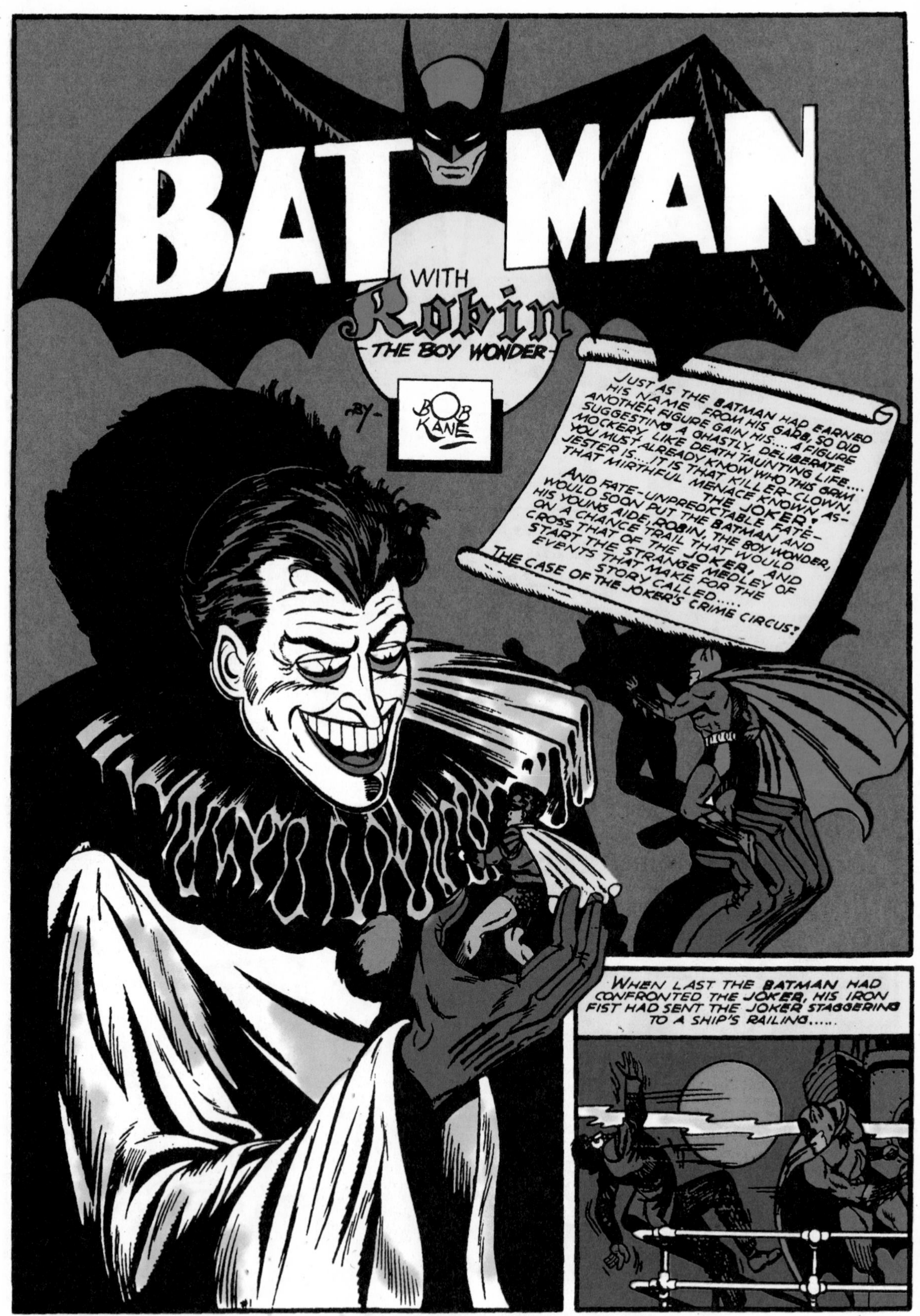
BAT-MAN
WITH Robin
-THE BOY WONDER-
-BY- BOB KANE
JUST AS THE BATMAN HAD EARNED HIS NAME FROM HIS GARB, SO DID ANOTHER FIGURE GAIN HIS.... A FIGURE SUGGESTING A GHASTLY, DELIBERATE MOCKERY, LIKE DEATH TAUNTING LIFE.... YOU MUST ALREADY KNOW WHO THIS GRIM JESTER IS....IT IS THAT KILLER-CLOWN, THAT MIRTHFUL MENACE KNOWN AS- THE JOKER!
AND FATE-UNPREDICTABLE FATE- WOULD SOON PUT THE BATMAN AND HIS YOUNG AIDE, ROBIN, THE BOY WONDER, ON A CHANCE TRAIL THAT WOULD CROSS THAT OF THE JOKER, AND START THE STRANGE MEDLEY OF EVENTS THAT MAKE FOR THE STORY CALLED.....
THE CASE OF THE JOKER'S CRIME CIRCUS!
WHEN LAST THE BATMAN HAD CONFRONTED THE JOKER, HIS IRON FIST HAD SENT THE JOKER STAGGERING TO A SHIP'S RAILING.....

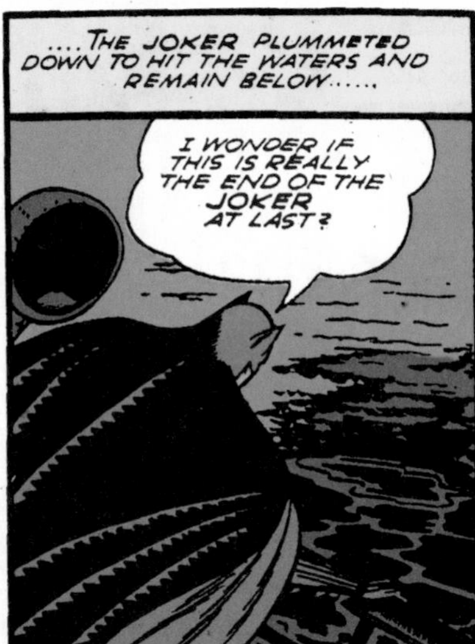
....THE JOKER PLUMMETED DOWN TO HIT THE WATERS AND REMAIN BELOW......
I WONDER IF THIS IS REALLY THE END OF THE JOKER AT LAST?

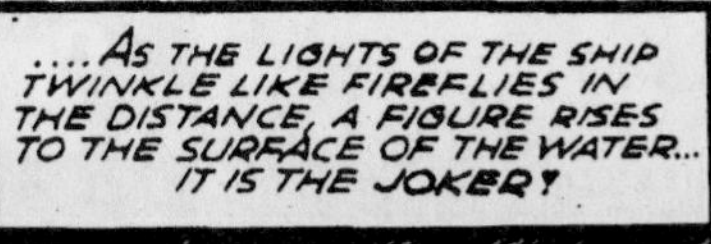
....AS THE LIGHTS OF THE SHIP TWINKLE LIKE FIREFLIES IN THE DISTANCE, A FIGURE RISES TO THE SURFACE OF THE WATER... IT IS THE JOKER!

.....HOURS LATER, A YACHT MAKES OUT HIS BOBBING FORM...
MAN AHEAD, SIR-- LOOKS LIKE HE'S CLINGING TO A BIT OF DRIFTWOOD!
GIVE THE NECESSARY ORDER TO PICK HIM UP!

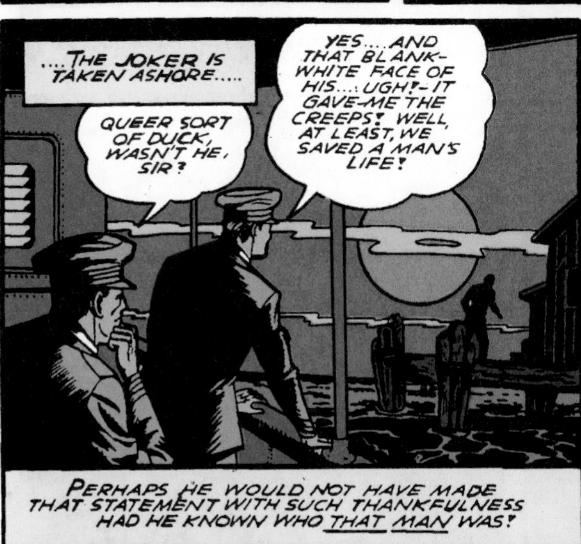
....THE JOKER IS TAKEN ASHORE.....
QUEER SORT OF DUCK, WASN'T HE, SIR?
YES....AND THAT BLANK-WHITE FACE OF HIS....UGH!--IT GAVE ME THE CREEPS! WELL, AT LEAST, WE SAVED A MAN'S LIFE!
PERHAPS HE WOULD NOT HAVE MADE THAT STATEMENT WITH SUCH THANKFULNESS HAD HE KNOWN WHO THAT MAN WAS!

UNOBSERVED, HE STEALS TO THE EDGE OF TOWN TO A SEEMINGLY DESERTED, GLOOMY OLD MANSION DUBBED BY THE PEOPLE AS "HAUNTED"....

BUT THE STRANGE-LOOKING MANSION IS NOT REALLY "HAUNTED" AND DESERTED..... IN REALITY, IT IS THE HIDDEN SANCTUM OF THE JOKER...

....THEN, THE JOKER LAUGHS... A WILD, JEERING LAUGH THAT MAKES THE VERY SILENCE OF THE ROOM CRAWL WITH MENACE.
I'M ALIVE! HA HA! I'M ALIVE! HA HA HA HA!
THE CLEVEREST AND THE MOST DANGEROUS CRIMINAL IN THE ANNALS OF CRIME WAS STILL AT LIBERTY!

THE BATMAN THINKS I'M DEAD. HE'LL KNOW DIFFERENTLY WHEN WE MEET AGAIN! ...AND WE SHALL MEET AGAIN!
THE TIME WAS CLOSE WHEN NEW FACTORS WOULD BRING ABOUT AN ACTUAL DUEL BETWEEN THE BATMAN AND THE JOKER!

1
TWO MONTHS PASS
AS NIGHT MAKES HER ENTRANCE WEARING HER GARMENTS OF BLACKNESS, TWO FIGURES DART THROUGH THE DARK OF HER SHADOW....

2
SUDDENLY THEY SEE.....
LOOK, ROBIN!
THREE MASKED MEN! -THIEVES!
3
THE THREE MEN BEND THEIR KNEES AS SOON AS THEY HIT THE GROUND, AND ROLL OVER.....

4
THEY ROLLED OVER TO ABSORB THE SHOCK OF HITTING THE GROUND!
JUST LIKE PROFESSIONAL ACROBATS WOULD DO IT!

5
THE TWO CRIME-FIGHTERS STRIKE!
PERHAPS YOU'RE NOT AWARE OF IT... BUT THERE'S A LAW AGAINST STEALING!

6
AS THEY BATTLE, THEY DO NOT NOTICE THE HUGE, HULKING FORM THAT COMES FROM THE CAR PARKED NEARBY.....

A HAND REACHES OUT TO SLAP ROBIN AND SEND HIM SPINNING...
HAH! JUST A BOY!

AGAIN, HE REACHES OUT, TO CLAMP STEEL HANDS UPON THE BATMAN!
I FIX YOU!
WHA...?

....HE LIFTS THE BATMAN HIGH IN THE AIR.......

....AND HURLS HIM AGAINST THE CONCRETE WALL!
I BREAK YOU TO PIECES!

I CRUSH HIM TO LITTLE BITS!
YEAH-YEAH...SOME OTHER TIME! C'MON!
LET'S GET AWAY FROM HERE!

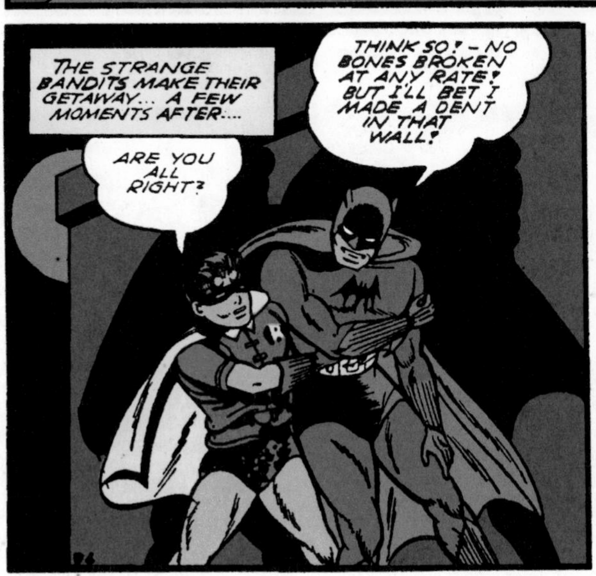
THE STRANGE BANDITS MAKE THEIR GETAWAY... A FEW MOMENTS AFTER:...
ARE YOU ALL RIGHT?
THINK SO! - NO BONES BROKEN AT ANY RATE! BUT I'LL BET I MADE A DENT IN THAT WALL!

MY FACE ACHES ALL OVER WHERE THAT GUY SMACKED ME! WAS HE STRONG!
ANYTIME THAT GUY WANTS A JOB AS STRONGMAN AT A CIRCUS HE CAN CALL ME TO VOUCH FOR HIM!

A WEEK LATER, ANOTHER RICH HOME IS ROBBED..
GOTHAM CITY GAZETTE
VAN PLATT HOM ROBBED......
FIFTH RICH HOME LOOTE IN LATEST ROBBERY EPIDEMIC
THOSE MYSTERIOUS BURGLARS, WHO HAVE BEEN STRIKING AT THE SOCIETY RICH THIS PAST MONTH, BRAZENLY ENTERED THE VAN PLATT MANSION LAST NIGHT, AND

.....IN HIS HOME, BRUCE WAYNE WEALTHY SCION OF SOCIETY, SCANS THE NEWS WITH UNUSUAL INTEREST.....
"THE FIFTH ROBBERY" HMM!
LETTER FOR YOU, BRUCE.
BEHIND THIS APPARENTLY PURPOSELESS LIFE OF PLAYBOY AND IDLER, LURKS ANOTHER STRANGER ONE... FOR.... BRUCE WAYNE IS THE BATMAN!

THE LETTER.....
You are cordially invited to attend a ball to be given this Saturday at eight thi o'clock
C.R. Darcey

ACCORDINGLY.....THAT SATURDAY NIGHT.....
AH, BRUCE-GLAD YOU COULD COME!
WILD HORSES COULDN'T KEEP ME AWAY, DARCEY.

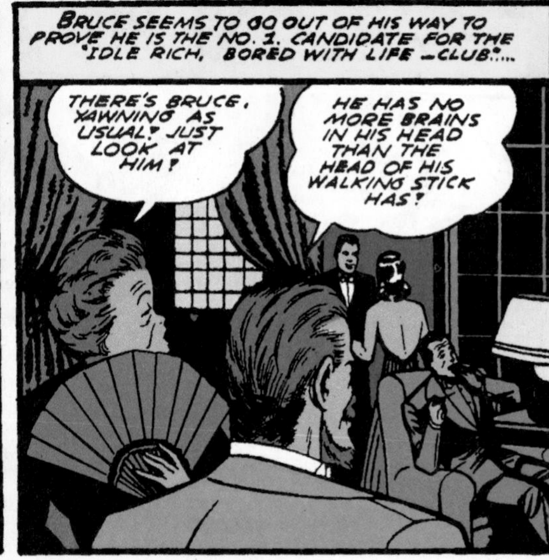
BRUCE SEEMS TO GO OUT OF HIS WAY TO PROVE HE IS THE NO. 1. CANDIDATE FOR THE 'IDLE RICH, BORED WITH LIFE -CLUB'....
THERE'S BRUCE, YAWNING AS USUAL! JUST LOOK AT HIM!
HE HAS NO MORE BRAINS IN HIS HEAD THAN THE HEAD OF HIS WALKING STICK HAS!

...SUDDENLY, THERE IS A ROLL ON THE DRUMS, AND DARCEY ADDRESSES HIS GUESTS..
FRIENDS-NOW I HAVE A TREAT IN STORE FOR YOU! THE BALL ROOM WILL BE CLEARED AND YOU WILL BE GIVEN SEATS SO THAT YOU MAY WATCH A CIRCUS!

.....A MINIATURE CIRCUS SHOW IS PUT ON IN THE BALLROOM... ACROBATS PERFORM
A STRONG MAN BENDS IRON BARS AND LIFTS TREMENDOUS WEIGHTS...
AJAX...THE STRONGEST, MIGHTIEST MAN IN THE WORLD!

REPLETE WITH ACROBATS, STRONG MAN, TRAPEZE ARTISTS, CLOWN, THE CIRCUS IS A HOWLING SUCCESS.....
ODD, HOW THAT CLOWN REMINDS ME OF SOMEONE!
HA HA! HA!
HA HA!

THAT NIGHT, WHEN THEIR ENGAGEMENT ENDS, THE CIRCUS TROUPE TOILS UP THE LONELY ROAD THAT LEADS TO THE "HAUNTED HOUSE"......

INSIDE, THE PERFORMERS RID THEMSELVES OF MAKE-UP.... ESPECIALLY THE CLOWN....
EVERY TIME I DO THIS, IT REMINDS ME OF THAT OLD SONG THAT GOES "AT NIGHT I LAY MY MASK ON THE SHELF AND SEE MYSELF AS I REALLY AM!...."

.....BE A PUNCHINELLO... LAUGH, CLOWN, LAUGH! HA HA HA HA!
UNDER THE HUMOROUS MAKE-UP IS THE REAL CLOWN...THE KILLER-CLOWN....THE JOKER!.....

.....AND EXACTLY THREE DAYS LATER.....
BRUCE! BRUCE! THE DARCEYS - THE PEOPLE WHOSE PARTY YOU WENT TO-THEY'VE BEEN ROBBED!
WH-AT? THAT MAKES THE SIXTH RICH FAMILY ROBBED THIS MONTH!

BRUCE INVESTIGATES, AND AT THE END OF THE DAY ANNOUNCES HIS FINDINGS AND SUSPICIONS TO DICK....
...YOU MEAN TO SAY YOU'VE FOUND OUT THAT EVERY RICH HOME THAT HAS BEEN ROBBED HAS HAD THIS CIRCUS PLAY AN ENGAGEMENT AT THEIR HOUSE?
YES .... AND REMEMBER WHEN WE HAD THAT RUN-IN THE OTHER NIGHT?.. THE CROOKS HOPPED AROUND LIKE PROFESSIONAL ACROBATS!

.... AND ONE WAS STRONG LIKE THE STRONG MAN OF A CIRCUS! NOW, WHAT'S TO PREVENT THIS CROOKED CIRCUS FROM PLAYING A RICH HOME AND "CASING" IT FOR A FUTURE ROBBERY? LOGICAL, ISN'T IT?

GOSH! THE SOCIETY COLUMN SAYS "THE MORGANBILTS' PARTY TONIGHT WILL FEATURE THE MINIATURE CIRCUS THAT IS THE CURRENT RAGE OF SOCIETY!"
WE CAN'T TELL WHEN THEY'LL STRIKE, SO WE'VE GOT TO PREVENT A FUTURE CRIME! DICK, WE'RE STEPPING OUT... TONIGHT!

THAT NIGHT.....IN THE "HAUNTED HOUSE".
....THE LAIR OF THE JOKER......
TONIGHT, WE PLAY THE MORGANBILT HOME. LOOK THE PLACE OVER. FIND OUT WHERE THEY HAVE THEIR SAFE HIDDEN. WORK FAST!

THIS IS TINO. HE HAS JUST JOINED UP WITH US. HE'LL BE OUR SURPRISE GUEST TONIGHT! NOW LET'S GO!
SO WAS THE STAGE SET, WITH THE BATMAN, ROBIN AND THE JOKER TO BE THE PRINCIPAL PLAYERS!

EVENING, AT THE MORGANBILT HOME...... THE JOKER'S CRIME CIRCUS HOLDS THE CENTER OF INTEREST......

THE HARLEQUIN OF HATE STEPS FORWARD.....
.....AND NOW WE HAVE A SURPRISE FOR YOU. WE PRESENT....

RA TA TA-TA!
....AND AS IF ON CUE, THE DYNAMIC DUO LEAPS INTO THE ROOM......
FANFARE, PLEASE!
LOOK! THE BATMAN!
AND ROBIN, THE BOY WONDER!

LOOK! THEY'RE PUTTING ON AN ACT!

MAKING BELIEVE HE IS AFRAID, THE BOY WONDER RACES AWAY, FOLLOWED BY THE ACROBATS, AND....

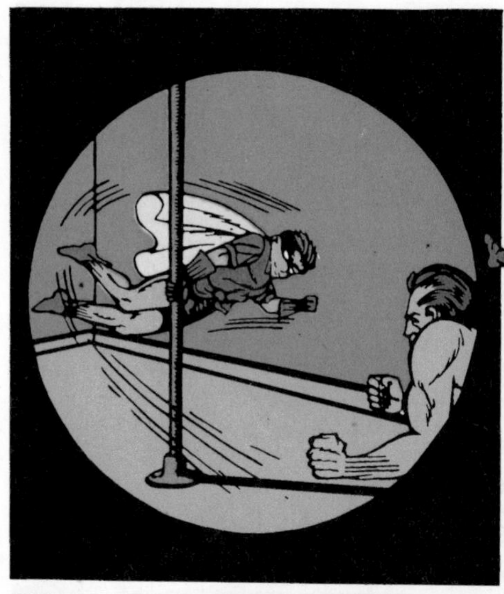

"SWING", EH, CHUMS?

MIGHT WORK AGAIN!
AGAIN HE SIMULATES FEAR, RACES UP A LADDER AND IS FOLLOWED BY THE TRAPEZE ARTISTS.....

WITH A QUICK HOP, THE BOY WONDER SLIDES THROUGH THE LADDER RUNGS, GRASPS THE ANKLES OF HIS NEAREST PURSUERS, AND.....

ELEVATOR-GOING DOWN!
8

MEANWHILE, THE BATMAN HAS BEEN SINGLED OUT FOR COMBAT BY AJAX, THE STRONG MAN!
YOU-AGAIN! I MAKE SURE I KILL YOU THIS TIME!
COME AHEAD, BIG BOY!

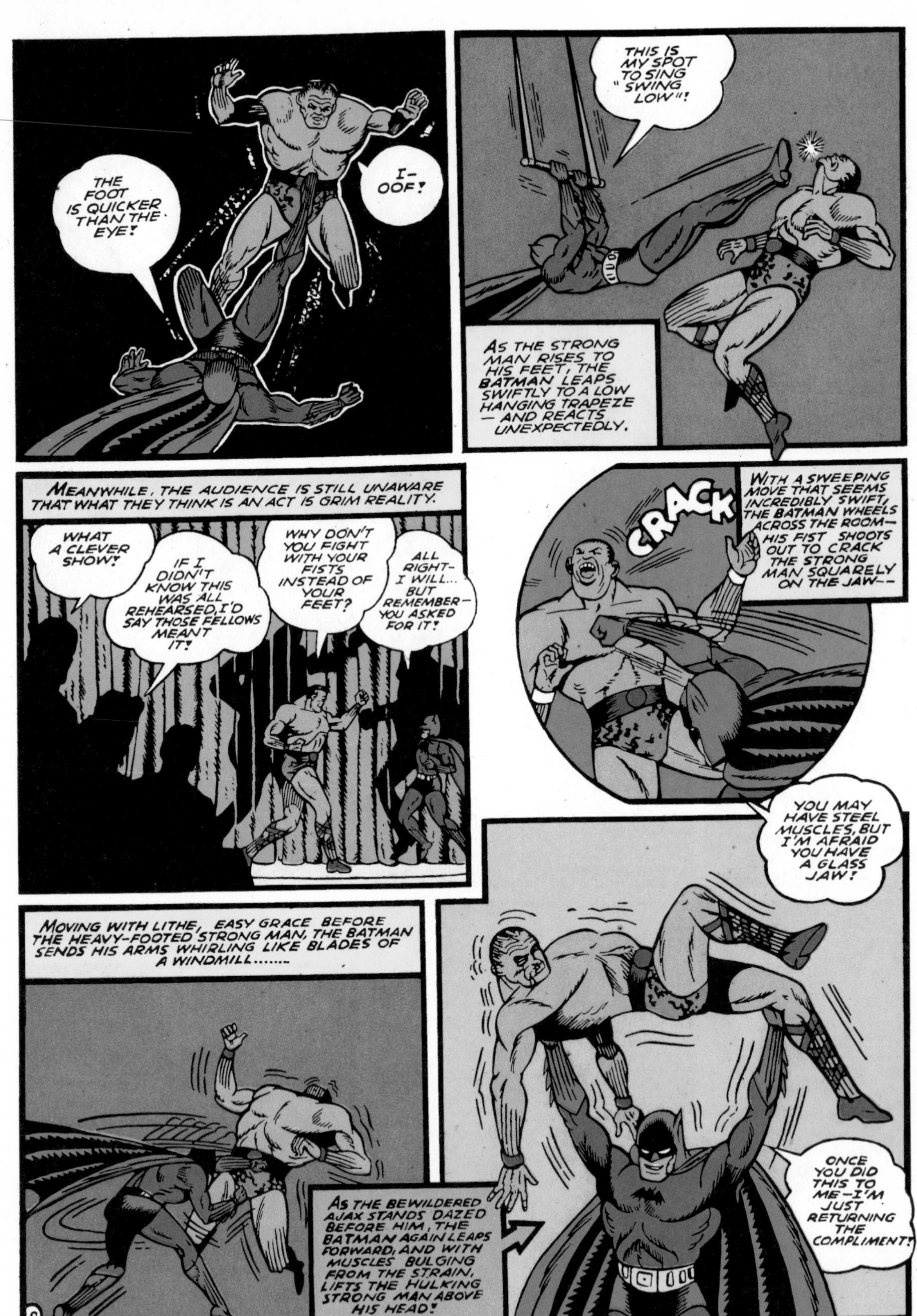

THE FOOT IS QUICKER THAN THE EYE!
I- OOF!
THIS IS MY SPOT TO SING "SWING LOW"!
AS THE STRONG MAN RISES TO HIS FEET, THE BATMAN LEAPS SWIFTLY TO A LOW HANGING TRAPEZE — AND REACTS UNEXPECTEDLY.
MEANWHILE, THE AUDIENCE IS STILL UNAWARE THAT WHAT THEY THINK IS AN ACT IS GRIM REALITY.
WHAT A CLEVER SHOW!
IF I DIDN'T KNOW THIS WAS ALL REHEARSED, I'D SAY THOSE FELLOWS MEANT IT!
WHY DON'T YOU FIGHT WITH YOUR FISTS INSTEAD OF YOUR FEET?
ALL RIGHT- I WILL... BUT REMEMBER- YOU ASKED FOR IT!
WITH A SWEEPING MOVE THAT SEEMS INCREDIBLY SWIFT, THE BATMAN WHEELS ACROSS THE ROOM— HIS FIST SHOOTS OUT TO CRACK THE STRONG MAN SQUARELY ON THE JAW--
CRACK
YOU MAY HAVE STEEL MUSCLES, BUT I'M AFRAID YOU HAVE A GLASS JAW!
MOVING WITH LITHE, EASY GRACE BEFORE THE HEAVY-FOOTED STRONG MAN, THE BATMAN SENDS HIS ARMS WHIRLING LIKE BLADES OF A WINDMILL.......
9
AS THE BEWILDERED AJAX STANDS DAZED BEFORE HIM, THE BATMAN AGAIN LEAPS FORWARD, AND WITH MUSCLES BULGING FROM THE STRAIN, LIFTS THE HULKING STRONG MAN ABOVE HIS HEAD!
ONCE YOU DID THIS TO ME—I'M JUST RETURNING THE COMPLIMENT!

WITH A SUDDEN, QUICK HEAVE OF HIS ARMS, THE BATMAN SLAMS THE GIANT BODY TO THE GROUND.....
ONCE AGAIN, THE DARK KNIGHT HAS GIVEN PROOF OF THE OLD ADAGE..... BRUTE STRENGTH CANNOT AVAIL AGAINST A QUICK MIND AND A QUICK BODY.

....THE JOKER CHOOSES THAT MOMENT TO EFFECT HIS ESCAPE......
LOOK! THAT CLOWN-HE'S GETTING AWAY!
THE CLOWN!- NOW, I KNOW WHY HE REMINDED ME OF SOMEONE... HE'S THE JOKER-- ALIVE!

THE AUDIENCE LEARNS THE TRUTH...
... AND IF THE POLICE WILL QUESTION THESE MEN, YOU'LL FIND THIS ENTIRE CIRCUS IS RESPONSIBLE FOR THESE ROBBERIES!
C'MON, ROBIN!
DID YOU HEAR THAT?
NO WONDER THAT FIGHT LOOKED SO REAL!

KEEPING THE JOKER'S CAR IN SIGHT, THE BATMAN AND ROBIN FOLLOW HIM TO HIS LAIR!.....
SO, -THIS IS HIS HIDEOUT!
SAY- THIS IS THE "HAUNTED HOUSE!"

AS THE BATMAN AND ROBIN DASH UP THE WINDING PATH, A FACE PEERS OUT AT THEM .....THE JOKER!
SO, THEY'RE COMING IN, ARE THEY? I'LL FIX THEM. I'LL SCARE THEM JUST AS I SCARE THE VILLAGERS WHEN THEY PRY INTO THIS HOUSE! HA HA HA!

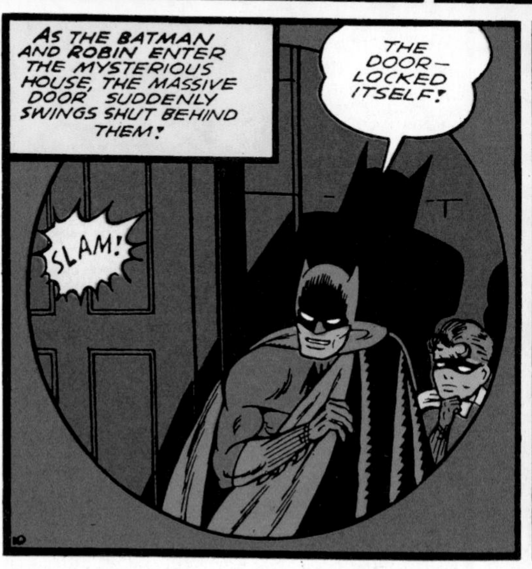
AS THE BATMAN AND ROBIN ENTER THE MYSTERIOUS HOUSE, THE MASSIVE DOOR SUDDENLY SWINGS SHUT BEHIND THEM!
THE DOOR-LOCKED ITSELF!
SLAM!
10

THE TWO MOUNT CREAKY, OLD STAIRS.....
PLEASANT LITTLE PLACE, ISN'T IT?
YES- IT MAKES A LOVELY BREEDING GROUND FOR GHOSTS!

AND THERE, WAITING FOR THEM ATOP THE STAIRS, IS AN AWESOME SIGHT......
INTRUDERS! GET OUT! GET OUT OF MY HOUSE ELSE I VENT MY WRATH UPON YOU!
THE BATMAN ATTACKS THE GHOST!
NEVER TACKLED A GHOST BEFORE— BUT THERE'S ALWAYS A FIRST TIME FOR EVERYTHING!
THE "GHOST" IS UNMASKED!
MY- WHAT A HEALTHY-LOOKING GHOST YOU ARE! FLESH AND EVERYTHING!
ABSORBED IN THE UNMASKING, THE BATMAN AND ROBIN DO NOT SEE A WALL PANEL SLIDE OPEN....AND AWAITING INSIDE IS THE JOKER!
AND WHEN THE BATMAN FINALLY DOES LOOK AROUND......
OUR "GHOST" FRIEND IS NONE OTHER........ ROBIN!—— GONE!—— AND HE WAS JUST STANDING HERE A MOMENT AGO!
THE "GHOST!" HE MUST KNOW WHERE HE IS! I'LL...OH-OH- HE'S GETTING AWAY!
RACING AFTER HIM, THE BATMAN DARTS INTO A ROOM IN WHICH THE "GHOST" HAS ENTERED......TO FIND THE "GHOST" IS GONE!
GONE!.... NOW, THIS DOOR HAS SHUT ON ME! I'LL SOON FIX THAT!
SLAM

......THE BATMAN SLAMS HIS POWERFUL FRAME AT THE DOOR AGAIN AND AGAIN......BUT IT DOES NOT EVEN BUDGE!
THIS DOOR — IT MUST BE STEEL, PAINTED TO LOOK LIKE WOOD! IT WON'T GIVE AN INCH!

SUDDENLY, THE LIGHTS GO OUT AND A SMALL LUMINOUS FACE GLOWS IN THE DARKNESS.... A WHISPERED LAUGH FILTERS THROUGH THE ROOM......
NOW WHAT?
HA HA HA HA

THE HEAD, HANGING DISEMBODIED IN THE DARKNESS, GROWS LARGER..... THE SNEERING LAUGH GROWS LOUDER.....
HA HA HA HA HA
JOKER!

HA HA HA HA HA HA HA HA
LARGER, LARGER SWELLS THE EERIE, MISTY FACE, UNTIL IT SEEMS TO FILL THE VERY ROOM....THE MAD LAUGHTER GROWS LOUDER, LOUDER.....IT THUNDERS, POUNDS AT THE BATMAN'S EARDRUMS......

WITH STARTLING SUDDENNESS THE BATMAN WHIRLS AND LEAPS AT THE WALL BEHIND HIM........

HE TEARS DOWN AN OBJECT FASTENED TO THE WALL....
I THOUGHT SO...... A MOTION PICTURE PROJECTOR THAT THREW THE IMAGE OF THE JOKER'S FACE ON THE WALL.... AND THERE MUST BE MICROPHONES HIDDEN ABOUT TO SEND OUT THAT LAUGH!
12

THEN, A VOICE....A SINISTER, MOCKING VOICE....THE VOICE OF THE JOKER!
QUITE RIGHT, BATMAN! AND NOW LISTEN, BATMAN— LISTEN FOR THE HISS OF GAS! IT MARKS YOUR END.... YOUR END!.... HA-HA-HA...

GAS! I'VE GOT TO GET OUT OF HERE!
THE BATMAN TAKES TWO PARTICULAR VIALS FROM HIS UTILITY BELT.....

PLACING THE CONTENTS OF ONE VIAL INTO THE OTHER, HE THROWS THE PELLET AT THE WALL....THERE IS A SHATTERING BLAST!....

....THE JOKER IS SENT SAILING OVER THE BATMAN'S HEAD.....

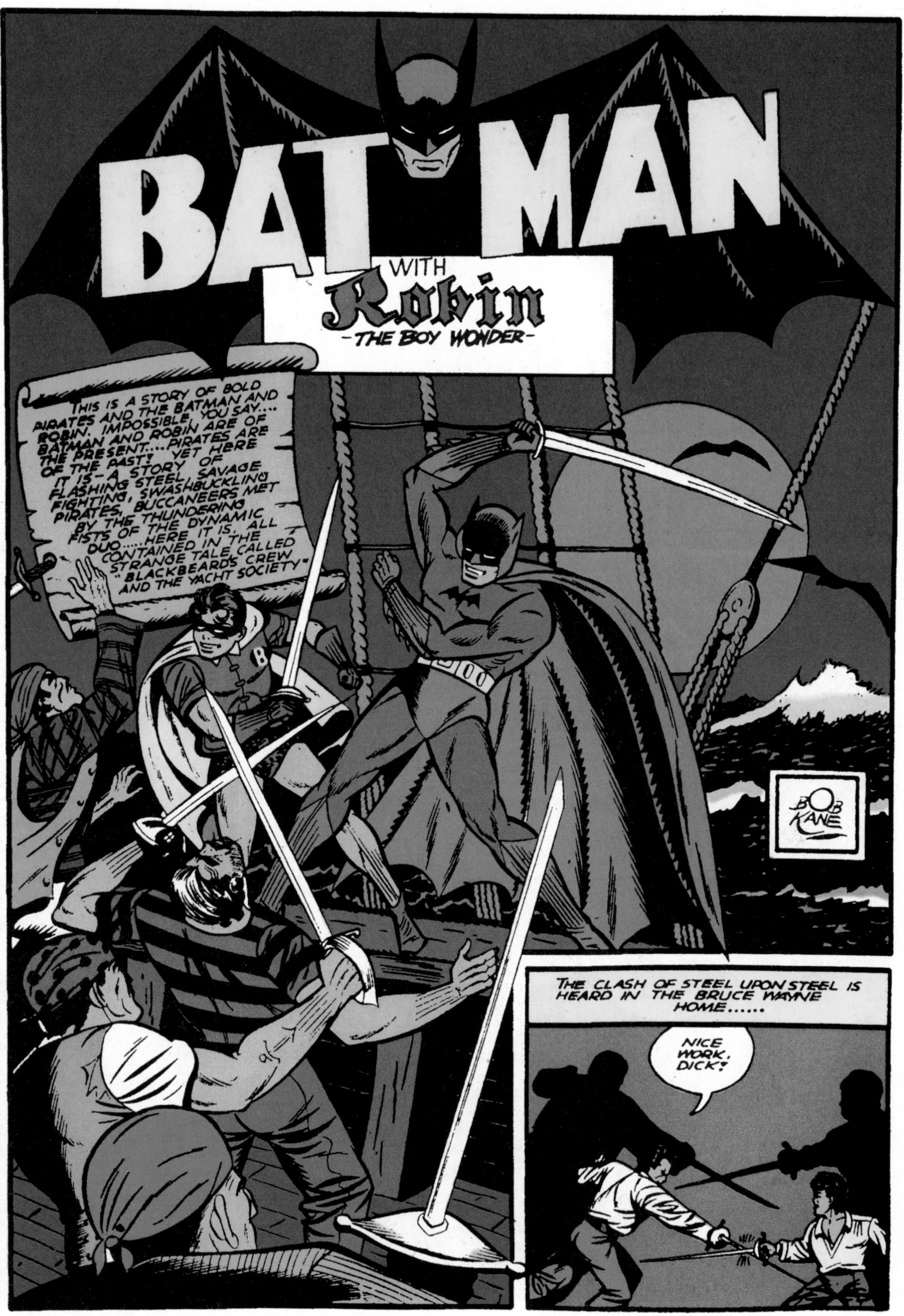
BATMAN
WITH
Robin
-THE BOY WONDER-
THIS IS A STORY OF BOLD PIRATES AND THE BATMAN AND ROBIN. IMPOSSIBLE, YOU SAY.... BATMAN AND ROBIN ARE OF THE PRESENT!...PIRATES ARE OF THE PAST! YET HERE IT IS--A STORY OF FLASHING STEEL, SAVAGE FIGHTING, SWASHBUCKLING PIRATES, BUCCANEERS MET BY THE THUNDERING FISTS OF THE DYNAMIC DUO.....HERE IT IS, ALL CONTAINED IN THE STRANGE TALE CALLED "BLACKBEARD'S CREW AND THE YACHT SOCIETY"
BOB KANE
THE CLASH OF STEEL UPON STEEL IS HEARD IN THE BRUCE WAYNE HOME......
NICE WORK, DICK!

SAY WHAT'S THE GOOD OF OUR KNOWING HOW TO FENCE? WE DON'T USE FOILS TO FIGHT WITH TODAY!
TRUE, BUT FENCING TEACHES YOU QUICKNESS OF MOVEMENT... AND BESIDES, IN OUR BUSINESS, IT HELPS TO KNOW THE USE OF ALL WEAPONS!
THE BUSINESS OF BRUCE WAYNE AND YOUNG DICK GRAYSON?..... FIGHTING CRIME! —FOR THEY ARE IN REALITY... THE BATMAN AND ROBIN THE BOY WONDER

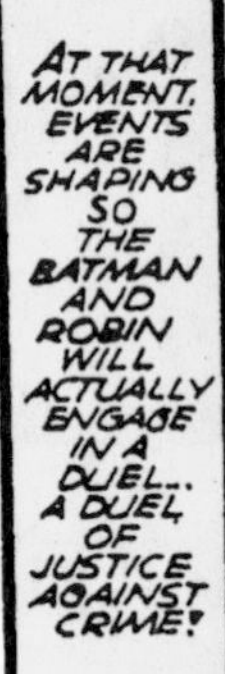
AT THAT MOMENT, EVENTS ARE SHAPING SO THE BATMAN AND ROBIN WILL ACTUALLY ENGAGE IN A DUEL... A DUEL OF JUSTICE AGAINST CRIME!

COME ALONG, STANLEY! STOP LAGGING BEHIND! I HAVE SOME LETTERS TO DICTATE!.... HURRY, CAN'T YOU!
Y-YES, SIR!
...ON A NEARBY PIER, PEOPLE BOARD A WAITING YACHT....
A CERTAIN MR HORN WITH HIS SECRETARY, STANLEY.....

A YOUNG, LOVELY GIRL, WITH HER TWO ARDENT ADMIRERS....
WHEN ARE YOU GOING TO BREAK DOWN AND MARRY ME, ELAINE?
BOYS... HOW CAN I MARRY EITHER ONE OF YOU WHEN I DON'T KNOW WHICH ONE OF YOU I LOVE THE MOST?
FORGET HIM-HOW ABOUT ME?

ALSO BOARDING THE YACHT IS A MR. COWDEN
THERE'S COWDEN! POOR CHAP WENT BANKRUPT! LOST EVERY CENT!
EVERYTHING I WORKED FOR- SWEPT AWAY OVERNIGHT! WHAT CAN I DO NOW! START ALL OVER AGAIN? NO—I'M BEATEN FOR GOOD!
LOOKS TIRED, DOESN'T HE?
WHO ARE THESE PEOPLE?.....MINOR PLAYERS, CERTAINLY..... BUT IT IS THE MINOR PLAYERS THAT MAKE UP THE CAST OF THE DRAMA OF LIFE.... FOR THEY ARE LIFE!

THAT'S THE EXCLUSIVE "YACHT SOCIETY," A CLUB COMPOSED OF YACHT OWNERS. ONCE A YEAR, ON A CERTAIN DAY, THEY GO FOR A LONG CRUISE ON ANOTHER MEMBER'S YACHT!
I HEAR THEY WEAR THE FANCIEST JEWELS......TRY TO COMPETE WITH EACH OTHER! WHAT A SETUP FOR CROOKS!

THEY'RE SAFE ENOUGH OUT AT SEA! ALL THEY HAVE TO WATCH OUT FOR ARE BUCCANEERS, PIRATES, HAW HAW!
YEAH!... PIRATES IN THE TWENTIETH CENTURY! SHADES OF CAPTAIN KIDD! HAW HAW!

AS SOON AS THE LAST GUEST IS ABOARD, THE YACHT HEADS FOR THE HIGH SEAS...... AND ONE OF THE STRANGEST OF MODERN ADVENTURES!

IN THE DAYS THAT FOLLOW, THE GUESTS LEAD THEIR NORMAL, EVERYDAY LIVES....
STANLEY...... STOP GAWKING AT THE SEA! YOU'RE NOT A GUEST HERE, YOU KNOW... BUT JUST MY SECRETARY! TAKE A LETTER
YES, MR HORN! YES, SIR!

DON'T KID YOURSELF! IT'S ME YOU REALLY LOVE!
IT'S VERY FLATTERING TO A GIRL TO BE LOVED BY TWO SUCH YOUNG MEN, BUT IT'S ALSO VERY DIFFICULT FOR HER!

..... AND MR COWDEN?
I'M TIRED.... BEATEN! I DON'T WANT TO FIGHT ANYMORE! THAT WATER...... DROWN YOUR TROUBLES, THEY SAY....

THAT NIGHT, THE MOON IS HIDDEN BY BLACK CLOUDS..... A HEAVY FOG ROLLS OVER THE CHURNING WAVES......

SUDDENLY, OUT OF THE MURKY MIST, THE GHOSTLY FORM OF A SCHOONER SAILS MAJESTICALLY ON THE HORIZON..... A BLACK FLAG WAVES DEFIANTLY, PROCLAIMING IT TO BE..... A PIRATE SHIP!

SMALL BOATS ARE LOWERED FROM HER SIDE, AND WITH MUFFLED OARS, MEN SLIP UP TO THE YACHT!......

THE DOOR OF THE CAPTAIN'S CABIN IS THRUST OPEN.......
WHA...... PIRATES! PIRATES!
PIRATES! ....WHY, IT MUST BE A MASQUERADE PARTY!

NOT EXACTLY, MATEY.... NOT EXACTLY! HAW-HAW!

1 THE PEOPLE ARE ALL BROUGHT UP ON DECK, WHERE THEY ARE STRIPPED OF THEIR VALUABLES, WHEN A TERRIBLE FIGURE APPEARS. A MAN WHO SEEMS TO BE A REINCARNATION OF THE DREADED BLACKBEARD, THE PIRATE!

IF THIS IS SOMEONE'S IDEA OF A JOKE....

I SHALL PROTEST TO THE AUTHORITIES... I....

HO HO.... WHAT A PRIZE CATCH THIS IS!

THERE'S THE YACHT! FUNNY— THERE'S NO ONE ON DECK! IT LOOKS DESERTED!
SOMETIME LATER... DAWN BEGINS TO BREAK.

LOOK! LOOK OVER THERE!
EITHER MY EYES ARE PLAYING TRICKS ON ME, OR THAT IS A PIRATE SHIP... A PIRATE SHIP, S'HELP ME!

WHAT ARE YOU SETTING HER DOWN FOR?
UNDOUBTEDLY, THAT'S WHERE THE PEOPLE FROM THE YACHT ARE BEING HELD!

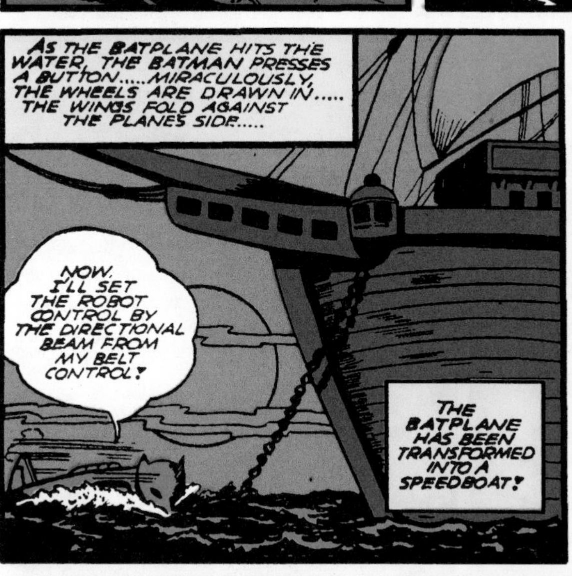
AS THE BATPLANE HITS THE WATER, THE BATMAN PRESSES A BUTTON.....MIRACULOUSLY, THE WHEELS ARE DRAWN IN..... THE WINGS FOLD AGAINST THE PLANE'S SIDE.....
NOW, I'LL SET THE ROBOT CONTROL BY THE DIRECTIONAL BEAM FROM MY BELT CONTROL!
THE BATPLANE HAS BEEN TRANSFORMED INTO A SPEEDBOAT!

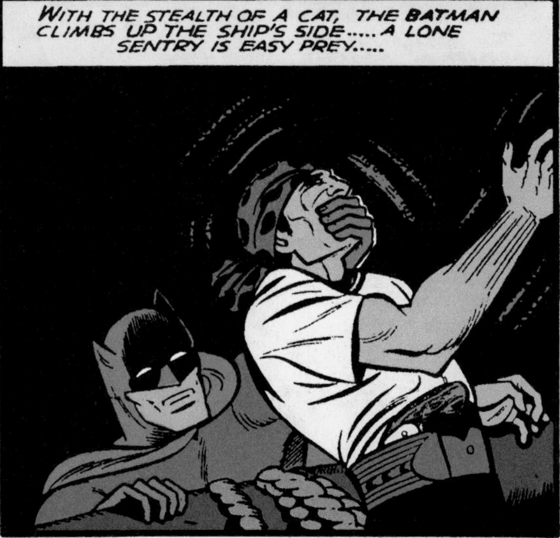
WITH THE STEALTH OF A CAT, THE BATMAN CLIMBS UP THE SHIP'S SIDE.....A LONE SENTRY IS EASY PREY.....

AS THE TWO SPRING LIGHTLY TO THE DECK, THEY ARE UNAWARE OF A RELIEF SENTRY'S WATCHING EYES......

SECONDS LATER, AS THEY PASS THE HOLD MANY FORMS FLING THEMSELVES OUT OF THE SHADOWS
GET 'EM!
WHA?

THOUGH THEY BATTLE VALIANTLY, THE BATMAN AND ROBIN ARE OVERWHELMED BY SUPERIOR NUMBERS.

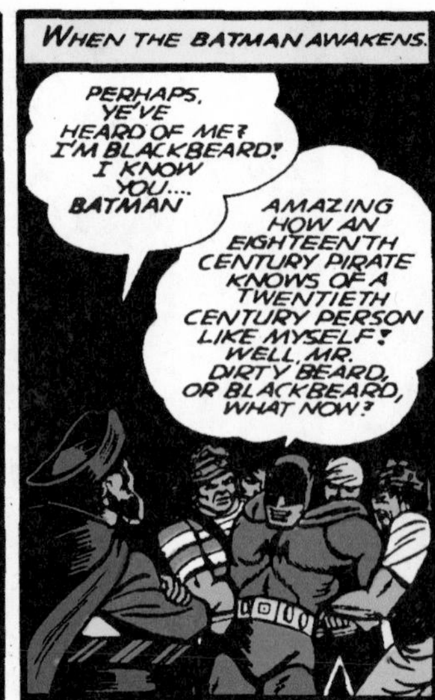
WHEN THE BATMAN AWAKENS.
PERHAPS, YE'VE HEARD OF ME? I'M BLACKBEARD! I KNOW YOU.... BATMAN
AMAZING HOW AN EIGHTEENTH CENTURY PIRATE KNOWS OF A TWENTIETH CENTURY PERSON LIKE MYSELF! WELL, MR. DIRTY BEARD, OR BLACKBEARD, WHAT NOW?

WHAT NOW? HO... HO! LOOK! YOUR LITTLE COMPANION IS GOING TA WALK THE PLANK!
ROBIN!

THE BATMAN GOES BERSERK AT THE SIGHT....
HO HO HO..... HO....
YOU ROTTEN SWINE! I'LL GET YOU FOR THIS! LET ME GO! LET ME GO!

A FINAL SHOVE .... AND ROBIN TOPPLES OFF THE PLANK!
IN YOU GO! HA HA!

NOTHING COULD HOLD THE BATMAN AFTER THIS..... NOT EVEN OVER-POWERING ODDS! WITH ALMOST SUPERHUMAN STRENGTH, HE TEARS HIMSELF LOOSE....ONE HAND DARTS TO A PIRATE BELT....
6

....A LITHE SPRING AND HE IS OVER THE SHIP'S SIDE....

A NEW MENACE APPROACHES - A TIGER SHARK APPEARS, CUTTING SHARPLY TOWARD ROBIN'S PLUMMETING FORM.....

A SUDDEN TWIST, AND THE BATMAN IS BENEATH THE DEMON OF THE DEEP, HIS BLADE BITING DEEP INTO THE MONSTER...

LOOK! BLOOD! THAT SHARK WE SEEN MUST HAVE GOT 'EM!
THAT'S THE END OF THE BATMAN!

BUT THE BATMAN AND ROBIN ARE VERY MUCH ALIVE....SWIMMING BENEATH THE SHIP, THEY CLIMB UP THE OTHER SIDE.....
THE HOLD IS OPEN ABOVE US! WE HEARD BLACKBEARD AND HIS MEN TALKING ABOUT YOU!
THANKS. BUT HOW DID YOU KNOW?

LEST THE CREW ABOVE MIGHT HEAR, THE PRISONERS GATHER IN A FAR CORNER OF THE HOLD.
YOU HAVE A PLAN TO FREE US?
YES, WHILE ROBIN AND I KEEP THE PIRATES OCCUPIED, I WANT TWO MEN TO GATHER ARMS FROM THE ROUNDHOUSE!

YOU CAN COUNT ME IN ON THIS!
IT MAY BE CRAZY, BUT IT'S THRILLING! GO TO IT, HENRY!
THIS IS CRAZY. THEY'LL GET YOU BEFORE YOU CAN GET STARTED!

EYES SHINING WITH EAGERNESS, COWDEN STEPS FORWARD.....
I'M YOUR OTHER MAN! I WANT TO FIGHT!
YOU'RE MAD, ALL OF YOU-- MAD! TRUSTING YOUR LIFE TO THIS-- THIS MASKED BANDIT!--

THE BATMAN! LIKE AS NOT HE'S.....
SHUT UP!

FOR TEN YEARS NOW, YOU'VE ORDERED ME AROUND! NOW, I'M GOING TO TELL YOU WHAT TO DO! IF YOU DON'T SHUT UP, I'M GOING TO SLAP YOU SILLY! NOW- SHUT UP!

IF YOU CAN USE AN EXTRA MAN..?
THANKS, BUT JUST TWO WILL BE ENOUGH! NOW. LISTEN CAREFULLY...

MOMENTS LATER, A PIRATE WHEELS AS A VOICE HAILS HIM....
HI THERE, UGLY!
IT'S HIM, THE BOY! ESCAPED- NOT DEAD!

DRAWING HIS CUTLASS, THE PIRATE LUNGES FORWARD...
I'LL MAKE SURE YOU DIE THIS TIME!

...BUT THE BOY WONDER NIMBLY LEAPS OVER THE SLASHING BLADE, WITH THE AGILITY OF A TRAINED ACROBAT!
WHAT SAY TO A GAME OF "HOP SCOTCH"?

TCH-TCH NO MANNERS! DON'T YOU KNOW IT'S NOT POLITE TO TURN YOUR BACK TO PEOPLE?
OW!
8

LOOK! THE GHOST OF THE BOY!
WE KNOW HOW TO SETTLE WITH "GHOSTS!" C'MON!

ROBIN SWEEPS UP THE FALLEN PIRATE'S SWORD.... THERE IS THE CLANG OF STEEL UPON STEEL AS THE BOY WONDER CLASHES WITH THE PIRATES!
COME AHEAD AND TRY IT!
GET THAT BOY!

MEANWHILE, THE BATMAN HAS BEEN QUITE BUSY...
UGH!
I'LL TAKE THAT SWORD, PLEASE!

A LITHE SPRING TO A DANGLING ROPE, AND HE SWINGS ACROSS THE DECK.....

MIND IF I BUTT IN?

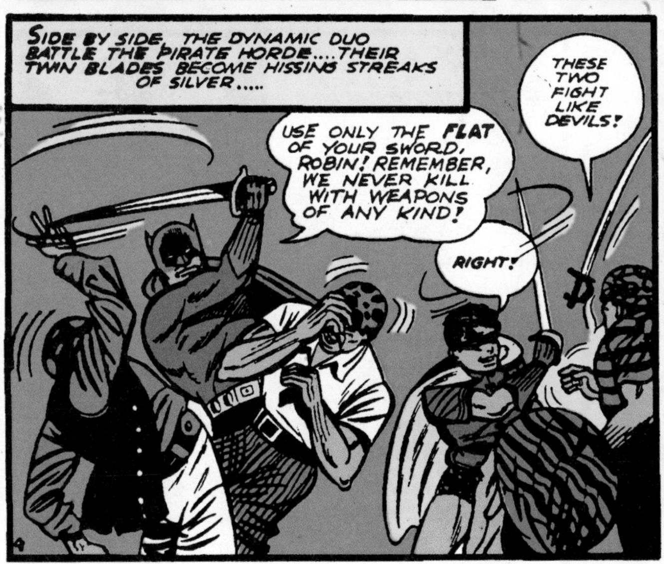
SIDE BY SIDE, THE DYNAMIC DUO BATTLE THE PIRATE HORDE....THEIR TWIN BLADES BECOME HISSING STREAKS OF SILVER.....
THESE TWO FIGHT LIKE DEVILS!
USE ONLY THE FLAT OF YOUR SWORD, ROBIN! REMEMBER, WE NEVER KILL WITH WEAPONS OF ANY KIND!
RIGHT!

AS MORE PIRATES CHARGE ON DECK, ROBIN SUDDENLY PUTS A PLAN INTO ACTION. HE RACES AWAY PURSUED BY A SHOUTING PIRATE....
FRIGHTENED, EH?

THE BOY WONDER GRASPS THE LOW-HANGING ROPE....
UP THE STAIRS,MEN... HE'S GETTING AWAY!

....SWINGS TO THE UPPER DECK.... A QUICK PIVOT....

....AND THE PIRATES GO SPRAWLING DOWN THE STAIRS!

THE BATMAN TRIES A LITTLE STRATEGY OF HIS OWN...WHIRLING SHARPLY, HE GRABS A LARGE WATER BARREL....

YOU BOYS LOOK LIKE YOU CAN USE A BATH, ANYWAY!

THEN, THE BATMAN CHARGES... AS HIS BLADE FLASHES.....THE PIRATES BREAK BEFORE HIM LIKE WATER, TUMBLING AGAINST ONE ANOTHER AS THEY RUN!
COME ON, YOU SPINELESS SWINE... FIGHT!

HA HA HA! LOOK AT THE JELLY FISH! TEN AGAINST ONE AND STILL THEY RUN! HA HA HA!

HIGH ABOVE, ROBIN SCRAMBLES UP THE SHIP'S RIGGING....

HIS KNIFE SLASHES AT THE RIGGING ROPES, AND THE SAILS DROP FROM THE MASTS IN GREAT WAVES......
THE SAILS! THEY'RE FALLING!

THE PIRATES ARE ENVELOPED BY THE HEAVY SAILS!

AT THAT VERY INSTANT, THE GREAT BLACKBEARD HIMSELF RUSHES FULL TILT AT THE BATMAN!
SO, YOU'VE RISEN FROM THE GRAVE, EH? — WELL, I'LL SEND YOU BACK TO IT!
WORDS, BLACKBEARD– JUST WORDS!

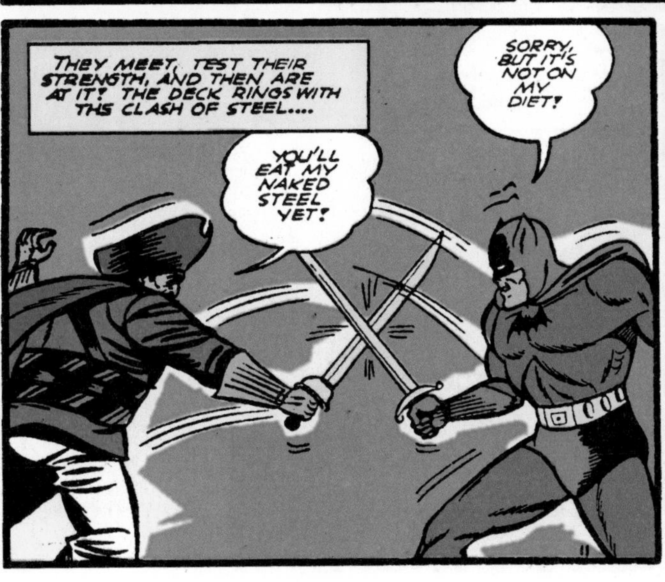
THEY MEET, TEST THEIR STRENGTH, AND THEN ARE AT IT! THE DECK RINGS WITH THS CLASH OF STEEL....
YOU'LL EAT MY NAKED STEEL YET!
SORRY, BUT IT'S NOT ON MY DIET!

SUDDENLY, THE BATMAN SLIPS ON A FALLEN KNIFE....
NOW, I HAVE YOU!

BLACKBEARD'S SWORD DARTS IN LIKE THE TONGUE OF A SNAKE, BUT THE BATMAN TWISTS ASIDE..
MY STEEL!

MY FOOT!

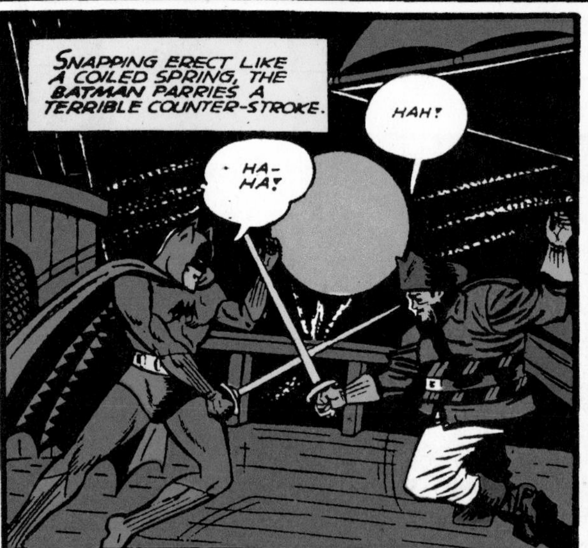
SNAPPING ERECT LIKE A COILED SPRING, THE BATMAN PARRIES A TERRIBLE COUNTER-STROKE.
HA-HA!
HAH!

....THEN, THE BATMAN'S HAND STREAKS FORWARD IN A DEADLY THRUST.....IT IS A MASTER-STROKE FOR BLACKBEARD'S SWORD FLIES FROM HIS HAND....
NOW!
HUH?

I DON'T NEED A SWORD NOW! THIS WILL BE JUST AS EFFECTIVE!
UGH!
12

HENRY AND COWDEN ROUND UP THE PIRATES....
...AND NOW, I'LL SHOW YOU WHO OUR FRIEND, BLACKBEARD, REALLY IS!

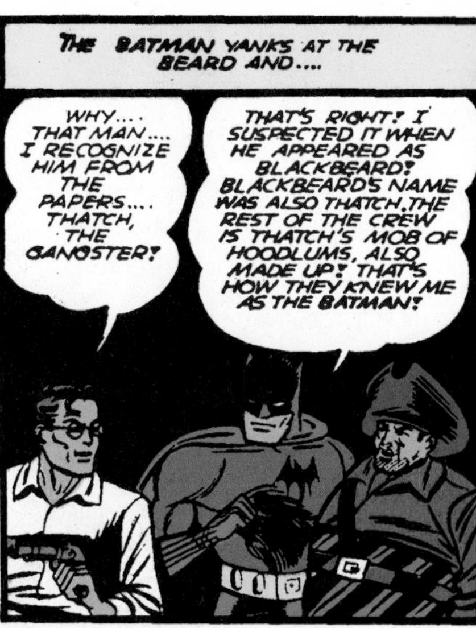
THE BATMAN YANKS AT THE BEARD AND....
WHY.... THAT MAN.... I RECOGNIZE HIM FROM THE PAPERS.... THATCH, THE GANGSTER!
THAT'S RIGHT! I SUSPECTED IT WHEN HE APPEARED AS BLACKBEARD! BLACKBEARD'S NAME WAS ALSO THATCH. THE REST OF THE CREW IS THATCH'S MOB OF HOODLUMS, ALSO MADE UP! THAT'S HOW THEY KNEW ME AS THE BATMAN!

THATCH CONFESSES....
SO, YOU KNEW OF THE "YACHT SOCIETY'S" TRIP A YEAR AGO?
SURE! AFTER LAST YEAR'S CRUISE, THE SOCIETY MENTIONED THE YACHT PICKED FOR THIS YEAR! I PLANNED IT THEN! WAS GOING TO ROB THE PEOPLE...

...AND HOLD THEM FOR A RANSOM! I GOT MY MEN TOGETHER AND HAD A FRIEND TEACH THEM TO DUEL! I BOUGHT THIS SHIP FOR CASH UNDER ANOTHER NAME!
AND NATURALLY, WHEN YOU RETURNED AS YOURSELVES AGAIN, NO-ONE WOULD SUSPECT THE SUDDENLY REINCARNATED BLACKBEARD AND HIS PIRATES ARE YOU GANGSTERS! CLEVER!

LATER THE BATMAN AND ROBIN, THE BOY WONDER, TAKE LEAVE OF THE SHIP.....
THATCH CERTAINLY WENT THROUGH A LOT OF TROUBLE! PIRATES... WHAT EVER MADE HIM PICK THAT?
THATCH USED TO BE AN ACTOR... COSTUMES AND FANTASY ALWAYS APPEALED TO HIM.....WELL, THAT'S ONE MORE CASE OFF THE BOOKS!

THE BATMAN'S ADVENTURE MAY BE FINISHED, BUT FOR OTHERS IT IS JUST BEGINNING...ABOARD THE YACHT.....
WHEN DID YOU KNOW IT WAS ME YOU REALLY LOVED?
WHEN YOU OFFERED TO HELP THE BATMAN, AND PAUL HESITATED— HIS HESITATION DECIDED ME!

I HEAR YOU'RE THINKING OF QUITTING THE FIELD, COWDEN!
I WAS, BUT THIS TRIP SUDDENLY SHOWED ME WHAT EXCITEMENT THERE IS IN FIGHTING INSTEAD OF QUITTING! NO SIR, I'M NOT QUITTING!

THEN, YOU'RE NOT GOING TO FIRE ME?
HM! HARUMPH! NO! OUR ORGANIZATION NEEDS MEN LIKE YOU! I RATHER LIKE THE WAY YOU SPOKE UP TO ME...SHOULD HAVE A LONG TIME AGO! HERE-HAVE A CIGAR!
AND SO, A SUDDEN TURN OF EVENTS BRINGS ABOUT CERTAIN REACTIONS IN PEOPLE! IMAGINE HOW THEY WOULD STILL BE ACTING IF THIS ADVENTURE HAD NOT HAPPENED?

Acclaimed
AMERICA'S NUMBER ONE ADVENTURE TEAM
THE AMAZING BATMAN WITH THAT SENSATIONAL YOUNG PHENOMENON, THE Original AND GREATEST WONDER BOY OF THEM ALL ROBIN — THRILL YOU EVERY MONTH — WITH THEIR ASTOUNDING, ACTION-A-MINUTE EXPLOITS IN DETECTIVE COMICS

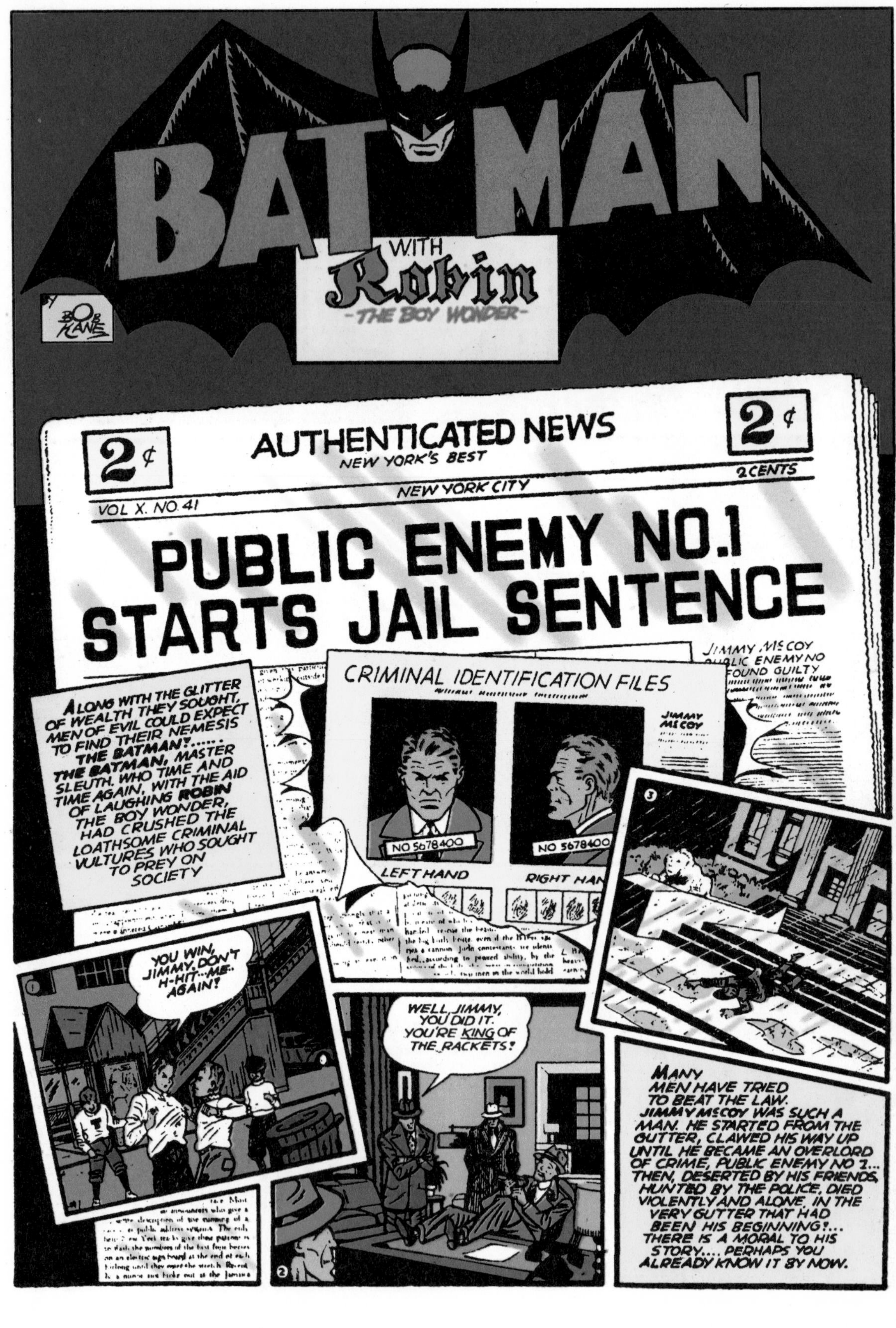
BATMAN
WITH Robin
-THE BOY WONDER-
BY BOB KANE
AUTHENTICATED NEWS
NEW YORK'S BEST
2¢
2¢
2 CENTS
NEW YORK CITY
VOL X. NO. 41
PUBLIC ENEMY NO.1 STARTS JAIL SENTENCE
JIMMY MC COY PUBLIC ENEMY NO FOUND GUILTY
CRIMINAL IDENTIFICATION FILES
JIMMY MC COY
NO 5678400
NO 5678400
LEFT HAND
RIGHT HAN
ALONG WITH THE GLITTER OF WEALTH THEY SOUGHT, MEN OF EVIL COULD EXPECT TO FIND THEIR NEMESIS THE BATMAN!...... THE BATMAN, MASTER SLEUTH, WHO TIME AND TIME AGAIN, WITH THE AID OF LAUGHING ROBIN THE BOY WONDER, HAD CRUSHED THE LOATHSOME CRIMINAL VULTURES WHO SOUGHT TO PREY ON SOCIETY
YOU WIN, JIMMY. DON'T H-HIT...ME... AGAIN!
WELL, JIMMY, YOU DID IT. YOU'RE KING OF THE RACKETS!
MANY MEN HAVE TRIED TO BEAT THE LAW. JIMMY MCCOY WAS SUCH A MAN. HE STARTED FROM THE GUTTER, CLAWED HIS WAY UP UNTIL HE BECAME AN OVERLORD OF CRIME, PUBLIC ENEMY NO 1... THEN, DESERTED BY HIS FRIENDS, HUNTED BY THE POLICE, DIED VIOLENTLY AND ALONE, IN THE VERY GUTTER THAT HAD BEEN HIS BEGINNING!... THERE IS A MORAL TO HIS STORY.... PERHAPS YOU ALREADY KNOW IT BY NOW.

UPON HEARING THE SENTENCE, HIS MOTHER GAVE A HEART-RENDING SHRIEK AND TOPPLED TO THE FLOOR! THE SHOCK WAS TOO MUCH, AND SHE DIED WITH HER SON'S NAME ON HER LIPS!

MOM.. MOM!

JIMMY... AHHHH!

IN JAIL JIMMY BECOMES ACQUAINTED WITH HARDENED CRIMINALS...MEN WHO HAD BUCKED THE LAW ALL THER LIFE!
WHEN WE GET OUT, KID, I'LL GET YOU IN WITH A MOB! I KNOW! YOU'RE A SMART KID! YOU CAN GET TO BE A BIG SHOT!

..AN' FROM NOW ON, YOU'RE GONNA BUY OUR BEER! - AN' IF YA DON'T....
SEE ED' FOR A TOM
NO TRUST
10
IN THE YEARS THAT FOLLOWED, JIMMY MCCOY CHANGED FROM AN EMBITTERED BOY, TO A SNEERING, CUNNING CRIMINAL

JIMMY WASN'T CONTENT TO BE A MERE MOBSTER. HE ORGANIZED HIS OWN MOB AND IT WASN'T LONG BEFORE HE WAS BEING CALLED THE "KING OF RACKETS!"
I WANT YOU BOYS TO PAY A VISIT TO AUGIE DAVIS! TELL HIM I'M TAKING OVER THE NORTH SIDE! GET GOIN'!

THEN ONE DAY, JIMMY'S BUBBLE BURST....PROHIBITION WAS REPEALED!
WHAT ARE WE GONNA DO? BOOTLEGGIN' WON'T GET US DOUGH ANYMORE!
WE'LL EXPAND OUR "PROTECTION" RACKET! THERE'S WAYS WE CAN GET DOUGH FROM THE SUCKERS! STOP WORRYIN'!

BUT, THE PUBLIC WAS AFTER JIMMY AND HIS LIKE!... G-MEN CALLED HIM "PUBLIC ENEMY NO. 1"!
DAILY TIMES.
2¢
2 CENTS
NEW YORK
VOL 14 NO 11
GOVERNMENT TO INVESTIGATE JIMMY 'RED' McCOY
RACKET BOSS TO BE HELD FOR INCOME TAX EVASION.
JIMMY 'RED' McCOY ENTERING THE ATTORNEY'S OFFICE

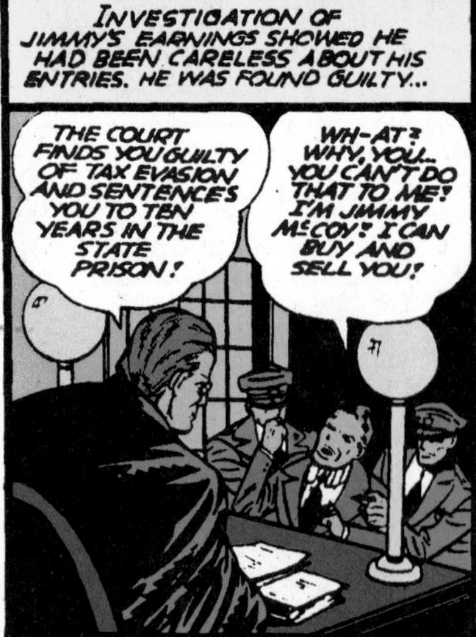
INVESTIGATION OF JIMMY'S EARNINGS SHOWED HE HAD BEEN CARELESS ABOUT HIS ENTRIES. HE WAS FOUND GUILTY...
THE COURT FINDS YOU GUILTY OF TAX EVASION AND SENTENCES YOU TO TEN YEARS IN THE STATE PRISON!
WH-AT? WHY, YOU.. YOU CAN'T DO THAT TO ME! I'M JIMMY McCOY! I CAN BUY AND SELL YOU!

BUT JIMMY'S THREATS DIDN'T HELP HIM... HE WAS SENT TO PRISON.. THE YEARS PASSED..
1931
19
19
19
19
19
1941

THEN. THE DAY CAME WHEN HE WAS RELEASED....JIMMY "RED" McCOY WAS FREE ONCE MORE!
NOW THAT I'M OUT, THE FIRST THING I'M GONNA DO IS GET MY OLD MOB TOGETHER! I'M GONNA RUN THIS TOWN JUST LIKE I USED TO!

THE NEWS OF McCOY'S RELEASE HITS THE NEWSPAPERS...
3¢ TRIBUNE 3¢
McCOY FREED
ONE TIME RACKETS KING SERVES SENTENCE
REFUSES TO TALK TO REPORTERS

AMONG THE MANY WHO DIGEST THIS PARTICULAR PIECE OF NEWS IS THE PRESENT "RACKETS KING"... BIG COSTELLO....
BOYS, I SEE THAT "RED" McCOY IS LOOSE! I DON'T LIKE THAT!
WHY, BOSS.. WHAT'VE YOU GOT TA BE AFRAID OF?
SURE- YOU'RE THE BIG SHOT NOW!

I KNOW JIMMY McCOY! THE FIRST THING THAT GUY'S GONNA DO IS GET A MOB TOGETHER AND TRY TO BE THE BIG SHOT HE ONCE WAS!

WELL, BEFORE McCOY GETS A CHANCE TO GET STARTED I WANT HIM RUBBED OUT! GET HIM... I DON'T CARE HOW.. BUT GET HIM!
YEAH.. JIMMY'S LIKE THAT!
GOTCHA, BOSS.

LATER THAT DAY, AS JIMMY McCOY WANDERS IDLY DOWN THE STREET THAT HE LIVED ON AS A BOY!..
SAME OLD BLOCK!... BUNCH O' KIDS STILL PLAYIN' THE SAME GAMES! CHEE..... IT GIVES ME A FUNNY FEELIN'!

SUDDENLY, A CAR WHIPS AROUND THE CORNER, THE SNOUT OF A MACHINE GUN CHATTERING SMOKE AND DEATH...

AT THE SOUND OF THE DEADLY CHATTER, McCOY THROWS HIMSELF TO THE GROUND AS BULLETS LANCE OVER HIM...
MAMA! MAMA.
LOOK OUT, KID!

BUT ONE STRAY BULLET FINDS A TARGET ... IN THE LEG OF A LITTLE GIRL RUNNING FOR SAFETY!

UGH!
....AND A SHOT BORES INTO THE BATMAN'S UNPROTECTED SHOULDER!

WITH A MOCKING LAUGH, MCCOY MAKES HIS ESCAPE.....
SO LONG, BATMAN! HAW... HAW!

MY FOLLOWING MCCOY TO SEE IF HE WAS GOING STRAIGHT, AT LEAST CONVINCED ME OF ONE THING..... MCCOY IS NOT GOING UP THAT NARROW PATH-BUT A VERY CROOKED ONE!

IF IT'S THE LAST THING I EVER DO, I'M GOING TO GET MCCOY! THE NEXT TIME WE MEET, THINGS WILL BE DIFFERENT!

THAT NIGHT...... MEN GATHER IN AN OLD DESERTED WAREHOUSE.....
WHAT'S THE IDEA O' GETTIN' US TOGETHER, MCCOY?
I SENT FOR YOU BOYS 'CAUSE I KNOW THAT EACH O'YA HAS A GRUDGE AGAINST BIG COSTELLO!...AN' SOME O'YA USED TO BE IN MY OLD MOB!

I WANT TO START A NEW MOB! YOU GUYS STICK WITH ME AN' YOU'LL BE EATIN' OUTA GOLD PLATES!
WHAT ABOUT BIG COSTELLO? HE RUNS THIS TOWN NOW!
YEAH! HE AIN'T GONNA LIKE IT!

WHATSA MATTER WITH YOU GUYS? COSTELLO'S GOT YOU SCARED?
DON'T GET SORE, MCCOY! I'M WITH YA!
COUNT ME IN!
ME, TOO!

AFTER LIGHTING HIS OWN CIGARETTE, A THUG HOLDS THE LIGHT FOR McCOY...
HERE'S A LIGHT, "RED."
HOLD THAT FOR ME!

AFTER LIGHTING UP, McCOY BLOWS THE FLAME!
HEY!.... WHAT'S THE IDEA? YOU KNEW I WANTED A LIGHT!
SHUT UP! I NEVER LIGHT THREE ON A MATCH! IT'S BAD LUCK!

SAME OLD JIMMY McCOY... STILL SUPERSTITIOUS! I'LL BET YOU STILL HAVE THAT OLD LUCKY RABBIT'S FOOT!
YOU BET YOUR SWEET LIFE I HAVE. THE DAY I LOSE THAT MY LUCK'S GONNA RUN OUT!

BUT I'VE BEEN PAYING ANOTHER PROTECTIVE ASSOCIATION! I.... ....
SHUT UP! FROM NOW ON, WE'RE PROTECTIN' YA! GET ME?
IN THE ENSUING DAYS, JIMMY McCOY BEGINS TO MOVE IN ON COSTELLO'S TERRITORY...

CAN'T PAY UP, EH?.. OKAY, BOYS..... THROW THAT ACID OVER THE CLOTHES!!
NO ONE SEEMS SAFE FROM HIS MEN...

AS THE RIVAL GANGS CLASH, BATTLES ARE FOUGHT....THE SMOKING GUN HOLDS SWAY....!
BOOM

WHILE IN HIS APARTMENT, BRUCE WAYNE, WHO IS IN REALITY THE BATMAN, SPEAKS WITH HIS WARD, DICK GRAYSON, WHOSE OTHER SELF IS ROBIN, THE BOY WONDER!
READING ABOUT THE GANGWAR AGAIN?
YES, AND I'VE GOT A FEELING THAT McCOY IS THE ONE WHO IS BUCKING BIG COSTELLO!—BUT NOBODY CAN PROVE IT. STORE OWNERS ARE AFRAID TO TALK. DICK, YOU'VE GOT A JOB TO DO— LISTEN...

THE NEXT DAY, A GRUBBY, DIRTY-FACED SHOE-SHINE BOY STANDS BEFORE THE HOUSE WHEREIN "RED" MC COY LIVES......
RED MC COY
SHINE. MISTER?
BEAT IT!
SCRAM!

BUT INSTEAD OF "SCRAMMING" THE BOY FOLLOWS THE GANGSTERS INTO THE HOUSE.....

HE STEPS SOFTLY TO THE DOOR AND LISTENS INTENTLY AT THE KEYHOLE.
CAN'T HEAR A WORD THEY'RE SAYING! THEY'RE TALKING TOO LOW!

APPLYING HIS EYE TO THE KEYHOLE, THE BOY BEGINS TO READ THE LIPS OF THE MEN......
...SO, IT'S THE PENGUIN CLUB TOMORROW NIGHT! THAT GUY IS NOT GONNA STALL US ANYMORE!
READING THE LIPS, AS WOULD A DEAF MAN, IS ONE OF THE MANY ACCOMPLISHMENTS USED BY THE BATMAN AND ROBIN IN THEIR FIGHT AGAINST CRIME

THE BOY WONDER QUICKLY REPORTS TO HIS CHIEF....
..AND THE OWNER OF THE PENGUIN CLUB REFUSES TO PAY PROTECTION MONEY TO MC COY BECAUSE HE SAYS HE'S PAYING COSTELLO FOR THAT!
SO, THEY'RE GOING TO SCARE HIM TOMORROW NIGHT! HMM! I'VE A HUNCH WE'LL BE THERE, TOO!

....BUT AT THAT VERY MOMENT, AN UNEXPECTED DEVELOPMENT IS TAKING PLACE.....THE NIGHT CLUB OWNER CALLS BIG COSTELLO!
...AND I'D LIKE TO KNOW WHERE THIS PROTECTION IS THAT I'M PAYING FOR! I DON'T WANT ANY TROUBLE!
SO, MC COY IS CALLING TOMORROW NIGHT!...DON'T WORRY, PAL. YOU'RE NOT GONNA HAVE ANY TROUBLE. MC COY IS! I'LL SEE TO THAT!

THE NEXT NIGHT, TWO FIGURES ON A NEARBY ROOF WATCH THE ENTRANCE OF THE PENGUIN CLUB.
LOOK!
MC COY AND HIS MEN!
BAR
N CLUB

A SCANT FEW MOMENTS LATER...
SAY-LOOK AT THOSE HARD-LOOKING TOUGHS GOING IN!
I RECOGNIZE THEM! THEY BELONG TO BIG COSTELLO'S MOB! C'MON.... THERE'S GOING TO BE SHOOTING.... AND THAT PLACE IS JAMMED WITH PEOPLE!

INSIDE THE PENGUIN CLUB
YOU— WHAT DO YOU WANT?
YOU KNOW WHAT I WANT? WHEN ARE YOU GONNA PAY OFF?
YOU'RE GONNA GET THE PAYOFF RIGHT NOW, MᶜCOY!
MᶜCOY AND HIS MEN WHIRL SWIFTLY, TUGGING AT THEIR GUNS! PANDEMONIUM BREAKS OUT WITH THE SOUND OF GUNFIRE!
OUCH! MY SHOULDER
ABRUPTLY, STREAKING TOWARD THE FRAY ARE TWO INSPIRING FIGURES.. IT IS THAT DYNAMIC DUO... BATMAN AND ROBIN, THE BOY WONDER!
MIND IF WE JOIN THE PARTY!
THE RIVAL GANGSTERS FORGET THEIR ENMITY AND WHEEL TO MEET THEIR COMMON FOE...
JUST LIKE FOOTBALL- TAKE OUT MEN, SO YOUR OWN MAN CAN COME THROUGH!
TCH-TCH! A GENTLEMAN NEVER RESTS HIS ELBOWS ON THE TABLE!
CRACK! THE STEEL FISTS OF THE BATMAN BEGIN THEIR DEADLY AND EFFECTIVE WORK....
MᶜCOY .. THOUGH NICKED IN THE SHOULDER - BLAZES AWAY FURIOUSLY AT THE RIVAL GANGSTERS
I'LL TEACH THE DIRTY CROOKS TO MIND THEIR OWN BUSINESS...

HOLDING A HEAVY DINING TABLE OVER HIS HEAD PROVES CHILD'S PLAY FOR THE DARK KNIGHT!

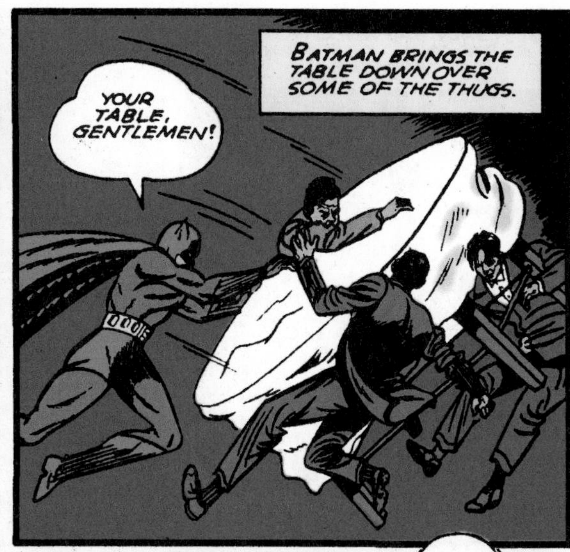
BATMAN BRINGS THE TABLE DOWN OVER SOME OF THE THUGS.
YOUR TABLE, GENTLEMEN!

AS THE GUNMEN BAND TOGETHER FOR A CONCERTED RUSH, THE MANTLED FIGHTERS HASTILY DECIDE UPON A PLAN OF ATTACK!
LOOK. ROBIN.... AMMUNITION!
I GET YOU!

THE THUGS ARE MET BY A BARRAGE OF HAND GRENADES!
OW!
AWK!
OUCH!
DO HAVE A PLATE OF SOUP!
...AND A CUP OF TEA!

THE THUGS ARE "OVERCOME" BY THE AMAZING DINNER!.
...PIE FOR DESSERT!

....WHILE ROBIN PROVIDES THE "ENTERTAINMENT"... SOME "AFTER-DINNER MUSIC"
...BET YOU NEVER KNEW I STUDIED THE BASS FIDDLE.... DOES IT "SHOCK" YOU?

SUDDENLY THE AIR IS PIERCED BY THE SOUND OF A POLICE WHISTLE ...
COPS! JIMMY!
C'MON! LET'S SCRAM OUTA HERE!
GRILL

THEIR WORK DONE, THE BATMAN AND ROBIN DECIDE UPON THEIR EXIT!
PENGUIN CLUB

UNDER PRESSURE FROM THE POLICE, THE NIGHT CLUB OWNER FORGETS HIS FEAR OF REPRISAL FROM THE RACKETEERS AND BABBLES HIS TALE OF WOE.
THEN, McCOY'S MEN STARTED SHOOTING! OH, MY PLACE IS RUINED.. . RUINED!
McCOY, EH? YOU'D BETTER COME ALONG FOR QUESTIONING COSTELLO!

ONE O'COSTELLO'S RATS GOT ME IN THE SHOULDER! I....
LISTEN!
ALL POLICE OFFICERS!... BE ON THE LOOKOUT FOR JIMMY "RED" McCOY! WANTED FOR ATTEMPTED EXTORTION RACKET! ALSO PICK UP "BIG" COSTELLO FOR QUESTIONING!
AS McCOY SPEEDS AWAY IN HIS CAR, HE TURNS ON THE RADIO TO THE POLICE CALLS AND HEARS.....

THIS IS WHERE I GET OFF! YOU'RE TOO "HOT" FOR ME TO BE STICKIN' TO!
YEAH- EVERY COP IN TOWN WILL BE LOOKIN' FOR YA!.. AN' I DON'T WANNA BE AROUND WHEN THEY GET YA!
"RED" McCOY! WANTED (AWK)
YOU YELLOW RATS! GET OUT!.. GET OUT BEFORE I PLUG YA!

"BIG" COSTELLO'S RESPONSIBLE FOR THIS! ... I'M GONNA GET THAT GUY!... THEY PROBABLY HAVE HIM OVER AT THE COURT-HOUSE FOR QUESTIONING BY NOW!.. I'LL GET HIM!

AS JIMMY STEPS FROM HIS CAR, CLOUDS GATHER IN LOWERING MASSES IN THE SKY... IT IS LIKE SOME OMINOUS FOREBODING OF THINGS TO COME. .
THE FIRST THINGS THE COPS WILL DO IS STOP EVERY CAR! BETTER WALK THERE!

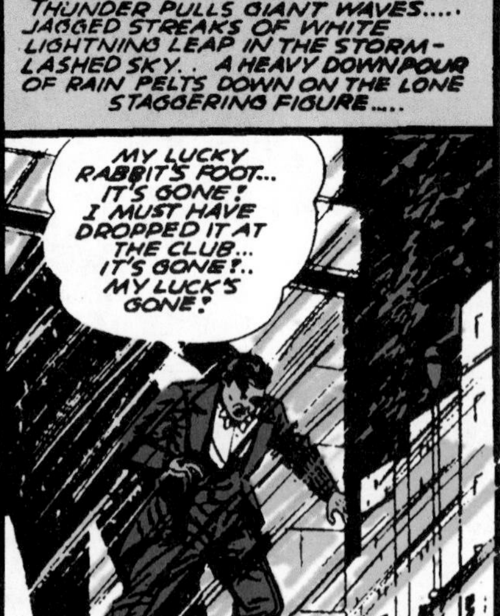
THUNDER PULLS GIANT WAVES..... JAGGED STREAKS OF WHITE LIGHTNING LEAP IN THE STORM-LASHED SKY.. A HEAVY DOWNPOUR OF RAIN PELTS DOWN ON THE LONE STAGGERING FIGURE.....
MY LUCKY RABBIT'S FOOT... IT'S GONE! I MUST HAVE DROPPED IT AT THE CLUB... IT'S GONE!.. MY LUCK'S GONE!

AT THAT VERY INSTANT, THE MANTLED FORM OF THE BATMAN STRIDES INTO McCOY'S ROOMS...
HE'S NOT HERE....I WONDER IF THAT HOT-HEADED...

THE NEXT MOMENT, HE AND ROBIN ARE RACING ALONG THE STREETS IN DESPERATE HASTE...
YOU THINK HE'S GONE TO THE COURTHOUSE TO GET COSTELLO?
I KNOW IT! HE'S HOT-HEADED, MAKES QUICK, RECKLESS DECISIONS! C'MON! ..THERE'S GOING TO BE MORE SHOOTING!

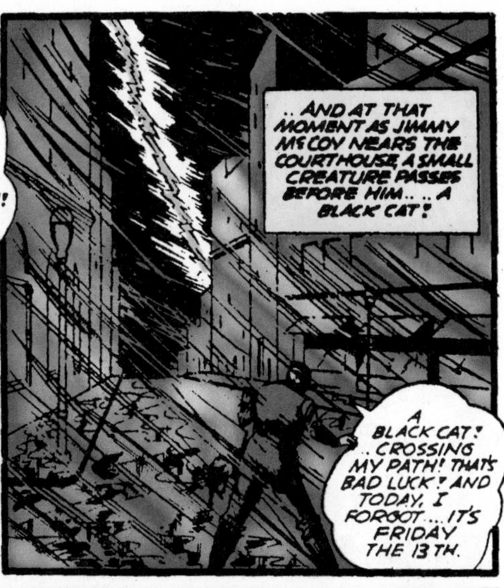
..AND AT THAT MOMENT AS JIMMY McCOY NEARS THE COURTHOUSE, A SMALL CREATURE PASSES BEFORE HIM... ...A BLACK CAT!
A BLACK CAT! ..CROSSING MY PATH! THAT'S BAD LUCK! AND TODAY, I FORGOT....IT'S FRIDAY THE 13TH.

THOUGH HIS SUPERSTITION IS GREAT, HIS HATRED OF COSTELLO IS GREATER...UP THE MANY STEPS OF THE COURTHOUSE WALKS JIMMY McCOY....

...THEN, THE GREAT DOORS OPEN AND CLOSE BEHIND THE FIGURES OF THREE MEN..."BIG" COSTELLO AND HIS BODYGUARDS!
THEY SURE FIND OUT THEY COULDN'T HOLD YOU, BOSS! HAW, HAW!
THEY DIDN'T HAVE A THING ON ME, AND THEY KNEW IT!
BOSS, LOOK! IT'S McCOY!

A SUDDEN CLASH OF LIGHTNING MERGED WITH THE ROAR OF GUNS...GUNS THAT LANCE FLAME AND SUDDEN DEATH!

TWO CLOAKED FIGURES LEAP UP THE STEPS AND PUT AN END TO THE GUN-FIGHT!
THAT'LL BE ENOUGH OF THAT!
LOOKS LIKE THE OTHER GUYS ARE ALL SHOT!

OKAY, MC COY!... I'M TAKING YOU IN! YOU'RE GOING TO A CELL AGAIN!
I'M NOT GOIN' TO ANY JAIL ANYMORE! HA HA! YOU'RE JUST A LITTLE TOO LATE! HA HA!

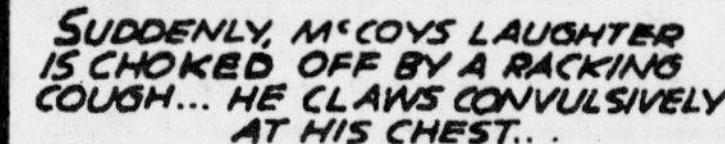
SUDDENLY, MC COY'S LAUGHTER IS CHOKED OFF BY A RACKING COUGH... HE CLAWS CONVULSIVELY AT HIS CHEST..

JUST A LITTLE TOO LATE! HA HA (COUGH) AHHH!!

...AND TUMBLES DOWN THE STEPS......

....ROLLS ALONG THE SIDEWALK ...

...AND SPRAWLS OVER THE CURB AND THE GUTTER!
JIMMY MC COY'S INFAMOUS CAREER HAS COME TO AN END AT LAST!

IT IS THE NEXT DAY IN THE WAYNE HOME!....
YOU KNOW— EVEN THOUGH MC COY WAS A CRIMINAL THERE WAS SOMETHING ...SOMETHING ABOUT HIM—
SOMETHING THAT SUGGESTED HE WAS A BOY TRYING TO ACT LIKE A BIG SHOT! YES, I FELT IT, TOO! TOO BAD....HE HAD TALENT. HE WOULD HAVE GONE FAR IN BUSINESS!

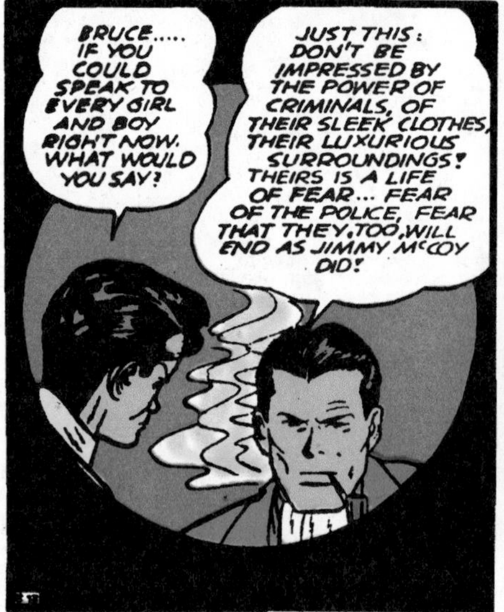
BRUCE..... IF YOU COULD SPEAK TO EVERY GIRL AND BOY RIGHT NOW, WHAT WOULD YOU SAY?
JUST THIS: DON'T BE IMPRESSED BY THE POWER OF CRIMINALS, OF THEIR SLEEK CLOTHES, THEIR LUXURIOUS SURROUNDINGS! THEIRS IS A LIFE OF FEAR... FEAR OF THE POLICE, FEAR THAT THEY, TOO, WILL END AS JIMMY MC COY DID!

LEST ALL OF YOU FORGET, THINK BACK NOW TO THAT DREADFUL NIGHT, THAT TERRIBLE SCENE WHEN JIMMY MC COY LAY FACE DOWN IN THE GUTTER, AS THE RAIN PELTED DOWN ON HIS SPRAWLED FIGURE! THINK BACK AND BE WISE!
YOU REMEMBER WE SAID THERE IS A MORAL TO THIS STORY. YOU MUST SURELY KNOW IT BY NOW! IT'S THAT OFTEN REPEATED PHRASE...THAT HORRIBLY TRUE PHRASE, "CRIME DOES NOT PAY!"

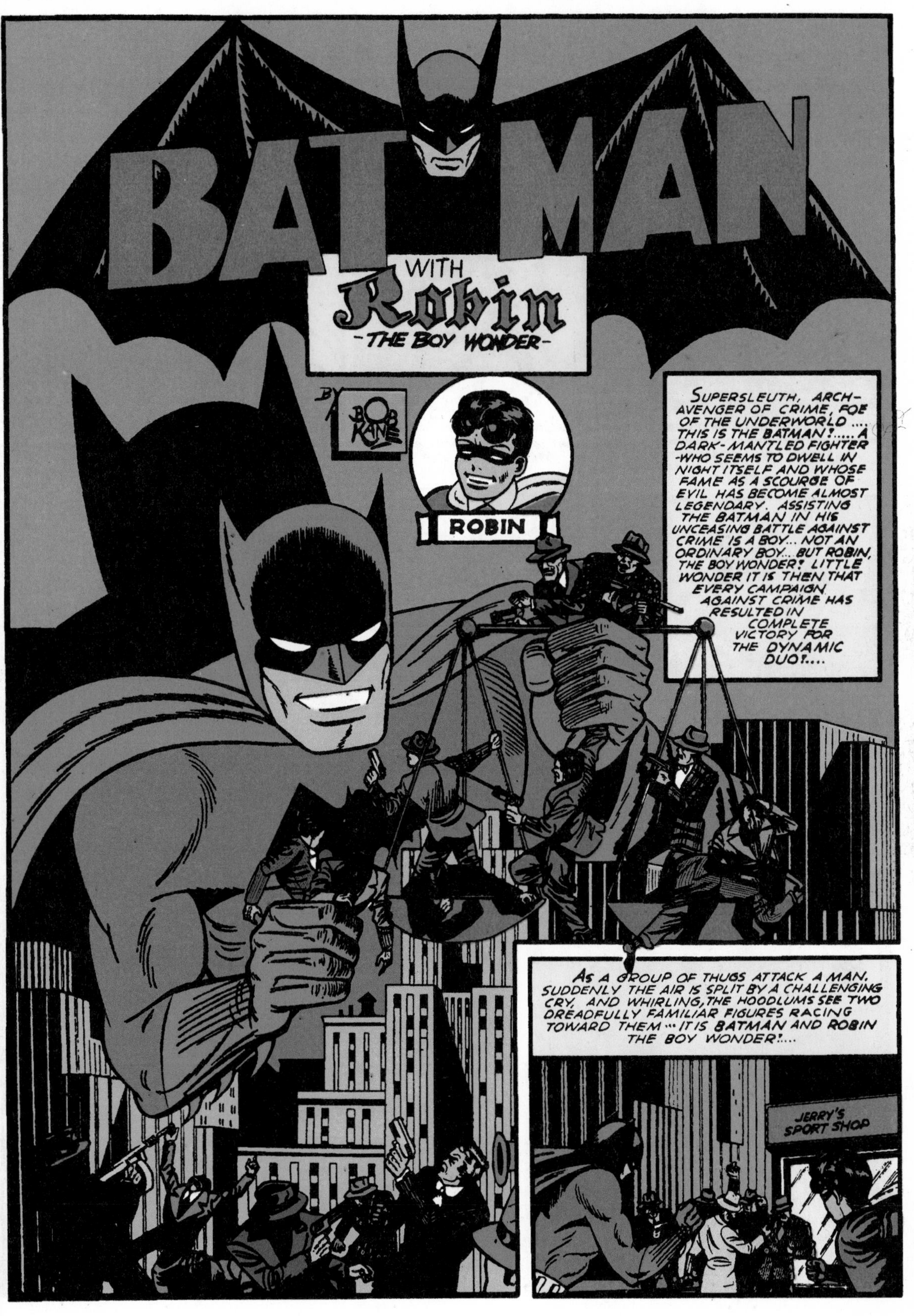
BATMAN
WITH
Robin
-THE BOY WONDER-
BY BOB KANE
ROBIN
SUPERSLEUTH, ARCH-AVENGER OF CRIME, FOE OF THE UNDERWORLD .... THIS IS THE BATMAN!..... A DARK-MANTLED FIGHTER -WHO SEEMS TO DWELL IN NIGHT ITSELF AND WHOSE FAME AS A SCOURGE OF EVIL HAS BECOME ALMOST LEGENDARY. ASSISTING THE BATMAN IN HIS UNCEASING BATTLE AGAINST CRIME IS A BOY... NOT AN ORDINARY BOY... BUT ROBIN, THE BOY WONDER! LITTLE WONDER IT IS THEN THAT EVERY CAMPAIGN AGAINST CRIME HAS RESULTED IN COMPLETE VICTORY FOR THE DYNAMIC DUO!....
AS A GROUP OF THUGS ATTACK A MAN, SUDDENLY THE AIR IS SPLIT BY A CHALLENGING CRY, AND WHIRLING, THE HOODLUMS SEE TWO DREADFULLY FAMILIAR FIGURES RACING TOWARD THEM ... IT IS BATMAN AND ROBIN THE BOY WONDER!....
JERRY'S SPORT SHOP

TWO WHIRLWINDS OF ACTION STRIKE!
NICE LITTLE RIOT, EH ROBIN?
NOT BAD AT ALL!

A BIG BOY LIKE YOU PLAYING WITH TOYS! TCH-TCH!

A SMALL BUT COMPACT FIST SHOOTS OUT WITH TRIP-HAMMER SPEED!

MEANWHILE, THE BATMAN FINDS HIMSELF BUSILY OCCUPIED........
CREEPING UP ON ME, EH?

WITH THE SPEED OF A STRIKING RATTLER, THE BATMAN'S HAND STREAKS FORWARD......

NEXT TIME DON'T BE SO COY!
....AND THE NEXT MOMENT, THE ASTOUNDED THUG FINDS HIMSELF SPINNING THROUGH THE AIR!

SUDDENLY, A CAR WHIPS AROUND THE STREET CORNER-FROM A WINDOW THE UGLY SNOUT OF A MACHINE GUN BEGINS ITS DEADLY CHATTER OF DEATH.....
GET DOWN!

A DOOR SWINGS OPEN AND THE SHAKY THUGS STAGGER TOWARD IT......
HURRY IT UP YOU GUYS!

AS THE CAR MAKES ITS GETAWAY, THE MACHINE GUN IS POINTED AT THE HUDDLED FIGURE OF THE RESCUED MAN....
LOOK OUT! THEY'RE GUNNING FOR YOU! BEHIND THE ASH CAN!

AS BULLETS WHINE OVER HIM LIKE ANGRY HORNETS, THE BATMAN PICKS UP A GUN DROPPED BY A THUG. TAKES CAREFUL AIM --- AND FIRES!
JUST WANT TO WING HIM!

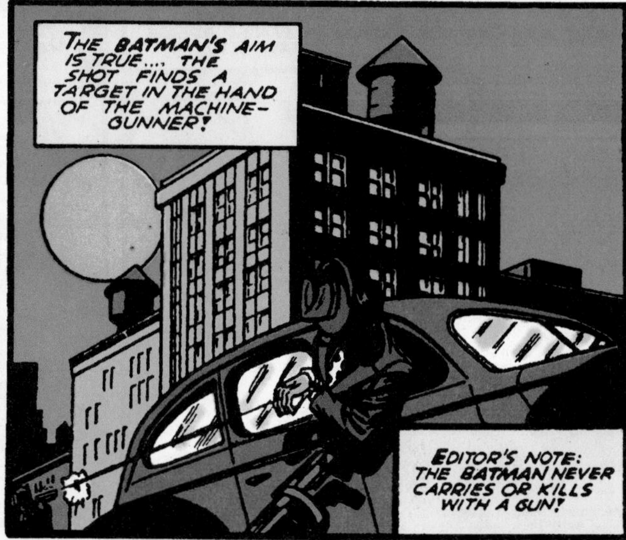
THE BATMAN'S AIM IS TRUE.... THE SHOT FINDS A TARGET IN THE HAND OF THE MACHINE-GUNNER!
EDITOR'S NOTE: THE BATMAN NEVER CARRIES OR KILLS WITH A GUN!

YOU CAN GET UP NOW! I DON'T THINK THEY WANT TO PLAY ANYMORE!

SAY, AREN'T YOU TIM BANNON, THE COACH OF THE PANTHERS -- THE PROFESSIONAL FOOTBALL TEAM?
YES- AND YOU'RE THE BATMAN! I'VE HEARD OF YOU!

ANY IDEA WHY THOSE MEN TRIED TO BEAT YOU UP?
MY TEAM IS PLAYING THE LIONS IN A COUPLE OF DAYS. THAT'S THE TEAM OWNED BY STACY THE GAMBLER! I THINK....

I KNOW-- YOU THINK THAT STACY WANTS TO MAKE SURE HIS TEAM IS GOING TO WIN. I HEARD HE HAS A LOT OF MONEY BET ON HIS TEAM FOR THAT GAME!
THAT'S IT! THAT GUY'S TRYING EVERY DIRTY TRICK TO HURT MY TEAM'S CHANCES! HE'S A DANGEROUS MAN!

SUDDENLY
THOSE SHOTS CAME FROM UP HERE!
OH-OH! SEE YOU AGAIN, BANNON-- WHEN WE'RE NOT SO PRESSED FOR TIME!

LATER..... IN A HOUSE ON THE SUBURBS.... EXIT BATMAN AND ROBIN -- ENTER BRUCE WAYNE AND YOUNG DICK GRAYSON!
DICKEY, M'LAD- I'VE A STRANGE FEELING WE'RE GOING TO HAVE A LITTLE EXCITEMENT IN THE NEXT COUPLE OF DAYS!
YOU'VE ONLY A FEELING-- I KNOW IT!

THAT NIGHT, STACY'S MEN REPORT AND TELL OF THEIR ENCOUNTER WITH THE BATMAN!
SO, THE BATMAN SHOWED UP, EH? THAT'S BAD---VERY BAD!
YEAH -- HE'S LIABLE TA MAKE TROUBLE FER US! THAT GUY'S POISON!
WE GOTTA GET THAT GUY OUTA THE WAY!

YOU'RE RIGHT! WE'VE GOT TO GET RID OF THE BATMAN-- AND I KNOW JUST THE WAY TO DO IT! YOU SEE-- I THINK I KNOW WHO THE BATMAN IS!
HUH!
WHA..?

ONE OF THE STOOLIES THAT WORKS FOR THE POLICE TELLS ME THAT THIS SOCIETY GUY, BRUCE WAYNE, IS ALWAYS HANGIN' AROUND HEADQUARTERS! SEEMS HE'S A FRIEND OF COMMISSIONER GORDON!

NOW WHAT'S A RICH PLAYBOY LIKE HIM HANGING AROUND THERE SO MUCH? MAYBE THIS "PLAYBOY" BUSINESS IS AN ACT SO THE POLICE DON'T GET WISE!
SOUNDS GOOD! WHAT'S YOUR PLAN, STACY?
WITH THESE FEW WORDS, THE STAGE IS BEING SET FOR A TITANIC STRUGGLE BETWEEN THE BATMAN AND THE MINIONS OF CRIME! WHO WILL WIN? WILL THE BATMAN BE EXPOSED?

THE NEXT MORNING, BRUCE RECEIVES A PHONE CALL....
YOU'VE GOT TO HELP ME! I KNOW YOU ARE THE BATMAN! I'M IN DANGER! THEY WANT TO KILL ME!
YES-THIS IS BRUCE WAYNE. WHO?

I LIVE AT 2255 GRAND STREET ON THE FOURTH FLOOR! DON'T FAIL TO COME THERE TOMORROW NIGHT AT TEN! CLICK!
WHA..? HELLO! HELLO!

HOW COULD ANYONE KNOW YOU'RE THE BATMAN?
I DON'T KNOW-- BUT I'M GOING TO FIND OUT-TOMORROW NIGHT AT TEN!

THE NEXT NIGHT - TWO MANTLED FIGURES ARE POISED AGAINST THE INKY SKY THAT FORMS THE BACKDROP OF THE GREAT STAGE THAT IS CALLED - GOTHAM CITY.....
THAT'S THE BUILDING DOWN THERE!

MOMENTS LATER, THE BATMAN EASES HIS BODY THROUGH THE WINDOW OF THE BUILDING.....
DARK! -FUNNY!

SUDDENLY, LIGHTS BLAZE ON.... THE BATMAN HAS WALKED INTO A TRAP!
"COME INTO MY PARLOR, SAID THE SPIDER TO THE FLY!" APPROPRIATE, EH, BATMAN?

NOW, WE'LL SEE IF YOU'RE REALLY BRUCE WAYNE... JOE! RIP THAT COWL OFF HIS HEAD!
WILL THE BATMAN'S REAL IDENTITY BE REVEALED? IS THIS THE END OF THE CAREER OF THE NEMESIS OF CRIME?

HELLO--
AM I
LATE?
NO- WE'VE
BEEN HOLDING
UP THE
PARTY FOR
YOU!
ABRUPTLY, A LIVING HURRICANE SWEEPS INTO THE ROOM...IT IS ROBIN, THE BOY WONDER!

CAN I GIVE YOU A LIFT, STACY?

THIS IS ONE MERRY-GO-ROUND THAT'S FREE, EH, BOYS?

AS THE DYNAMIC DUO STREAKS OUT OF THE ROOM TOWARD THE STAIRS, THEY FIND THEIR EXIT IS BLOCKED!
OH-OH- WE'VE GOT MORE COMPANY!

ALLOW ME TO WELCOME OUR.... GUESTS!

AS THE MEN SPILL DOWN THE STAIRS, THE BATMAN AND THE WONDERBOY TAKE A LONG HEADLONG DIVE....
LOW BRIDGE!

....ROLL OVER THEM IN MID-AIR....

...AND LIKE TWO CANNONBALLS LEAVING THE MUZZLE OF A SPRING-GUN, THEY BOMBARD THE CREW OF THUGS MASSED AT THE BOTTOM OF THE STAIRS!

FOLLOW THEM! DON'T LET THEM GET AWAY!

LIKE TWO FOXES ELUDING THE HOWLING PACK, THE DYNAMIC DUO LEADS THE THUGS A MERRY CHASE!
IF IT'S A CHASE THEY WANT, WE'LL GIVE IT TO THEM!

THERE THEY GO! -TOWARD THAT OLD BARN!
WE'VE GOT 'EM CORNERED - C'MON!
.....AFTER WHAT SEEMS HOURS TO THE WEARY GUNMEN, THE BATMAN AND ROBIN LEAD THEIR PURSUERS TO AN OPEN FIELD AT THE EDGE OF TOWN....

BUT WHEN THE GANGSTERS ENTER THE BARN.....
FINE! THAT'S BRUCE WAYNE'S HOME OVER THERE! I PLANTED SOME BOYS THERE EARLIER THIS EVENING IN CASE THIS SHOULD HAPPEN!
THEY MUST'VE GONE THROUGH THE WINDOW!
GONE! THERE'S NOBODY HERE!

STACY QUESTIONS TWO OF THE MEN HE HAS POSTED AROUND THE WAYNE HOUSE.
DID THE BATMAN OR ANYBODY TRY TO GET IN THE HOUSE?
NAW! NOBODY!
A FLEA COULDN'T GET PAST THE BOYS! WE'RE WATCHIN' LIKE HAWKS!

JUST THEN, THE HOODLUMS HEAR A VOICE, AND WHEEL ABOUT TO SEE THE MAN THEY SUSPECT IS THE BATMAN... BRUCE WAYNE!
I DON'T KNOW WHO YOU PEOPLE ARE, BUT YOU'RE DISTURBING ME!
ULP!
IT'S HIM!-- BRUCE WAYNE!

WITH A FINAL ADMONISHING, BRUCE CLOSES THE DOOR ON THE BEWILDERED MEN!
THAT GUY CAN'T BE THE BATMAN! NOBODY GOT PAST US!
IT MUST BE A TRICK! LOOK THROUGH THE WINDOW AND SEE WHAT HE'S DOING!

WHAT THE MEN SEE WHEN THEY PEER THROUGH THE WINDOW.
THAT'S HIM! LET'S WATCH HIM AWHILE...
YEAH! HE'S READIN' A BOOK

IDLY, THE MEN WATCH FOR A FEW MINUTES...... WHEN SUDDENLY.. ...
HYA BOYS! LOOKING FOR ME?
THE BATMAN!
ULP! THEN, THIS WAYNE GUY CAN'T BE HIM! HE'S STILL SITTIN' IN THE CHAIR READIN' A BOOK!

THE CHASE BEGINS ALL OVER AGAIN!
C'MON, BOYS-- YOU'RE SLOWING UP!
(PUFF-PUFF) A GRASSHOPPER'S GOT NOTHIN' ON THAT GUY. HE SURE DOES HOP AROUND! (PUFF-PUFF)

"PERHAPS YOU ARE WONDERING HOW THE BATMAN MANAGED TO GET INTO THE HOUSE WITHOUT BEING SEEN BY THE THUGS?... IT'S ALL VERY SIMPLE...... "
"WHEN THE BATMAN DARTED INTO THE BARN, HE RAISED A CLEVERLY HIDDEN TRAPDOOR WHICH LEADS TO A TUNNEL BELOW...... "
#8

"THIS TUNNEL RAN DIRECTLY TO THE WAYNE HOUSE WHERE THE BATMAN MOUNTED STEPS, AND SLIPPED THROUGH A SECRET PANEL INTO HIS HOME.... . "
"THEN, HE SIMPLY DISCARDED HIS COSTUME AND OPENED THE FRONT DOOR!"

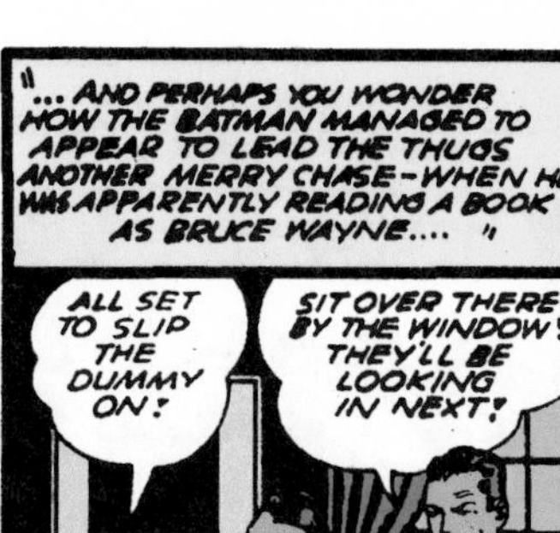
"...AND PERHAPS YOU WONDER HOW THE BATMAN MANAGED TO APPEAR TO LEAD THE THUGS ANOTHER MERRY CHASE-WHEN HE WAS APPARENTLY READING A BOOK AS BRUCE WAYNE.... "
ALL SET TO SLIP THE DUMMY ON!
SIT OVER THERE BY THE WINDOW! THEY'LL BE LOOKING IN NEXT!
" EXPLANATION..AN ESPECIALLY CONSTRUCTED LIFE-LIKE DUMMY WHICH IS SLIPPED OVER ROBIN'S FORM... "

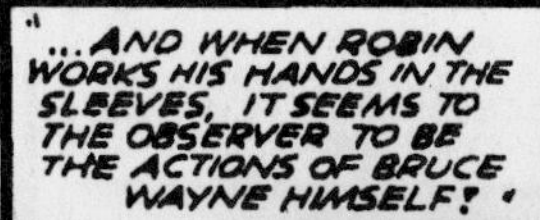
"...AND WHEN ROBIN WORKS HIS HANDS IN THE SLEEVES, IT SEEMS TO THE OBSERVER TO BE THE ACTIONS OF BRUCE WAYNE HIMSELF! "

" WHILE ROBIN MANIPULATED THE DUMMY, BRUCE SLIPPED ON HIS COSTUME AND RACED THROUGH THE TUNNEL AND OUT IN THE NIGHT! "

MEANWHILE, THE ELUSIVE BATMAN THROWS A PARTING WORD AT STACY AND HIS THUGS.
PERHAPS, YOU ARE WONDERING HOW I MANAGED TO SHOW UP TONIGHT, WHEN IT WAS BRUCE WAYNE WHO RECEIVED THAT PHONE CALL-IT MIGHT INTEREST YOU TO KNOW THAT I LISTENED IN ON YOUR LITTLE CONFAB LAST NIGHT, AND ACTED ACCORDINGLY!
OH, THAT'S HOW..?

THAT VERY NIGHT, STACY AND HIS MEN ARE WEARY AND FOOTSORE AFTER A FUTILE EFFORT TO CATCH THE BATMAN!
WELL, STACY, ARE YA CONVINCED NOW THAT BRUCE WAYNE AIN'T THE BATMAN!
YEAH-YEAH!-BUT THAT ISN'T GOING TO STOP ME FROM GOING AHEAD WITH MY PLANS! I'VE GOT TOO MUCH MONEY BET TO STOP NOW!
OKAY! WE KNOW WHAT TO DO!

THE MORNING OF THE BIG GAME.....
WHAT'S THE IDEA OF SLIPPING OVER TO SEE STOCKTON, THE STAR QUARTERBACK OF THE PANTHERS?
JUST WANT TO MAKE SURE THAT STACY'S MEN HAVEN'T INTIMIDATED HIM-THREATENED TO HURT HIM UNLESS HE FUMBLES A FEW PLAYS!

BUT WHEN THEY STEP INSIDE..
BARTON! STOCKTON'S ROOM-MATE... STABBED TO DEATH!...
AND STOCKTON'S NOT AROUND! THEY'VE KIDNAPPED HIM! STACY'S MEN HAVE KIDNAPPED HIM TO KEEP HIM FROM PLAYING!

SEATING HIMSELF BEFORE A MIRROR, THE BATMAN PROPS UP A PICTURE OF THE KIDNAPPED STAR..
SAY--WHAT ARE YOU DOING?
STOCKTON'S MY HEIGHT AND ABOUT MY BUILD. I THINK IT WILL WORK!

DEFT FINGERS APPLY MAKEUP FROM THE UTILITY BELT...SLOWLY MOULD AND CHANGE THE CONTOURS OF THE FACE...
MMM! NOSE NEEDS A LITTLE MORE PUTTY TO GET THAT SHAPE!

UNTIL AT LAST..
HOW DO I LOOK?
YOU'RE STOCKTON! YOU'RE HIM EXACTLY!
THE BATMAN WAS NOW READY TO MAKE THE FINAL MOVE IN HIS CAMPAIGN AGAINST STACY AND HIS COHORTS!

LATER THAT DAY..... HUGE THRONGS FILL THE STADIUM-CHEER WILDLY AS THE PLAYERS DASH ONTO THE FIELD.
EXIT

IN HIS BOX, STACY GETS A DECIDED SHOCK AS HE PEERS THROUGH HIS OPERA GLASSES......
NO 34?...STOCKTON? ...THAT'S HIM

SOMETHING'S WRONG! BETTER GET OUT TO THE HIDEOUT RIGHT AWAY!
STACY LEAVES, AND IN HIS HASTE DOES NOT NOTICE THE YOUNGSTER WHO FOLLOWS HIM.....

STACY UNWITTINGLY LEADS THE BOY TO THE HIDEOUT!
IT WORKED! THE BATMAN'S PLAN WORKED!
GARAGE

STACY GETS ANOTHER SHOCK....
WHAT'S THE MATTER WITH YOU MUGGS? I THOUGHT I TOLD YOU TO SNATCH STOCKTON AND.... STOCKTON? —HERE?

BUT IT CAN'T BE?..... I JUST SAW HIM ON THE FOOTBALL FIELD!
YOU'RE NUTS, BOSS! THIS GUY'S BEEN HERE ALL THE TIME!
SURE, BOSS-WE'VE WATCHED 'IM LIKE A HAWK!
SUDDENLY, A FIGURE CRASHES THROUGH THE SKYLIGHT. IT IS THAT AMAZING YOUNG PHENOMENON... ROBIN, THE BOY WONDER!
PARDON MY FEET!

GET THAT KID! HE WORKS WITH THE BATMAN!
THIS WILL TAKE CARE OF HIM!

GOOD THING NOBODY WAS SITTING IN IT!

YOU LOOK VERY TIRED! DO HAVE A CHAIR!

AS STACY AND A THUG SEND SHOTS WINGING TOWARD HIM, THE QUICK-THINKING BOY WONDER DROPS TO THE FLOOR....
(OH-OH! THE FLOOR IS THE BEST PLACE FOR ME RIGHT NOW!)

UH- I'M SHOT!
BUT STACY IS IN LINE OF THE FIRE FROM HIS THUG-- AND A LEADEN PELLET BORES INTO HIS BODY!
?

STACY IS FINISHED... .. AND SO ARE YOU!

ROBIN FREES STOCKTON...
DON'T TELL ME A KID LIKE YOU TOOK CARE OF THESE TOUGHS?!

ROBIN TELLS STOCKTON HOW THE BATMAN HAS TAKEN HIS PLACE AT THE BIG GAME..
TOOK MY PLACE?..I'LL BET HE'S FUMBLING EVERY PLAY! I BETTER GET BACK THERE AND STOP HIM IN TIME!
YOU GO THERE ALONE. I WANT TO DELIVER THESE MUGGS TO JAIL. ONE OF THEM IS GUILTY OF THE MURDER OF YOUR ROOM-MATE!

MEANWHILE.... AT THE STADIUM, THE TWO TEAMS HAVE BEEN BATTLING, WITH EITHER SIDE FAILING TO SCORE
34

THE RIVAL TEAM GETS THE BALL..... THE PLAY IS PUT INTO ACTION..... THE QUARTERBACK THROWS A LONG PASS TO AN END.....
34

....BUT A MAN SUDDENLY LEAPS UP AND LITERALLY PLUCKS IT FROM HIS HANDS..... IT IS THE BATMAN...... "STOCKTON"

.....A STIFF STRAIGHT ARM TAKES CARE OF THE END......
SORRY, BUDDY-- I'VE GOT A DATE WITH THE GOAL POSTS!

.....DOWN THE FIELD STREAKS THE BATMAN, WEAVING IN AND OUT OF THE OPPOSITION IN A PERFECT EXAMPLE OF BROKEN FIELD RUNNING....
34
HAVEN'T DONE THIS SINCE MY COLLEGE DAYS!

AS THREE OF THE OPPOSITION CLOSE IN ON HIM AT THE GOAL, THE BATMAN'S POWERFUL FRAME SLAMS INTO THEM LIKE A BATTERING RAM.

...AND HE IS OVER FOR A TOUCHDOWN!
WH-WHAT WENT THROUGH US?
I DIDN'T KNOW THEY HAD CYCLONES IN THIS PART OF THE COUNTRY!

THE BATMAN'S KICK FOR THE EXTRA POINT IS GOOD! THE PANTHERS LEAD 7 TO 0!
....AT THAT MOMENT, THE REAL STOCKTON ENTERS THE STADIUM TO HEAR CHEER AFTER CHEER FOR HIS BRILLIANT PERFORMANCE ON THE FIELD....
STOCKTON
STOCKTON
YEA
YEA!
SAY-I MUST HAVE DONE ALL RIGHT!...THAT IS-I MEAN-HE DID ALL RIGHT!

AT THE END OF THE HALF, THE BATMAN MEETS STOCKTON IN A SECLUDED CORNER....
G-GOSH! YOU'RE MORE LIKE ME THAN I AM MYSELF!
NOW THAT YOU'RE HERE, YOU CAN GO OUT AND DO YOUR OWN PLAYING!

THEY CHANGE CLOTHES ....
I-I DON'T KNOW HOW TO THANK YOU FOR EVERYTHING!
FORGET IT! I LIKE TO KEEP MY SPORTS CLEAN AND HONEST! NOW, GO OUT THERE AND PLAY!

STOCKTON GOES ONTO THE FIELD AND PLAYS LIKE A MAN INSPIRED!

WHILE UP IN THE STANDS TWO FIGURES WATCH WITH INTEREST.....THEY ARE BRUCE WAYNE AND YOUNG DICK GRAYSON......
NICE GAME, EH, BRUCE?
NOT BAD-NOT BAD AT ALL!
BOB KANE

No. 48
A DC PUBLICATION
The BATMAN
Detective
FEB.
COMICS
Reg. U.S. Pat. Off.
10¢
BOB KANE

BATMAN
WITH
Robin
THE BOY WONDER
BY
BOB KANE
WHEN CRIMINALS PLOT TO ROB THE GREAT VAULT HOUSING THE NATION'S GOLD RESERVE, THEN IT IS THAT THE CLOAKED BATMAN AND YOUNG, LAUGHING ROBIN THE BOY WONDER, STEP IN TO NULLIFY CRIME'S THRUST AND DRAW BACK THE CURTAIN THAT VEILS THE MYSTERY OF
THE SECRET CAVERN
OUR STORY BEGINS IN KENTUCKY, WHEN A MAN IDLY ROWING ON A STREAM, SUDDENLY DRIFTS INTO A GASH IN THE SIDE OF A MOUNTAIN.....
WONDER WHERE THIS LEADS TO?
1

THE MAN IS STUNNED BY THE VASTNESS AND STRANGENESS OF THE WORLD HE HAS ENTERED INTO.....
WHA....? A CAVERN.... A GREAT LIMESTONE CAVERN!

AS HE ROWS, THE GREAT NATURAL WONDERS STRETCH BEFORE HIM MILE UPON MILE.....
I'VE DISCOVERED IT! I'VE DISCOVERED A LIMESTONE CHAMBER THAT IS EVEN GREATER THAN THE MAMMOTH CAVE OR THE CARLSBAD CAVERNS! IT'S MAGNIFICENT!

TAKING OUT HIS SURVEYING INSTRUMENTS, THE MAN STEPS ON THE CAVE'S FLOOR, AND SOON HAS MORE CAUSE FOR EXCITEMENT..
WHY..., FROM MY CALCULATIONS, THIS CAVERN PASSES DIRECTLY UNDER THE GREAT GOLD TREASURY VAULT OF FORT STOX!

WHEN THE MAN GETS BACK TO TOWN, HE CAN HARDLY CONTROL HIS EXCITEMENT....
IF I DON'T TELL SOMEONE, I'LL BUST! LISTEN TO ME, MEN.....
WHAT'S GOT YOU ALL HOPPED UP, MISTER?

HE TELLS OF HIS GREAT DISCOVERY.....
SO YOU FOUND A BIG LIMESTONE CAVE! SO WHAT?
BUT IT GOES DIRECTLY BENEATH THE GOVERMENT GOLD VAULT AT FORT STOX!

WHAT?.... THE GOLD VAULT?.... ARE YOU KIDDIN'?
SAY- WHERE- ABOUTS IS THIS PLACE, MISTER?
AH- I--ER- DOUBT IF I CAN FIND IT AGAIN! AH-GOOD DAY!
AT THE GLITTER OF GREED IN THE STRANGERS' EYES, THE MAN REALIZES THE SIGNIFICANCE OF HIS DISCOVERY.....
2

HE SHUT UP LIKE A CLAM! HE KNOWS WHERE THAT PLACE IS!
GOOD THING WE DECIDED TO COME TO THIS BURG TO HIDE OUT FROM THE COPS!
YEAH- LOOKS LIKE WE STUMBLED ONTO SOMETHING BIG!

THE CRIMINALS FIND OUT THE MAN, HENRY LEWIS, IS ROUGHING IT ALONE IN A LOG CABIN IN THE WOODS AND.....THE NEXT MORNING.....
WHA..... WHAT IS THIS?
TAKE IT EASY, LEWIS! WE DECIDED TO SEE IF WE COULD PERSUADE YA TO TELL US WHERE THE OPENING TO THE CAVE IS!

WHEN LEWIS REFUSES, HE IS BEATEN. TORTURED.... BUT HE STOUTLY MAINTAINS HIS SILENCE...
HE'S OUT AGAIN! I WONDER IF HE'D TALK IF WE PROMISED TO GIVE HIM A SHARE OF THE HAUL?
NAW! THIS GUY IS A MILLIONAIRE. HIS HOBBY IS SURVEYIN'! HE'S WORTH PLENTY!

SAY, AIN'T THIS GUY LEWIS GOT A KID NAMED LINDA, SINGIN' IN RENALDO'S TOP HAT CLUB?
YE-AH! THEY BILL HER AS A SOCIETY SINGER!
SAY-IT OUGHTA BE A CINCH FOR US TO COOK UP A WAY FOR LEWIS TA TALK NOW!

TWO NIGHTS LATER ... GOTHAM CITY.... IN A PRIVATE OFFICE OF THE TOP HAT CLUB.
LISTEN, RENALDO.... THIS CLUB OF YOURS AIN'T DOING SO HOT. NOW, HOW WOULD YOU LIKE A CHANCE TO MAKE SOME DOUGH-BIG DOUGH?
YOU INTEREST ME STRANGELY, NICK.... KEEP TALKING!

LATER THAT EVENING..... AS LINDA LEWIS WALKS TO THE BAND PLATFORM, SHE STOPS FOR A WORD WITH A WEALTHY, SOCIETY PLAYBOY NAMED BRUCE WAYNE.....
HOW ABOUT A MOVIE AFTER YOU FINISH YOUR NUMBER, LINDA?
ALL RIGHT, BRUCE. WAIT FOR ME!

...AND LATER, WHEN SHE HAS FINISHED, AND HAS CHANGED CLOTHING.... SUDDENLY....
I HAVE BEEN WAITING FOR YOU! COME WITH ME!
WHO..?

WITH THE INSTINCT FOR SELF PRESERVATION STRONG, THE GIRL DIPS HER HAND IN HER DRESSER DRAWER AND BRINGS OUT A SMALL PEARL-HANDLED REVOLVER...
YOU'RE MAD! STAY AWAY FROM ME! STAY AWAY OR I'LL SHOOT!
COME WITH ME!
3

AS THE MAN NEARS HER LINDA AUTOMATICALLY PULLS THE TRIGGER .....THERE IS A SHOT!
I-I WAS ONLY FOOLING! YOU SHOULDN'T HAVE.... OHHH!

THE DOOR IS THRUST OPEN.....
THAT SHOT!... NICK!
SHE SHOT HIM!
I DIDN'T MEAN TO-HE...HE WAS CRAZY! HE WOULD HAVE KILLED ME!

YOU LITTLE FOOL! NICK WAS ONLY HAVING SOME FUN-HE'S A PRACTICAL JOKER! THE THREE OF US WERE IN ON IT!
HE'S DEAD! GOT IT RIGHT THROUGH THE HEART!
I KILLED HIM! I KILLED A MAN! OH-WHAT AM I GOING TO DO?

NOBODY HEARD THE SHOT. THE BAND WAS PLAYING TOO LOUD!
GIVE ME THAT GUN. YOU GET OUT OF THE CITY-TO YOUR FATHER IN KENTUCKY! WE'LL TAKE CARE OF THIS. NO ONE WILL KNOW!

BLINDLY, THE DISTRACTED, BEWILDERED GIRL FOLLOWS INSTRUCTIONS.... AND WHEN SHE LEAVES....
OKAY. NICK-YOU CAN GET UP NOW!
BOY-DID SHE FALL FOR OUR LITTLE ACT!

FOR A MINUTE I WAS WORRIED IF SHE HAD REAL SLUGS IN THAT GUN!
I SHOVED THE BLANKS IN WHILE SHE WAS OUT SINGIN'!
NOW, ALL I HAVE TO DO IS SHOW LEWIS THIS GUN WITH THE GIRL'S PRINTS ON IT, AND HE'LL SPILL EVERYTHING!

AFTER WAITING IN VAIN FOR LINDA, BRUCE WAYNE QUESTIONS RENALDO.....
SHE'S GONE? BUT SHE HAD AN APPOINTMENT WITH ME!
AH-ER-I ALMOST FORGOT! SHE SAID SHE COULDN'T MAKE IT TONIGHT-SOME OTHER TIME, PERHAPS!

FUNNY SHE DIDN'T COME TO TELL ME THAT HERSELF! LINDA'S NOT LIKE THAT! WONDER IF ANYTHING IS WRONG?
4

A STREAKING EXPRESS TRAIN ROARS TOWARD KENTUCKY CARRYING LINDA LEWIS...

WHEN LINDA REACHES HER FATHER'S SECLUDED CABIN....
RENALDO! YOU-HERE?
YOU TOOK A TRAIN...I CAME BY PLANE, AND BEAT YOU BY A FEW HOURS!

FATHER-THESE MEN-THOSE GUNS AT YOUR BACK? WHY?
NEVER MIND THAT! RENALDO HERE TELLS ME YOU KILLED A MAN! IS IT TRUE? TELL ME!

YES, FATHER, I DID.... BUT IT WAS IN SELF-DEFENSE! I SWEAR IT! YOU'VE GOT TO BELIEVE ME!
I BELIEVE YOU, LINDA!

OKAY, RENALDO-YOU WIN! I'LL DO ANYTHING TO KEEP LINDA FROM JAIL!
I KNEW YOU'D GET SMART
TIE THE DAME UP,TOO! THEN, LEWIS WILL LEAD US TO THE TUNNEL! - AND THE GOLD!

MEANWHILE, BRUCE WAYNE HAS BEEN A BIT UNEASY ABOUT LINDA LEWIS - HE CALLS AT HER HOME....
SHE JUST PACKED HER BAGS AND LEFT? DIDN'T SHE SAY WHERE?
NO, SIR... AND YOU KNOW SOMETHING SIR? SHE LOOKED WORRIED, LIKE SHE HAD SOMETHING ON HER MIND!

AT HIS HOME, BRUCE SPEAKS WITH HIS YOUNG WARD, DICK GRAYSON.....
DICK, I CAN'T HELP FEELING SOMETHING IS WRONG! ALL THE CIRCUMSTANCES SEEM TO INDICATE IT!... AND THE WAY RENALDO ACTED THAT NIGHT.......
WELL-WHAT ARE WE WAITING FOR? LET'S GO!

IN THE PLACE OF BRUCE WAYNE AND DICK GRAYSON.... THE DYNAMIC DUO- BATMAN AND ROBIN, THE BOY WONDER!
SHE WORKED FOR RENALDO-RENALDO WENT OUT OF TOWN-SHE WENT OUT OF TOWN-IT ALL ADDS UP!
RENALDO-HERE WE COME!

DESCENDING A FLIGHT OF STAIRS, THE TWO RACE ALONG A SECRET TUNNEL UNDER THE WAYNE HOME....

THEY ASCEND STAIRS AND SLIDE AWAY A PANEL THAT LEADS INTO A SEEMINGLY OLD DESERTED BARN......
OPEN THOSE DOORS, ROBIN!
RIGHT!
5

THERE IS THE QUIET PURR OF A SUPERCHARGED MOTOR - AND THE BATMOBILE STREAKS OUT INTO THE NIGHT!

THE BATMOBILE FLASHES THROUGH THE STREETS WITH BULLET SPEED....

HEY- DID YOU SEE THAT?
SURE I SAW IT- BUT THAT DON'T SAY I HAVE TO BELIEVE IT!
Z-I-N-G

THE CAR COMES TO A STOP IN THE BACK ALLEY OF RENALDO'S APARTMENT HOUSE.....
THAT'S RENALDO'S APARTMENT. YOU STAY HERE. I'LL CALL YOU IF I NEED HELP!

SWIFTLY AND NOISELESSLY, THE BATMAN MOVES UP THE FIRE ESCAPE!

YEAH, NICK- RENALDO IS DOWN IN KENTUCKY, TAKIN' CARE O' LINDA LEWIS AND HER OLD MAN! YOU STAY HID-REMEMBER, YOU'RE SUPPOSED TO BE DEAD!
6

AS THE BODYGUARD HANGS UP, A SHADOW SEEMS TO CREEP ALONG THE FLOOR....
HUH? THAT SHADOW- LIKE A BAT-- THE BATMAN! HE'S HERE!

WHIRLING IN TERROR, THE THUG WHIPS OUT A GUN, AND FIRES.....

A WEIRD FIGURE SPRINGS FROM THE SHADOWS....
I'M NOT THERE... HERE I AM!

LINDA LEWIS AND HER FATHER ARE IN TROUBLE...

....AND YOU KNOW WHY!

TALK, YOU WHIMPERING WRETCH-TALK! WHAT ABOUT RENALDO AND LEWIS? TALK!
DON'T HIT ME LIKE THAT AGAIN! DON'T

THE COWARDLY THUG BABBLES AS THE BATMAN STARES AT HIM GRIMLY....
SO THAT'S THE SCHEME, IS IT?.... AND WHERE IS NICK HIDING OUT? TELL ME OR I'LL....
I'LL TELL... HE'S HIDING ON MARKER PLACE IN AN OLD GARAGE. IT'S SUPPOSED TO BE A GARAGE... BUT IT'S REALLY A GAMBLING JOINT.

I'VE ALREADY MET NICK BEFORE- HE'S A FIRST CLASS RAT WITH A THIRD RATE CONSCIENCE! IT'LL BE A PLEASURE TO NAB HIM!

MOMENTS LATER, AS THE BATMOBILE WHIZZES TOWARD ITS DESTINATION...
SOMETHING ON YOUR MIND?
I JUST REMEMBERED THAT I DIDN'T TIE THAT HOODLUM UP. I'LL BET HE'S ON THE PHONE RIGHT NOW, SPEAKING WITH NICK!

THE BATMAN'S HUNCH IS CORRECT!
I HADDA TALK. HE WOULD A KILLED ME. HE'S ON HIS WAY OVER!
YOU DIRTY SQUEALER! OKAY..... THE BOYS AND I WILL TAKE CARE O' HIM!

HOODLUMS, EAGER TO SETTLE OLD SCORES WITH THEIR NEMESIS, TAKE THEIR PLACES AT WINDOWS..... WHEN.....
WE'LL GET 'IM WHEN... HEY-WHAT'S, THAT COMIN THIS WAY?
IT'S-IT'S THE BATMOBILE..... AND IT'S COMIN' STRAIGHT AT THE GARAGE!

THERE IS A SUDDEN RENDING, SMASHING OF WOOD AS THE BATMOBILE CRASHES THROUGH THE BARRED GARAGE DOORS!
CRACK!

I'M COMING FOR YOU, NICK!
DON'T LET 'IM GET ME! PLUG 'IM! GIVE 'IM ALL THE BULLETS YOU'VE GOT!

WITH A SUDDEN LITHE MOVEMENT, THE BATMAN SCOOPS UP THE HEAVY TABLE.....
8

....AND BEARS IT FORWARD LIKE A BATTERING RAM!
YOU GAMBLED ON THE TABLE, BUT I'LL BET YOU DIDN'T GAMBLE ON THIS!

THE BATMAN'S STEEL FISTS LASH OUT IN PILE-DRIVER BLOWS!
KEEP SCORE FOR ME ROBIN!

C'MON-LET'S GET THAT KID!
GANGING UP ON ME, EH?

TIME TO RE-TIRE, EH, BOYS?
OOF!!!

PANIC-STRICKEN AT THE SUDDEN DEFEAT OF HIS MOBSTER PALS, NICK FLEES IN TERROR.....
THEY AIN'T GONNA GET ME! NOT ME!
NICK DOESN'T WANT TO PLAY ANYMORE!

A QUICK TWIRL, AND A ROPE WHISTLES OUT AT NICK....
HE WANTS TO LEAVE US....
9

...BUT I THINK HE CHANGED HIS MIND!

AFTER PHONING THE POLICE AND TELLING THEM TO PICK UP THE GANGSTERS, THE BATMAN BLINDFOLDS NICK AND SPEEDS BACK TO THE SECRET BARN.....
WH-WHERE ARE YOU TAKING ME?
TO KENTUCKY, NICK-TO KENTUCKY!

MOMENTS LATER A WEIRD SHAPE R SES IN THE AIR... IT'S THE BATPLANE!

LIKE SOME ANCIENT, FABLED BIRD, IT WINGS THROUGH THE SKY.

MILES ARE COVERED IN MOMENTS AS THE BATPLANE DASHES THROUGH THE HEAVENS, UNTIL AT LAST THE BATPLANE FLUTTERS DOWN TO A STOP A SHORT DISTANCE AWAY FROM THE LEWIS CABIN
WE'RE HERE! — KENTUCKY!

LATER AS A GUARD STANDS BEFORE THE CABIN, A MUSCULAR ARM ENCIRCLES HIS THROAT

INSIDE THE CABIN, A SECOND GUARD STARTS AT THE SOUND OF A KNOCK AT THE DOOR....
MUST BE BLACKIE! WONDER WHAT HE WANTS?

AS THE GUARD OPENS THE DOOR, A FIST SUDDENLY WHIPS IN WITH BLURRING SPEED

UGH!

SAY "HELLO" TO THE LADY, NICK!
WHY-WHY, IT'S THE MAN I KILLED... ONLY HE ISN'T DEAD! HE'S ALIVE!
WHA-AT?

THE BATMAN FREES LEWIS AND ACQUAINTS THEM WITH THE TRUE FACTS
THEN, IT WAS ALL A SCHEME SO DAD WOULD REVEAL THE LOCATION OF THE CAVERN!
FRAME MY DAUGHTER, WOULD THEY?
YES... AND INCIDENTALLY, I THINK WE HAD BETTER GET THERE RIGHT AWAY!

MOMENTS LATER, A BOAT SLIPS ALONG THE WATER THAT WINDS THROUGH THE TWISTING LABYRINTH OF THE GREAT CAVERN...
WHAT A SOLEMN, AWESOME PLACE!
SO MAJESTIC AND SO SOMBRE!
HOW DEADLY QUIET IT IS!

BETTER HURRY- RENALDO AND HIS MEN MUST BE DIGGING INTO THE VAULT BY NOW!

WHILE FURTHER ON, RENALDO'S MOBSTERS DIG LIKE MOLES THROUGH THE ROCK......UNTIL
RENALDO! THIS IS IT! WE'RE THROUGH!
OKAY! WE'LL GO UP NOW!

NOISELESSLY, THE MOBSTERS SCAMPER UP THE LADDER INTO FORT STOX ITSELF.
VAULT

THOSE BATS GIVE ME THE CREEPS. THEY REMIND ME TOO MUCH OF THE BATMAN! LIKE HE WAS HERE!
YOU NUTS? I SUPPOSE YOU EXPECT THE BATMAN TO STEP OUT OF THE SHADOWS AND SAY....

.... GOOD EVENING GENTLEMEN!
I- I'M SEEIN' THINGS! I MUST BE!
AWK

AS ROBIN USES AN OAR WITH A PURPOSE OTHER THAN THAT FOR THE ONE IT WAS INTENDED, THE BATMAN SPRINGS FORWARD TOWARD THE UPRIGHT LADDER...
NOW YOU'RE SEEING THINGS... STARS!

DOWN COMES THE LADDER, AND THE GUNMEN WITH IT!
JUST LIKE HUMPTY DUMPTY-- YOU HAD A GREAT FALL!

THE MEN RISE SHAKILY TO THEIR FEET.....

....ONLY TO GO DOWN AGAIN!
YOU CERTAINLY DO HAVE YOUR UPS AND DOWNS, DON'T YOU?

MEANWHILE, THE BOY WONDER GIVES A GOOD ACCOUNTING OF HIMSELF.....
A LITTLE SOMETHING FOR YOU, BUDDY!
12

....AND YOU'RE NO EXCEPTION, HORSEFACE!

AN UNTHINKING GUNMAN IN THE VAULT TAKES A POT SHOT AT THE DYNAMIC DUO....
I'LL GET THAT BATMAN YET!
I HEARD A SHOT!
LOOK! OVER THERE!
YOU NUTS? WANTA BRING THE SOLDIERS OUT?

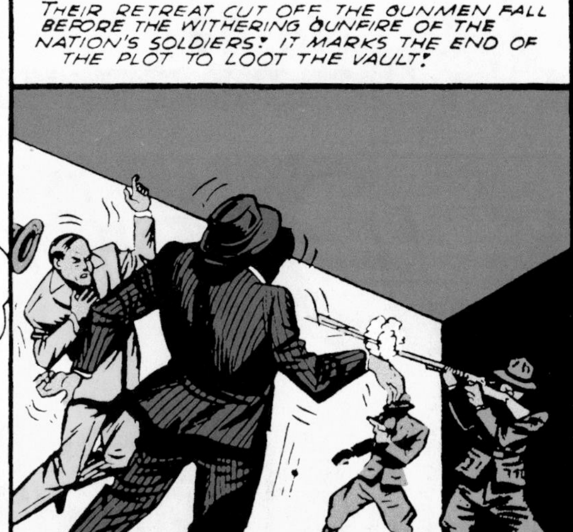
THEIR RETREAT CUT OFF THE GUNMEN FALL BEFORE THE WITHERING GUNFIRE OF THE NATION'S SOLDIERS! IT MARKS THE END OF THE PLOT TO LOOT THE VAULT!

.....WHILE BELOW, AS RENALDO TRIES TO FLEE, A MANTLED FIGURE SEEMS TO WIND ITSELF AROUND HIS BODY...
TAKE IT EASY, RENALDO...

YOU'RE NOT GOING ANYWHERE.... FOR MAYBE TWENTY YEARS OR SO.

WHEN THE BATMAN TURNS TO FIND MR. LEWIS, HE DISCOVERS THE GENTLEMAN IS QUITE BUSY.....
WHAT ?
THESE ARE THE MUGGS THAT TIED ME UP AND BEAT ME! NOW, LET'S SEE HOW THEY LIKE IT FOR A CHANGE!

WHEN ALL IS EXPLAINED TO THE FORT STOX COMMANDER, THE BATMAN AND ROBIN PREPARE TO TAKE LEAVE OF LEWIS AND LINDA......
YOU'VE DONE YOUR COUNTRY A GREAT SERVICE! I'LL SEE THAT THE PRESIDENT HEARS OF THIS AND GIVES YOU BOTH A SUITABLE AWARD!
THAT'S NOT NECESSARY. BEING AMERICANS IS ENOUGH OF AN AWARD!

I SALUTE TWO GREAT AMERICANS!
OUTLINED AGAINST THE MOON IS A CRAFT CARRYING TWO FIGURES... THE BATMAN AND ROBIN, THE BOY WONDER!
BOB KANE

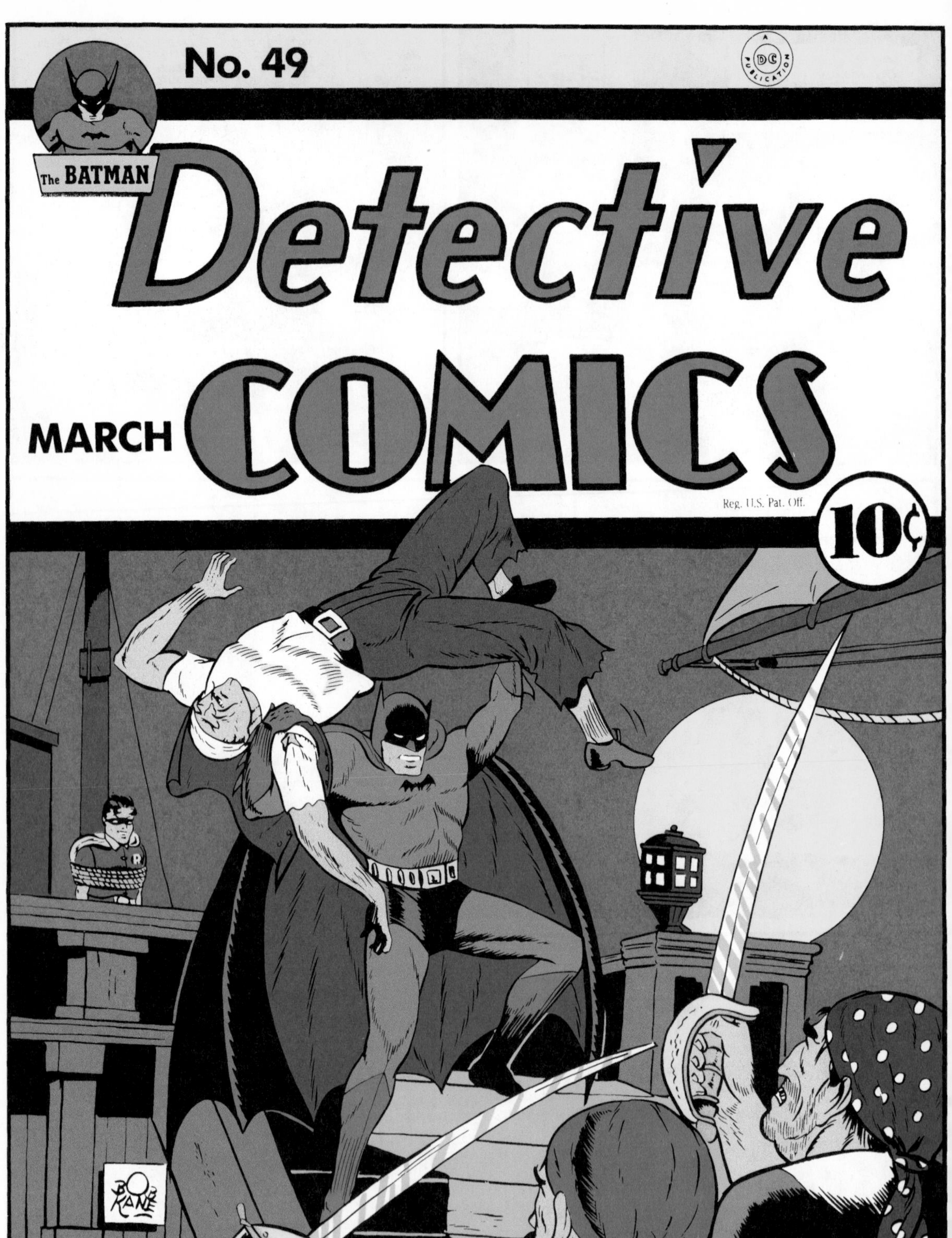
No. 49
A DC PUBLICATION
The BATMAN
Detective
MARCH
COMICS
Reg. U.S. Pat. Off.
10¢
BOB KANE

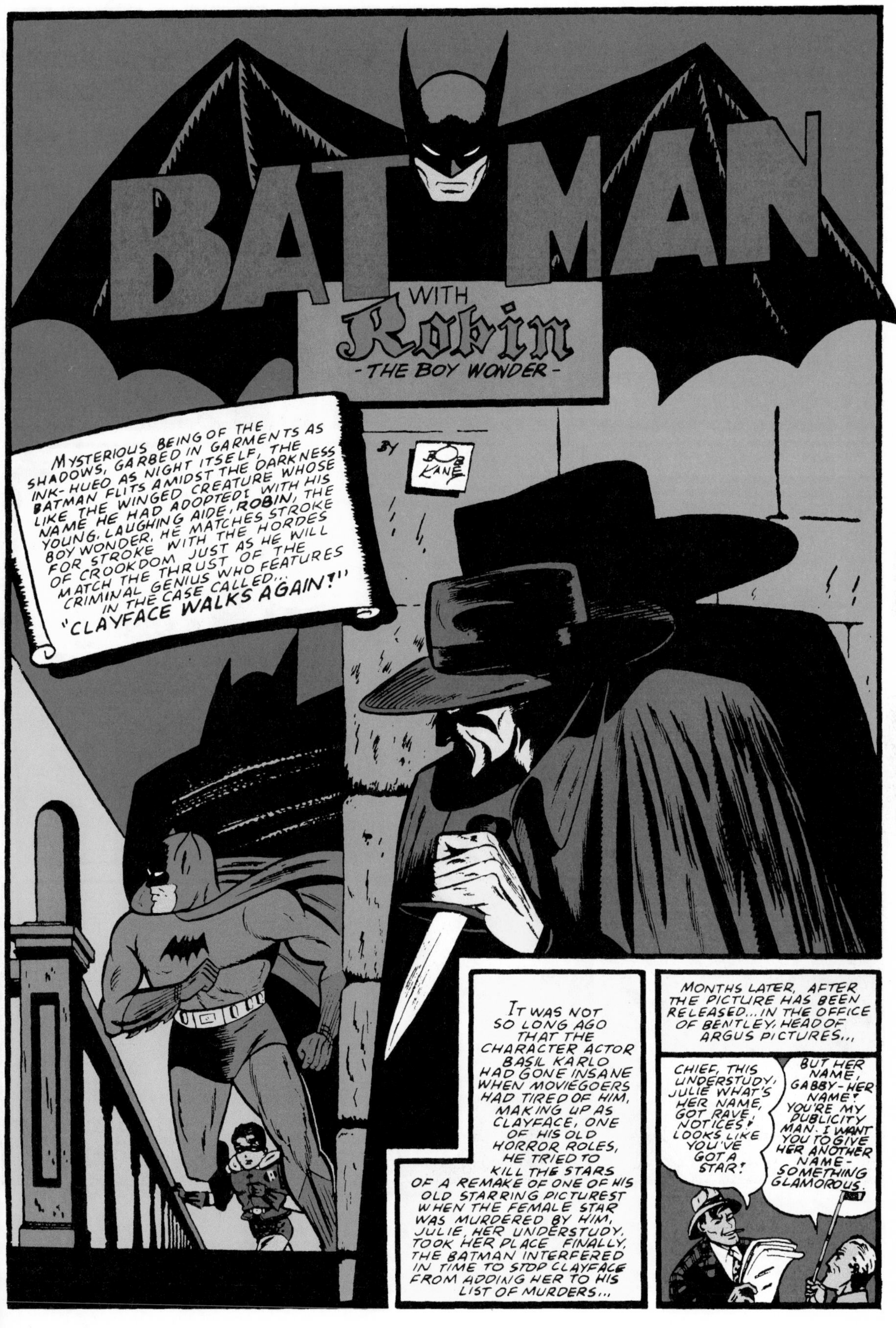

BATMAN
WITH
Robin
-THE BOY WONDER-
MYSTERIOUS BEING OF THE SHADOWS, GARBED IN GARMENTS AS INK-HUEO AS NIGHT ITSELF, THE BATMAN FLITS AMIDST THE DARKNESS LIKE THE WINGED CREATURE WHOSE NAME HE HAD ADOPTED! WITH HIS YOUNG, LAUGHING AIDE, ROBIN, THE BOY WONDER, HE MATCHES STROKE FOR STROKE WITH THE HORDES OF CROOKDOM JUST AS HE WILL MATCH THE THRUST OF THE CRIMINAL GENIUS WHO FEATURES IN THE CASE CALLED... "CLAYFACE WALKS AGAIN!"
BY BOB KANE
IT WAS NOT SO LONG AGO THAT THE CHARACTER ACTOR BASIL KARLO HAD GONE INSANE WHEN MOVIEGOERS HAD TIRED OF HIM. MAKING UP AS CLAYFACE, ONE OF HIS OLD HORROR ROLES, HE TRIED TO KILL THE STARS OF A REMAKE OF ONE OF HIS OLD STARRING PICTURES! WHEN THE FEMALE STAR WAS MURDERED BY HIM, JULIE, HER UNDERSTUDY, TOOK HER PLACE. FINALLY, THE BATMAN INTERFERED IN TIME TO STOP CLAYFACE FROM ADDING HER TO HIS LIST OF MURDERS...
MONTHS LATER, AFTER THE PICTURE HAS BEEN RELEASED... IN THE OFFICE OF BENTLEY, HEAD OF ARGUS PICTURES...
CHIEF, THIS UNDERSTUDY, JULIE WHAT'S HER NAME, GOT RAVE NOTICES! LOOKS LIKE YOU'VE GOT A STAR!
BUT HER NAME, GABBY-HER NAME! YOU'RE MY PUBLICITY MAN. I WANT YOU TO GIVE HER ANOTHER NAME-SOMETHING GLAMOROUS.

SHE TOOK THE PUBLIC BY STORM, AND ...
"STORM" THAT'S IT! —BUT LET'S SPELL IT "S-T-O-R-M-E!"
SNAP!

"STORME"— NOT BAD! NOW A FIRST NAME. ONE THAT WILL BE IN CONTRAST! SOMETHING GENTLE, KIND, SWEET!
WHO WAS IT IN BOOKS THAT WAS GENTLE, KIND!

"PORTIA"? SHAKESPEARE'S "PORTIA!" HOW DO YOU LIKE THIS? "PORTIA STORME!"
ITS A NATURALY A NATURAL! CALL UP THE NEWSPAPERS, THE MOVIE MAGS! SPREAD THAT NAME FROM HERE TO TIMBUCTOO!
SNAP!

A STAR IS BORN!
GOTHAM GAZETTE
PORTIA STORME
SCREEN STARS
10¢
NEWS
PORTIA STORME
MOVIE MAG
10¢
PORTIA STORME
A STAR IS BORN
PORTIA STORME
MOVIE
10¢
Starring PORTIA STORME TRUE STORY

A FEW DAYS LATER, JULIE, NOW PORTIA STORME, TALKS WITH HER FIANCÉ, BRUCE WAYNE...
YOU'RE ON YOUR WAY UP, A NEW STAR, A NEW NAME!
...AND A NEW CAREER! OH, BRUCE, IF ONLY YOU WOULD DO SOMETHING!

...IF ONLY YOU'D FIND YOURSELF A CAREER INSTEAD OF BEING THE PUBLIC'S NUMBER ONE PLAYBOY!
SORRY, HONEY. I'M HAVING TOO GOOD A TIME TO BE BOTHERED WITH ANYTHING REMOTELY CONNECTED WITH WORK! (YOU'D BE MIGHTY SURPRISED IF YOU KNEW I HAD A CAREER— AS THE BATMAN!)

THEN I'M SORRY, BRUCE. UNTIL YOU DECIDE TO MAKE SOMETHING OF YOURSELF, I'M AFRAID OUR ENGAGEMENT IS OFF!
I-I SEE.

I'M NOT WALKING OUT ON YOU, BRUCE. ANYTIME YOU DECIDE TO CHANGE YOUR WAYS, I'LL COME BACK TO YOU GLADLY!
I UNDERSTAND! IT'S ALL RIGHT!

IN CASE YOU EVER NEED ME FOR ANYTHING, JUST HOLLER. IF EVER THERE'S ANYTHING I CAN DO...
THANK YOU, BRUCE, BUT I DON'T THINK I'LL EVER BE IN MUCH TROUBLE.

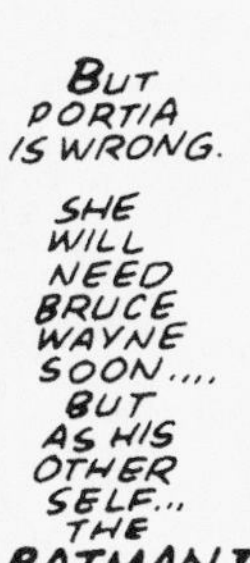

BUT PORTIA IS WRONG.
SHE WILL NEED BRUCE WAYNE SOON.... BUT AS HIS OTHER SELF... THE BATMAN!

THAT VERY NIGHT, AS THUNDER YELLS OUT IN BASS, AND LIGHTNING GLITTERS IN THE HEAVENS, A PRISON AMBULANCE ROLLS SLOWLY ALONG A WET ROAD...
WHO IS THAT GUY IN THE BACK?
BASIL KARLO, THAT HORROR MOVIE ACTOR! WHAT A NIGHT TO BE TRANSFERRING HIM TO THE STATE ASYLUM! SORTA FITS DOESN'T IT?

AS THE RAIN RUSHES DOWN WITH INCREASING FORCE, THE TRUCK SUDDENLY SKIDS MADLY ON THE SLIPPERY ROAD AND PLUNGES OFF THE EMBANKMENT...

THERE IS A CRASH - A SUDDEN STILLNESS! MINUTES PASS. THEN, A LONE FIGURE RISES SHAKILY FROM THE TWISTED MASS OF STEEL AND WOOD...

A FLASH OF JAGGED LIGHTNING MOMENTARILY ILLUMINATES THE MACABRE SCENE, AND REVEALS THE FACE OF THE SURVIVOR... BASIL KARLO, THE PRISONER!
YOU SEE? IT'S ME - KARLO! AND I'M FREE! FRE-EE -EEE!

MOMENTS LATER, THE OWNER OF A MOVIE MAKE-UP SUPPLY STORE FALLS BACK IN UTTER TERROR AS A TERRIBLE FIGURE NEARS HIM...
WHO- WHAT DO YOU WANT?

THERE IS A STRANGLED SCREAM, THE FALL OF A BODY! THEN KARLO LOOKS ABOUT, SITS BEFORE A MIRROR, AND DEFTLY APPLIES MAKEUP...
HA! IT FEELS GOOD TO USE MAKEUP AGAIN!
WIG

...FIRST THE WAY, THEN CLAY... WIG... AND FINALLY THE HAT AND CAPE. IN PLACE OF THE FACE OF KARLO... THE GROTESQUE ONE OF... CLAYFACE!
THE WORLD WILL ONCE AGAIN HEAR OF ME!

GOTHAM GAZETTE
KARLO "CLAYFACE" ESCAPES
A SMASHUP, WHICH STUNNED TWO PRISON GUARDS, GAVE BASIL KARLO THE CHANCE FOR ESCAPE--
KARLO GAINED FOR HIMSELF THE NAME OF CLAYFACE WHEN HE FIGURED IN THE MANY MURDERS OF
AN UNIDENTIFIED MAN YESTERDAY ATTACKED THE OWNER OF A MAKEUP STORE AND
F. MILLER ARRIVES

THE HOME OF BRUCE WAYNE AND HIS WARD, YOUNG DICK GRAYSON-
YOU THINK IT WAS KARLO WHO ATTACKED THAT MAKEUP STORE OWNER?
RIGHT! KARLO IS PROBABLY WEARING MAKEUP RIGHT NOW-THE MAKEUP OF CLAYFACE! DICK, GET OUT OUR WORK CLOTHES-WE'VE GOT A JOB TO DO!
KARLO CLAYFACE ESCAPES

ONCE AGAIN, BRUCE AND DICK REVERT TO THEIR OTHER SELVES... THE BATMAN AND ROBIN, THE BOY WONDER!
DO I DETECT THE EAGER LIGHT OF BATTLE IN YOUR EYES?
YOU DO -AND HOW!

THEY PAD THROUGH THE SECRET TUNNEL BELOW THE HOUSE...

A MOMENT LATER, THE BATMOBILE ZOOMS THROUGH THE NIGHT!
GOING OVER TO ARGUS STUDIOS, AREN'T YOU?
GOOD GUESS, ROBIN. I FIGURE THAT'S THE ONE PLACE CLAYFACE WOULD BE LIKELY TO GO!

THE DYNAMIC DUO SCALES THE ARGUS STUDIO WALL AND DROPS INSIDE THE GROUNDS.

MAYBE CLAYFACE IS AROUND AND MAYBE HE'S NOT, BUT AT ANYRATE IT DOES'T HURT TO LOOK! WE'LL SPLIT UP... BE ABLE TO COVER MORE TERRITORY THAT WAY!

WALKING ACROSS A "YACHT" SET IS A MYSTERIOUS FIGURE... CLAYFACE!
THIS STUDIO FIRED ME! ME-KARLO! I'LL DESTROY IT BY FIRE! THIS INCENDIARY BOMB SHOULD DO IT VERY NICELY!

THEN CLAYFACE SEES...
THE BATMAN! THE MAN RESPONSIBLE FOR MY CAPTURE!

CLAYFACE REACHES ON THE "YACHT" WALL AND SEIZING A FIRE HOOK, HURLS IT AT THE BATMAN!

SOME SIXTH SENSE, SOME INSTINCTIVE FEELING OF DANGER, WARNS THE BATMAN AND HE DUCKS...
WHA..?

THE BATMAN SEES HIS ENEMY AND GIVES CHASE...
CLAYFACE!

A LOW, SWEEPING TACKLE BRINGS CLAYFACE DOWN, ON A SET OF A MINIATURE CITY...
STICK AROUND CHUM!

LIKE TWO TITANS, THEY BATTLE OVER THE MINIATURE CITY...

SUDDENLY, CLAYFACE SCOOPS UP A TINY RAILROAD TRAIN AND MANAGES TO CATCH THE BATMAN ON THE SIDE OF THE HEAD...

THE BATMAN DROPS!
NOW'S MY CHANCE TO FINISH HIM OFF! ...THAT TRUCK-THAT'S THE ANSWER!

CLAYFACE SETS THE TRUCK SPEEDING AT THE BATMAN AND LEAPS OFF...
IS THE BATMAN DOOMED TO A MANGLED DEATH! WILL THE HURTLING MONSTER CLAIM THE BATMAN AS ITS VICTIM?

CLAYFACE, CERTAIN THAT THE BATMAN IS AS GOOD AS DEAD, WALKS THE STUDIO GROUNDS BENT ON MORE DESTRUCTION...
'IF THE BATMAN IS HERE, THEN THAT ROBIN BOY MUST BE AROUND! I'VE A SCORE TO SETTLE WITH HIM ALSO!

IT IS AS IF FATE WERE DIRECTING THE SCENE, FOR ROBIN HIMSELF PASSES NEARBY.
I'M IN LUCK TONIGHT LOOK AT HIM! SO SURE OF HIMSELF! BAH! I'LL TAKE THAT OUT OF HIM!

A PIECE OF SKY SEEMS TO FALL ON ROBIN'S HEAD! A LIGHT, WHITE AND PAINFUL, FLASHES BEFORE HIS EYES-THEN ALL IS BLACKNESS!

CLAYFACE DRAGS THE UNCONSCIOUS BOY TO A SET CONSTRUCTED OF WOOD.
NOW THE INCENDIARY BOMB!

THERE IS A SHARP EXPLOSION, THEN-FIRE!
HA HA-BURN! -LIKE THE HATE IN MY HEART! BURN! HA HA HA!
NOW IT IS ROBIN WHOM DEATH TAPS ON THE SHOULDER! IS THIS NIGHT TO SEE THE END OF THE DYNAMIC DUO?

MEANWHILE, WHAT OF THE DARK KNIGHT?... AS THE ENGINE OF DESTRUCTION ROARS AT HIM, THE BATMAN DECIDES UPON QUICK ACTION...
GOT TO DO SOMETHING FAST OR I'M A GONER!

THE BATMAN DIVES INTO THE PATH OF THE TRUCK!

BUT LIES SAFE BETWEEN THE MASSIVE WHEELS!
THE BATMAN HAS MET CLAYFACE AND CHECKMATED HIS FIRST MOVE!

MEANWHILE - BACK AT THE FIRE...
IF THERE'S A BOY IN THERE, I'M AFRAID HE'S A GONER!
I TELL YOU I SEEN HIM! IT WAS CLAYFACE - AND HE LEFT A KID WITH A COSTUME ON INSIDE!
CLAYFACE!

NOT YET, HE ISN'T!
BATMAN!

THE BATMAN DOUSES HIMSELF WITH WATER...
I'M GOING IN THERE!

HE LASSOES A NEARBY PROJECTION...
YOU CAN'T GO IN THERE - IT'S SHEER SUICIDE!
LISTEN, THE BEST FRIEND I'VE GOT LIES IN THERE - GET OUT OF MY WAY! I'M GOING IN!

THE DAUNTLESS BATMAN SWINGS TOWARD THE RAGING INFERNO...

THROUGH THE VERY FIRE, HE SWINGS... THROUGH SMOKE. THROUGH UNBEARABLE HEAT... THROUGH TONGUES OF FLAME THAT LICK AT HIS FIGURE...

-UNTIL HE DROPS INTO THE VERY MIDST OF THE ROARING FIRE... HE FIGHTS HIS WAY THROUGH LEAPING YELLOW TENDRILS, CALLING... ALWAYS CALLING...
ROBIN! ROBIN!

THEN...
ROBIN! THE FLAMES HAVEN'T REACHED HIM YET!

IT TOOK NERVE TO GO IN THERE!
MORE THAN NERVE, CHIEF-IT WAS THE LOVE FOR THAT KID!
NO SIGN OF THEM YET! IT-IT LOOKS HOPELESS!

LOOK!

THE BOY! -HOW IS HE?
HE'S ALL RIGHT! MY WET CAPE PROTECTED HIM!
DOUSING YOUR CLOTHES WITH WATER WAS A SMART STUNT-BUT YOUR GOING IN THERE WAS STILL SOMETHING I'M GOING TO REMEMBER A LONG, LONG TIME!

LATER...THE WAYNE HOME...
LOOK AT THE SIZE OF THAT EGG WHERE CLAYFACE GOT ME!
I'M GOING TO GET THAT GUY-I'M GOING TO GET HIM IF IT'S THE LAST THING I DO!

THAT NIGHT, AS PORTIA STORME RIDES HOME IN HER CAR, SHE IS STARTLED BY THE MOMENTARY GLIMPSE OF A FACE...
CLAYFACE!

...AT THE STUDIO, THE NEXT MORNING...
I TELL YOU IT WAS CLAYFACE! HE WAS WATCHING ME! I'M IN DANGER!
HE STILL HATES YOU BECAUSE HE FAILED TO KILL YOU BEFORE! HE'LL TRY AGAIN!

BUT THAT NEW PICTURE WE'RE SHOOTING...
WE'LL CONTINUE SHOOTING! IF YOU STOP NOW, YOU'LL LOSE A FORTUNE!
ATTA GIRL-JUST POST A LOT OF GUARDS AROUND, AND CLAYFACE WON'T DARE TO SHOW UP!

GABBY FEST'S LOVE FOR PUBLICITY IS TOO STRONG, AND THE NEXT DAY...
DAILY TROTTER
CLAYFACE THREATENS PORTIA STORME
BRAVE YOUNG ACTRESS TO CONTINUE WORK UNDER GUARD
STUDIO POSTS SPECIAL DETAIL ABOUT SET...
PORTIA STORME

SO THEY THINK MERE GUARDS CAN STOP ME! FOOLS! THE UTTER FOOLS!

PORTIA-THREATENED! WE'VE GOT TO DO SOMETHING!

...THAT NIGHT, PORTIA STORME HAS A VISITOR....
WHO..? -THE BATMAN!
WE MEET AGAIN! NOW LISTEN CAREFULLY-I'VE GOT SOMETHING I WANT TO SPEAK TO YOU ABOUT....

EARLY THE NEXT MORNING, A HAND REACHES THROUGH A WINDOW IN THE STUDIO COSTUME DEPARTMENT.

ANOTHER FIGURE JOINS THE MANY EXTRAS THAT STROLL PAST THE GUARDS ONTO THE SET...
NOW DON'T WORRY ABOUT A THING, PORTIA - WITH ALL THE POLICE I'VE GOT POSTED, CLAYFACE WON'T DARE TO SHOW UP!
...I'LL TRY NOT TO, MR. BENTLEY... BUT I HAVE A QUEER FEELING THAT HE WILL.

SUDDENLY, TWO MANTLED FORMS RACE TOWARD THE GUARDED SET....THEY ARE THE BATMAN AND ROBIN!
LET US THROUGH! PORTIA STORME IS IN TERRIBLE DANGER!

YEAH - FROM MASKED GUYS LIKE YOU!
LET'S GRAB 'EM, BOYS!
OKAY, BUDDY - YOU ASKED FOR IT!

I SAID, WE'RE GOING THROUGH!

...AND HE'S NOT KIDDING!

I REPEAT, GENTLEMEN - WE'RE GOING THROUGH!

ONTO THE SET RACES THE DYNAMIC DUO....
STOP THEM! STOP THEM!

I'LL STAND THESE BABIES OFF, ROBIN!

AS ROBIN DISAPPEARS WITH PORTIA STORME INTO A SMALL ALCOVE OF THE CASTLE, THE BATMAN HOLDS OFF THE ATTACKING GUARDS...
I'M AFRAID THERE'S SOME SORT OF MISTAKE, BUT I CAN'T STOP TO EXPLAIN NOW!

HOWEVER, THE NUMBER OF GUARDS PROVES TOO OVERWHELMING, AND THE DYNAMIC DUO RETREATS....

UP IN ONE OF THE TOWERS, CLAYFACE GLOATS....
THEY'RE RUNNING AWAY, LEAVING PORTIA STORME BEHIND! HA! NOW I CAN TAKE CARE OF HER WITHOUT ANY DISTURBANCE!

CLAYFACE GRIMLY PLACES AN ARROW INTO HIS GIANT BOW...DRAWS IT FULL BACK AND....
NOW... PORTIA STORME ...DIE!

THERE IS A TWANG.. A HISS... AND THE SHAFT OF DEATH BURIES ITSELF IN THE BACK OF PORTIA STORME!

THAT'S HIM— CLAYFACE!

THE BATMAN RACES UP THE STEPS LIKE A WHIRLWIND...

BUT IS MET BY CLAYFACE....

KNIFE IN HAND, CLAYFACE LEAPS....
THIS TIME YOU WILL DIE, BATMAN!

BRACING HIS BODY, THE BATMAN MEETS THE MADMAN'S CHARGE...

THE TWO LOCK IN A DEATH GRIP AND TUMBLE DOWN THE STEPS.
I'M GOING TO KILL YOU YET!
I'LL DO MY BEST TO ALTER YOUR PLANS!

CLAYFACE IS TAKEN INTO POLICE CUSTODY....
-PORTIA! -PORTIA! SHE'S DEAD! DEAD!
CAREFUL, BENTLEY- HER GHOST IS RISING!

WAIT I ASKED YOU ONCE BEFORE ABOUT A CAREER IN THE MOVIES! HOW ABOUT IT?
WHEN THERE'S NO MORE CRIME IN THIS WORLD, I'LL BE GLAD TO- UNTIL THEN I'M BUSY!
THAT'S THE SORT OF CAREER I WISH BRUCE WOULD PICK FOR HIMSELF! BUT I GUESS THAT'S WISHING FOR THE IMPOSSIBLE!

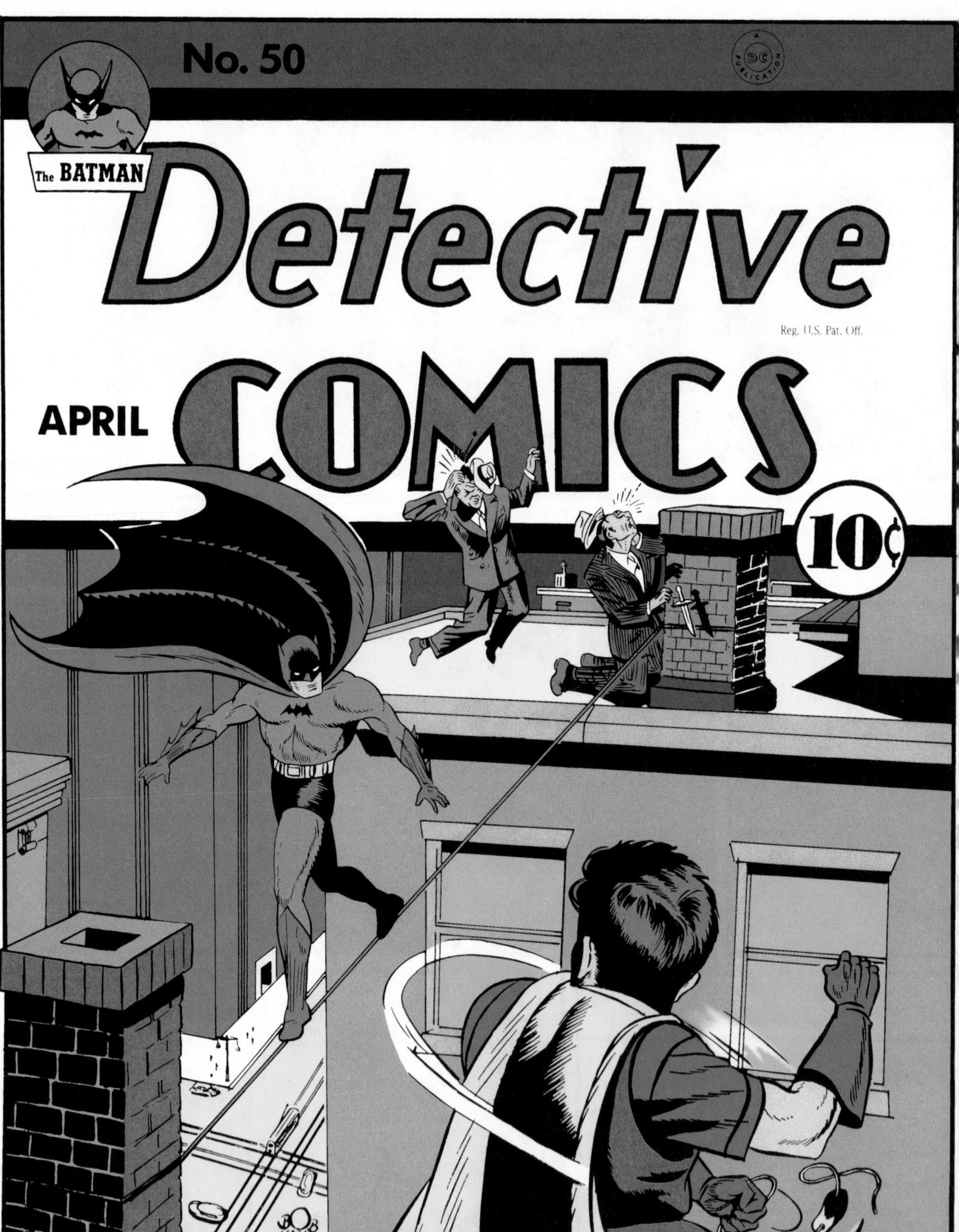
No. 50
The BATMAN
Detective
Reg. U.S. Pat. Off.
APRIL
COMICS
10¢
BOB KANE

BATMAN
WITH Robin
-THE BOY WONDER-
BY- BOB KANE
TO MANY PEOPLE, THE BATMAN IS A BEING OF MYSTERY, AN EERIE POWER. YET, HE IS A MAN-A MAN WHO HAS DEVELOPED HIS BRAIN AND HIS MUSCULAR FRAME TO THE HIGHEST DEGREE. A LIVING BEING OF THE DARKNESS, HE COMES AND GOES UNSEEN. HIS AIM IN LIFE-THE BLOTTING OUT OF ALL CRIME! ASSISTING THE BATMAN IS THAT PHENOMENAL BOY WONDER, ROBIN! IT IS THESE TWO WHO WILL SOLVE AND METE OUT JUSTICE IN.....
"THE CASE OF THE THREE DEVILS!"
ONE STILL NIGHT, AS THE BATMAN AND ROBIN GHOST OVER THE ROOFTOPS, THEY SPY THREE BIZARRE FIGURES IN FLIGHT. WITHOUT A MOMENT'S HESITATION, THE DYNAMIC DUO SWINGS DOWN TO DO BATTLE WITH THE STRANGELY-CLAD FIGURES.
AS ROBIN DROPS TO AID THE BATMAN, HE IS TACKLED IN MID-AIR BY A DEVIL-LIKE FIGURE, AND THE TWO PLUNGE TO THE ROOFTOP BELOW.....

AS ROBIN STARTS TO RISE SOMEWHAT UNSTEADILY TO HIS FEET, THE DEVIL-GARBED ATTACKER PUNISHES HIM CRUELLY WITH A WRESTLER'S TRICK....

THEN, THE MAN SPRINGS FORWARD AND BRINGS A GUN BUTT DOWN ON THE BATMAN'S HEAD....

THE THREE DEVILS CONTINUE THEIRFLIGHT ACROSS THE ROOFTOPS....

LUCKILY, THE GUN BUTT ONLY GRAZED THE BATMAN, AND HE AND ROBIN GIVE CHASE....

AS THE THREE DEVILS PERCEIVE THEIR PURSUERS DRAWING CLOSE, ONE DIVES HEADLONG OFF THE ROOF, HIS HANDS REACHING FOR A JUTTING FLAGPOLE.....

WHEN HE GAINS THE FLAGPOLE, HE HOOKS HIS LEGS AROUND IT AND DANGLES HEAD DOWN.....

A DARING PLUNGE BY THE SECOND DEVIL......
ALLEY OOP!

.....A GIANT SWING THROUGH EMPTY SPACE, HE GRASPS THE HANDS OF THE FIRST DEVIL.....

...DOES A SOMERSAULT IN MID-AIR AND STREAKS TOWARD A FIRE-ESCAPE RUNG ON THE NEXT BUILDING.....

THE SCENE IS REPEATED BY THE LAST THIEF.....

....AND THE THIRD DEVIL IS CAUGHT BY THE SECOND DEVIL......
GOT YOU!

......THEN THE FIRST MAN LEAVES THE FLAGPOLE AND DIVES TOWARD HIS COMPANION, WHOSE DANGLING FORM SWINGS OUT TO MEET HIM...

THE THREE, THEN, SCRAMBLE UP THE LADDER AND CONTINUE THEIR SUCCESSFUL FLIGHT!
OKAY! STEP ON IT!

THE BATMAN AND ROBIN ARRIVE TOO LATE!
BOY, DID YOU SEE HOW THEY GOT AWAY?
YES- AND VERY NEATLY DONE! ROBIN. LOOKS LIKE WE'RE IN FOR SOME STIFF COMPETITION! THOSE DEVILS ARE DARE-DEVILS!

IN THE ENSUING WEEKS, THE NAME OF THE "THREE DEVILS" BECOMES WELL KNOWN-TOO WELL KNOWN FOR COMFORT!
RECORD
THREE DEVILS LOOT JEWELRY STORE
NEWS
THREE DEVILS M DARING ESCAPE AFTER HOLDUP
ATROU
VILS STEAL FAMOUS 'S RUBY...

WELL, CAN YOU TELL ME WHY YOU DIDN'T CATCH THE THREE DEVILS THIS TIME?
CATCH THEM? WE CAN'T EVEN GET CLOSE TO THEM!
THEY HOP AROUND LIKE MEXICAN JUMPING BEANS!

AT HIS HOME, BRUCE WAYNE CHATS WITH HIS YOUNG WARD, DICK GRAYSON...
THOSE THREE DEVILS SEEM TO BE GIVING THE POLICE A VERY DEVIL OF A TIME! A BAD PUN, DICK, BUT QUITE TRUE, NEVERTHELESS!

DICK, WHAT DO YOU THINK THE THREE DEVILS DO WITH ALL THE JEWELS THEY'VE STOLEN?
WHY- WHY, THEY SELL THEM FOR MONEY, OF COURSE!

BUT WAIT- THEY CAN'T SELL THEM TO JEWELRY STORES.
EXACTLY! THEY MUST SELL THE STUFF TO A "FENCE"! -A MAN WHO BUYS STOLEN DIAMONDS!

THERE ARE ONLY TWO FENCES IN THE CITY BIG ENOUGH TO BUY AND CUT UP THE DIAMONDS THE DEVILS HAVE STOLEN!
I SEE- AND WE'RE GOING TO KEEP AN EYE ON THE TWO FENCES! HERE WE GO AGAIN!

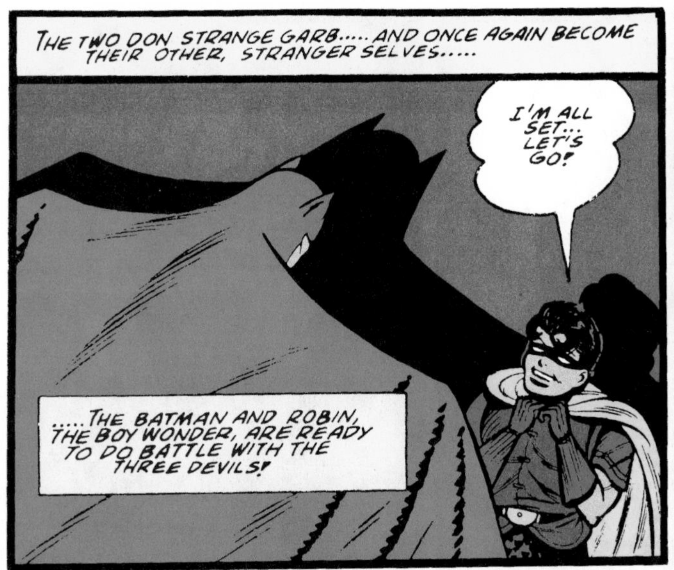
THE TWO DON STRANGE GARB..... AND ONCE AGAIN BECOME THEIR OTHER, STRANGER SELVES.....
I'M ALL SET... LET'S GO!
.....THE BATMAN AND ROBIN, THE BOY WONDER, ARE READY TO DO BATTLE WITH THE THREE DEVILS!

TAKING ALONG THOSE NEW ROCKET-ROLLER SKATES WE DEVELOPED?
YES, I FIGURE THEY MIGHT COME IN HANDY!

NIGHTFALL! THE MOON IS LIKE AN UNWINKING EYE AS IT LOOKS DOWN AT THE TWO MANTLED FIGURES WHO SLINK SILENTLY IN THE SHADOWS ACROSS THE GREY CITY STREETS....

THE DENS OF THE TWO NOTORIOUS FENCES ARE WATCHED.....

NOTHING YET! WE'LL JUST HAVE TO KEEP WATCHING.

NIGHT AFTER NIGHT, THE DYNAMIC DUO MOVES DEEP IN DARKNESS, KEEPING THEIR CONSTANT VIGIL.
NO SIGN OF THEM!
IT LOOKS LIKE MY SCHEME HAS LAID AN EGG-AND A LARGE EGG AT THAT!

THEN....
NOT YET IT HASN'T -LOOK!
THE THREE DEVILS! ACTION AT LAST!

INSIDE THE DEN OF FRANKIE THE FENCE...
HERE'S SOME MORE STUFF FOR YOU, FRANKIE!
LET'S TAKE A LOOK AT IT!

NOT BAD-NOT BAD!
WHAT DO YA MEAN NOT BAD? THAT STUFF WAS TAKEN FROM THE VAN DEEKES' SAFE!

-AND IT'S GOING RIGHT BACK AGAIN!
THE BATMAN!

WITH ONE LIGHTNING MOVE, THE BATMAN WHEELS ACROSS THE ROOM-HIS MUSCULAR FRAME RAMS INTO THE THREE DEVILS!...

THE BOY WONDER BRINGS HIS LITHE BODY INTO PLAY....
HELP! MIKE! TRIGGER! JOE!
ME FOR YOU!

A SIDE DOOR BANGS OPEN AND THREE THUGS BURST INTO THE ROOM.....
WHAT...? WHAT'S GOIN' ON-A RIOT?
THE BATMAN! NOW'S OUR CHANCE TO GET THAT GUY!
LOOK-THE BATMAN!

A THUG HURLS HIMSELF AT THE BATMAN. BUT FINDS HIMSELF TACKLING EMPTY AIR!
GETTING ME IS NOT GOING TO BE SO EASY!

THAT'S WHAT I WANT! OOPS... PARDON ME!

THE BATMAN AND ROBIN HOLD THEIR OWN AGAINST ODDS!
NICE LITTLE RIOT WE STARTED, EH, ROBIN?
IT'S NOT SO BAD!
I'D BE SAFER FIGHTING A TIGER THAN THE BATMAN, WOW!?!

FRANKIE WHIPS OUT A GLEAMING KNIFE, AND CIRCLING BEHIND THE BATMAN, RAISES IT ALOFT FOR THE PLUNGE.....

I DON'T KNOW HOW THIS BOOK GOT MIXED UP IN YOUR PLACE, BUT IT'S A CINCH YOU NEVER READ IT!
CRIME DOES NOT PAY!
AWK!
BONK!

TRIGGER GETS DESPERATE AND LIVES UP TO HIS NAME.... AVOIDING THE WHINING BULLETS, THE BATMAN GRAZES HIS HEAD ON THE EDGE OF THE TABLE!
I'LL STOP YA!

YOU FOOL! THAT SHOT WILL BRING THE POLICE!
I FORGOT!
THIS SIDE DOOR-HURRY! IT LEADS TO THE STREET!

WHAT'S THE IDEA OF THE CAR?
GET IN! THE STREET WILL BE ALIVE WITH POLICE! WE CAN'T LET OURSELVES BE SEEN WITH OUR COSTUMES ON!

AS THE CAR BOLTS FROM THE CURB, A FIGURE LOOKS AFTER IT.... ROBIN, THE BOY WONDER!
THE BATMAN WILL BE ALL RIGHT. I'VE GOT TO FOLLOW THE DEVILS! NOW FOR MY ROCKET-SKATES!

ON GO THE STRANGE ROLLER SKATES. A LEVER IS PUSHED ON EACH, AND ROBIN IS WHIZZING AFTER THE CAR!
BOY-THESE THINGS CAN TRAVEL!
Thrifty

THE BOY WONDER LEANS FORWARD TO KEEP HIS BALANCE AS HE STREAKS LIKE A FLASH OVER THE PAVED STREET....
ROBIN'S ROCKET-SKATES! NOT A BAD NAME!

MEANWHILE, WHAT OF THE BATMAN? ....AS HE RISES TO HIS FEET, A BLUE-UNIFORMED FIGURE CONFRONTS HIM......
THE LAW!
WHA....THE BATMAN! I'VE GOT THE BATMAN!
8

COULD YOU BE TELLIN' ME WHAT'S BEEN GOIN' ON HERE?
THAT'S EASY! THE THREE DEVILS HAVE BEEN DISPOSING OF THEIR LOOT BY WAY OF FRANKIE THE FENCE! I TRIED TO BREAK UP THE COMBINATION-BUT THEY GOT AWAY!

IF I EVER MEET THEM AGAIN THEY WON'T GET AWAY!
I'M SURE THEY WON'T. 'TIS A FUNNY THING, MR. BATMAN. BUT I HAVE A LOT OF RESPECT FOR YE-EVEN THOUGH YOUR METHODS AIN'T EXACTLY PEACEFUL!

YE KNOW, IF YOU WAS TA BE HITTIN' ME ONCE, I GUESS THEN I COULDN'T HOLD YE- AND I'D STILL BE CARRYIN' OUT ME DOOTY!
SAY, YOU'RE OKAY!

SOCK AWAY!
AS LONG AS YOU SAY SO- HERE IT IS!

...AND WHEN OTHER POLICE BREAK IN....
IT'S RILEY! HE'S UNCONSCIOUS!
...AND WILL YOU LOOK AT THE MAN.... HE-HE LOOKS LIKE HE WAS GRINNING AT SOMETHING!

IN THE MEANTIME, ROBIN HAS TRAILED THE DEVILS TO THE EDGE OF TOWN....
THEY'RE GOING INTO THAT TUNNEL!

ROBIN FOLLOWS...
WHY- WHY, THIS IS THE ABANDONED TUNNEL THAT CONNECTS WITH THE SUBWAY!

AS THE THREE DEVILS TURN A CORNER, ROBIN IS CLOSE BEHIND, WHEN SUDDENLY SOMETHING LANDS ON HIS HEAD WITH A PARALYZING THUD!

I'LL PLUG THE KID AND GET IT OVER WITH!
NO! IF HIS BODY IS DISCOVERED WITH A SLUG IN IT, THE COPS WILL INVESTIGATE AND MAYBE FIND OUR HIDEOUT!
LET'S SHOVE HIM ON THE SUBWAY TRACK. THE TRAIN WILL FINISH HIM AND IT WILL LOOK LIKE AN ACCIDENT -LOOK LIKE HE FELL OFF THE STATION.

A MOMENT LATER, ROBIN'S INERT FORM IS LYING ACROSS A SUBWAY EXPRESS TRACK.....IN THE DISTANCE, THE WAIL OF A TRAIN WHISTLE IS HEARD....
WoOOO

AS ROBIN GAINS CONSCIOUSNESS, HE IS AWARE OF A THROBBING NOISE... THE GROUND SHIVERS... A SUBWAY TRAIN IS APPROACHING!!

DEATH- CRUSHING DEATH IS HURTLING AT HIM AS THE TRAIN ROARS OUT OF THE TUNNEL...
TRAIN-- GROGGY- CAN'T MOVE- GOT NO STRENGTH!

THE TERRIBLE BLOW ON THE HEAD HAS LEFT ROBIN STILL DIZZY AND WEAK! THE TRAIN LEAPS AT HIM AT A TERRIFYING SPEED...
GOT TO MOVE- GOT TO.....
IT POUNDS OVER THE RAILS, ITS WHEELS SCREAMING LIKE TORTURED BEASTS....

SUDDENLY, AS THE TRAIN RUSHES AT HIM LIKE A GIGANTIC MONSTER OF STEEL, ROBIN MAKES A DESPERATE TRY... ROLLS AND SLIPS DOWN IN THE GRAVEL PIT THAT RUNS BETWEEN THE TRACKS....

HE IS NOT A SECOND TOO SOON, FOR AN INSTANT LATER THE TRAIN IS DASHING OVER HIM AT BULLET SPEED!

LATER, WHEN HE IS ABLE, ROBIN RACES HOME TO RELATE EVERYTHING TO THE BATMAN....
...SO I'M ALL RIGHT NOW. ANYWAY, WE KNOW WHERE THE HIDEOUT OF THE THREE DEVILS IS!
APPROPRIATE THAT THE DEVILS SHOULD HAVE A HIDEOUT UNDERGROUND -SORT OF IN KEEPING WITH THEIR CHARACTER! WE'LL TAKE A LOOK TOMORROW AFTER YOU'VE RESTED!

THE NEXT NIGHT, THE DYNAMIC DUO RETRACE ROBIN'S STEPS AND ENTER THE HIDDEN ABODE OF THE THREE DEVILS!
THEY'RE GONE!
PROBABLY OUT PULLING ONE OF THEIR JOBS!

THE BATMAN IDLY INSPECTS THE BOOK ON THE TABLE.
A BOOK FULL OF NEWSPAPER CLIPPINGS - ALL ABOUT CIRCUS ACROBATS! NOW I'VE GOT IT-THE THREE DEVILS ARE FORMER CIRCUS ACROBATS!
NO WONDER THEY WERE ABLE TO HOP AROUND LIKE THEY DID!

LOOK- THIS ARTICLE TELLING ABOUT A JEWELRY CONCERN OPENING ON THE TOP FLOOR OF THE CAPITOL STATE BUILDING-IT'S UNDERLINED!
THAT MEANS THEY'VE GONE TO LOOT THE PLACE! C'MON-THERE'S NOT A MOMENT TO LOSE!

ATOP THE OBSERVATION TOWER OF THE CAPITOL STATE BUILDING....
OKAY-I'LL LOWER YOU DOWN TO THE WINDOW!
RIGHT! THIS WILL BE A CINCH FOR US!

SUDDENLY, TWO FIGHTING WHIRLWINDS FLASH IN THEIR MIDST...
THE BATMAN! HE KNOWS ABOUT US!
I'LL MAKE YOU REGRET YOU LEFT THE CIRCUS TO BECOME CROOKS!
THAT KID- HE'S STILL ALIVE!

OVER THE ROOF TOP THEY BATTLE, WHEN SUDDENLY A DEVIL MANAGES TO HIT ROBIN A TERRIBLE BLOW...
HAH!
UGH!

THE BOY TUMBLES BACK OVER THE BALUSTRADE AND PLUNGES DOWN!....

AS THE BOY'S TWISTING BODY FLASHES PAST THE NEARBY BUILDING, HIS MANTLE BILLOWS OUT, CATCHES HOLD ON THE HOUR HAND OF THE GIANT CLOCK ON THE BUILDING FACE....

...AND ROBIN DANGLES IN MID AIR!
WHEW! SAVED IN THE NICK OF "TIME"!

THE BATMAN MAKES A DESPERATE LEAP FOR THE BELFRY TOWER....
THAT CAPE WON'T STAND THE STRAIN VERY LONG! I'VE GOT TO HELP! THAT BELFRY TOWER... I MAY BE ABLE TO REACH HIM FROM THERE!

THE THREE DEVILS SPRING AFTER THE BATMAN!
HE'S THE ONLY ONE WHO KNOWS WHO WE ARE!
WE'VE GOT TO KILL HIM TO PROTECT OURSELVES!

HIGH UP ON THE BELL TOWER CROSS-BEAMS, THERE IS A TITANIC STRUGGLE...

MEANWHILE, AS ROBIN DANGLES PERILOUSLY IN SPACE, A MURDEROUS DEVIL LEVELS A GUN AT HIS HELPLESS FIGURE...
NOW'S MY CHANCE TO GET THAT KID- I CAN'T MISS...

A CREAKING BOARD WARNS ROBIN, WHOSE HAND DARTS IN HIS JERKIN AND PRODUCES THE SLING-SHOT!
NOT A SECOND TO LOSE...

EVEN FROM HIS DIFFICULT POSITION, ROBIN'S AIM IS TRUE! THE DEVIL TOPPLES FROM HIS PERCH AS THE STEEL PELLET CATCHES HIM SQUARELY IN THE FOREHEAD!
YAAAAAAAA
Z-I-N-G..

SUDDENLY, THE CLOCK INDICATES NINE O'CLOCK! UP IN THE BELFRY, MACHINERY SETS THE BELL IN MOTION TO TOLL THE HOUR...
THE HOUR- NOW'S MY CHANCE!

THE BATMAN SPRINGS...
?
?

AS THE BATMAN CATCHES THE CLAPPER, THE BELL SWINGS OUT...
RING OUT, WILD BELLS!
RING! RING! RING!

...THEN AS IT SWINGS BACK AGAIN INTO THE BELFRY, THE BATMAN LASHES OUT WITH BOTH FEET!
...AND HERE'S WHERE I RING THE BELL WITH YOU FELLOWS!

...THE MURDERING DEVILS TOPPLE TO THE FLOOR BELOW!

WITH THE AID OF HIS SILK ROPE, THE BATMAN RESCUES ROBIN!

LATER...
WHEW! I'VE HAD ENOUGH EXCITEMENT TO DO ME FOR A LONG TIME!
THOSE DEVILS DID GIVE US A BIT OF TROUBLE, DIDN'T THEY?
BOB KANE

THEY WOULD HAVE BEEN MUCH BETTER OFF IF THEY HAD STAYED WITH THE CIRCUS.
LIKE A LOT OF OTHER PEOPLE, THEY THOUGHT THEY COULD PICK UP WEALTH THE EASY WAY. THEY SHOULD HAVE REALIZED THAT'S THE HARDEST WAY —WHICH ONCE AGAIN PROVES THAT CRIME DOESN'T PAY!

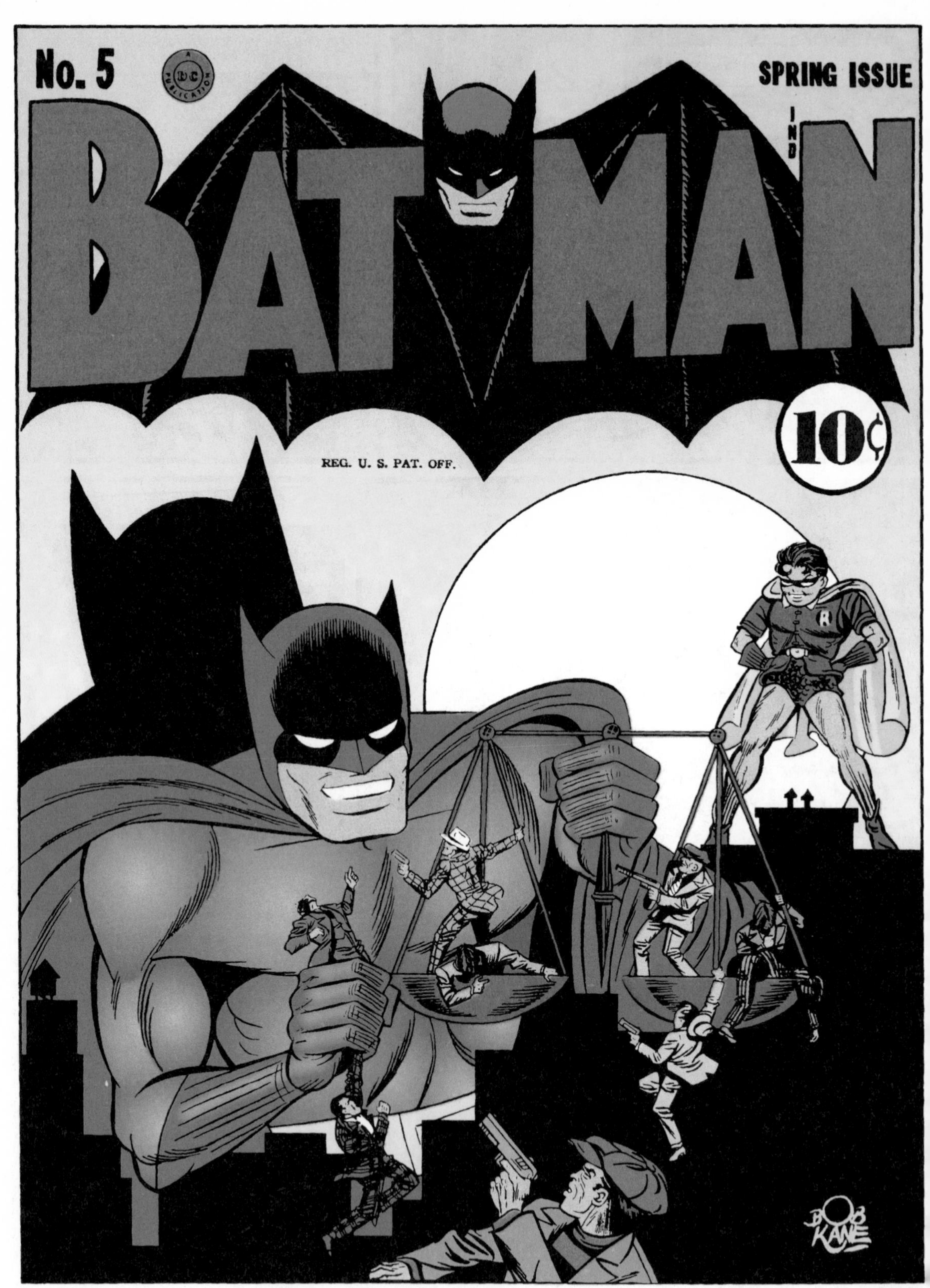
No. 5
A DC PUBLICATION
SPRING ISSUE
BATMAN
IND
10¢
REG. U. S. PAT. OFF.
R
BOB KANE

BATMAN
WITH Robin THE BOY WONDER
BY BOB KANE
THE BATMAN, MYSTERIOUS FIGURE OF NIGHT, WHO HAS MATCHED WITS WITH MINIONS OF CRIME, AT LAST PLAYS A GAME OF CARDS WITH THAT SUPREME MASTER OF EVIL.... THE JOKER! A GAME SO DEEP, SO CRAFTY THAT THE ONLY WAY TO WIN IT WAS TO.....REACH ITS CLIMAX! CAN THE BATMAN DEFEAT A GAME WHICH EVERYONE ELSE HAD THOUGHT WON? READ ON.... READ ON AND FIND THE ANSWER IN....
"THE RIDDLE OF THE MISSING CARD!"
IN THE APARTMENT OF BRUCE WAYNE AND YOUNG DICK GRAYSON, WHO ARE, IN REALITY, THE BATMAN AND ROBIN THE BOY WONDER....
NOTHING MUCH DOING IN TOWN SINCE THE JOKER'S FINISH- HO HUM!
I GUESS THE JOKER DID DIE AFTER ALL, WHEN HE PLUNGED DOWN THAT TRAP-DOOR. AT LEAST, WE HAVEN'T HEARD OF HIM SINCE!
BUT IS THE JOKER REALLY DEAD? OR IS THIS MASTER CRIMINAL OF ALL TIME STILL ALIVE?
LET US SEE WHAT ACTUALLY DID BEFALL THE JOKER WHEN HE PLUMMETED THROUGH THE TRAP-DOOR TO THE SEWAGE WATERS SO FAR BELOW....

A CLINGING FOG HANGS LIKE A PALL OVER THE WATERFRONT. A SMALL BOAT LOOMS IN THE FOG AND RIDES STEALTHILY ON THE BLACK WATER THAT LAPS GENTLY AT THE DOCK-POSTS. A VOICE CALLS OUT...
HE-LP... HE-LP....
LISTEN... SOMEONE IN TROUBLE!
SO WHAT? WE CAN'T STOP TO PICK HIM UP.

HEY.... YOU GONE CRAZY? PUT OUT THAT LIGHT? THE COPS WILL SEE US?
SHUT UP.... CAN'T YOU SEE WHO IT IS? IT'S THE JOKER?

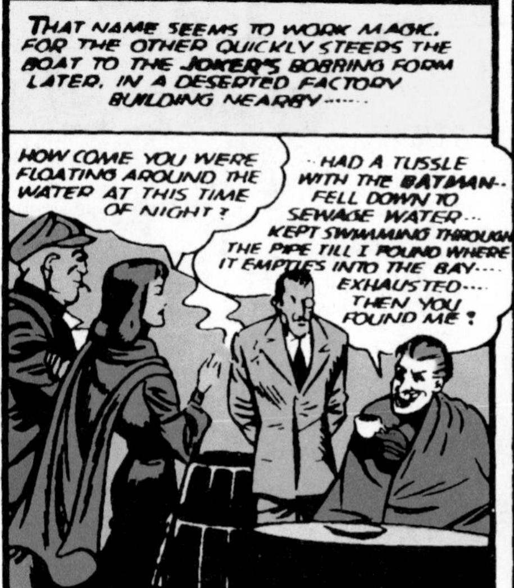
THAT NAME SEEMS TO WORK MAGIC, FOR THE OTHER QUICKLY STEERS THE BOAT TO THE JOKER'S BOBBING FORM LATER, IN A DESERTED FACTORY BUILDING NEARBY.......
HOW COME YOU WERE FLOATING AROUND THE WATER AT THIS TIME OF NIGHT?
...HAD A TUSSLE WITH THE BATMAN... FELL DOWN TO SEWAGE WATER... KEPT SWIMMING THROUGH THE PIPE TILL I FOUND WHERE IT EMPTIES INTO THE BAY.... EXHAUSTED.... THEN YOU FOUND ME!

AFTER THE JOKER HAS REGAINED SOME OF HIS STRENGTH...
I'M CURIOUS TO KNOW WHY YOU HESITATED TO PICK ME UP AT FIRST... HIDING SOMETHING FROM THE POLICE?
YOU GUESSED IT. WE HAD A STEWARD HIDE SOME DIAMONDS ON AN INCOMING STEAMER.
...AND THEN WE SMUGGLE THEM IN... BUT THE DIAMOND SMUGGLING BUSINESS IS PRETTY WELL SHOT.... WHAT WITH THE WAR GOING ON!

WHY DID YOU CHANGE YOUR MIND ABOUT PICKING ME UP AFTER YOU SAW WHO I WAS!
WE THINK MAYBE YOU CAN FIGURE OUT A NEW RACKET FOR US
WE NEED A NEW RACKET. YOU'RE A GUY WITH BRAINS.

I'LL INTRODUCE US. I'M QUEENIE. THIS IS DIAMOND JACK DEEGAN... AND THE BIG LUG IS CLUBSY
DEY CALLS ME DATS ON ACCOUNTA I AM AN EXPOIT AT CONKIN' GUYS OVER DA BEAN!
2.

I'VE JUST HAD A DROLL THOUGHT I'M THE JOKER... WE HAVE BLACK-HAIRED QUEENIE... THE BLACK QUEEN.... DIAMOND JACK -- THE JACK OF DIAMONDS....

... AND CLUBSY, HERE THE KING OF CLUBS! FOUR CARDS... FOUR CARDS ABOUT TO PLAY A GAME OF CHANCE WITH THE POLICE!
I DON'T LIKE TO PLAY WID DE COPS. YA CAN'T CHEAT WID DEM. DE LAST TIME I PLAYED RUMMY WID SERGEANT CASEY, HE....
SHUT UP, CLUBSY!

GOT ANY IDEAS, JOKER?
YES....FOR A GAMBLING SHIP! A GAMBLING SHIP OUT SIDE THE THREE MILE LIMIT SO THE LAW CAN'T TOUCH US.

OUR PATRONS WILL BE THE SOCIETY RICH. QUEENIE CAN GET PLAYBOYS DRUNK AND JACK CAN MIX WITH THE GUESTS. YOU PUMP THEM FOR INFORMATION ABOUT THEIR JEWELS--
I GET IT! WE TAKE THEIR DOUGH AWAY AT THE GAMBLING TABLES, AND TAKE AWAY THEIR JEWELS AT THEIR HOMES. OK-AY.... OK-AY!

AND NOW A TOAST TO THE SUCCESS OF THE FOUR CARDS! THE JOKER!
THE BLACK QUEEN!
THE JACK OF DIAMONDS!
AND DE KING O' CLUB

TWO MONTHS LATER.... THE GAMBLING SHIP, "THE DECK," HAS BECOME FRONT PAGE NEWS... ALONG WITH THE NEWS OF RECURRING ROBBERIES.....
CITY EDITION
CITY DEMANDS CLOSING OF GAMBLING SHIP
VAN SNOOT HOME ROBBED OF $50,000 IN GEMS
CAFE SOCIETY APPEARS CONSTANTLY ON SHIP

AT THE WAYNE HOME.....
SO YOU'RE GOING TO HAVE A LOOK AT THE GAMBLING SHIP, EH?
UHUH....I'VE GOT MY SUSPICIONS ABOUT THAT BOAT. IT...OUCH.. I CUT MYSELF! OH, WELL....IT'S JUST A NICK!
"JUST A NICK"? YET IT IS THIS LITTLE NICK THAT WILL SAVE THE BATMAN FROM DEATH AND ENABLE HIM TO BRING ABOUT THE DOWNFALL OF AN ARCH-CRIMINAL. SUCH IS THE IRONY OF LIFE!

EARLY THAT EVENING, BRUCE IS AMONG THE GUESTS THAT THRONG THE GAMBLING SHIP....
MY-MY...LOOK AT ALL THE PEOPLE ANXIOUS TO LOSE THEIR MONEY.
5
13

BY CHANCE, HE MAKES THE ACQUAINTANCE OF QUEENIE, WHO ACTS THE PART OF HOSTESS ON THE SHIP...
TELL ME....WHAT DOES ONE DO AROUND HERE FOR EXCITEMENT? JUST STANDING AT A TABLE AND THROWING AWAY MY MONEY SEEMS RATHER TIRESOME.
I'M SORRY YOU'RE BORED!
GOOD-LOOKING CHAP...NASTY CUT IN HIS CHIN.. FROM SHAVING PROBABLY.

I DARE SAY YOU'RE ABOUT THE ONLY EXCITING THING ABOARD THIS SHIP. YOU'RE QUITE PRETTY, YOU KNOW.
THANKS FOR THE COMPLIMENT. SURE YOU CAN SPARE IT?
FUNNY THING..I GET TO FEELING HIS BOREDOM IS AN ACT...AS IF HE WERE PLAYING A PART. GUESS I'M CRAZY... BUT HE IS NICE—

LATER, BRUCE STROLLS ABOUT THE DECK. HE STEPS INTO A DARK SHIP CORNER TO LIGHT A CIGARETTE....
WIND KEEPS BLOWING OUT MY MATCH. BETTER TRY TO LIGHT IT IN THIS CORNER.

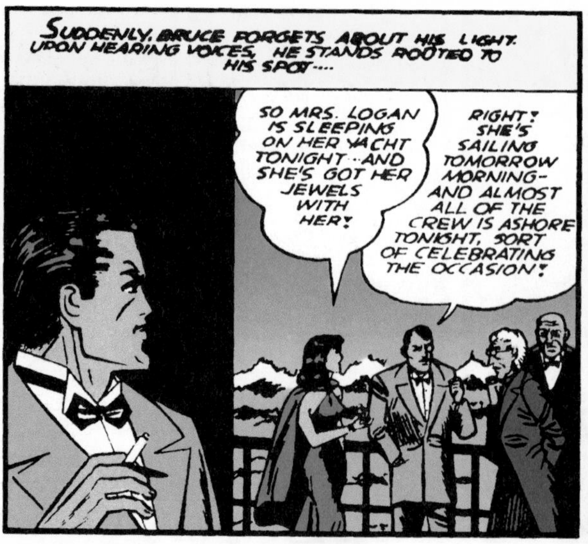
SUDDENLY, BRUCE FORGETS ABOUT HIS LIGHT. UPON HEARING VOICES, HE STANDS ROOTED TO HIS SPOT....
SO MRS. LOGAN IS SLEEPING ON HER YACHT TONIGHT--AND SHE'S GOT HER JEWELS WITH HER!
RIGHT! SHE'S SAILING TOMORROW MORNING-AND ALMOST ALL OF THE CREW IS ASHORE TONIGHT, SORT OF CELEBRATING THE OCCASION!

IT'S A SWEET SET-UP. DO WE GO AFTER IT, JOKER?
UH?
YES...I--SOMEONE'S IN THAT CORNER! COME OUT OF THERE!

BRUCE HAS BEEN UNABLE TO CONTROL HIS SUDDEN EXCLAMATION UPON HEARING THE NAME OF THE MAN HE HAD THOUGHT DEAD. WHAT NOW?
HELLO THERE! JUST STEPPED IN THE CORNER TO LIGHT MY CIGARETTE. A VERY DEVIL OF A WIND.
YOU!

I QUITE UNDERSTAND. BUT I REGRET THAT THIS MUST HAPPEN TO YOU- NOW
HOID YA DE FOIST TIME, JOKER

THE LIMP FORM OF BRUCE WAYNE IS DROPPED OVER THE SIDE....
WHA.... WHAT ARE YOU DOING? HE'LL DROWN!
EXACTLY!... DEAD MEN TELL NO TALES. HE OVERHEARD OUR PLANS, AND YOU CALLING ME THE JOKER! I MUST PROTECT MYSELF!

THE WATER MUST HAVE REVIVED HIM! HE'S TRYING TO SWIM!
I'LL FIX THAT--NO ONE WILL HEAR.... MY GUN IS EQUIPPED WITH A SILENCER!

BULLETS STAB AT BRUCE WAYNE AND KICK SPRAY ABOUT HIS FACE. SUDDENLY, HE THROWS UP HIS ARMS IN A DESPAIRING GESTURE AND SINKS BENEATH THE BLACK WATER-
HA HA HA HA HA!

MOMENTS LATER, A DRIPPING FIGURE CLIMBS ONTO THE WHARF.... IT IS BRUCE WAYNE...
GOOD THING I HAD PRESENCE OF MIND TO PRETEND I WAS HIT. NOW HOME...AND SOME DRY CLOTHES!

AFTER ACQUAINTING YOUNG DICK WITH THE FACTS, HE AND THE BOY DON STRANGE GARB TO BECOME THE BATMAN AND ROBIN, THE BOY WONDER....
THEY RACE THROUGH A SECRET TUNNEL THAT RUNS UNDER THE WAYNE HOME....

....TO A BARN HOUSING A SUPER-CHARGED CAR. THE BATMAN STEPS ON THE THROTTLE AND THE BATMOBILE LEAPS AWAY AND OUT INTO THE NIGHT!

IT RACES THROUGH THE STREETS LIKE A RUNAWAY COMET AND FINALLY SKIDS TO A HALT BEFORE THE LOGAN YACHT.....
WE MAY BE TOO LATE!

JUST IN TIME, I SEE!
THE BATMAN?

GREETINGS, JOKER! NICE TO SEE YOU AGAIN!
UGH!
BRING THAT POP-GUN BACK TO THE TOY COUNTER!

THE JOKER WHIRLS SWIFTLY, AND SEIZING A FIRE-AXE SLASHES WILDLY AT THE BATMAN....
HERE. TAKE THIS!
THANKS!

BUT I DON'T THINK I LIKE YOUR GIFT VERY MUCH!

MEANWHILE, CLUBSY IS KEEPING ROBIN BUSY.... HE HURLS HIS TREMENDOUS HULK AT THE BOY WONDER....
I'M GONNA TEAR YA APART WID ME BARE HANDS!
NICE FELLA!

ROBIN DROPS ON HIS BACK, AND BRACING HIMSELF, MEETS CLUBSY'S BULL-LIKE CHARGE WITH A BIT OF STRATEGY---
OOPS-UP YOU GO!

JUST A LITTLE STUNT I LEARNED WHILE I WAS WITH THE CIRCUS!
6

W-WHO SHOVED ME INTA A REVOLVIN' DOOR?

THE JOKER IS GETTING AWAY!
TRY AND HOLD YOUR OWN, ROBIN. I'M GOING AFTER HIM!

THE JOKER RACES ONTO THE WHARF. HE JUMPS INTO HIS CAR PARKED NEARBY. THE CAR TEARS AWAY JUST AS THE BATMAN LEAPS INTO THE BATMOBILE... AND THE CHASE IS ON!

THE TWO CARS WHIP MADLY AROUND DANGEROUS CURVES ON TWO WHEELS. TIRES SCREAM IN PROTEST AS IF RELUCTANT TO LEAVE THE GROUND.
SCREECH!

THE SUPER-CHARGED BATMOBILE OVERTAKES THE JOKER. WITH STARTLING SUDDENESS, THE JOKER WHEELS HIS CAR ABOUT.
WHA.... I'M CUT OFF! I'LL NEVER BE ABLE TO STOP IN TIME! I'LL CRASH!

DESPERATELY, THE BATMAN TWISTS HIS WHEEL, TRYING TO AVOID THE INEVITABLE CRASH. THE CAR CAREENS CRAZILY... SMASHES THROUGH FLIMSY WOODEN FENCING....

...AND HURTLES OFF THE STEEP CLIFF IN A TERRIBLE DIVE INTO A DEEP RAVINE!!

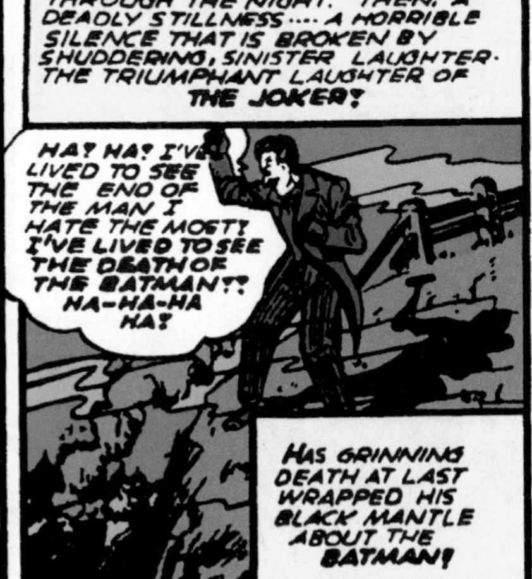
A DEAFENING CRASH REVERBERATES THROUGH THE NIGHT. THEN, A DEADLY STILLNESS.... A HORRIBLE SILENCE THAT IS BROKEN BY SHUDDERING, SINISTER LAUGHTER. THE TRIUMPHANT LAUGHTER OF THE JOKER!
HA! HA! I'VE LIVED TO SEE THE END OF THE MAN I HATE THE MOST! I'VE LIVED TO SEE THE DEATH OF THE BATMAN!! HA-HA-HA HA!
HAS GRINNING DEATH AT LAST WRAPPED HIS BLACK MANTLE ABOUT THE BATMAN!

THE JOKER LAUGHS TOO SOON. FOR HANGING FROM A JUTTING BRANCH, WHICH HE HAD GRASPED IN HIS DOWNWARD PLUNGE, IS THE BATMAN!
STEPPED OUT JUST IN TIME---

MEANWHILE, ROBIN, TOO, HAS HIS TROUBLES. AS HE STEPS BACK TO AVOID DIAMOND JACK'S GUN, CLUBSY WRAPS HIS HUGE ARMS ABOUT HIM---
THAT BRAT IS TOUGHER TO HANDLE THAN A DOZEN COPS!
DAT'S FINE! GOTCHA!
UH!

HOLD HIM! HAH! THIS'LL QUIET HIM FOR AWHILE!

WHEN THE JOKER ARRIVES BACK ON THE GAMBLING SHIP...
HELLO! YOU BACK? WHAT HAPPENED?
I--ROBIN-- THIS HAS BEEN A FORTUNATE DAY FOR ME. THE BATMAN AND ROBIN-- BOTH IN ONE DAY!

WE WERE GOING OVER HIM FOR ANY SECRET WEAPONS AN' LOOK WHAT WE FOUND.... A WIRELESS... BUILT IN HIS BELT-BUCKLE-
SO THAT'S HOW THEY CONTACT EACH OTHER! NOW I CAN TELL FOR SURE WHETHER THE BATMAN IS REALLY DEAD....
BATMAN-- DEAD?

ROBIN'S BELT IS REMOVED BY THE JOKER AND---
IF HE ANSWERS THIS CALL....
WHA-- MY WIRELESS! MUST BE ROBIN!

YES, ROBIN-- WHAT IS IT?
BATMAN-- ALIVE! I KNEW IT! I FELT IT!

YES--I'M ALIVE?--BUT YOU'RE USING ROBIN'S WIRELESS--IF YOU'VE HURT HIM I'LL--
I HAVEN'T--YET? WHY NOT COME AND SEE HOW HE IS ...ALONE?
I SEE--THE OLD COME-ON GAME? OKAY--I'LL BE THERE?
I'LL BE EXPECTING YOU? I MAY EVEN PROVIDE SOME ENTERTAINMENT FOR YOU?
BATMAN? DON'T COME--IT'S A TRAP--DON'T?

I MUST GO ALONE. AT THE FIRST SIGN OF A POLICEMAN, ROBIN WOULD BE SHOT?

HE'LL COME... HE'LL COME... AND WHEN HE DOES--HA-HA-HA?

SHORTLY AFTER, THE DOOR OF THE CABIN IS THRUST OPEN....
AH...A MAN OF YOUR WORD, BATMAN? COME RIGHT IN?

ALLOW ME TO INTRODUCE MY COMPANIONS--THE BLACK QUEEN... THE JACK OF DIAMONDS... AND THE KING OF CLUBS?
NOT FORGETTING THE JOKER, OF COURSE? MY-MY, AREN'T YOU ALL JUST CARDS--MARKED CARDS? HI, ROBIN?

AT THE JOKER'S INVITATION, THE BATMAN SEATS HIMSELF AT THE TABLE FOR A GAME OF CARDS....
WE PLAY FOR HIGH STAKES. PERHAPS A LIFE MAY BE LOST.
ALL LIFE IS A GAMBLE. START DEALING, JOKER.... AND NOT FROM THE BOTTOM OF THE DECK?
...HIS CHIN... A NICK IN IT.. JUST LIKE BRUCE WAYNE'S. THEN HE'S NOT DEAD.. AND HE.. HE'S THE BATMAN?
AT LAST, ONE PERSON OTHER THAN ROBIN KNOWS THE TRUE IDENTITY OF THE BATMAN... AND ALL BECAUSE OF A SHAVING NICK?
9

CARDS ARE SHUFFLED. WHO WILL WIN THIS GAME WITH A HUMAN LIFE AT STAKE?
I'M AFRAID YOU LOSE. I HOLD THE WINNING CARD--THE JOKER?
I KNEW YOU WOULDN'T ALLOW ME TO WIN?

...SO I'M GOING TO SHOW YOU A CARD TRICK.... HERE?

GET HIM! DON'T LET HIM GET AWAY!
DON'T WORRY-- I'M NOT GOING, NOT WITHOUT ROBIN!

AS HIS COHORTS BUSY THEMSELVES WITH THE BATMAN, THE JOKER SCOOPS UP THE JEWEL CASE OF MRS. LOGAN AND SETS FIRE TO A PILE OF GREASY RAGS HE PULLS FROM A CHEST NEARBY.....
I'VE BEEN PREPARING FOR AN EMERGENCY JUST LIKE THIS!

THE TREACHEROUS JOKER STEPS OUT OF THE DOOR AND LOCKS THE DOOR BEHIND HIM!
THIS DOOR IS OF STEEL.... AND I'VE LOCKED THE STEEL SHUTTERS OUTSIDE THE WINDOWS. THEY'LL BURN TO DEATH....MY STUPID HELP AND THE BATMAN AND ROBIN, THEY'LL BURN AND THERE'S NO ESCAPE! HA-HA-HA!

FIRE.... AND WE'RE LOCKED IN! THE JOKER DOUBLE-CROSSED US! LET'S GET OUT OF HERE!
YEAH... AFTER I PLUG THE BATMAN!

HE'S GOING TO KILL HIM!
YOU CAN'T KILL HIM! THAT'S MURDER!
DON'T I KNOW IT! GET OUT OF MY WAY!

YOU'RE-NOT GOING-- TO-- KILL-- HIM!
UGH! WHA...!

WH-WHY DID YOU SAVE MY LIFE? I-I DON'T UNDERSTAND....
I-I-COULDN'T LET HIM KILL YOU! STOP-STOP ASKING ME SO MANY QUESTIONS!

SUDDENLY, THERE IS A SHOT--AND THE BLACK QUEEN SLUMPS IN THE BATMAN'S ARMS.
SHE'S BEEN SHOT!
THAT'LL FIX YA-- DOUBLE-CROSSING-AAAH!

1
THIS IS MY FINISH. I GUESS I···· LOVED YOU ALL THE TIME. MR. BRUCE WAYNE. I'M GOING····· PLEASE, KISS ME···KISS ME BEFORE IT'S TOO LATE-
SHE KNEW I WAS BRUCE WAYNE??

2

3
THANKS-- OHH--
DEAD····

4
BUT NOW THE BATMAN MUST TURN TO THE TROUBLE AT HAND, FOR THE FIRE NOW RAGES FIERCELY. QUICKLY, HE FREES ROBIN.
MIXING TWO VIALS FROM YOUR BELT?
YES···· THIS WILL BLAST THE DOOR RIGHT OFF ITS HINGES!

5
A TERRIFIC EXPLOSION, AND THE DYNAMIC DUO IS FREE.
COME ON··· MAYBE WE CAN STILL SEE WHERE THE JOKER HAS HEADED!
HE CAN'T HAVE GONE FAR IN THIS SHORT WHILE!

6
THERE HE GOES!
MY SPEEDBOAT CAN RUN CIRCLES AROUND THAT TUB OF HIS! IT'S DOWN BELOW WHERE I LEFT IT! C'MON!

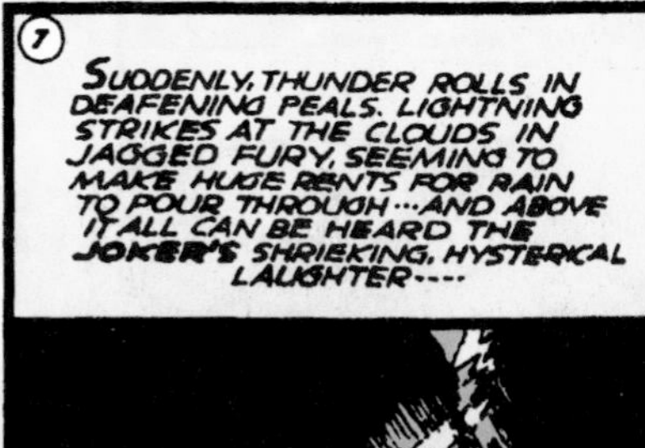
7
SUDDENLY, THUNDER ROLLS IN DEAFENING PEALS. LIGHTNING STRIKES AT THE CLOUDS IN JAGGED FURY, SEEMING TO MAKE HUGE RENTS FOR RAIN TO POUR THROUGH···AND ABOVE IT ALL CAN BE HEARD THE JOKER'S SHRIEKING, HYSTERICAL LAUGHTER····

HA HA HA HA! RAIN---THUNDER--- LIGHTNING--- THEY CAN'T STOP ME NOW---I LAUGH AT IT! HA HA HA HA!
AND NOW, THE JOKER HIMSELF SEEMS A PART OF THE ELEMENTS····WILD AND VIOLENT!

1
THE JOKER BECOMES AWARE OF THE BATMAN'S SPEEDBOAT CUTTING THROUGH THE WATER, SHORTENING HIS LEAD....
BLAST THEM... I'VE GOT TO FIND A PLACE WHERE I CAN HOLD THEM OFF. THAT LIGHTHOUSE... JUST THE SPOT! HA HA HA!

2
THERE HE GOES... TOWARDS THAT LIGHTHOUSE!
...AND THAT'S JUST WHERE WE'RE GOING!

3
THE LIGHTHOUSE KEEPER FALLS PREY TO THE MADMAN'S WRATH---
WHO?
HA HA HA! FOOL! GET OUT OF MY WAY!

4
BUT THE BATMAN ARRIVES ON THE SCENE. IN ONE BURST OF SPEED, HE IS AFTER THE JOKER ---CHASING HIM UP THE WINDING, LIGHTHOUSE STAIRCASE---
HI, PAL-- YOU DIDN'T REALLY THINK YOU COULD LOSE ME THAT EASY, DID YOU?

5
UP THE TWISTING STAIRS THEY RACE, UNTIL THEY REACH THE WINDSWEPT TOWER. A SINGLE BOUND BRINGS THE BATMAN TO GRIPS WITH THE GRIM JESTER!
WE'RE PLAYING THE SAME GAME, JOKER.. BUT NOT WITH CARDS THIS TIME

6
WITH SUDDEN FURY, THE JOKER TEARS HIMSELF FREE-A TERRIBLE BLOW SENDS THE BATMAN REELING BACK, AND HE TOPPLES OVER THE TOWER RAILING--
HA-HA THE JOKER WILL STILL WIN IN ANY GAME! HA-HA!

7
WITH QUICK PRESENCE OF MIND, THE BATMAN REACHES OU IN ONE DESPERATE TRY.... AND MANAGES TO MAKE GOOD HIS CLUTCH FOR SAFETY!
YOU WON'T HOLD ON THAT RAIL TOO LONG... HA-HA-HA-HA AFTER I CRUSH YOUR FINGER TIPS. HA-HA HA!
CAN THE JOKER SEND THE BATMAN PLUNGING TO A WATERY GRAVE?
12

ABRUPTLY, A SMALL FIGURE HURLS HIMSELF AT THE JOKER...IT IS ROBIN THE BOY WONDER!
YOU FORGOT ABOUT ME!
YOU!

ENRAGED, THE KILLER-CLOWN CATAPULTS TOWARD THE BOY WONDER....BUT ROBIN SUDDENLY DROPS TO ONE KNEE...
I'LL ATTEND TO YOU FIRST!
BROTHER, ARE YOU DUE FOR A SURPRISE!

UP-- AND OVER!
AS THE JOKER'S HURTLING BODY LOOMS ABOVE HIM, ROBIN QUICKLY THRUSTS UP HIS HANDS... BRACES HIMSELF...AND WITH ONE SWIFT MOVEMENT, THROWS THE MADMAN OVER HIS HEAD!

OUT INTO EMPTY SPACE FLIES THE JOKER...AND DOWN, DOWN HE PLUNGES, HIS BODY TWISTING AND TURNING.....

...DOWN INTO THE GREEDY WATERS THAT SWALLOW UP HIS HURTLING FORM!
THIS IS ONE GAME THE JOKER LOST!
...AND HE LOST BECAUSE HE LOST TRACK OF ONE CARD.... BUT NEVER MIND THAT...LET'S RETURN THESE JEWELS!

LATER THAT EVENING.....
WHAT DID YOU MEAN WHEN YOU SAID THE JOKER LOST BECAUSE HE DIDN'T KEEP TRACK OF ONE CARD?
I MEAN THE FOUR CARDS! THERE SHOULD HAVE BEEN FIVE! HE HAD THE KING OF CLUBS--THE JACK OF DIAMONDS--THE BLACK QUEEN OF SPADES--- AND, OF COURSE, THE JOKER. HE FORGOT ONE CARD.

....HE FORGOT ABOUT HEARTS.....AND THERE WAS A HEART.... THE HEART OF THAT GIRL WHO DIED BACK THERE. HE DIDN'T COUNT ON THAT...AND THAT DEFEATED HIM!

BUT IS THE JOKER REALLY DEFEATED? OR DOES HE STILL LIVE TO HOLD A HIDDEN TRICK? ONLY THE STORM-LASHED, TURBULENT SEA CAN ANSWER THAT QUESTION!
BOB KANE

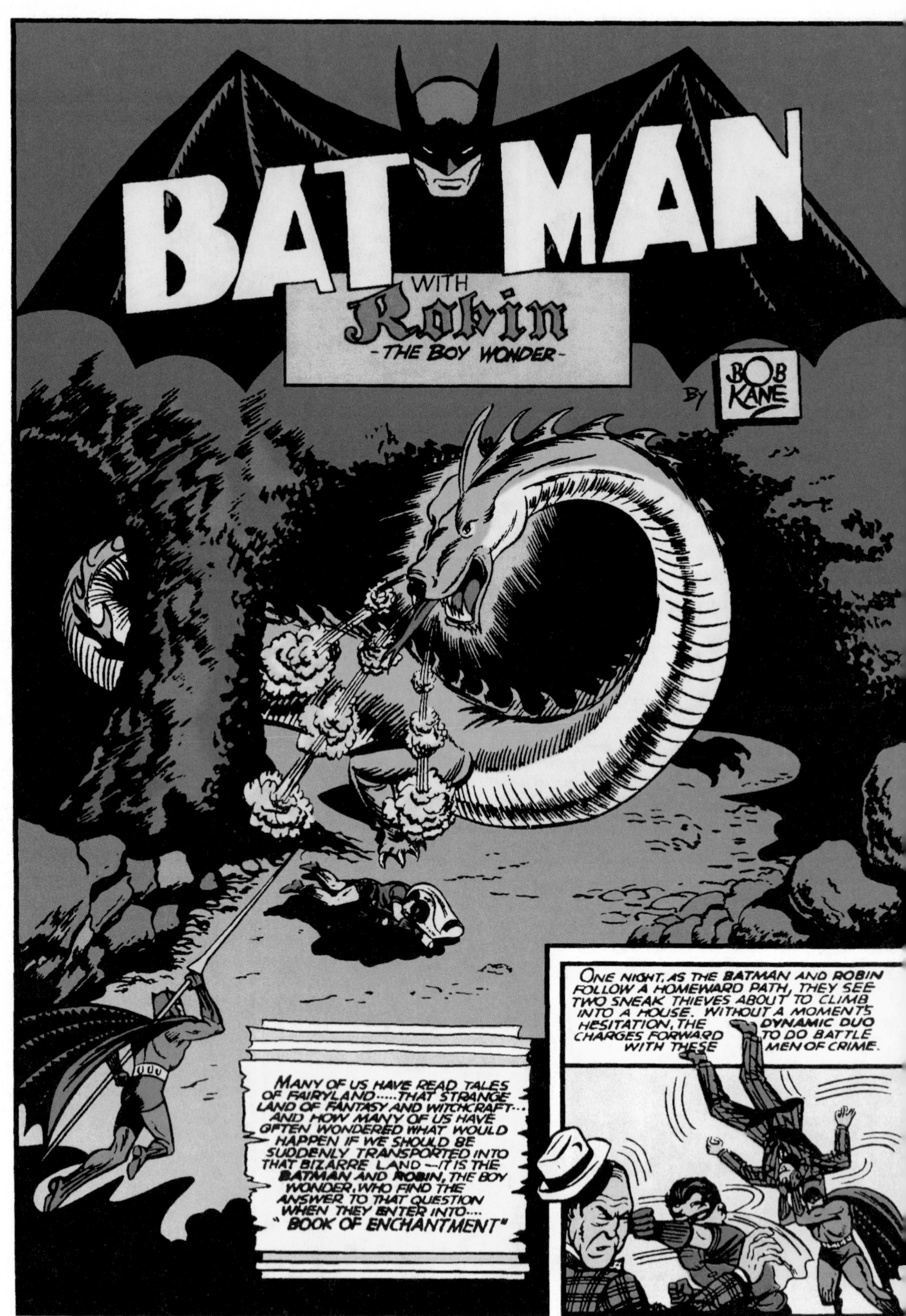
BATMAN
WITH Robin -THE BOY WONDER-
BY BOB KANE
MANY OF US HAVE READ TALES OF FAIRYLAND.....THAT STRANGE LAND OF FANTASY AND WITCHCRAFT... AND HOW MANY OF US HAVE OFTEN WONDERED WHAT WOULD HAPPEN IF WE SHOULD BE SUDDENLY TRANSPORTED INTO THAT BIZARRE LAND --IT IS THE BATMAN AND ROBIN, THE BOY WONDER, WHO FIND THE ANSWER TO THAT QUESTION WHEN THEY ENTER INTO.... "BOOK OF ENCHANTMENT"
ONE NIGHT, AS THE BATMAN AND ROBIN FOLLOW A HOMEWARD PATH, THEY SEE TWO SNEAK THIEVES ABOUT TO CLIMB INTO A HOUSE. WITHOUT A MOMENT'S HESITATION, THE DYNAMIC DUO CHARGES FORWARD TO DO BATTLE WITH THESE MEN OF CRIME.

1 THE THIEVES ARE QUICKLY PUT TO ROUT-- SUDDENLY, A FIGURE APPEARS ON THE THRESHOLD OF THE HOUSE AND CALLS OUT...
WHA...! THE BATMAN!?.. COME INTO MY HOUSE! I NEED YOUR HELP! I AM PROFESSOR ANDERSON!

2 PLEASE DON'T THINK I AM ONE OF THOSE CRACKPOT, MAD SCIENTISTS ONE READS ABOUT IN MYSTERY STORIES AND COMIC BOOKS.... ALTHOUGH YOU WILL THINK I'M MAD WHEN I SHOW YOU MY MACHINE!

3
MY MACHINE.. MY LIFE'S WORK!
IT LOOKS IT!... BUT WHAT IS IT FOR?

4 IF YOU WERE TO SIT IN THIS CHAIR AND READ THIS BOOK, BY PRESSING A SERIES OF BUTTONS I COULD SEND YOU INTO THE WORLD OF THE BOOK YOU ARE READING!
Anthology of FAIRY TALES

5 INTO THE LAND OF THE BOOK.... WHY-WHY, IT COULDN'T BE DONE-- IT'S IMPOSSIBLE!!
FOR MAN TO BE ABLE TO FLY WAS ONCE THOUGHT IMPOSSIBLE... RADIO, THE TELEPHONE WERE ONCE IMPOSSIBILITIES!

6 ALL RIGHT- SUPPOSE IT IS POSSIBLE-- WHAT HAS IT GOT TO DO WITH US?
MY DAUGHTER, ENID...I SENT HER INTO FAIRYLAND TWO DAYS AGO..SHE HASN'T COME BACK! BRING HER BACK TO. ME- PLEASE!

7 WHY PICK ON US? WHY NOT GET SOMEONE ELSE - OR GO GET HER YOURSELF?
I MUST STAY TO WATCH THE MACHINE. I CAN'T ASK ANYONE ELSE. WHY, THEY'D LAUGH AT ME!

8 YOU WHO HAVE SEEN SO MANY STRANGE THINGS-- YOU WILL NOT LAUGH - YOU-- YOU MUST HELP ME! PERHAPS, ENID IS IN TROUBLE!
FAIRYLAND WITH ITS GIANTS AND WITCHES AREN'T EXACTLY OUR LINE, BUT YOU NEED HELP. WE'LL DO IT!

3 THE PROFESSOR THROWS A SWITCH. THE MACHINE SHIVERS, THROBS WITH ENERGY... A CURIOUS PRESSING, SHRINKING FEELING IS FELT BY THE BATMAN AND ROBIN.

... AND THE WITCH POINTED WITH A LONG, BONY FINGER AND THE....

4 THEN THEIR SENSES BEGIN TO SWIM... THEY SEEM TO BE LOST IN YAWNING SPACE--WORLDS, COMETS SEEM TO WHIZ PAST THEM. FAR OFF THERE IS A ROLL OF THUNDER AND ALL THE WHILE THEY FEEL THAT TERRIBLE SHRINKING SENSATION...

SUDDENLY, THERE IS A BLINDING, WHITE FLASH OF LIGHTNING, A CRASHING THUNDERCLAP..... AND THEY ARE IN THE STRANGE WORLD OF FAIRYLAND! 5

IT WORKED-- WE'RE IN THE LAND OF THAT BOOK!

GOLLY!

THE BATMAN AND ROBIN QUICKLY INSPECT THE LAND ABOUT THEM, THEN DECIDE TO START THEIR QUEST FOR THE MISSING GIRL, ENID. 6

THE FIRST THING WE OUGHT TO DO IS FIND OUT IF ANYONE HAS SEEN THE GIRL.

LET'S ASK THAT OLD MAN COMING UP THE ROAD.

7 WILL YOU STOP A MOMENT, OLD MAN?... I WANT TO ASK YOU A QUESTION!

I NEVER STOP-- I NEVER CAN! I AM TIME-- FATHER TIME!

FATHER TIME! TIME SEES EVERYTHING THAT HAPPENS. TELL ME -- ENID ANDERSON-- SHE ARRIVED HERE TWO DAYS AGO-- WHERE IS SHE?

AH, YES, I HAVE SEEN HER. SHE HAS BEEN CAPTURED BY GRUEL... GRUEL, THE BLACK WITCH!

8

THE BLACK WITCH?
YES--AND YOU MUST RESCUE THE GIRL BEFORE THIS DAY ENDS. ANYONE WHO REMAINS IN FAIRYLAND FOR THREE DAYS IS COMPELLED TO REMAIN HERE FOREVER!!

YOU HAVE TILL SUNDOWN TO TAKE HER BACK TO YOUR OWN LAND, ELSE SHE MAY NEVER LEAVE..... REMEMBER-- SUNDOWN!!

LOOKS LIKE WE HAVE A MAN-SIZED JOB ON OUR HANDS.
YES, AND-WHAT'S THAT UP THERE IN THE SKY?

FRAMED AGAINST THE SKY IS A WEIRD SIGHT.... A WITCH ON A BROOMSTICK!
THERE THEY ARE -- HEE HEE!

THE BROOMSTICK HALTS BEFORE THE BATMAN AND ROBIN, AND THE WITCH JUMPS OFF WITH A QUICK LITTLE HOP.....
A WITCH-- THE BLACK WITCH!
HEE HEE...I LOOKED INTO MY MAGIC CRYSTAL AND SAW YOU ARRIVE ...GOING TO TRY TO TAKE THE GIRL FROM ME, EH? HEE HEE!

LET US SEE HOW YOUR MIGHT SHALL AVAIL AGAINST MY MAGIC. IF YOU WOULD FIGHT... HERE-- FIGHT TWO OF MY SERVANTS--

A PUFF OF SMOKE. IT CLEARS SLOWLY, AND IN ITS PLACE STAND TWO STRANGE LOOKING CREATURES....
HERE ARE TWO OPPONENTS FOR YOU--BURN-THE MAN OF FIRE... AND FREEZE-THE MAN OF ICE! HEE HEE!

DEFEAT THEM --IF YOU CAN! HEE HEE HEE!
WITH THE EMBRACE OF EITHER OF THEIR OPPONENTS MEANING DEATH, THE BATMAN AND ROBIN FACE A SUPREME TEST--CAN THEY WIN?

4
QUICK AS THOUGHT, THE BATMAN DROPS TO THE GROUND... HIS OUT-THRUST FOOT TRIPS THE MAN OF FIRE.....
OUCH! I'M GIVING MYSELF THE HOT-FOOT!

5
WHILE AT THAT VERY INSTANT, THE MAN OF ICE LUNGES AT THE BOYWONDER WHO SIDESTEPS AND.....
BRRR! LIKE GRABBING AN ICICLE!

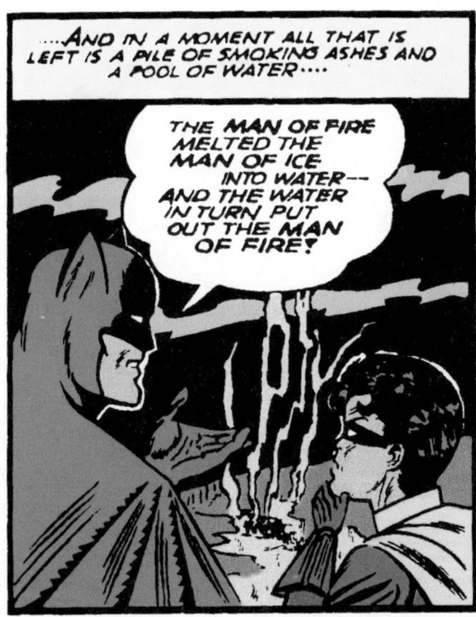
....AND IN A MOMENT ALL THAT IS LEFT IS A PILE OF SMOKING ASHES AND A POOL OF WATER....
THE MAN OF FIRE MELTED THE MAN OF ICE INTO WATER-- AND THE WATER IN TURN PUT OUT THE MAN OF FIRE!

OUR TWO TRAVELERS CONTINUE ON THEIR JOURNEY. AT LAST, THEY STOP BEFORE A YOUNG BOY WHO SKIPS MERRILY ALONG THE ROAD...
HEY, BOY!
CAN'T STOP NOW, MISTER. I'M SIMPLE SIMON, AND I'M ON MY WAY TO THE FAIR!

LOOK, SIMP-- I MEAN SIMON-- IS THIS THE ROAD TO THE CASTLE OF THE BLACK WITCH?
YEP--BUT YA GOTTA FOLLY IT THROUGH THE MOUNTAIN. THE GREAT DRAGON GUARDS IT! GOOD LUCK HAW-HAW!

ON THEY TRAVEL TILL THEY COME TO THE MOUNTAIN OF THE DRAGON....
THIS IS THE MOUNTAIN- SEE-THE PATH GOES RIGHT THROUGH IT!
YES- BUT I DON'T SEE ANY DRAGON-

...AND THEY ARE FORCED TO FLEE FOR THEIR LIVES. THE DRAGON HAS EMERGED!
RUN- RUN!

CAUTIOUSLY, THEY ADVANCE TOWARD THE HOLE--SUDDENLY, THEY HEAR A BELLOWING ROAR--THERE IS A SMELL OF SULPHUR....

ROBIN TRIPS AND FALLS IN THE PATH OF THE MONSTER!!
ROBIN!

DISREGARDING DANGER TO HIMSELF, THE BATMAN RACES BACK TOWARD HIS YOUNG AIDE......A GIANT PAW DESCENDS.....

.....AND MISSES ITS INTENDED VICTIMS BY SCANT INCHES!
WOW!

PLACING ROBIN IN A SAFE SPOT, THE BATMAN DRAWS TWO VIALS FROM HIS UTILITY BELT AND MIXES THEIR CONTENTS.... FEARLESSLY, HE DARTS BACK BEFORE THE FURIOUS DRAGON AND HURLS THE VIAL WITH ITS CONTENTS AT THE MONSTER'S GAPING MOUTH
THIS WILL FIX THAT BIG LIZARD ONCE AND FOR ALL!

THERE IS A TREMENDOUS BLAST AND THE HEAD OF THE DRAGON IS BLOWN TO BITS!

AND SO THE BATMAN AND ROBIN ARE ABLE TO TRAVEL THE ROAD THAT LEADS THROUGH THE MOUNTAIN TO THE OTHER SIDE....
WE GOT THROUGH ALL RIGHT, BUT NOW WHAT?
I'LL ASK DIRECTIONS OF THAT FAT FELLOW ON THE WALL OVER THERE!

THE WITCH'S CASTLE? YOU'LL HAVE TO CLIMB JACK'S BEAN-STALK, FOR IT IS THE LAND AT THE END OF IT!!
SAY-- YOU LOOK VERY FAMILIAR-- HAVEN'T I SEEN YOU SOMEPLACE BEFORE?
VERY POSSIBLY-- VERY POSSIBLY! MY NAME IS VERY, VERY IMPORTANT. I'M CONNECTED WITH THE KING'S SOLDIERS. I AM HUMPTY DUMPTY!
BETTER NOT BE TOO IMPORTANT, HUMPTY DUMPTY- YOU'RE RIDING FOR A FALL!
LEAVING HUMPTY DUMPTY, THE BATMAN AND ROBIN WANDER UNTIL THEY FIND THEMSELVES BEFORE A LARGE FIELD. A GIGANTIC BEAN-STALK IS GROWING BEFORE THEIR VERY EYES....
LOOK! THAT BEAN-STALK!
THAT'S IT! THAT'S JACK'S BEAN-STALK! GRAB HOLD OF IT! HURRY!
THE DYNAMIC DUO MANAGES TO SECURE A FIRM GRIP. THE BEAN-STALK CONTINUES TO GROW AT A TREMENDOUS RATE-HIGHER, HIGHER THAN THE TALLEST BUILDING....
HOLD TIGHT, ROBIN-- AND DON'T LOOK DOWN!
HIGHER, HIGHER AND STILL HIGHER, UNTIL IT PIERCES THE VERY CLOUDS... UNTIL IT REACHES THE STRANGE LAND ABOVE EARTH!
WELL, HERE WE ARE- THE LAND ABOVE THE CLOUDS!
WE MUST BE NEAR THE WITCH'S CASTLE NOW!
A GIANT! A ONE-EYED GIANT!
FEE FI FOE FUM! FOOD-FRESH FOOD! WHAT A MEAL YOU TWO WILL MAKE! HO HO!
HOLY CATS! MORE TROUBLE!
THE CYCLOPS CARRIES THE DYNAMIC DUO TO HIS COTTAGE AND PLACES THEM INSIDE A CAGE---
WHAT ARE YOU DOING?
NO ONE'S GOING TO MAKE ME INTO BOILED BEEF. THE ACID IN THIS VIAL SHOULD EAT AWAY THESE BARS EASILY ENOUGH!
HO HO, I GO TO GET WATER TO BOIL YOU IN!

FREE-FOR A MOMENT--FOR THE GIANT HAS RETURNED!
WHA.... TRY TO ESCAPE, WILL YOU! I'LL FIX YOU GOOD!
I WONDER WHAT HE'D CHARGE TO HAUNT A GHOST!
..AND HE MEANS IT, TOO! IF I ONLY HAD A WEAPON-OH-OH--

THE BATMAN SPIES A FALLEN FORK, AND HURLS IT LIKE A JAVELIN AT THE GIANT'S SINGLE EYE.....
AAGH!
BULL'S-EYE!

HIS SINGLE ORB USELESS, THE GIANT BELLOWS IN PAIN. HIS WILDLY FLAILING ARMS MANAGE TO CATCH ROBIN...JUST THEN ANOTHER GIANT ENTERS....
HO, COUSIN-- WHAT GOES ON?
MY FOOD HAS STAGED A MUTINY! I'LL KILL THEM! THEY HAVE BLINDED ME!

THE MADDENED GIANT HURLS ROBIN FROM HIM, BUT ROBIN IS ABLE TO CLOSE ONE HAND ABOUT THE CHAIN FROM WHICH A LAMP DANGLES....
9

THE LAMP SWINGS LIKE A PENDULUM. AS IT REACHES THE END OF ITS SWING, IT ARCS BACK AND CRASHES INTO THE TEMPLE OF THE OTHER GIANT!
BONK!

WHERE IS THE OTHER ONE! WHERE ARE YOU! I'LL MASH YOU FLAT!
HERE I AM-- RIGHT HERE!

NOW I GOT YOU!
OOPS-- YOU MISSED!

EASILY MAKING THEIR ESCAPE FROM THE DEFEATED GIANTS, THE BATMAN AND ROBIN AT LAST ARRIVE BEFORE THE CASTLE OF THE BLACK WITCH!
THE BLACK WITCH'S CASTLE! AND SURROUNDED BY A WALL OF FIRE!
AND LOOK AT THIS DEEP GORGE! HOW CAN WE EVER EXPECT TO GET TO THE OTHER SIDE AND PENETRATE THAT FIRE?

THE BATMAN GIVES DIRECTIONS, AND HE AND ROBIN PROCEED TO BEND DOWN A SPRINGY SAPLING---THE SAPLING IS TIED DOWN, AND PROVIDES A RUDE CATAPULT!
THINK IT WILL WORK?
I'M SURE IT WILL! WHEN I CUT THE ROPE, THE CATAPULT SHOULD HURL YOU OVER THE GORGE AND THROUGH THE FIRE!

BREATHING A SILENT PRAYER, THE BATMAN CUTS THE ROPE! THE SAPLING SPRINGS UPWARD AND ROBIN STREAKS THROUGH THE AIR LIKE A RELEASED ARROW!

THE BOY WONDER TWISTS HIS BODY IN MIDAIR AND LANDS CAT-LIKE ON THE BALLS OF HIS FEET!

THE BATMAN PREPARES TO TRAVEL THE SAME, DANGEROUS WAY--
HERE GOES NOTHING!

AGAIN A FORM IS FLUNG THROUGH THE BARRIER OF FIRE.....

3
BUT THE WITCH IS QUICK····ONE SWIFT MOTION OF HER BONY HANDS AND THE STAIRS SUDDENLY BECOME SMOOTH····DOWN TUMBLE THE BATMAN AND ROBIN····

HEE HEE HEE!

4
...A STONE MOVES IN THE FLOOR···THEY TUMBLE THROUGH, INTO THE TORTURE DUNGEON OF THE BLACK WITCH.

WITCH HAS STARVED US···· WE EAT!

HO HO, NEW VICTIMS!

YEAH-- AND A HANDSOME LOT, TOO.

A PLAYFUL BUNCH, AREN'T THEY?

5
THE DYNAMIC DUO IS NOT TO BE TAKEN SO EASILY--

HI THERE, FATTY!

6
NOW TO CRACK A COUPLE OF NUTS!

NOW, MY LITTLE PIPSQUEAK, WHAT IS THE WAY TO DEFEAT THE WITCH'S POWER? TELL ME OR I'LL WRING YOUR SCRAWNY LITTLE NECK!
YOU MUST WRESTLE WITH HER...SHE WILL CHANGE INTO DIFFERENT BEASTS...BUT YOU MUST HOLD ON_TILL AFTER THE THIRD CHANGE. DO THAT AND HER POWER IS LOST!
BEARING THIS IN MIND, THE BATMAN MAKES HIS WAY TO THE HIGH TOWER....
WANNA WRESTLE?
YOU! ESCAPED AGAIN! THIS TIME I SHALL DEAL WITH YOU– HEE HEE!

AS THE WITCH HURLS HERSELF AT THE BATMAN, HE FEELS HER UNDERGO A CHANGE. SHE HAS TURNED INTO A LION!
WHA...?

BUT REMEMBERING THE DWARF'S WORDS, THE BATMAN HOLDS ONTO THE VICIOUS BEAST.
LION OR NO LION, I'M STICKING TO YOU LIKE GLUE!

AGAIN THE WITCH TRIES TO SHAKE THE BATMAN, THIS TIME AS A GRINNING CROCODILE.
THAT'S NOT GOING TO DO YOU ANY GOOD!
12

....THE THIRD DESPERATE CHANGE... A SNARLING, CLAWING, MAN-EATING TIGER!
HOLD THAT TIGER.... HOLD THAT TIGER....

THE BATMAN HOLDS ON LIKE GRIM DEATH. THE TIGER CANNOT SCARE HIM OR SHAKE HIS TENACIOUS GRIP... AND THE WITCH BECOMES HERSELF AGAIN!
YOU'VE DEFEATED ME! MY POWER IS GONE... GONE!

4 UP OVER MOUNTAINS RISES THE CARPET. IT SOARS LIKE A SWIFT BIRD OVER THE LAND--

BOB KANE

5 AT LAST---
WE'RE SETTLING-RIGHT ON THE EXACT SPOT WE FIRST ARRIVED AT!
AND JUST IN TIME, TOO-- THE SUN IS GOING DOWN!

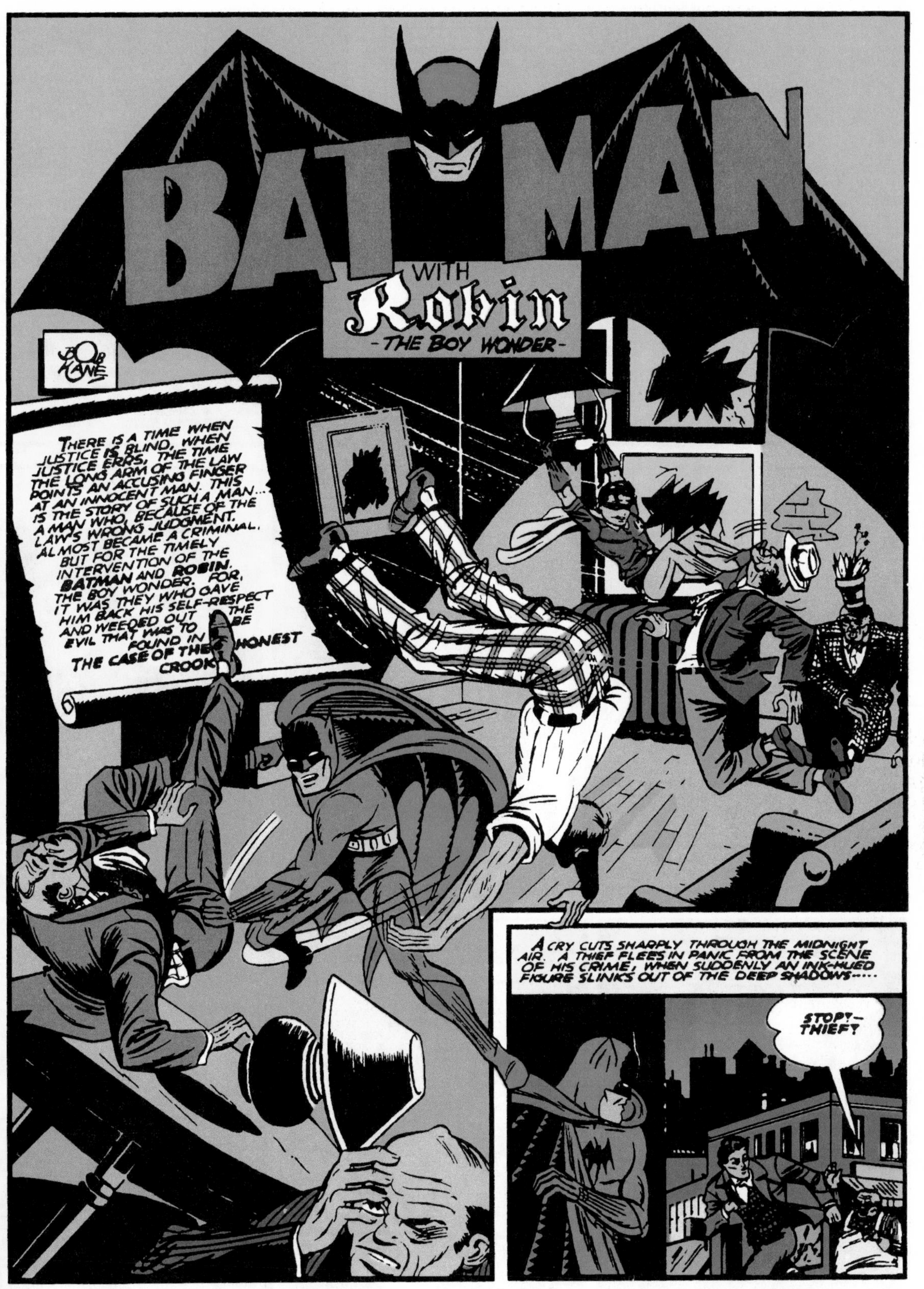
BATMAN
WITH Robin
-THE BOY WONDER-
BOB KANE
THERE IS A TIME WHEN JUSTICE IS BLIND, WHEN JUSTICE ERRS, THE TIME THE LONG ARM OF THE LAW POINTS AN ACCUSING FINGER AT AN INNOCENT MAN. THIS IS THE STORY OF SUCH A MAN... A MAN WHO, BECAUSE OF THE LAW'S WRONG JUDGMENT, ALMOST BECAME A CRIMINAL. BUT FOR THE TIMELY INTERVENTION OF THE BATMAN AND ROBIN, THE BOY WONDER. FOR, IT WAS THEY WHO GAVE HIM BACK HIS SELF-RESPECT AND WEEDED OUT THE EVIL THAT WAS TO BE FOUND IN
THE CASE OF THE HONEST CROOK
A CRY CUTS SHARPLY THROUGH THE MIDNIGHT AIR. A THIEF FLEES IN PANIC FROM THE SCENE OF HIS CRIME, WHEN SUDDENLY AN INK-HUED FIGURE SLINKS OUT OF THE DEEP SHADOWS....
STOP!—THIEF!

A SHORT RUN, A LOW TACKLE, AND THE MANTLED FIGURE BRINGS DOWN THE FUGITIVE THIEF.
HOTEL

HOLD HIM! HOLD HIM!
AS THE BATMAN IS ABOUT TO STRIKE THE THIEF, SOMETHING IN THE BOY'S EYES STAYS HIS FIST, FOR THEY REVEAL A DESPERATE, TORTURED SOUL.

(PUFF-PUFF) SUCH A CRAZY CROOK.....HE HELD ME UP AND ONLY TOOK SIX DOLLARS....THERE WAS MORE, BUT HE WOULDN'T TAKE IT! (PUFF-PUFF)

SIX DOLLARS!-- WHY ONLY SIX DOLLARS WHEN YOU COULD HAVE HAD MORE!
I'M NOT REALLY A CROOK. I-I JUST NEEDED SIX DOLLARS. MY WIFE IS SICK. I NEEDED MEDICINE AND-AND-

WITH THESE FEW WORDS, THE BOY BURIES HIS FACE IN HIS HANDS.
HERE-- HERE! TAKE IT EASY. WHY NOT TELL US ALL ABOUT IT?
POOR BOY.

MY NAME IS JOE SANOS! IT ALL STARTED ABOUT TWO YEARS AGO. I HAD A GOOD JOB IN A GARAGE AND WAS ENGAGED TO BE MARRIED....
2

"BUT MY GIRL, ANN, DIDN'T WANT TO GET MARRIED UNTIL WE HAD $ 1000 IN THE BANK!"
LET'S WAIT UNTIL WE'VE GOT ENOUGH MONEY TO BUY FURNITURE AND EVERYTHING ELSE, JOE. LET'S PLAY SAFE!
OKAY, HONEY. WE ONLY NEED $ 200 MORE. IT WON'T BE LONG NOW!

"EVERYTHING WAS GOING ALONG SWELL, WHEN ONE NIGHT WHILE I WAS ALONE IN THE GARAGE, A CAR CAME TEARING UP THE RAMP...."

"THREE HARD-LOOKING MEN JUMPED OUT. ONE WALKED OVER TO ME...."
LISTEN, KID, THE COPS ARE ON OUR TRAIL. WE JUST PULLED A BIG JOB, AND WE WANTA TO KEEP THIS HOT CAR HERE FOR THE NIGHT?

KEEP YOUR MOUTH SHUT, AND I'LL SLIP YOU A COUPLE HUNDRED BUCKS TOMORROW WHEN I GET THE CAR-- OTHERWISE--
$200? WE'D HAVE THE $1000! ANN AND I COULD GET MARRIED!

"I MUST HAVE BEEN CRAZY BECAUSE I AGREED TO IT. EARLY THE NEXT MORNING, I RAN UP ANN'S HOUSE TO TELL HER THE GOOD NEWS...."
ANN, ANN-- WE CAN GET MARRIED! I'LL HAVE THAT $200 BY TONIGHT!
BUT JOE-- WHERE DID YOU GET IT?

"I COULDN'T LIE TO ANN. I TOLD HER THE TRUTH -- AND BOY, DID SHE LACE IT INTO ME!"
IF YOU THINK I'M GOING TO START THE FOUNDATION OF OUR MARRIED LIFE ON THAT KIND OF MONEY, YOU'RE MISTAKEN, JOSEPH SANDS!
ALL RIGHT-ALL RIGHT! I WON'T TAKE THE MONEY.... I PROMISE!

"I TOLD THE MOBSTER ABOUT IT THAT NIGHT WHEN HE CAME FOR HIS CAR. I COULD SEE HE DIDN'T LIKE THE IDEA...."
SO THAT'S HOW IT IS MISTER. YOU DON'T HAVE TO WORRY--I WON'T TELL ANYBODY ABOUT THE JOB YOU PULLED!
OKAY-OKAY! JUST MAKE SURE O' THAT!

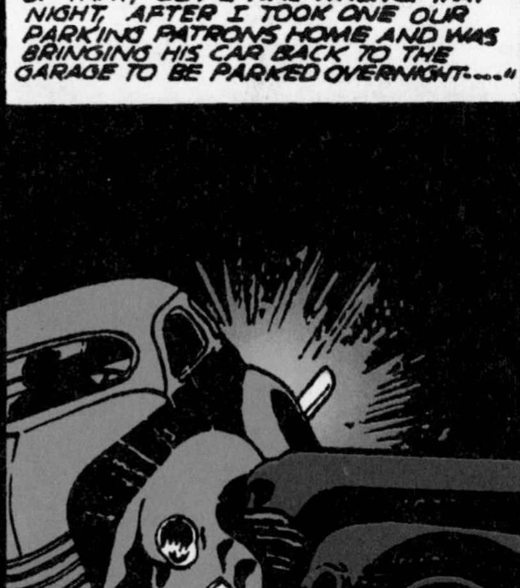
"I THOUGHT THAT WAS THE END OF THAT, BUT I WAS WRONG. THAT NIGHT, AFTER I TOOK ONE OUR PARKING PATRONS HOME AND WAS BRINGING HIS CAR BACK TO THE GARAGE TO BE PARKED OVERNIGHT...."

"I WAS PRETTY DAZED, BUT COULD TELL THAT ONE OF THE MEN FROM THE OTHER CAR WAS THE GANGSTER WHO HAD APPROACHED ME.... SOMEBODY CALLED HIM MATTY!"
WHY DON'T WE PLUG 'IM! THAT'LL SHUT HIM UP!
NO, THE BOSS DON'T LIKE THAT. WE JUST FIX HIM LIKE THIS..... LIQUOR.... SEE?

"THEN THEY HIT ME OVER THE HEAD WITH A GUNBUTT, AND STEPPING ON THE GAS, SENT THE CAR SPEEDING THROUGH THE STREET........"

"I WAS STILL UNCONSCIOUS, AND WITH NOBODY STEERING IT, THE CAR SWERVED AND CRASHED INTO A STORE----"
VICS BA
CRASH!

"A COP PULLED ME OUT OF THE WRECK."
DRUNK-- DRUNK AS A LORD!

"I WAS BROUGHT BEFORE A JUDGE WHO DECIDED TO MAKE AN EXAMPLE OF ME. OF COURSE, HE WOULDN'T BELIEVE MY STORY..."
YOU DRUNKEN DRIVERS ARE A PUBLIC MENACE. I'M GOING TO SENTENCE YOU TWO YEARS IN THE STATE PRISON!
YOU CAN'T! I WAS FRAMED, I TELL YOU! I WAS FRAMED!
OHHHH-

"ANN WAS WAITING FOR ME WHEN I GOT OUT. I WAS BROKE. THEY HAD TAKEN MY SAVINGS TO PAY FOR THE DAMAGES TO THE STORE AND THE CAR."
THE FIRST THING I'M GOING TO DO IS GET THAT GANGSTER WHO FRAMED ME TO GET ME OUT OF THE WAY!
NO-NO! THEY'LL KILL YOU! JOE, IF YOU FORGET ABOUT HIM- I'LL MARRY YOU- MARRY YOU TODAY! PLEASE- FOR ME!

"A SWELL GIRL, ANN. I AGREED, AND WE WERE MARRIED AS SOON AS I GOT MYSELF A JOB."
....DO YOU, ANN DAVIS, TAKE THIS MAN TO....

"I GUESS WE THOUGHT ALL OUR TROUBLES WERE OVER THEN, BUT WE WERE WRONG. ONE DAY, MY BOSS CALLED ME INTO HIS OFFICE....."
I'VE JUST LEARNED YOU HAVE A PRISON RECORD. WE CAN'T ALLOW THAT IN THIS COMPANY. YOU'RE DISCHARGED.

"...AND IT WAS THE SAME WITH EVERY OTHER JOB. AS SOON AS THEY FOUND OUT I WAS ONCE IN JAIL---"
ARUMPH! IN VIEW OF YOUR PAST RECORD-- ARUMPH--
YEAH-- I KNOW-- I'M FIRED!

"....IT GOT SO I COULDN'T HOLD ANY JOB. WE WERE ALMOST FLAT BROKE THE DAY ANN FELL SICK---"
SHE'LL BE ALL RIGHT, DOC-- SHE'LL BE ALL RIGHT!
GET THIS PRESCRIPTION FILLED AND BUY THESE MEDICINES. THAT'LL DO IT!

"I GAVE THE DOCTOR OUR LAST TWO DOLLARS. I DIDN'T KNOW WHAT I WAS GOING TO DO ABOUT THE MEDICINES--"
ABOUT HOW MUCH DO YOU GUESS ALL THAT WILL BE?
MM-I SHOULD SAY ABOUT-SIX DOLLARS!

"SIX DOLLARS... AS FAR AS I WAS CONCERNED IT MIGHT HAVE BEEN SIX MILLION."
SIX DOLLARS TO SAVE ANN. WHERE CAN I GET SIX DOLLARS?.....I CAN'T STEAL IT.... OR....OR CAN I?

THAT'S IT! I-I DIDN'T EVEN HAVE A GUN... I JUST SHOVED MY HAND IN MY POCKET! I-I'M SORRY MISTER, IF I--
I FORGET ALL ABOUT IT. YOU DO THE SAME THING!

THIS FELLOW, MATTY....DID HE HAVE A FACE THAT REMINDED YOU OF A SNAKE? DID HE WEAR SLEEK CLOTHES?
YES, HE DID. HOW DID YOU KNOW?

I KNOW A LOT OF THINGS— HERE... HERE'S SOME MONEY TO TIDE YOU OVER FOR A WHILE. NOW JUST GIVE ME YOUR ADDRESS AND I'LL BE OFF!
GOSH-- I DON'T KNOW WHAT TO SAY!

LATER, WHEN THE GRATEFUL BOY HAS GONE, THE BATMAN'S LITHE FORM DARTS THROUGH THE DARKENED STREETS....
ONLY ONE GUNMAN IS CALLED MATTY, AND LOOKS LIKE A SNAKE. MATTY LINK.... AND HE BELONGS TO SMILEY SIKES' MOB!

AS A MOBSTER STANDS GUARD BEFORE THE SANCTUM OF THE GANGLORD....SILENTLY, AN ARM OF STEEL ENCIRCLES HIS THROAT....

EVENING, SMILEY! THOUGHT I'D COME TO PAY A SOCIAL CALL!
THE BATMAN!
4F

BATMAN, I GOTTA HAND IT TO YA- MY MEN ALL OVER THE PLACE AN' YOU WALK IN AS BOLD AS BRASS? WHAT'S ON YOUR MIND?
LEMME...

MATTY LINK FRAMED A KID I KNOW--JOE SANDS. WOULD YOU BY ANY CHANCE HAVE BEEN THE ONE WHO FIXED UP THE FRAME?
NOW, THAT'S A KINDA PERSONAL QUESTION. I DON'T LIKE THAT--SO YA KNOW WHAT I'M GONNA DO--?

...I'M GONNA LET THE BOYS MUSS YOU UP A BIT SO YOU DON'T ASK ME THINGS LIKE THAT NO MORE. NO SHOTS, BOYS- WE DON'T WANT THE POLICE IN OUR PRIVATE PARTY!

I'M GONNA SIT BACK IN MY RINGSIDE SEAT AND ENJOY THIS!
MAKE YOURSELF COMFORTABLE!

TAKE DIS!
MISSED? TCH TCH! NOW IS THAT NICE...TRYING TO HIT A MAN WHEN HE'S SITTING DOWN!

NICE OF YOU TO PROVIDE ENTERTAINMENT AT YOUR PARTY, SMILEY...WHEN ARE YOU SERVING TEA!

THE BATMAN SHOOTS UP OUT OF THE CHAIR LIKE AN UNLEASHED BOLT OF LIGHTNING!
BETTER TELL YOUR BOYS TO PUT AWAY THEIR POPGUNS, SMILEY, BEFORE THEY HURT THEMSELVES!

ENJOYING YOUR LITTLE RIDE?

TCH-TCH! HOW CARELESS OF ME..... SLIPPED RIGHT OUT OF MY HANDS!

AU REVOIR, GENTLEMEN-- I HOPE I HAVENT CAUSED YOU ANY INCONVENIENCE!

BY THE WAY, SMILEY, I GUESS YOU DID FRAME THE KID, AFTER ALL! THANKS FOR TELLING ME!
SLAM!

A FEW MOMENTS AFTER THE BATMAN HAS LEFT, ANOTHER ENTERS SMILEY'S HEAD-QUARTERS....IT IS MATTY LINK!
H'YA, SMILEY? SAY-WHAT HIT THIS PLACE...A CYCLONE?
YEAH- AND ITS NAME WAS BATMAN!

THE BATMAN WAS ASKIN' ABOUT YOU.... AN' ABOUT JOE SANDS!
BATMAN- JOE SANDS! I-I THINK I BETTER GET OUTA TOWN FOR A COUPLA MONTHS! ER-I'LL BE SEEIN' YA!

AFTER MATTY LEAVES....
I GOTTA HUNCH THE BATMAN IS GONNA TRY TO MAKE MATTY TALK. MAYBE MATTY OUGHTA TAKE A VACATION-- A PERMANENT ONE!
YE-AH!

AND SO THE NEXT MORNING, BRUCE WAYNE, IN REALITY THE BATMAN, READS STARTLING NEWS....
I SHOULD HAVE EXPECTED THIS. SMILEY COVERS HIMSELF WELL!
DAILY
MOBSTER SHOT TO DEATH
THE BULLET-RIDDLED BODY OF MATTY LINK

HE SPEAKS WITH HIS YOUNG WARD, DICK GRAYSON, WHOSE OTHER SELF IS ROBIN, THE BOY WONDER!
DICK, I WANT YOU TO SEARCH MATTY LINK'S ROOMS. MAYBE YOU CAN DIG UP SOMETHING LINKING HIM AND SMILEY WITH JOE SANDS.
SURE THING, BRUCE!

MAYBE THE POLICE FOUND SOMETHING ON MATTY'S BODY--SO-O-O.... I SHALL VISIT MY GOOD FRIEND, POLICE COMMISSIONER GORDON, AS BRUCE WAYNE, SOCIETY PLAYBOY--AND SEE WHAT I CAN FIND OUT!

NIGHT HAS THROWN ITS BLACK CLOAK OVER THE CITY. A SLIM FIGURE MOVES SWIFTLY AND SILENTLY UP THE FIRE-ESCAPE OF THE LATE MATTY LINK'S BOARDING HOUSE....

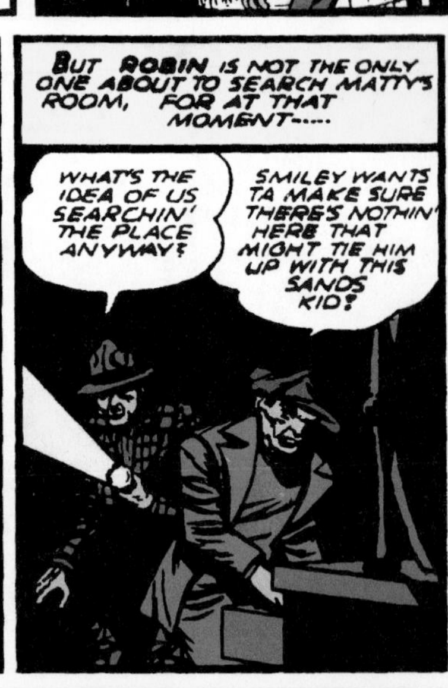
BUT ROBIN IS NOT THE ONLY ONE ABOUT TO SEARCH MATTY'S ROOM, FOR AT THAT MOMENT-----
WHAT'S THE IDEA OF US SEARCHIN' THE PLACE ANYWAY?
SMILEY WANTS TA MAKE SURE THERE'S NOTHIN' HERE THAT MIGHT TIE HIM UP WITH THIS SANDS KID!

HEY--LOOK-- A SHADOW-- SOMEONE'S COMIN' UP THE FIRE ESCAPE!
DOUSE THE LIGHTS! LET'S DUCK, IN ONE O' THESE CLOSETS.
"CLICK!"

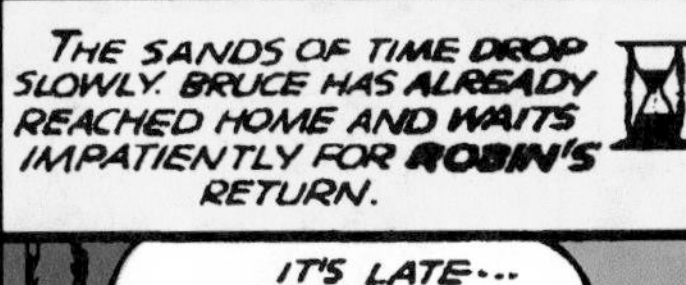
THE SANDS OF TIME DROP SLOWLY. BRUCE HAS ALREADY REACHED HOME AND WAITS IMPATIENTLY FOR ROBIN'S RETURN.

IT'S LATE... HE SHOULD HAVE BEEN BACK HOURS AGO...

HASTILY, HE DONS HIS COSTUME. AN INSTANT LATER, HE SENDS THE WEIRD BATMOBILE STREAKING THROUGH THE CITY STREETS--

SOMETHING'S HAPPENED TO HIM-- I FEEL IT!

MOMENTS LATER, THE BATMAN STOPS BEFORE THE DOOR OF MATTY'S ROOM.....
THE STRANGEST FEELING JUST CAME OVER ME. I-I SEEM TO DREAD OPENING THIS DOOR-

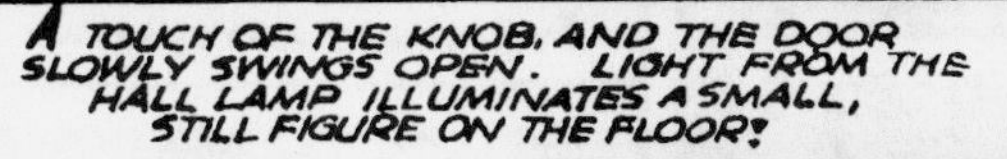
A TOUCH OF THE KNOB, AND THE DOOR SLOWLY SWINGS OPEN. LIGHT FROM THE HALL LAMP ILLUMINATES A SMALL, STILL FIGURE ON THE FLOOR!

ROBIN!

HIS HEAD... ALL BLOODY.... HE'S BEEN CLUBBED... CLUBBED TO DEATH! ROBIN'S DEAD!!

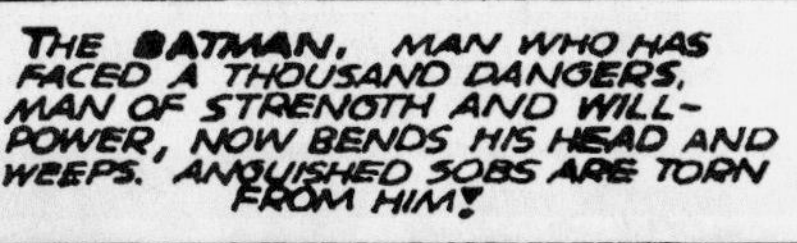
THE BATMAN, MAN WHO HAS FACED A THOUSAND DANGERS, MAN OF STRENGTH AND WILL-POWER, NOW BENDS HIS HEAD AND WEEPS. ANGUISHED SOBS ARE TORN FROM HIM!

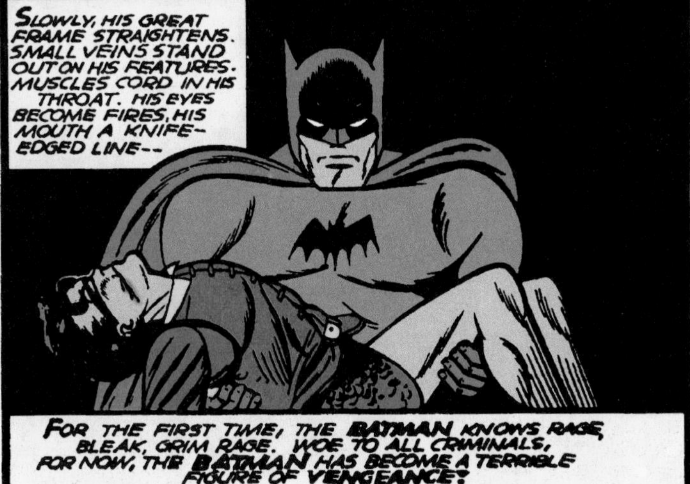
SLOWLY, HIS GREAT FRAME STRAIGHTENS. SMALL VEINS STAND OUT ON HIS FEATURES. MUSCLES CORD IN HIS THROAT. HIS EYES BECOME FIRES, HIS MOUTH A KNIFE-EDGED LINE--
FOR THE FIRST TIME, THE BATMAN KNOWS RAGE, BLEAK, GRIM RAGE. WOE TO ALL CRIMINALS, FOR NOW, THE BATMAN HAS BECOME A TERRIBLE FIGURE OF VENGEANCE!

THEN, AS HE PLACES ROBIN IN THE BATMOBILE....
UH?--HE'S ALIVE... HE'S ALIVE!? I'VE GOT TO GET HIM TO A DOCTOR --A DOCTOR!
OOOOOH!

AN INSISTENT THUMPING ON HIS FRONT DOOR ROUSES A DOCTOR FROM SLEEP....
THIS BOY IS HURT....BAD! HE NEEDS AN OPERATION! HURRY!
WHA.... SEE HERE..... I CAN'T!

LISTEN....IF THIS BOY DIES BECAUSE YOU REFUSED TO OPERATE--I'LL COME BACK AND KILL YOU WITH MY BARE HANDS!

I'LL OPERATE.... BUT NOT BECAUSE OF YOUR THREATS..... BUT BECAUSE IT IS THE DUTY OF A DOCTOR TO COME TO THE AID OF ANYONE WHO NEEDS HIS SERVICES!
OKAY!...I'LL BE BACK LATER. I'VE GOT TO SEE A MAN NAMED SMILEY ABOUT SOMETHING!

A SECOND LATER, THERE IS THE ROAR OF A MOTOR....AND THE BATMOBILE LEAPS AWAY AND TEARS UP THE STREET LIKE A CYCLONE!

IN SMILEY'S RETREAT....
YEAH...AS SOON AS I SEEN HIM I KNEW IT WAS THAT ROBIN KID THAT WORKS WITH THE BATMAN!
NICE WORK! THAT'LL WARN HIM TO KEEP AWAY!
SMILEY! THE BATMOBILE JUST PULLED UP!

A SUDDEN TINKLING OF GLASS. A BULLET BORES INTO THE BATMAN'S SHOULDER, BUT MERE BULLETS CANNOT STOP THE BATMAN NOW....
2200
10

THE GANG LORD HYSTERICALLY YELLS ORDERS AT HIS GUNMEN....
WATCH THAT DOOR KNOB-AS SOON AS YOU SEE IT TURN-FIRE THROUGH THE DOOR!

BUT THE BATMAN DOESN'T EVEN BOTHER WITH OPENING THE DOOR. THERE IS A CRASH.... THE WOOD SPLINTERS AS HIS BROAD SHOULDERS SMASH THROUGH.....
YOU MURDERING RATS--YOU WON'T FORGET THIS DAY!
ANOTHER BULLET LODGES IN THE BATMAN'S SHOULDER BUT IT IS NO MORE THAN A FLEA BITE TO HIM NOW--
LONG AGO, THE BATMAN HAD PERMANENTLY DISCARDED HIS BULLET-PROOF VEST BECAUSE IT HAMPERED FREEDOM OF MOVEMENT.
BY NOW, THE BATMAN HAS THROWN ALL CAUTION TO THE WINDS. HE IS MAD, FIGHTING MAD!
RATS-- DIRTY RATS!
PICKING UP ONE HELPLESS THUG, THE BATMAN USES HIM AS A HUMAN BLUDGEON.
I'D LIKE TO BEAT YOU ALL TO A PULP BEFORE I GET TO WORK ON YOU!
A BULLET SINGS ITS SONG OF DEATH AS IT HUMS PAST HIS EAR....
SMILEY! YOU'RE THE MAN I WANT!

A BULLET SKIDS OFF THE BATMAN'S RIBS. BUT HE DOES NOT FALTER....
HA HA HA HA!
I'M GOING TO WIPE THAT SMILE OFF YOUR FACE!

AS SMILEY SEES THAT THE BATMAN ADVANCES IN THE FACE OF DEATH, HE GROWS NERVOUS, AIMS HASTILY....
I KNOW ONE OF MY SHOTS HIT. BUT HE DOESN'T STOP. HE ISN'T HUMAN!
I'M GOING TO GET YOU, SMILEY!

UGH!

DRAGGING SMILEY TO HIS FEET, THE BATMAN BLASTS A VICIOUS UPPERCUT TO HIS CHIN....
NOT SMILING NOW, ARE YOU!

AND FOLLOWS UP WITH A TERRIFIC RIGHT CROSS.....

ALMOST FORGOT MY ORIGINAL REASON FOR HUNTING YOU UP IN THE FIRST PLACE. I WANT A WRITTEN CONFESSION FROM YOU...ABOUT HOW YOU FRAMED JOE SANDS, OR BY GODFREY I'LL...
DON'T.. DON'T HIT ME AGAIN! I'LL DO ANYTHING... BUT DON'T HIT ME!

CONFESSION IN HAND, THE BATMAN DRAGS SMILEY ACROSS THE FLOOR OF HIS DEN. NO ONE OFFERS RESISTANCE. THEY ARE TOO AWED BY THIS MAN WITH HIS FACE SET IN AN UNYIELDING MASK....
THINK WE OUGHTA TAKE A SHOT AT THE BATMAN?
NOT ME! I AIN'T TACKLIN' WITH HIM TODAY!

HERE....HERE'S SMILEY....AND HERE'S SOMETHING YOU MIGHT BE INTERESTED IN.... A CONFESSION!
WANTED

THE POLICE ARE TOO ASTOUNDED TO EVEN HALT THE MASKED FIGURE....
DID-DID YOU SEE HIS FACE?
YEAH! THAT'S THE FIRST TIME I EVER SAW IT LOOK LIKE THAT! IT-IT WAS TERRIBLE ...LIKE A DEMON'S!

A FEW MOMENTS LATER....
HOW IS HE.. HOW IS ROBIN?
HE'LL BE ALL RIGHT HE'LL LIVE!

I-I---I THINK I'M GOING TO BE A SISSY AND FAINT, DOC.... SORRY!

"SISSY AND FAINT" I DON'T KNOW HOW HE KEPT GOING THE WAY HE DID.... WITH THREE BULLETS IN HIM! AMAZING.... AMAZING....

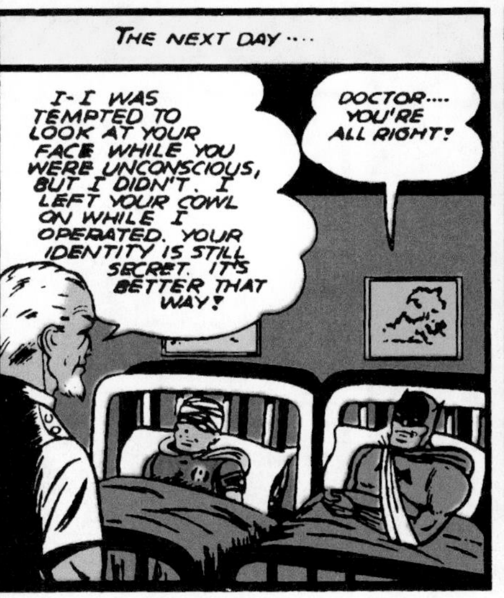
THE NEXT DAY....
I-I WAS TEMPTED TO LOOK AT YOUR FACE WHILE YOU WERE UNCONSCIOUS, BUT I DIDN'T. I LEFT YOUR COWL ON WHILE I OPERATED. YOUR IDENTITY IS STILL SECRET. IT'S BETTER THAT WAY!
DOCTOR.... YOU'RE ALL RIGHT!

BY THE WAY....THOSE PEOPLE YOU WANTED ME TO GET IN TOUCH WITH ARE WAITING OUTSIDE!
13

THANKS TO YOU, MY NAME IS CLEARED NOW AND ANN WILL BE ALL RIGHT!
....AND ME, I GAVE HIM A JOB IN MY STORE! HE IS A NICE BOY!
ALL'S WELL THAT ENDS WELL, EH, ROBIN?
BOB KANE

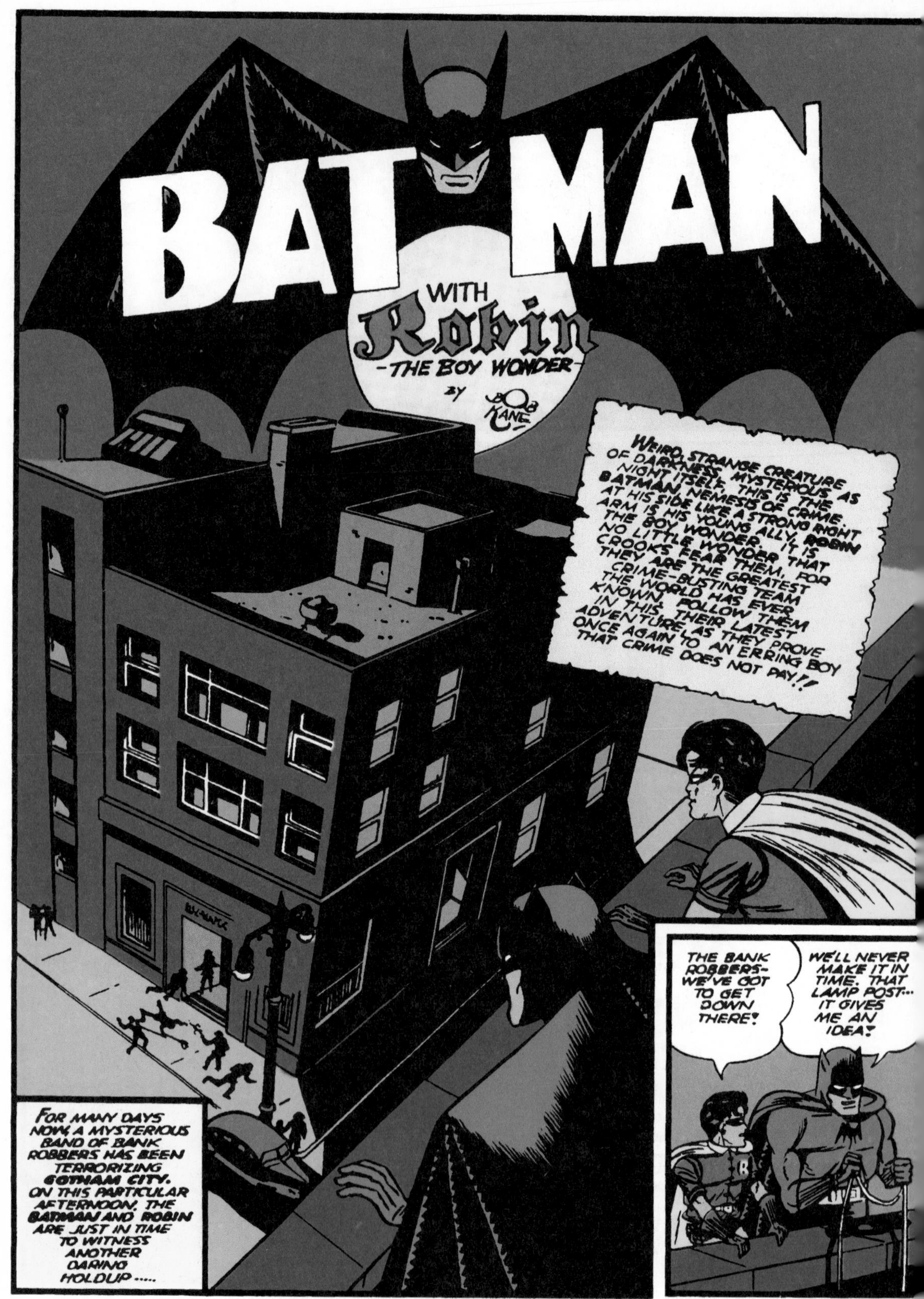
BATMAN
WITH Robin
-THE BOY WONDER-
BY BOB KANE
WEIRD, STRANGE CREATURE OF DARKNESS, MYSTERIOUS AS NIGHT ITSELF. THIS IS THE BATMAN, NEMESIS OF CRIME. AT HIS SIDE LIKE A STRONG RIGHT ARM IS HIS YOUNG ALLY, ROBIN THE BOY WONDER. IT IS NO LITTLE WONDER THAT CROOKS FEAR THEM, FOR THEY ARE THE GREATEST CRIME-BUSTING TEAM THE WORLD HAS EVER KNOWN. FOLLOW THEM IN THIS, THEIR LATEST ADVENTURE, AS THEY PROVE ONCE AGAIN TO AN ERRING BOY THAT CRIME DOES NOT PAY!!
FOR MANY DAYS NOW, A MYSTERIOUS BAND OF BANK ROBBERS HAS BEEN TERRORIZING GOTHAM CITY. ON THIS PARTICULAR AFTERNOON, THE BATMAN AND ROBIN ARE JUST IN TIME TO WITNESS ANOTHER DARING HOLDUP.....
THE BANK ROBBERS-WE'VE GOT TO GET DOWN THERE!
WE'LL NEVER MAKE IT IN TIME. THAT LAMP POST... IT GIVES ME AN IDEA!

① THE BATMAN TWIRLS HIS STRONG, SILKEN ROPE OVER HIS HEAD.....
WE'LL BE TAKING A TERRIBLE CHANCE. BUT IT'S THE ONLY WAY.

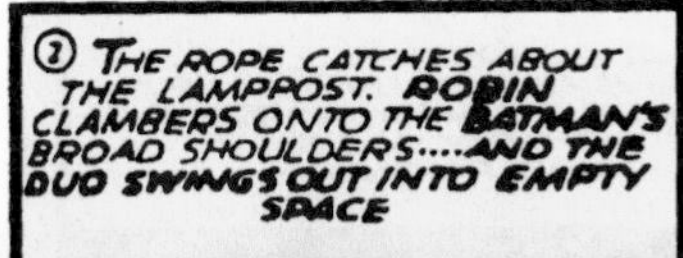
② THE ROPE CATCHES ABOUT THE LAMPPOST. ROBIN CLAMBERS ONTO THE BATMAN'S BROAD SHOULDERS.....AND THE DUO SWINGS OUT INTO EMPTY SPACE

HERE WE GO!

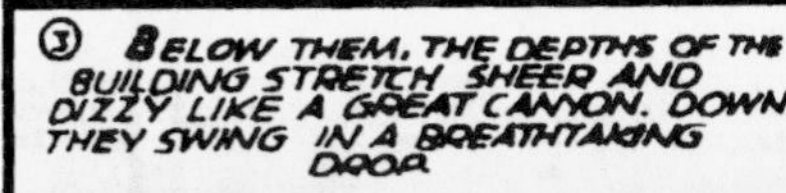
③ BELOW THEM, THE DEPTHS OF THE BUILDING STRETCH SHEER AND DIZZY LIKE A GREAT CANYON. DOWN THEY SWING IN A BREATHTAKING DROP

④ THE TIGHT HOLD IS SUDDENLY RELEASED AS THE BATMAN AND ROBIN DROP LIKE TWO BIRDS OF PREY ATOP THE BACKS OF THE ASTONISHED THIEVES.
DO WE INTRUDE?
BANK

⑤
PLEASANT DREAMS. RAT!

⑥ AS THE BATMAN MOVES TOWARD A HOODLUM, SUDDENLY ANOTHER DARTS FORWARD AND, PUSHING THE OTHER OUT OF HARM'S WAY, TURNS TO FACE THE CRIME-FIGHTER HIMSELF
WHA...?
THAT'S THE FIRST TIME I'VE EVER SEEN A CROOK FACE DANGER FOR ANOTHER. VERY QUEER.

IN THE MELEE, THE RESCUED HOODLUM'S KERCHIEF FALLS AND THE **BATMAN** CATCHES A QUICK GLIMPSE OF HIS FACE....

IT IS THE FACE OF A BOY ... A BOY WHO IS SCARED STIFF!

NEARER AND NEARER DRAWS THE **BATMOBILE** AS THE CHASE TAKES THE CARS WHIPPING AROUND CORNERS, ROARING UP STREETS...

JAKE MILLER SECOND HAND BOOKS

BUT THEY CAN BE TRACED BY THE CAR... AND THEN THE POLICE WILL SEARCH THESE HOUSES...

THE CAR WAS PROBABLY STOLEN... AND THEY'RE SMART ENOUGH TO KNOW THE POLICE WON'T BELIEVE THEY'LL BE STUPID ENOUGH TO REVEAL THEIR NEIGHBORHOOD!

I'M CURIOUS TO KNOW WHY THAT BANDIT PROTECTED THE OTHER AT THE RISK OF HIMSELF--- SO I'M COMING BACK TO INVESTIGATE TOMORROW-- AS **BRUCE WAYNE**!

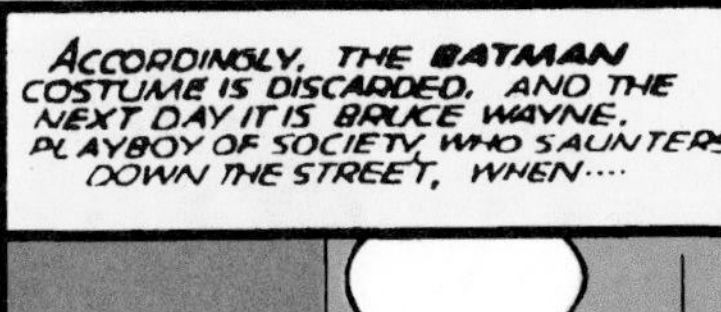
ACCORDINGLY, THE BATMAN COSTUME IS DISCARDED, AND THE NEXT DAY IT IS BRUCE WAYNE, PLAYBOY OF SOCIETY, WHO SAUNTERS DOWN THE STREET, WHEN....

OOF!
UGH!

YOU BIG APE...WHY DON'T YOU LOOK--- BRUCE---- BRUCE WAYNE!
LINDA PAGE! WELL, WELL! I HAVEN'T SEEN YOU IN A DOG'S AGE. THE WHOLE CROWD HAS BEEN ASKING ABOUT YOU!

TELL THE CROWD I WOKE UP ONE DAY TO REALIZE THERE ARE MORE IMPORTANT THINGS THAN CAFE SOCIETY- SO-O-O... I'VE MOVED OUT AND BECOME A NURSE!
A NURSE? YOU...YOU GAVE UP A PLACE IN SOCIETY TO WORK FOR A LIVING? IT'S...IT'S STUPID!

YOU'RE THE ONE WHO'S STUPID --- WASTING YOUR LIFE AS THE GREAT SOCIETY PLAYBOY. YOU'VE GOT TALENT. IF YOU WANTED TO YOU--
AH-AH! DON'T TRY TO REFORM ME. I'M HAVING TOO GOOD A TIME TO KILL MYSELF WITH WORK!

IT'S NO USE TALKING TO YOU- C'MON- AT LEAST, YOU CAN WALK ME HOME.
SURE- I WANT TO SEE THIS LITTLE FLAT OF YOURS- "WOIKING GOIL."
ARMY & NAVY STORE

AS THEY NEAR LINDA'S MODEST APARTMENT BUILDING....
HELLO, MRS. GROGAN. WHAT'S WRONG? YOU LOOK WORRIED.
IT'S MY BOY, TOMMY-- IF ONLY HIS FATHER WERE ALIVE, HE'D PUT A STOP TO HIS RUNNING AROUND.

TOMMY- BOY GIVING HER TROUBLE?
TOMMY IS REALLY A GOOD KID AT HEART. BUT LATELY HE'S BEEN MIXING WITH THE MOB DOWN AT THE POOL PARLOR POOR WOMAN.... I FEEL SORRY FOR HER!

TOMMY HAS AN OLDER BROTHER, MIKE, WHO IS A GANGSTER. TOMMY IDOLIZES HIS BROTHER MIKE BECAUSE HE'S GOOD TO HIM AND.....
AND HIS MOTHER IS AFRAID HE'LL FOLLOW IN MIKE'S FOOTSTEPS. THE USUAL STORY!

SPEAKING OF THE DEVIL... THERE'S MIKE AND TOMMY NOW!
IT'S THE BOY.... AND THE OTHER IS THE ONE WHO SAVED HIM YESTERDAY! BROTHERS... NO WONDER!

LATER THAT VERY AFTERNOON, THE MIDTOWN BANK...
IT'S THESE BANK ROBBERS AGAIN!
HELP! POLICE! AAAH...

A POLICEMAN'S SHOT FINDS ITS MARK!
OOOH!

THEIR WOUNDED COMPANION IS HUSTLED INTO THE CAR AND THE HOODLUMS MAKE GOOD THEIR ESCAPE AGAIN!

2¢
GOT
VOL. II NO 16
MYSTERY GANG LOOTS FIFTH BANK.
HERO POLICEMAN WOUNDS MEMBER OF GANG IN DARING...

THAT NIGHT AS LINDA PAGE SITS IN HER APARTMENT, THE DOOR IS SUDDENLY THRUST OPEN---
OKAY, BABE.... GRAB YOUR INSTRUMENT BAG---YOU'RE GOING FOR A LITTLE RIDE!
WHA-WHAT'S THE IDEA?
5

WE GOT A PATIENT FOR YA! C'MON!
HEY... WHATCHA DOIN!
YOU-YOU CAN'T EXPECT ME TO GO OUT WITHOUT PUTTING SOME FRESH LIPSTICK ON, DO YOU?

LINDA IS BLINDFOLDED AND TAKEN TO A CAR.
THE COAST IS CLEAR! OKAY, PETE... LET'S GO!

AFTER WHAT SEEMS AN ENDLESS RIDE, LINDA IS LED DOWN RICKETY STEPS. HER BLINDFOLD IS REMOVED AND SHE SEES---
MIKE GROGAN--- AND TOMMY-- HE'S BEEN WOUNDED!
YEAH--- A SLUG GOT HIM AND YOU'RE GONNA TAKE IT OUT! WE GOT YOU CAUSE A DOC HAS TO MAKE A REPORT--- AND YOU DON'T!

ARE YOU GONNA FIX TOMMY UP AND KEEP YOUR MOUTH CLOSED?
YOU KNOW I WON'T TALK. IF I DID, IT WOULD KILL YOUR MOTHER TO KNOW TOMMY WAS--- A BANK ROBBER!

YOU KNOW I WOULDN'T DO ANYTHING TO HURT TOMMY. HE KEPT HANGIN' AROUND. YOU KNOW HOW IT IS. YA GOTTA BELIEVE ME!
I BELIEVE YOU. TOMMY JUST WANTED TO BE WHAT YOU ARE BECAUSE HE IDOLIZES YOU. BUT YOU LET HIM DOWN, MIKE---YOU LET HIM DOWN!

AT THAT VERY MOMENT, THE BATMOBILE DARTS THROUGH THE CITY STREETS------
WHAT'S THE IDEA OF GOING TO SEE THIS GIRL, LINDA?
SHE KNOWS MIKE GROGAN AND TOMMY WELL. MAYBE SHE CAN GIVE ME SOME INFORMATION ABOUT THEM!

MINUTES LATER, A BAT-LIKE SHAPE MOVES SILENTLY AND SWIFTLY UP THE FIRE-ESCAPE LEADING TO LINDA'S ROOM-

NOBODY HOME. MIGHT AS WELL GO---- WAIT----WHAT'S THIS?

A MESSAGE IN LIPSTICK---- WRITTEN HURRIEDLY ON THE DRESSER!
TWO GUNMEN HAVE KIDNAPPED ME—

DOWN TO THE BATMOBILE RACES THE BATMAN. FROM A HIDDEN COMPARTMENT, HE TAKES MAKEUP---AND A PICTURE.
LINDA MENTIONED A POOLROOM ON THE CORNER WHICH TOMMY AND MIKE FREQUENT, SO WHAT?
SO THIS! I'M GOING IN THERE. BUT NOT AS THE BATMAN!

FROM A CLOSET BUILT IN THE REAR OF THE BATMOBILE, HE EXTRACTS CLOTHING.
HOLY CATS! YOU LOOK LIKE A DIFFERENT MAN!
I AM! I'M GOING TO IMPERSONATE A CERTAIN TRIGGER BURNS, AN OUT-OF-TOWN MOBSTER I KNOW OF!

AND SO IT IS "TRIGGER BURNS" THAT WALKS INTO THE POOL ROOM....
I'M TRIGGER BURNS. I WANTA TALK TA MIKE GROGAN. WHERE IS HE?
TRIGGER BURNS! MIKE GROGAN.... SURE...SURE... HE'S IN THE BACK!

I'LL TAKE YA TA MIKE. HE OUGHTA BE GLAD TA SEE YA.

AS THE BATMAN DESCENDS THE BACK STAIRS, SUDDENLY....
THEY THINK I'M A DETECTIVE!
YOU AIN'T TRIGGER, WISE GUY. TRIGGER WAS BUMPED OFF THE OTHER DAY. REACH... COPPER!

THE BATMAN SWINGS INTO ACTION.....
UGH!

KNOCKING YOU MUGGS AROUND IS GETTING TO BE A HABIT!
HEY GANG- GET THIS COPPER!!
COME AND GET ME... IF YOU CAN!

THE BATMAN'S FISTS LASH OUT IN PILE-DRIVER BLOWS....
YOUR POSTURE IS BAD. PARDON ME WHILE I STRAIGHTEN IT FOR YOU!
SUDDENLY, THE DOOR IS THROWN BACK AS IF BY A CYCLONE--- AND THAT CYCLONE IS ROBIN, THE BOY WONDER!
I KIND OF THOUGHT SOMETHING WAS UP WHEN I HEARD THAT SHOT! LET ME IN ON THIS!
AH.... AMMUNITION!
BEHIND THE EIGHTBALL, EH, CHUM?
ROBIN PUTS A CUE STICK TO GOOD USE...
THE CORNER POCKET... FOR MR. CUE "BALD" HERE!
OKAY.... WE'VE DONE ENOUGH DAMAGE HERE — LET'S GO!
RIGHT!

AFTER THE BATMAN AND ROBIN ARE GONE ....
GET THE NUMBER O' THE TRUCK THAT HIT ME!
LISTEN.... THAT DICK WAS AFTER MIKE! WE GOTTA GET WORD TO 'IM!
I'LL GET TO THE HIDEOUT RIGHT AWAY!

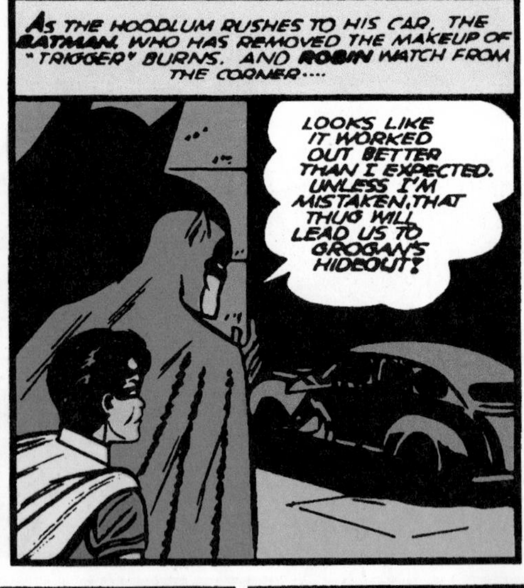
AS THE HOODLUM RUSHES TO HIS CAR, THE BATMAN, WHO HAS REMOVED THE MAKEUP OF "TRIGGER" BURNS, AND ROBIN WATCH FROM THE CORNER....
LOOKS LIKE IT WORKED OUT BETTER THAN I EXPECTED. UNLESS I'M MISTAKEN, THAT THUG WILL LEAD US TO GROGAN'S HIDEOUT!

SHUTTING DOWN THE HEADLIGHTS, THE BATMAN AND ROBIN CAUTIOUSLY FOLLOW THE THUG... TO THE HIDEOUT ON THE WATERFRONT!

MIKE DOWNSTAIRS?
YEAH! HE'S DOWN WIT' DE GANG! ME...I'M UP HERE WATCHIN' ALL ALONE!

CHEE... DEM SHADOWS GIMME DE CREEPS. THEY GOT SUCH FUNNY SHAPES. DAT ONE LOOKS JUST LIKE A BAT!

BROTHER, YOU WERE NEVER MORE RIGHT IN YOUR WHOLE LIFE!

DOWNSTAIRS....
SURE... THAT COPPER WAS ASKIN' FOR YOU, MIKE.
THEY MUST BE WISE TO US!
YEAH-- WE BETTER ALL SCRAM OUTA HERE. GRAB THE KID AND LET'S GO!

TOMMY CAN'T BE MOVED! IT MIGHT BE FATAL!
THAT MEANS I STAY. YOU GUYS CAN GO!
WHAT-AN' LEAVE YOU BEHIND TO SPILL EVERYTHING WHEN THE COPS START WORKIN' ON YOU?

YOU MUST BE OUTA YOUR HEAD. C'MON, GRAB THAT KID...WE'RE GETTIN' OUTA HERE!
PULL A GUN ON ME, WILL YOU....?

THERE IS A SUDDEN ROAR OF A GUN-- MIKE CLAWS AT HIS CHEST AND SLUMPS TO TO THE FLOOR

YOU...YOU KILLED HIM!
SURE...AND I'M GONNA LET YOU AND THE KID HAVE IT, TOO. THAT'LL TAKE CARE O' ALL THE LOOSE ENDS!
MIKE... MIKE...

PULL THAT TRIGGER AND ONE OF THOSE LOOSE ENDS WILL BE A ROPE-AROUND YOUR NECK!
THE BATMAN!

THE BATMAN'S FIST LANDS WITH TERRIFIC IMPACT ON THE KILLERS CHIN.
A FIRST-CLASS PUNCH FOR A FIRST-CLASS RAT!

SENSING DANGER, THE BATMAN SUDDENLY WHIRLS AND.....
IT'S NOT NICE TO TRY TO SHOOT PEOPLE IN THE BACK, OR DIDN'T YOU KNOW?

MEANWHILE, ROBIN IS HAVING SOME FUN....
HEY! LEGGO MY SUSPENDERS-- LEGGO-- YOU HEAR?

...WITH PLEASURE!
OWW!
-- S-N-A-P--

ENOUGH KIDDING AROUND--NOW TO GET TO WORK!

UNNOTICED, A FIGURE DROPS OFF THE COT, PICKS UP A GUN AND STAGGERS TO THE DOOR WAY---IT IS TOMMY--

THE WOUNDED BOY DRAGS HIS PAIN-WRACKED, WEAKENED BODY UP THE STAIRS. ONCE--TWICE, HE FALTERS, BUT UP----UP HE CLIMBS----

UNTIL HE STEPS ONTO THE DOCK ITSELF. HIS FINGERS TUG AT THE PISTOL'S TRIGGER. A SHOT RINGS OUT.
CRACK!

DOWN BELOW, THE BATMAN AND ROBIN BATTLE FURIOUSLY WHEN A THUG SUDDENLY PLACES A PISTOL AGAINST LINDA'S HEAD AND SHOUTS----
YOU--- YOU---
OKAY--CUT OUT THE HORSE PLAY OR I PLUG THIS DAME!

NICE WORK, JOE! NOW I'M GONNA DO SOMETHIN' I ALWAYS WANTED TO DO--GIVE IT TO THE BATMAN!

A SHOT BLASTS THROUGH THE ROOM---BUT THE BATMAN STILL STANDS ERECT. IT IS THE KILLER WHO MEETS HIS END!
JUST IN TIME, EH, BATMAN?
POLICE!

YOU BOYS CAN TAKE OVER NOW. OUR JOB IS FINISHED! C'MON ROBIN!

As the policemen inspect the scene....
Mike Grogan--shot!
Listen... my kid brother. Tommy he didn't have anything to do with the holdups. He didn't even carry a gun!

He wanted to be like me. He didn't mean no harm. He's a good kid!
I guess he is. He called us here. Don't worry--I'll put a good word in for him to the judge!

Do something for me, Tommy. Go straight... Don't be a sucker like me. Promise me you'll go straight promise.. prom-- aaah!
I promise, Mike... I promise!
Mike Grogan has robbed his last bank!

Was that fellow with the boy the famous Batman I've heard so much about?
That was him. All right. Quite a guy, isn't he?

I should say so! He-- he's wonderful!

A few days later in court....
..and because you aided in the capture of a vicious group, the jury recommends you be pardoned in your mother's hand
Gosh th-thanks.. thanks!

And in a restaurant...
Look, you've been talking about the Batman all evening. What's he got that I haven't got? I've got money, good looks...
A girl isn't always interested in that... he-- he represents excitement, color, daring--I can't exactly explain it

Bob Kane
Bruce is nice... and I do like him... a lot, but if he only were a little more like the Batman. But I guess that's asking too much!
Ho-ho! It looks very much like the Batman will be seeing more of Linda Page in the future.. I'll see to that!

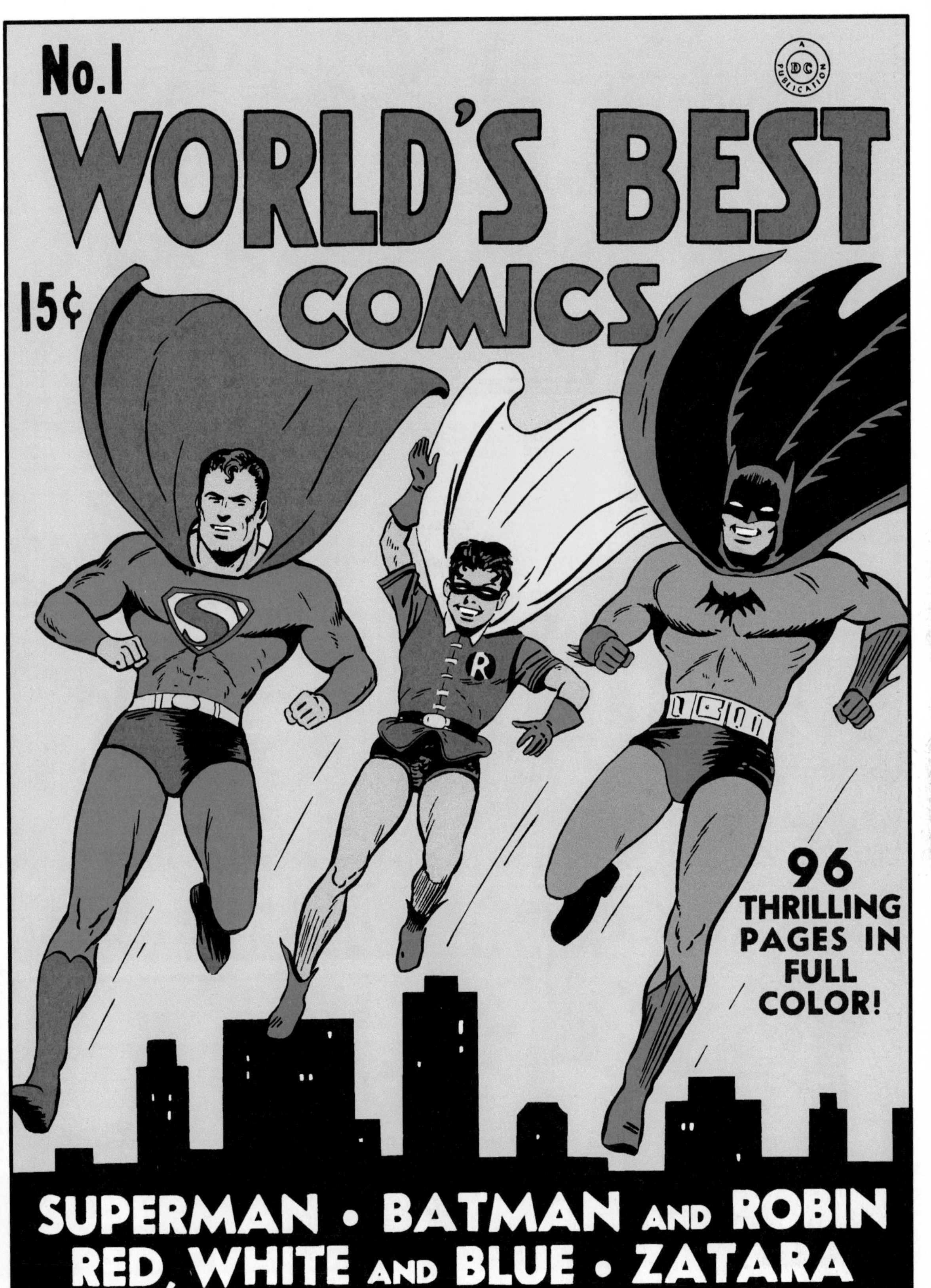

No. 1
A DC PUBLICATION
WORLD'S BEST COMICS
15¢
96 THRILLING PAGES IN FULL COLOR!
SUPERMAN • BATMAN AND ROBIN
RED, WHITE AND BLUE • ZATARA

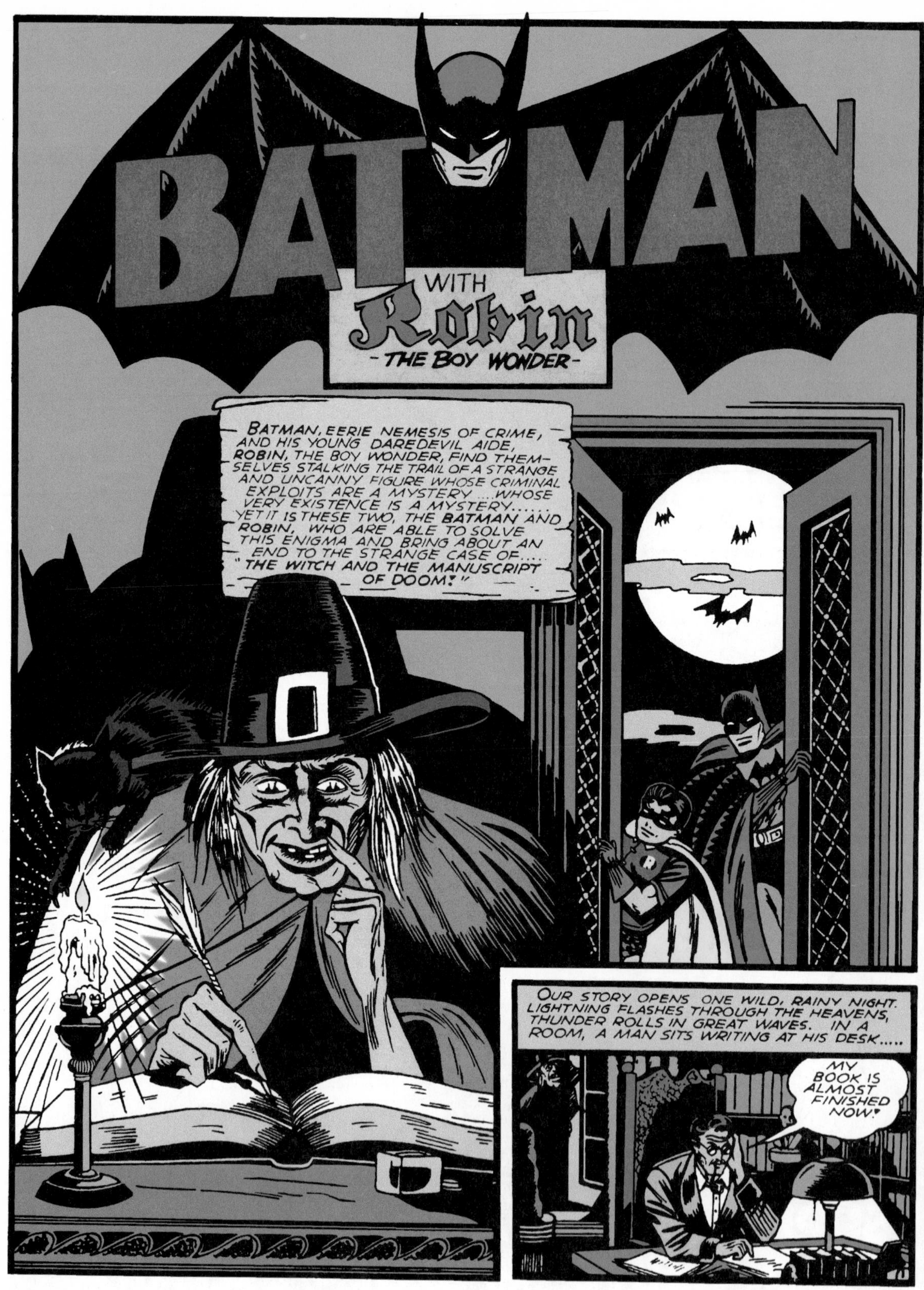
BATMAN
WITH
Robin
-THE BOY WONDER-
BATMAN, EERIE NEMESIS OF CRIME, AND HIS YOUNG DAREDEVIL AIDE, ROBIN, THE BOY WONDER, FIND THEMSELVES STALKING THE TRAIL OF A STRANGE AND UNCANNY FIGURE WHOSE CRIMINAL EXPLOITS ARE A MYSTERY ... WHOSE VERY EXISTENCE IS A MYSTERY...... YET IT IS THESE TWO, THE BATMAN AND ROBIN, WHO ARE ABLE TO SOLVE THIS ENIGMA AND BRING ABOUT AN END TO THE STRANGE CASE OF.... "THE WITCH AND THE MANUSCRIPT OF DOOM!"
OUR STORY OPENS ONE WILD, RAINY NIGHT. LIGHTNING FLASHES THROUGH THE HEAVENS, THUNDER ROLLS IN GREAT WAVES. IN A ROOM, A MAN SITS WRITING AT HIS DESK.....
MY BOOK IS ALMOST FINISHED NOW!

A BENT SHAPE CREEPS SILENTLY TOWARD THE MAN...

THERE IS A DULL THUD AND THE MAN SLUMPS FORWARD....
THIS IS WHAT I WANT!

SUDDENLY, THE DOOR SWINGS OPEN........ THE BUTLER BLUNDERS UPON THE SCENE.....
MR. DORNE, I...... WHA...?

WITH A LOUD CRY, THE BUTLER HURLS HIMSELF UPON THE INTRUDER.....
HELP! MURDER!

THERE IS A FURIOUS STRUGGLE, BUT THE STAFF DESCENDS AGAIN AND THE BUTLER LIES MOANING ON THE FLOOR!

THE HIDEOUS FIGURE VANISHES IN THE PROTECTING DARKNESS, LEAVING BUT A SINGLE CLUE.... PART OF A SHEET OF PAPER WHICH HAD BEEN TORN OFF IN THE STRUGGLE......
2

PAINFULLY, THE BUTLER DRAGS HIMSELF TO THE TELEPHONE.....
GET ME THE POLICE! MY MASTER-ERIK DORNE-HAS BEEN MURDERED!

IN HEADQUARTERS, POLICE COMMISSIONER GORDON CHATS WITH HIS OLD FRIEND, BRUCE WAYNE, A WEALTHY SOCIETY PLAYBOY.
TELL ME, BRUCE, IS GOING OUT TO NIGHTCLUBS THE ONLY THING YOU'RE INTERESTED IN?
OH, NO-I LIKE TO PLAY A LITTLE POLO NOW AND THEN!
A CALL JUST CAME IN, COMMISSIONER -A MURDER!

IT'S ERIK DORNE, SIR. HIS BUTLER WAS ATTACKED, TOO!
ERIK DORNE, THE MYSTERY STORY WRITER? WHERE'S MY COAT?
MYSTERY STORY WRITER MYSTERIOUSLY MURDERED? SOUNDS MELODRAMATIC -THINK I'LL TODDLE ALONG WITH YOU!

A POLICE CAR SPEEDS THEM TO THE SCENE......
.....YOU MEAN TO SAY A PERSON THAT LOOKED LIKE A WITCH ATTACKED YOU?
YES- LIKE A WITCH- VERY UGLY- TOOK MANUSCRIPT- AAAH!

FAINTED! HE'S IN A BAD WAY! I'M AFRAID HE WON'T STAND ANY MORE QUESTIONING FOR A TIME!
FOUND THIS ON THE FLOOR, SIR! LOOKS LIKE PART OF A MANUSCRIPT!

THE PAPER......
This story is about a witch- a witch that lives. This is a true story. It is the story of

THIS- THIS IS INCREDIBLE! FROM ALL APPEARANCES IT LOOKS LIKE THE WITCH OF THE MYSTERY STORY KILLED DORNE! IT'S FANTASTIC.
WELL, DORNE SAYS THE WITCH REALLY LIVES. NOW YOU HAVE PROOF OF IT!

DID I HEAR SOMEONE MENTION- A WITCH?

WHO ARE YOU?
JOSHUA GRIMM- AUTHOR OF MANY BOOKS ON WITCHCRAFT AND DEMONOLOGY! THE POLICEMAN OUTSIDE TELLS ME ERIK DORNE WAS MURDERED! TCH-TCH!

WHAT ARE YOU DOING HERE?
WHEN I SAW ERIK TODAY AT THE PUBLISHING OFFICE, HE ASKED ME, "WHEN IS A WITCH NOT A WITCH?"- AND THEN SMIRKED AND WALKED AWAY! I CAME DOWN TO FIND OUT WHAT HE MEANT BY THAT! MY WORK, YOU KNOW!
3

WHY–WHAT IS THIS?.... ERIK..... WHAT HAS HAPPENED TO HIM?
HE'S BEEN MURDERED! WHO ARE YOU?
THIS IS MR. WRIGHT, THE MAN WHO PUBLISHES DORNE'S BOOKS!

AND WHAT MADE YOU COME AROUND THIS PARTICULAR NIGHT?
ERIK DID! SAID HE HAD A NEW MYSTERY NOVEL FOR ME! I CAME TO PICK UP THE MANUSCRIPT!

LOOKS LIKE THE MURDERER BEAT YOU TO IT! THE MANUSCRIPT IS GONE!
GONE!? WHY, THAT'S TERRIBLE–TERRIBLE! BUT WHY SHOULD ANYONE WANT TO STEAL IT?
THAT'S EXACTLY WHAT I WANT TO FIND OUT!

COME ALONG, BRUCE. ERIK DORNE WASN'T EXACTLY A LOVABLE FELLOW, SO I'M GOING TO QUESTION SOME SUSPECTS.
SUSPECTS! SOUNDS JUST LIKE A MYSTERY STORY!

GORDON QUESTIONS ERIK DORNE'S AUNT... MELISSA BRUNT!
SO MY NEPHEW WAS MURDERED, EH? WELL, GOOD RIDDANCE TO BAD RUBBISH, I ALWAYS SAY!
HOW CAN YOU SPEAK LIKE THAT OF THE DEAD? HE WAS YOUR NEPHEW!

HE WAS A NO-GOOD NEPHEW! WHILE WE SCRIMPED, HE SQUANDERED MONEY WITHOUT GIVING A THOUGHT TO ME OR HIS TWO COUSINS HERE!
YOU BETTER GO NOW! SHE GETS VERY EXCITED WHEN ERIK IS MENTIONED!

IF EVER THERE WAS A WOMAN WHO LOOKED LIKE A WITCH, THERE'S ONE! DID YOU SEE THAT CAT OF HERS?
C'MON. WE'RE GOING TO SEE JANE WARE, THE ACTRESS! SHE'S ERIK'S WIFE, BUT THEY HAVEN'T BEEN LIVING TOGETHER FOR QUITE A WHILE.

AS THEY GO BACKSTAGE AND ENTER JANE WARE'S DRESSING ROOM, THEY GET A DECIDED SHOCK...
LOOK! A WITCH!

WITH A LAUGH, THE WITCH PEELS OFF HER "FACE"......
THAT'S MAKEUP! MISS WARE PLAYS A WITCH IN THE PLAY SHE IS STARRING IN.
WHAT IS IT YOU WANT TO TELL ME, COMMISSIONER?
I DON'T KNOW HOW TO SAY IT, BUT YOUR HUSBAND-- HE'S DEAD!

SO HE'S DEAD! THAT MEANS YOU'RE FREE AT LAST!
BUT YOU ARE OF THE POLICE! DOES THAT MEAN....?
YES! MURDER! AND PERHAPS, NOW, YOU CAN EXPLAIN THIS GENTLEMAN'S REMARK!

I WANTED A DIVORCE FROM ERIK SO I COULD MARRY HARVEY MORROW, HERE --
-- BUT HE WOULDN'T GIVE IT TO HER! NOW WE CAN GET MARRIED AT LAST!
NOT A BAD EXCUSE FOR A MURDER, EH, MR. MORROW?

WHEN BRUCE AND GORDON LEAVE.....
YOU KNOW, JANE WARE COULD HAVE SNEAKED OFF DURING STAGE INTERMISSION, KILLED DORNE, AND GOT BACK IN TIME TO CONTINUE HER ROLE.
PERHAPS SHE, IN HER MAKEUP, WAS THE WITCH THE BUTLER SAW.

LOOK: DORNE'S STORY CONCERNS A REAL WITCH-- JOSHUA GRIMM WRITES BOOKS ABOUT WITCHES-- WRIGHT PUBLISHES THEM-- MISS BRUNT LOOKS LIKE A WITCH, AND JANE WARE'S STAGE ROLE IS THAT OF A WITCH! LORD!
THE TROUBLE IS YOU DON'T KNOW WHICH WITCH IS WHICH!

DORNE WAS KILLED BECAUSE HIS STORY WAS GOING TO EXPOSE A PERSON WHO WAS A WITCH! THAT'S WHY THE MANUSCRIPT WAS STOLEN!
SOMEONE LIVING TWO SEPARATE LIVES, EH? WELL, COMMISSIONER, IT'S TOO DEEP FOR ME! PARDON ME WHILE I GO HOME AND DREAM ABOUT WITCHES! TA-TA!
5

UPON REACHING HIS HOME, BRUCE ACQUAINTS HIS YOUNG WARD, DICK GRAYSON, WITH THE FACTS OF THE CASE...
WHAT'S THAT IN YOUR HAND? LOOKS LIKE HAIR!
IT IS! I PICKED IT UP FROM THE MURDER ROOM FLOOR! IT'S HAIR FROM A WIG -- PROBABLY TORN OFF WHEN THE BUTLER STRUGGLED WITH THE WITCH!

I WANT YOU TO GET ME A SAMPLE OF HAIR FROM THE WIG WORN BY JANE WARE IN HER "WITCH" STAGE ROLE.
I GET IT-- IF THE HAIRS MATCH, THAT MEANS JANE WARE IS GUILTY!

THE NEXT NIGHT, THE TWO DON CLOSE-FITTING COSTUMES, WHICH REVEAL PHYSIQUES OF BREATH-TAKING SYMMETRY....
IF MISS BRUNT KILLED DORNE, THEN SHE MUST HAVE HIDDEN THE MANUSCRIPT! I'M GOING TO LOOK IN HER HOME!
WHEN THE DYNAMIC DUO, THE BATMAN AND ROBIN, INVESTIGATE, EVEN PERFECT CRIMES CAN BE SOLVED!

MOMENTS LATER, A SLIM FIGURE DARTS PAST THE UNWARY STAGE-DOOR WATCHMAN....

THE BOY WONDER MOVES SWIFTLY UP THE STAIRS THAT LEAD TO THE DRESSING ROOMS....
THIS IS THE ROOM! NOW, FOR THAT WIG!

AS ROBIN PULLS HAIRS FROM THE WIG, THE DOOR SUDDENLY SWINGS OPEN....
THE FIRST ACT IS.... WHA...?
A SNEAK THIEF?

MOVING INCREDIBLY SWIFT, ROBIN BOUNDS ACROSS THE ROOM...
SORRY I HAVE TO DO THIS, MISTER!
MPH!

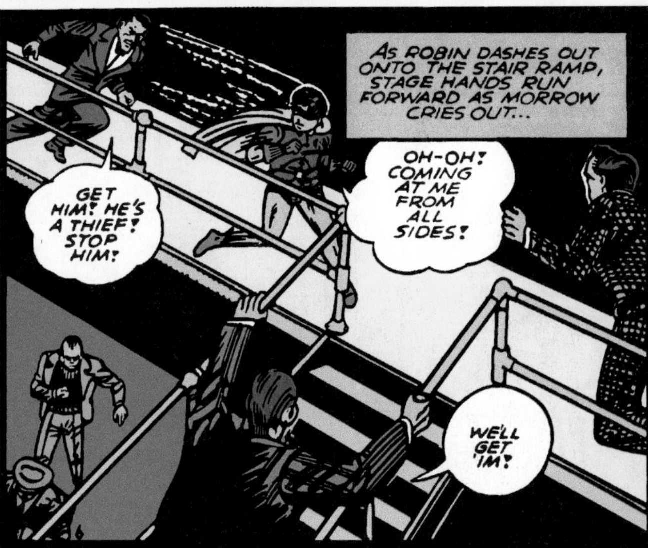
AS ROBIN DASHES OUT ONTO THE STAIR RAMP, STAGE HANDS RUN FORWARD AS MORROW CRIES OUT...
GET HIM! HE'S A THIEF! STOP HIM!
OH-OH! COMING AT ME FROM ALL SIDES!
WE'LL GET 'IM!

ROBIN DECIDES UPON A HEADLONG DIVE INTO SPACE....
BETTER THIS WAY!

THE BOY WONDER DOES A COMPLETE SOMERSAULT IN MID-AIR....

.....DROPS ONTO A STAGE-SET BED... BOUNCES OFF....
BOY, AM I THE BOUNCING BABY!

....AND LANDS SMACK INTO OTHER STAGE HANDS, WHO HAVE JUST RUN TOWARD HIM!
I'LL BET YOU NEVER EXPECTED THIS! NEITHER DID I!

A MAD DASH ACROSS THE STAGE PROPELS THE WONDER BOY THROUGH MEMBERS OF THE CAST- AND HE IS AWAY!
A PLAY ABOUT PIRATES AND A WITCH--- SOUNDS GOOD.... WISH I HAD TIME TO STAY!

AT THAT INSTANT, A BLOTTED SHAPE SLIPS INTO THE BRUNT HOUSE....

MUST BE A WALL SAFE ABOUT SOME PLACE!

LIGHTS SUDDENLY BLAZE ON!...
YOU WERE RIGHT, AUNT, WHEN YOU SAID YOU HEARD SOMEONE PROWLING AROUND THE HOUSE!
HE'S MASKED! SHOOT HIM — SHOOT HIM BEFORE HE ATTACKS US!

MOVING WITH THE SWIFTNESS OF A MONGOOSE DARTING AT A COBRA, THE BATMAN'S HAND SLAPS AT THE VASE ON THE TABLE......
THIS CALLS FOR ACTION! SOME FLOWERS FOR YOU!

THE FLYING VASE FINDS A TARGET!

MIGHTY MUSCLES LAUNCH THE DARK KNIGHT CLEAR ACROSS THE TABLE......
NOW FOR THE OTHER "CHARMING" GENT!

DROP YOUR GUN AND LET'S ARGUE!

A SHORT, CHOPPY UPPERCUT LIFTS THE MAN OFF HIS HEELS!
I'VE CHANGED MY MIND. I DON'T FEEL LIKE TALKING!

YOUR NEPHEWS ARE SO IMPETUOUS! ADIEU, MISS BRUNT!

LATER.....
HERE ARE THOSE HAIRS! I RAN INTO A LITTLE TROUBLE GETTING THEM!
NOW, ISN'T THAT STRANGE? I RAN INTO JUST A WEE BIT OF TROUBLE MYSELF!

THE BATMAN PLACES THE DIFFERENT HAIRS UNDER HIS MICROSCOPE FOR COMPARISON...
HMM!
WHAT HAS THE BATMAN DISCOVERED ABOUT THE TWO HAIRS?

AT THAT VERY MOMENT, THE MYSTERIOUS WITCH LAUGHS.....
IT WOULD NEVER DO FOR THE POLICE TO READ THIS MANUSCRIPT! NEVER! HEE HEE!

THE NEXT DAY.....
I'VE BEEN THINKING OVER WHAT EACH SUSPECT SAID, AND I THINK I KNOW NOW WHO IS GUILTY! ...AND I'VE GOT A PLAN TO PROVE IT!

BRUCE DIALS A NUMBER.......
YOU SAY YOU ARE A POLICE REPORTER?
YES! I'VE JUST COME FROM THE HOSPITAL. THE BUTLER IS STILL IN A BAD WAY, BUT HE KEEPS MUMBLING ABOUT A DUPLICATE MANUSCRIPT HIDDEN IN ERIK DORNE'S ROOM!

NATURALLY, THIS WOULD AFFECT YOUR OCCUPATION! HAVE YOU ANY COMMENT ON THOSE PAPERS?
NO COMMENT! SORRY! CLICK!

I'VE PLANTED THE BAIT! NOW, LETS HOPE OUR PARTY TAKES A NIBBLE AT IT!
WHO DID BRUCE PHONE? WHO DO YOU THINK IS THE WITCH?

THAT NIGHT, A SHADOWY FIGURE POISES OUTSIDE THE WINDOW OF THE LATE ERIK DORNE'S ROOM......
9

NOISELESSLY, IT GLIDES INTO THE ROOM....... AT THAT MOMENT, THE MOON SLIPS OUT FROM BEHIND DARK CLOUDS AND REVEALS IN ITS LIGHT...... THE WITCH!
THAT HIDDEN MANUSCRIPT MUST BE AROUND SOMEPLACE!

ABRUPTLY, TWO FIGURES LEAP OUT OF DARKENED CORNERS.....THE BATMAN AND ROBIN, THE BOY WONDER!
HUH?
GOOD EVENING, WITCH!

THEN, ONE OF THOSE UNFORESEEN LITTLE THINGS HAPPENS..... THE BATMAN TRIPS OVER A FOOTSTOOL IN HIS PATH.....
WHA..?

THE WITCH IS QUICK TO TAKE ADVANTAGE, AND WHIRLING SWIFTLY, BRINGS THE STAFF DOWN ON ROBIN...
NOT SO FAST, BOY!

THE WITCH SPRINGS OUT OF THE WINDOW, RACES TOWARD A WAITING CAR, AND SPEEDS AWAY!

THE DYNAMIC DUO PURSUES....
WE'LL HAVE TO BORROW THIS CAR HERE.
LUCKY THAT STAFF ONLY GRAZED ME!

JAGGED STREAKS OF WHITE LIGHTNING LEAP IN THE SKY AS THE MAD CHASE BEGINS...
IF THIS WERE THE BATMOBILE, WE'D BE ON TOP OF THAT CAR IN NO TIME!
THIS IS ONE DEVELOPMENT IN THE CASE I NEVER EXPECTED!
10

IT IS A WEIRD SCENE AS THE WITCH'S SHRIEKING, INSANE LAUGHTER IS HEARD ABOVE THE STORM'S FURY...
HEE-HEE-HEE-

ON THEY RACE, MILE AFTER MILE... UNTIL....
LOOK! THE WITCH IS GOING INTO THAT HOUSE!

A BIG, GABLED HOUSE LOOMS SULLEN AGAINST THE GREY BLUR OF THE STORMY SKY....
C'MON!

.....BUT AS THE WITCH REACHES THE HOUSE, SHE YANKS HARD AT A ROPE THAT DANGLES FROM A NEARBY TREE.....
MEDDLERS.. ...I'LL TEACH THEM! HEE HEE....

TOO LATE! THE BATMAN AND ROBIN FEEL THE GROUND GIVE WAY.....

....AND FALL THROUGH THE CAMOUFLAGED TRAP DOOR!

WHEN THE DUO AWAKENS....
WHA...? A PRINTING PRESS!
YES, MR. BATMAN! I AM WHAT YOUR NEWSPAPERS CALL A "FIFTH COLUMNIST!" WE TURN OUT PAMPHLETS DEALING WITH THE GREATNESS OF OUR FATHERLAND'S CAUSE!

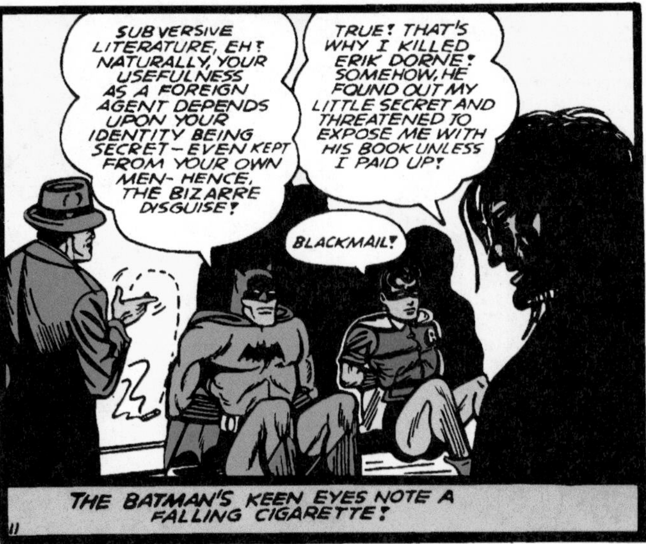
SUBVERSIVE LITERATURE, EH? NATURALLY, YOUR USEFULNESS AS A FOREIGN AGENT DEPENDS UPON YOUR IDENTITY BEING SECRET-- EVEN KEPT FROM YOUR OWN MEN-- HENCE, THE BIZARRE DISGUISE!
TRUE! THAT'S WHY I KILLED ERIK DORNE! SOMEHOW, HE FOUND OUT MY LITTLE SECRET AND THREATENED TO EXPOSE ME WITH HIS BOOK UNLESS I PAID UP!
BLACKMAIL!
THE BATMAN'S KEEN EYES NOTE A FALLING CIGARETTE!
11

WHEN THE WITCH AND THE FOREIGN AGENTS BUSY THEMSELVES WITH THEIR PAMPHLETS, THE BATMAN'S HANDS CLOSE ABOUT THE CIGARETTE.....
THE LIGHTED STUB BURNS THROUGH THE ROPE.....

AS SOON AS HIS HANDS ARE LOOSE, THE BATMAN SLIDES A BLADE FROM HIS BELT AND FURTIVELY SLICES ROBIN'S BONDS.....

ABRUPTLY, ROBIN SPRINGS FROM THE FLOOR.......
IF THIS WORKS, IT'S GOING TO BE A HONEY!

HIS STRONG HANDS CLOSE ABOUT THE CHANDELIER, HE SWINGS OUT, RELEASES HIS GRIP.....
HERE SHE GOES!

DOWN COMES ROBIN.....

THE TABLE ACTS LIKE A SEE-SAW AS THE WEIGHTED END GOES DOWN — AND THE OTHER END SNAPS UP......
YIPEEE! IT WORKED!

THE STAFF CATCHES THE BATMAN ON THE SIDE OF THE HEAD.
YOU'LL NEVER TAKE ME!

THE WITCH PULLS AT THE STAFF, AND A GLEAMING SWORD FLASHES IN THE LIGHT....

THE BATMAN TUGS AT THE CARPET STRIP AND.....

THE WITCH DRAWS A GUN....

AND THE BATMAN AND WITCH LOCK IN A DEATH STRUGGLE....

SUDDENLY.... WITH A MIGHTY HEAVE.....THE WITCH GOES FLYING....

THE BATMAN RIPS AWAY THE DISGUISE AND REVEALS....

WITH THE WITCH, ALIAS WRIGHT, IN CUSTODY, BRUCE AND DICK DISCUSS THE CASE AT HOME...

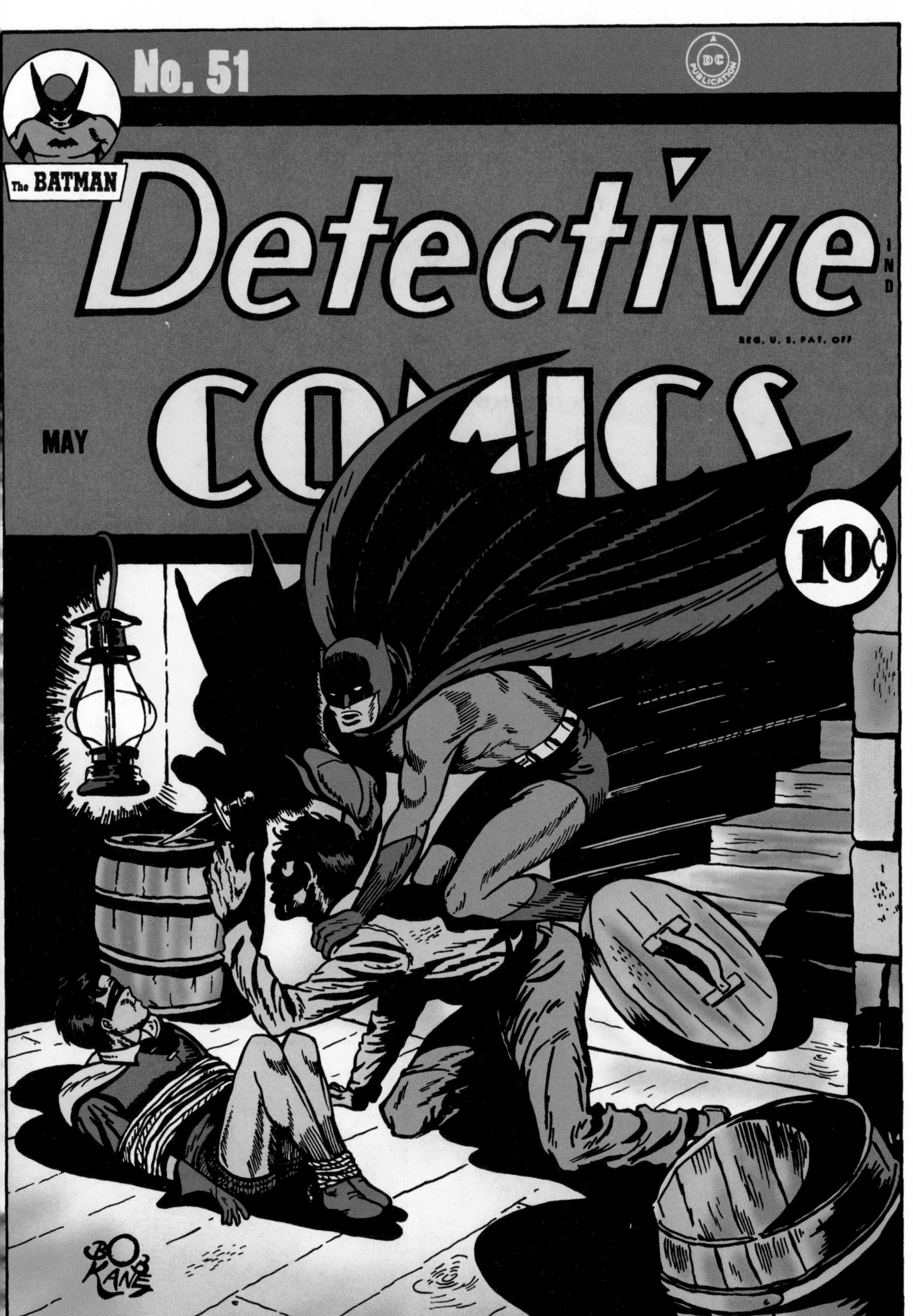
No. 51
A DC PUBLICATION
The BATMAN
Detective
IND
REG. U. S. PAT. OFF
COMICS
MAY
10¢
BOB KANE

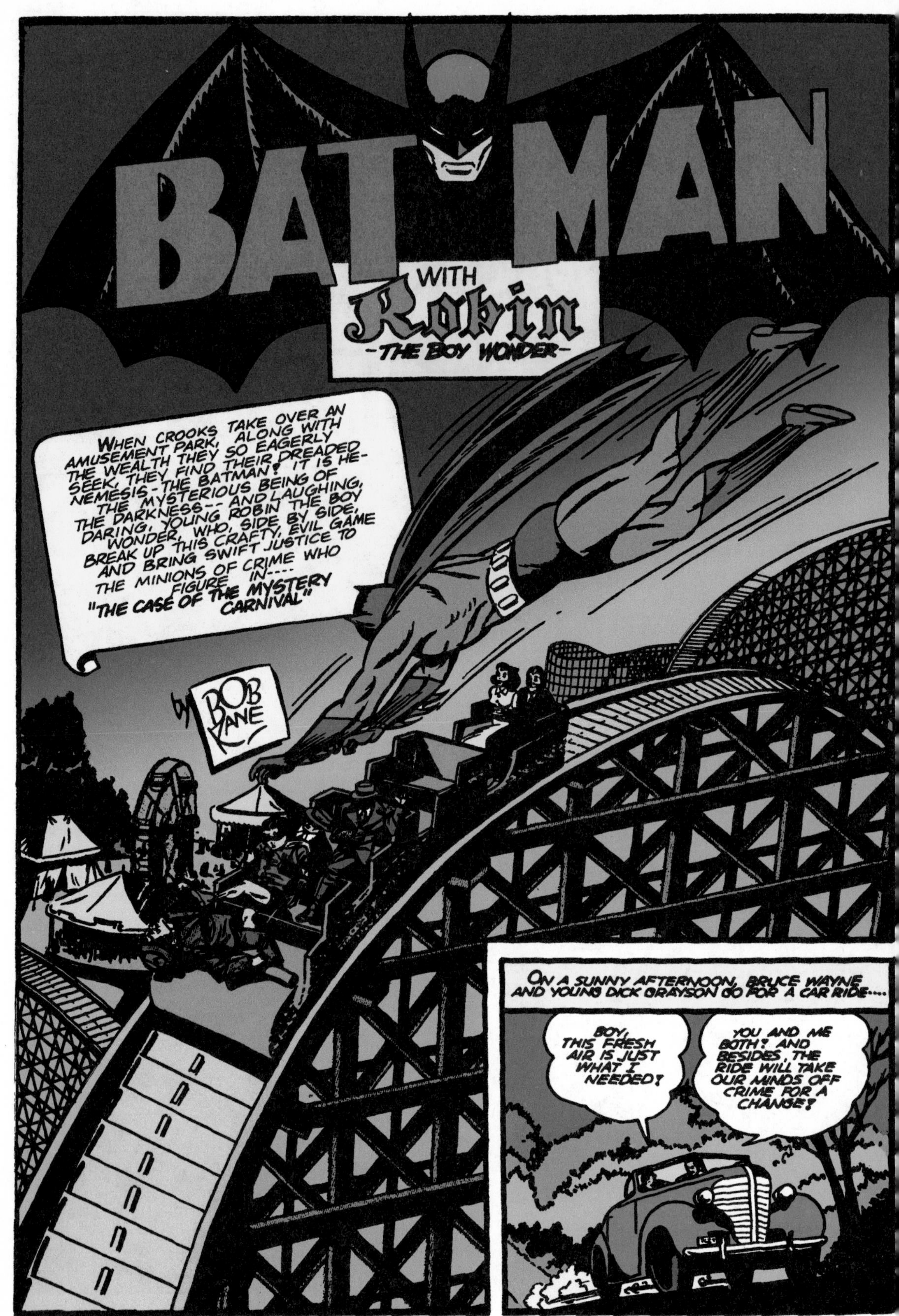
BATMAN
WITH Robin
-THE BOY WONDER-
WHEN CROOKS TAKE OVER AN AMUSEMENT PARK, ALONG WITH THE WEALTH THEY SO EAGERLY SEEK, THEY FIND THEIR DREADED NEMESIS - THE BATMAN! IT IS HE - THE MYSTERIOUS BEING OF THE DARKNESS -- AND LAUGHING, DARING, YOUNG ROBIN THE BOY WONDER, WHO, SIDE BY SIDE, BREAK UP THIS CRAFTY, EVIL GAME AND BRING SWIFT JUSTICE TO THE MINIONS OF CRIME WHO FIGURE IN---- "THE CASE OF THE MYSTERY CARNIVAL"
by BOB KANE
ON A SUNNY AFTERNOON, BRUCE WAYNE AND YOUNG DICK GRAYSON GO FOR A CAR RIDE....
BOY, THIS FRESH AIR IS JUST WHAT I NEEDED!
YOU AND ME BOTH! AND BESIDES, THE RIDE WILL TAKE OUR MINDS OFF CRIME FOR A CHANGE!

LOOK-AN AMUSEMENT PARK! LET'S GO! WHAT DO YOU SAY?
WHY NOT? AND I KNOW THE OWNER, COLONEL DAWES- HE'S AN OLD FRIEND! I'LL DROP IN ON HIM!

FLASHY SIDESHOWS, PITCHMEN, BARKERS, FREAKS, SHRIEKS, YELLS, LAUGHTER, ALL ARE PART OF THE GREAT AMUSEMENT PARK....
HURRY HURRY. HURRY! ONLY THE TENTH PART OF A DOLLAR, FOLKS-ONE DIME!
C'MON, BRUCE... LET'S GO ON THE CHUTE-THE CHUTES!
THE SCENIC RAILWAY? SURE!

YEE-EE-EE!
HEY- TAKE IT EASY- MY EARS!

BOY.... WAS THAT EXCITING!
YOU'RE A FUNNY KID. YOU FIGHT GUNMEN, LEAP OVER ROOFTOPS, WALK TELEPHONE WIRES, AND YOU CALL A RIDE ON THE CHUTES EXCITING!

KNOCK DOWN THE BOTTLES AND GET A PRIZE- ONLY TEN CENTS!
I'D LIKE TO TRY THAT, BRUCE.
OKAY.

DICK MAKES THREE THROWS AND THREE BULLS-EYES!
LET ME HAVE THREE MORE!

DICK KEEPS THROWING BALLS, AND WITH EVERY THROW HE SCORES A DIRECT HIT!
LAY OFF, KID- LAY OFF! HERE'S YOUR PRIZE! JUST GO AWAY AND LET ME ALONE SO I CAN FAINT IN PEACE!
GO EASY ON THE POOR FELLOW, DICK-- WANT TO RUIN HIM?
CANDY

SAY, THAT KID SURE CAN THROW A BALL! HE-HE'S A REGULAR BOY WONDER!
BROTHER, YOU SAID A MOUTHFUL!

AS THEY PASS ANOTHER CONCESSION.....
I JUST MISSED IT! IF I MADE THAT, I WOULDA GOT TWENTY FIVE CENTS!
TRY AGAIN! MAYBE YOU'LL MAKE IT THIS TIME!
SLOT MACHINES!
THAT'S ODD! COLONEL DAWES IS AS HONEST AS THEY COME! HE WOULDN'T USUALLY ALLOW THEM IN THE PARK! LET'S GO SEE HIM!

THEY ENTER THE ADMINISTRATION OFFICE..
COL. DAWES? --JUST A MOMENT. I'LL SEE...
DON'T BOTHER. HERE'S THE COLONEL NOW!
JOHN! HOW ARE YOU, YOU OLD WARHORSE!
EH?

JUST PASSING THROUGH SO I THOUGHT.....
AH-ER-IT'S NICE TO SEE YOU AGAIN, BUT I'M-ER-QUITE BUSY! AH-ER-DROP IN AGAIN SOMETIME! GOOD-BYE!

WHAT DO YOU THINK OF THAT ?
BOY, DID HE GIVE YOU THE OLD BRUSH-OFF!

OUTSIDE THE BUILDING, AS BRUCE LOOKS AFTER THE COLONEL....
LOOK! COLONEL DAWES IS SCRATCHING HIS LEFT LEG!
SO WHAT? A LOT OF PEOPLE SCRATCH THEIR LEFT LEG!

BUT-BUT COLONEL DAWES HAS NO LEG! HE LOST IT IN THE WORLD WAR! HE WEARS A FALSE ONE!
HUH?

A PERSON ONLY SCRATCHES HIS LEG IF IT ITCHES, NOW, HOW CAN A FALSE LEG ITCH?
IT CAN'T! TH....THAT MEANS THAT MAN IS NOT COLONEL DAWES!

RIGHT! AND THAT MAN WITH HIM- I'VE SEEN HIS FACE BEFORE, THAT'S "MOUSE" DOCKER--A SMALL TIME CROOK! C'MON, LET'S GET BACK TO OUR CAR!

BRUCE PULLS OPEN THE BACK TRUNK OF THE CAR AND PRODUCES TWO COSTUMES....
GOOD THING WE ALWAYS CARRY OUR COSTUMES ALONG JUST IN CASE!
WE'LL WAIT FOR NIGHTFALL AND THEN WE'LL INVESTIGATE OUR BOGUS FRIEND!
THE BATMAN AND ROBIN THE BOY WONDER ARE READY TO MEET SERVERS OF CRIME!

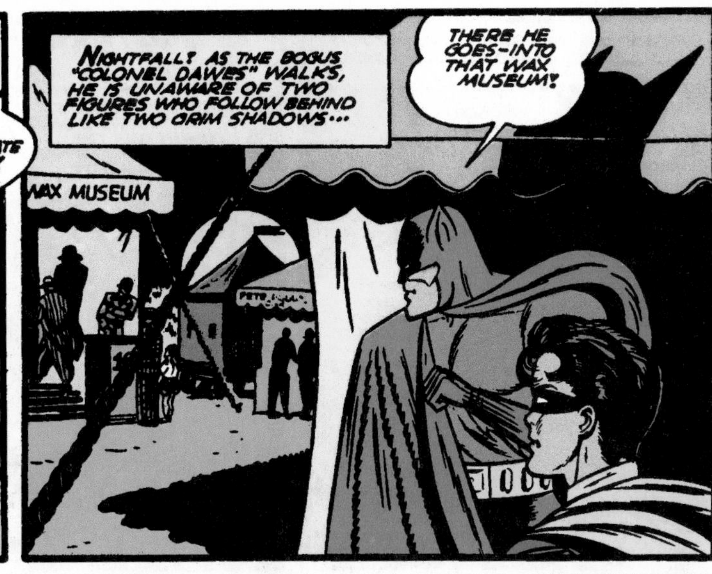
NIGHTFALL! AS THE BOGUS "COLONEL DAWES" WALKS, HE IS UNAWARE OF TWO FIGURES WHO FOLLOW BEHIND LIKE TWO GRIM SHADOWS...
THERE HE GOES-INTO THAT WAX MUSEUM!
WAX MUSEUM

THEY DART PAST THE UNWARY BARKER AND FIND THEMSELVES INSIDE....
SHH! SOMEONE'S COMING!

TWO FIGURES JOIN THE EXHIBIT...
LOOK, HENRY-- WAX FIGURES OF THE BATMAN AND ROBIN THE BOY WONDER! MY, DON'T THEY LOOK REAL!
I SHOULD SAY THEY DO. ANYONE WOULD THINK THEY WERE ALIVE!

WHEN THE PATRONS HAVE GONE, THE TWO FIGURES COME TO LIFE....
THAT WAS A CLOSE ONE!
CLOSE ENOUGH! NOW LETS GET GOING- HE WENT DOWN THIS WAY!

THEY PUSH OPEN A DOOR.....
WHAT A CREEPY PLACE! MUST BE THE STORE ROOM!
QUIET! FOOTSTEPS!
CLOP CLOP CLO

THE OLD CARETAKER SHUFFLES NEAR....
HELLO, NAPOLEON! I JUST SAW THE DUKE OF WELLINGTON. HE WAS ASKING ABOUT YOU!... AND YOU, HUNCHBACK-- IT'S TIME TO RING THE BELLS OF NOTRE DAME!

I NEVER SAW YOU TWO BEFORE, BUT NO MATTER... YOU ARE WELCOME TO JOIN MY LITTLE FAMILY. I'LL COME BACK AND TALK TO YOU LATER..... HEE HEE...

AGAIN THE BATMAN AND ROBIN FLIT SILENTLY IN THE GLOOM... WHEN --
VOICES?
HOW DID YOU BOYS DO SO FAR TODAY?
NOT BAD, MINDY-- NOT BAD?

THE BATMAN PLACES HIS EYES AGAINST A CRACK IN THE DOOR AND SEES.....
GETTING CHARLIE, HERE, TO IMPERSONATE DAWES WAS THE BEST IDEA YOU EVER HAD, MINDY?
SURE? WITH DAWES LOCKED AWAY, CHARLIE COLLECTS ALL THE GATE RECEIPTS, AND WE JUST SIT BACK AND GROW RICH?
AN' DON'T FORGET THE COMMISSION FROM THE CONCESSIONAIRES.

OKAY, BOYS. LINE UP, AND LET'S GET DOWN TO BUSINESS? HOW DID YOU DO WITH THE SLOT MACHINES, JOE?
PRETTY GOOD?
I HAD A CINCH IN PICKIN' POCKETS?
ME, TOO?

AS THE ILLEGAL PROFITS ARE SHARED, OUTSIDE, ROBIN ACCIDENTALLY LEANS AGAINST A WAX FIGURE....
LOOK OUT!
UH?

TOO LATE? THE FIGURE TOPPLES AND CRASHES TO THE FLOOR.
WHAT WAS DAT?
THAT NUTTY WATCHMAN MUSTA KNOCKED SOMETHIN' OVER IN THE DARK?
CRASH!
NOT HIM? HE KNOWS THIS PLACE LIKE A BOOK? OPEN THAT DOOR?

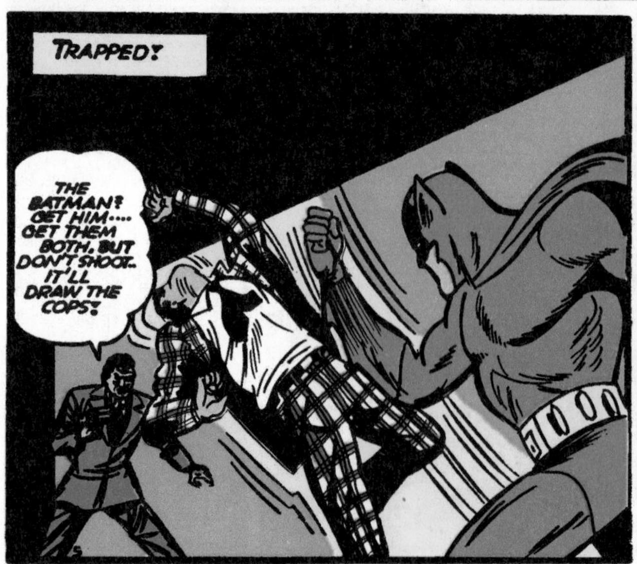
TRAPPED?
THE BATMAN? GET HIM.... GET THEM BOTH, BUT DON'T SHOOT-- IT'LL DRAW THE COPS?

THE BATMAN AND ROBIN FIGHT LIKE TWO TIGERS, BUT THE ODDS ARE TOO OVERWHELMING
THAT'S IT? WE GOT 'EM NOW?

THEY ARE SECURELY TRUSSED AND TOSSED INTO A ROOM....
I DON'T LIKE THIS, MINDY... SOMETHIN'S WRONG!
YEAH-- HOW DID THE BATMAN KNOW OUR GAME?
WE'VE GOT TO WORK FAST. YOU GUYS GO OUT AND PULL AS MANY HOLDUPS AS YOU CAN-- THEN WE'LL GET OUTA HERE!

THE MEN LEAVE.....
THIS IS NOT SO... LOOK-- OVER THERE ON THE BED!
DAWES? THE REAL COLONEL DAWES!

THE BATMAN CALLS DAWES BUT HE DOES NOT ANSWER....
SOMETHING'S WRONG, HE DOESN'T EVEN WAKE UP.
YET, HE'S ALIVE! I CAN HEAR HIM BREATHING. IF ONLY I COULD GET FREE!

HOURS PASS, WHEN SUDDENLY THE DOOR OPENS-- AND A BENT FIGURE ENTERS THE ROOM-
TIED YOU UP, DIDN'T THEY? HEE HEE
THE CARETAKER-
...AND HE'S GOT A KNIFE!

THE KNIFE DESCENDS--TO CUT THEIR BONDS!
I SAW THEM-- I SAW THEM TIE YOU UP! I MUST FREE YOU SO YOU CAN GO BACK TO YOUR PLACES AND JOIN MY LITTLE FAMILY AGAIN!
THE POOR MAN THINKS WE'RE STILL WAX FIGURES-- FROM HIS LITTLE FAMILY, AS HE CALLS IT!

HE'S BREATHING HEAVILY, BUT HIS HEART ACTION IS WEAK! HE'S BEEN DRUGGED!
WE'D BETTER GET HIM TO A DOCTOR RIGHT AWAY!
HEE HEE!

I'LL TAKE HIM TO ONE. YOU STAY HERE AND TRY TO STOP MINDY'S GANG WITHOUT GETTING HURT.
RIGHT!

AFTER THE BATMAN HAS GONE, ROBIN CAUTIOUSLY STEPS OUT INTO THE WAX MUSEUM WHEN...
LOOK..... THE KID THAT WORKS WITH THE BATMAN!
GET HIM BEFORE HE CALLS THE COPS! C'MON!
OH-OH!

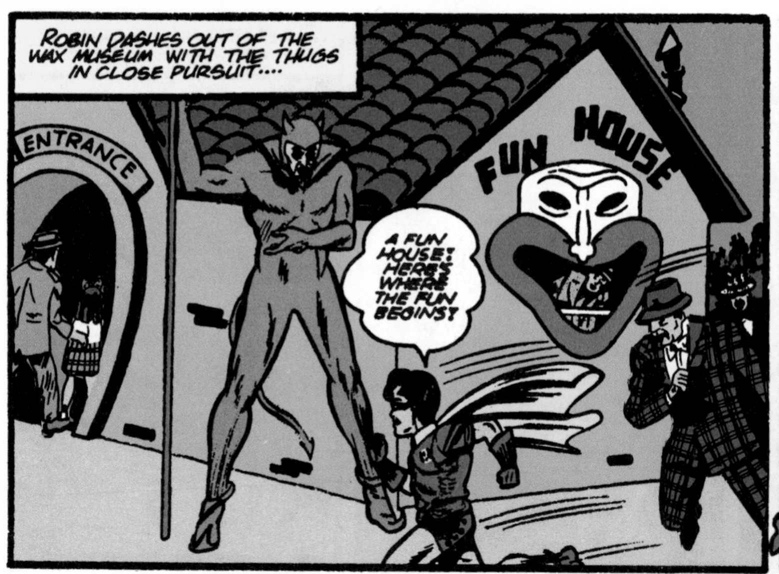
ROBIN DASHES OUT OF THE WAX MUSEUM WITH THE THUGS IN CLOSE PURSUIT....
ENTRANCE
FUN HOUSE
A FUN HOUSE! HERE'S WHERE THE FUN BEGINS!

ROBIN SPRINGS...
I CAN SEE WHERE I'M GOING TO HAVE QUITE A PARTY!

AS ROBIN SWINGS UP, THE THUGS' MOMENTUM CARRIES THEM PAST THE BOY WONDER...WHO PIVOTS AROUND THE PITCHFORK AND....
?
OHH... THERE HE IS?...

LEFT YOURSELVES WIDE OPEN, DIDN'T YOU?

ROBIN DARTS INSIDE AND BOLTS THROUGH ONE OF THE MANY DOORS CONFRONTING HIM.....
LET'S SEE WHERE THIS LEADS TO....

THE THUGS RACE UP AND ARE CONFUSED BY THE MANY SIMILAR FUN HOUSE DOORS.
THEY'RE ALL THE SAME! WHICH ONE DID HE GO THROUGH?
I DUNNO- I'LL TRY THIS ONE!

BOOO!

1 AT LAST THEY FIND THE RIGHT DOOR AND ENTER ANOTHER ROOM....
WHERE'D DAT BRAT GO NOW?
YEAH-- WHERE IS HE?

2
FUN HOUSE
FUNNY MIRRORS
GIANT SLIDE
HEY, BOYS-- HERE I AM!
HUH?

3 THE GUNMEN GO DOWN AGAIN!
WHAT'S THE MATTER WITH YOU FELLAS--YOU'RE ALWAYS FALLING DOWN!

WHEN THE THUGS RISE TO THEIR FEET AGAIN, THEY SEE ROBIN CALMLY RIDING AROUND ON THE SPINNING FLOOR....
DERE HE IS!
LEMME AT 'IM! I'LL MOIDER 'IM!
LET'S SEE YOU GET OUTA THIS!

THEY RANGE THEMSELVES ABOUT THE SPINNING FLOOR, READY TO POUNCE ON HIM WHEN HE STEPS OFF....
GET OUT? REALLY, IT'S SO SIMPLE!

ROBIN MERELY STICKS OUT HIS BALLED FISTS---AND THE SPINNING FLOOR DOES THE REST!

THE THUGS WEARILY PICK THEMSELVES UP AND GIVE CHASE···AND STEP ON A RUBBER FLOOR THIS TIME!
I GET A KICK OUT OF THIS- HOW ABOUT YOU BOYS?
DE FLOOR IS MOVIN'!
HELP!
IT MUST BE A EART'QUAKE!

THE BOY WONDER BOUNCES UP AND DOWN LIKE A JACK-IN-THE-BOX.
SO SORRY- SOMEBODY MUST BE ROCKING THE BOAT!
OOF!

LIFE HAS ITS UPS AND DOWNS, HASN'T IT?

THEN AS THE HOODLUMS GAIN THE STATIONARY FLOOR, ROBIN GREETS EACH ONE-PERSONALLY!
HYA-CHUM! I'LL PUNCH THE BUTTON FOR THE NEXT TRIP!

ONE GOES INTO A SPINNING BARREL····
GO AHEAD··· HAVE YOUR BARREL OF FUN!

ANOTHER IS UNWILLINGLY SEATED IN A CHAIR FITTED WITH AN ELECTRIC SHOCKER.
SHOCKING THING, ISN'T IT?
OWW! I'VE BEEN ELECTROCUTED!

AFTER ROBIN LEAVES THE THUGS AND GOES ON HIS WAY····
FUNN ORS
SHUT UP, DOPEY! THIS IS ONE O' THEM FUNNY MIRRORS!!
WHAT A SOCK DAT KID HAS! HEY! LOOK AT WHAT HE DONE TO MY FACE! IT'S ALL OUT A SHAPE!
OH, YEAH···· WELL, I AIN'T LAUGHIN'! I REALLY GOT LUMPS!

MEANWHILE, MINDY'S MOBSTERS HAVE BEGIN A SERIES OF DARING HOLDUPS.... WHEN SUDDENLY ONE LOOKS VERY FOOLISH AND SLUMPS TO THE GROUND.....
OKAY-- LETS---WHA... WHAT'S THE MATTER WITH JOEY?

AND ANOTHER .....
BONG!
UGH!

HELLO, CHUM-- JUST A LITTLE PRACTISE TO KEEP MY ARM IN TRIM!
THE-- THE BATMAN!

FRANTIC, THE THUG STARTS TO RUN, WHEN THERE IS A HUMMING NOISE AND.....
THIS OUGHT TO PROVE I'M JUST AS GOOD AS ROBIN IS AT THROWING A BALL!

LATER, THE BATMAN CROUCHES ATOP A CIRCUS TENT.... HE LOOKS DOWN UPON THE VAST THRONGS BELOW HIM...
A HOLDUP NEAR THE AIRPLANE RIDE! BY THE TIME I GET THROUGH THE CROWD, THE COMMOTION WILL WARN THEM! AH-- I'VE GOT A BETTER IDEA!

THE BATMAN RACES TOWARD THE "AIRPLANE RIDE"... A LITHE SPRING...
GOOD THING THE RIDE IS JUST STARTING!

ROUND AND ROUND GO THE PLANES... GATHERING MORE MOMENTUM.... AND CLINGING FAST IS THE BATMAN.....

ABRUPTLY, THE BATMAN RELEASES HIS TENACIOUS GRIP. THE CENTRIFUGAL FORCE SENDS HIS FORM WHIPPING OVER THE CROWD LIKE A RELEASED ARROW.....

.... AND HE DROPS LIKE A PLUMMET TO THE BACKS OF THE HOLD-UP MEN!!
GREETINGS, RATS! YOU'VE GOT COMPANY!
UGH!
OOF!

THE BATMAN'S FIST SNAKES OUT..... ONE.... TWO!
BE GOOD BOYS AND YOU'LL ONLY GET HIT ONCE!

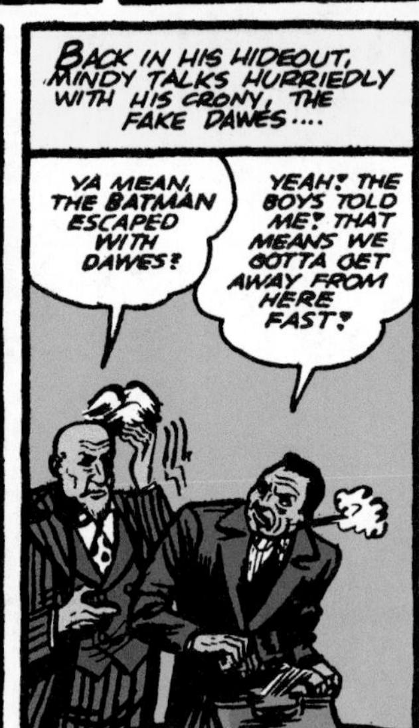
BACK IN HIS HIDEOUT, MINDY TALKS HURRIEDLY WITH HIS CRONY, THE FAKE DAWES....
YA MEAN, THE BATMAN ESCAPED WITH DAWES?
YEAH! THE BOYS TOLD ME! THAT MEANS WE GOTTA GET AWAY FROM HERE FAST!

SUDDENLY, A LIVING WHIRLWIND SWEEPS INTO THE ROOM...
YOU TWO ARE NOT GOING ANYPLACE-YET!
THE BATMAN!

DESPERATELY, MINDY TUGS AT HIS GUN. THE BATMAN THROWS HIMSELF TO THE SIDE AS A BULLET SCREAMS PAST HIS CHEEK....

HOLDING THE BATMAN AT BAY WITH A CEASELESS BARRAGE OF BULLETS, THE CRAZED MAN RACES TO THE DOOR....
GOTTA GET AWAY FROM HIM.... GOTTA GET AWAY!
I'M COMING FOR YOU, MINDY!!

HIS TERROR GROWING, MINDY DARTS TOWARD THE SCENIC RAILWAY, HOPING TO SHAKE HIS RELENTLESS PURSUER....
HERE--A DOLLAR--I WANT THE WHOLE CAR TO MYSELF---START HER OFF RIGHT NOW!
YES, SIR!

TOO LATE!
GOT TO GET UP TO HIM. THE FERRIS WHEEL-THAT WILL DO IT!

THE BATMAN LEAPS TOWARD A RISING CAR OF THE FERRIS WHEEL....
COME TO POPPA!

UP--UP--UP GOES THE BATMAN AS THE CAR ASCENDS.

THE CAR REACHES ITS HIGHEST POINT. THE BATMAN FLINGS HIMSELF TOWARD THE SCENIC RAILWAY STRUCTURE....
I'D BETTER NOT MISS!

...AND HIS FISTS CLOSE VISE-LIKE ABOUT A SUPPORTING BEAM!
NOW FOR MINDY!

THE BATMAN CLIMBS TO THE UPPER PORTION OF THE RAILWAY AND WAITS FOR THE CAR MINDY IS ON.....

As it passes beneath, the Batman dives headlong off his perch...
YOU!
High above the earth in a rocketing car, the Batman and Mindy lock in a death struggle!
Suddenly, as the car screams about a curve, the Batman is hurled off balance.
HERE'S WHERE YOU GET YOURS BATMAN!
UGH!
YOU MEAN, YOU GET YOURS!
I'M FALLING-- I'M FALLING!
NOT VERY FAR! CAN'T EVEN LET DEATH TAKE YOU AWAY FROM ME!
MINDY, THIS IS THE END OF THE RIDE FOR YOU!
Later, after Mindy and his mob are in the hands of the police and the plot is exposed, Bruce and Dick ride homeward....
GEE, I SURE HAD A LOT OF FUN AT THAT AMUSEMENT PARK!
I DID, TOO-- IT DID OFFER ABOUT THE MOST AMAZING AMUSEMENTS!

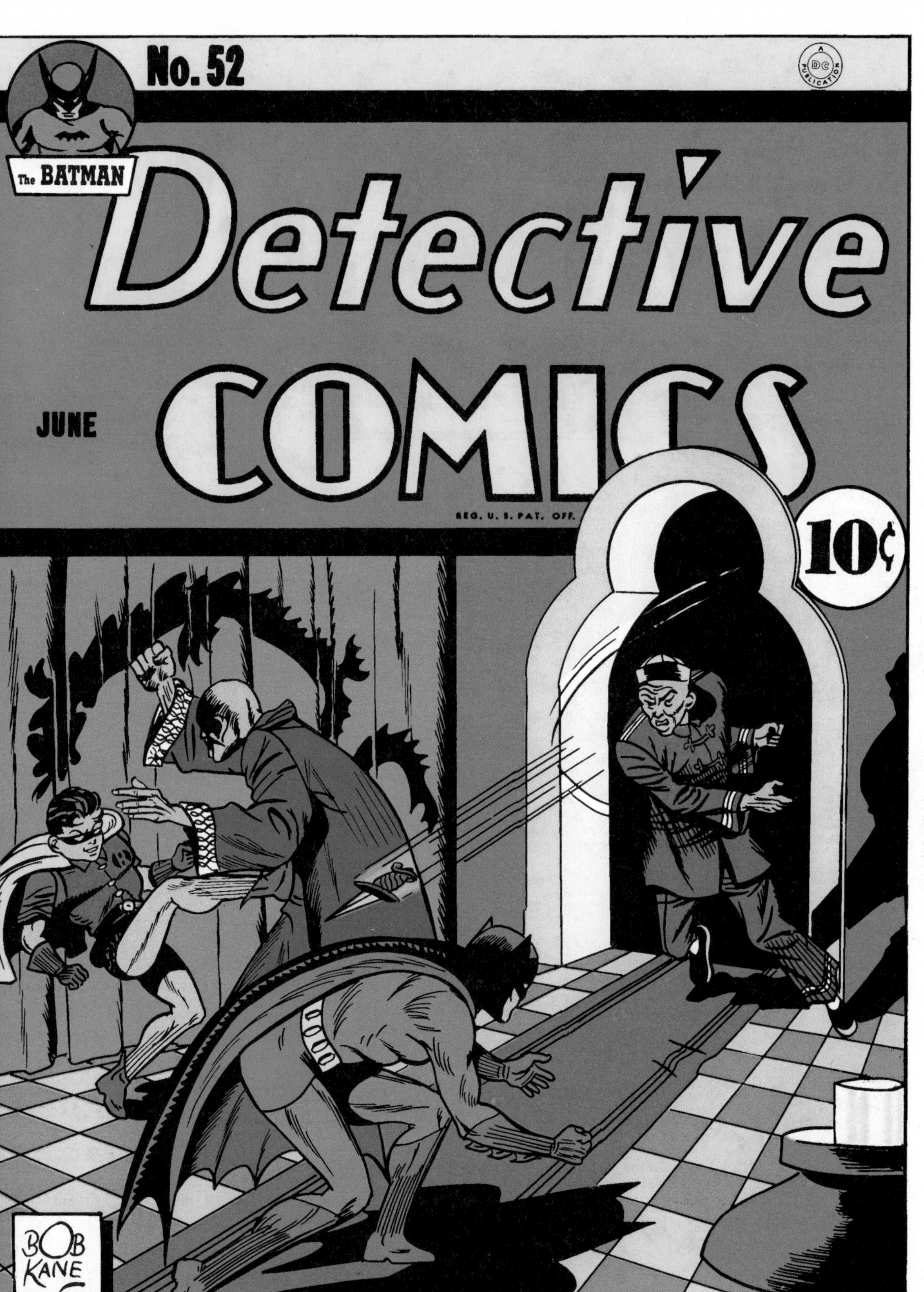
No. 52
A DC PUBLICATION
The BATMAN
Detective
COMICS
JUNE
REG. U. S. PAT. OFF.
10¢
BOB KANE

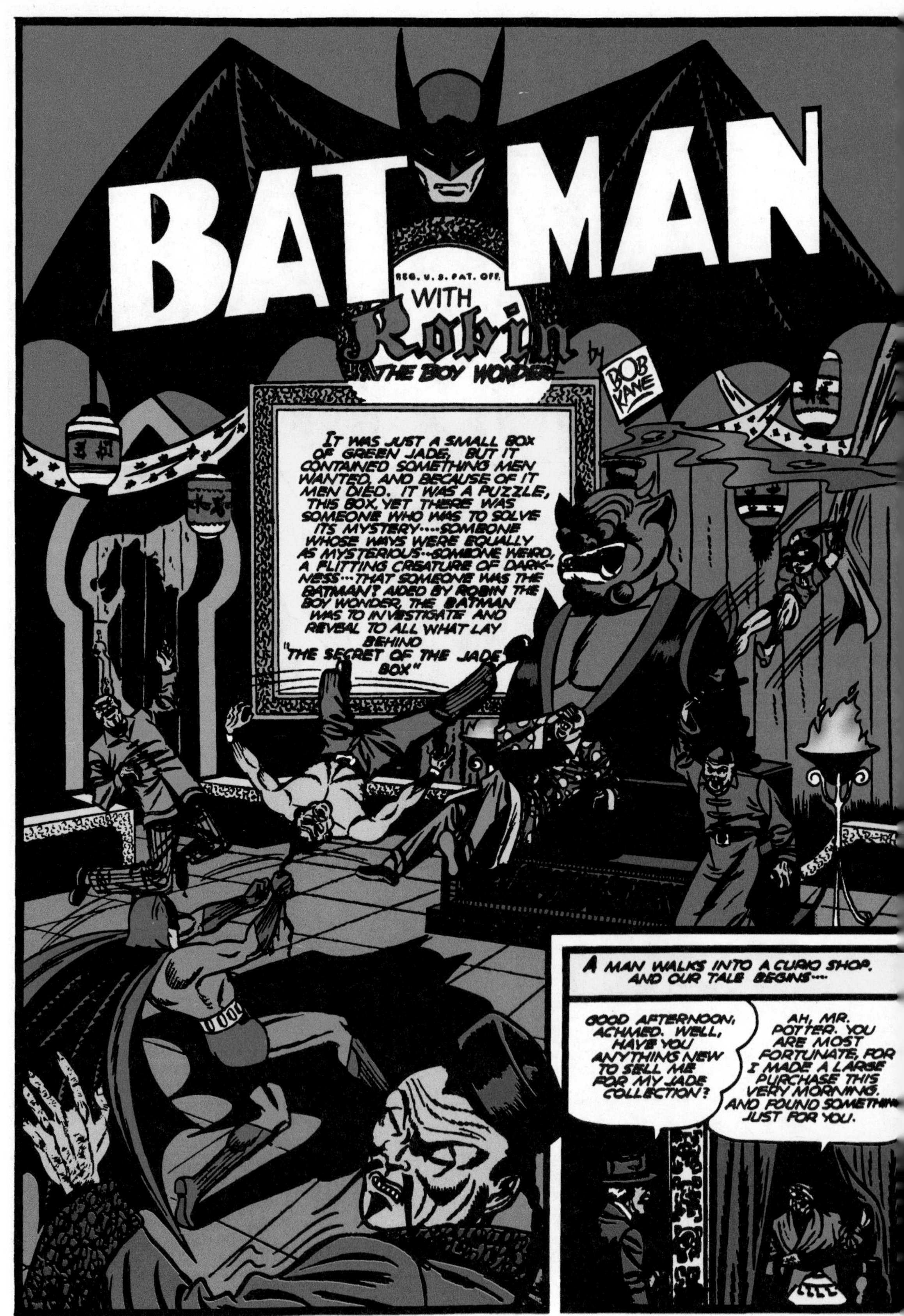
BATMAN
REG. U.S. PAT. OFF.
WITH Robin THE BOY WONDER
by BOB KANE
IT WAS JUST A SMALL BOX OF GREEN JADE, BUT IT CONTAINED SOMETHING MEN WANTED, AND BECAUSE OF IT MEN DIED. IT WAS A PUZZLE, THIS BOX, YET THERE WAS SOMEONE WHO WAS TO SOLVE ITS MYSTERY.... SOMEONE WHOSE WAYS WERE EQUALLY AS MYSTERIOUS--SOMEONE WEIRD, A FLITTING CREATURE OF DARKNESS... THAT SOMEONE WAS THE BATMAN! AIDED BY ROBIN THE BOY WONDER, THE BATMAN WAS TO INVESTIGATE AND REVEAL TO ALL WHAT LAY BEHIND "THE SECRET OF THE JADE BOX"
A MAN WALKS INTO A CURIO SHOP, AND OUR TALE BEGINS....
GOOD AFTERNOON, ACHMED. WELL, HAVE YOU ANYTHING NEW TO SELL ME FOR MY JADE COLLECTION?
AH, MR. POTTER. YOU ARE MOST FORTUNATE, FOR I MADE A LARGE PURCHASE THIS VERY MORNING, AND FOUND SOMETHING JUST FOR YOU.

HERE....A BOX OF PUREST JADE! IS IT NOT A BEAUTY?
HMM? YOU KNOW I CAN'T RESIST IT, YOU OLD ROGUE...
AND SO THE JADE BOX IS BOUGHT WITH MONEY NOW... BUT MANY LIVES WILL PAY ITS PRICE.... BEFORE LONG....

THAT NIGHT.... IN POTTER'S HOME...
I'M EXPECTING BRUCE WAYNE, THOMAS. SHOW HIM IN HERE WHEN HE ARRIVES.
VERY GOOD, SIR!

WHILE EXAMINING THE BOX, POTTER'S FINGERS ACCIDENTALLY PRESS A BIT OF CARVING. THERE IS A SUDDEN CLICK...
WHY... THERE IS A SECRET BOTTOM UNDER THE OTHER ONE! BY ALL THAT'S HOLY.... WHAT'S THIS INSIDE..... IT'S......

A SHADOW CROSSES THE DESK..... POTTER LOOKS UP, HIS EYES OPEN WIDE, STARE FIXEDLY IN FASCINATED HORROR....

A SUDDEN, LOW MOAN.. A DULL THUMP. AS SWIFTLY AS THEY CAME, THE INTRUDERS DEPART. ALL IS SILENCE EXCEPT FOR THE MONOTONOUS TICKING OF A CLOCK.. AND ON THE FLOOR LIES A FALLEN OBJECT.. THE JADE BOX!
TICK TOCK TICK

MINUTES PASS... THE DOOR SWINGS OPEN.
I THOUGHT MR. POTTER WOULD BE IN THE STUDY, THOMAS.
HE SAID HE WOULD BE HERE, MR WAYNE. PERHAPS HE WENT TO ANOTHER ROOM.

THIS NEW JADE BOX MR. POTTER BOUGHT THIS AFTERNOON.. ON THE FLOOR. TCH-TCH!
ALWAYS THE STICKLER FOR NEATNESS, AREN'T YOU, THOMAS?

AS HE LAYS THE BOX UPON THE DESK, POTTER GASPS. INSTANTLY, BRUCE WAYNE IS AT HIS SIDE.... AND THERE BEHIND THE DESK....
GOOD LORD! POTTER!
HE.. HE'S BEEN MURDERED!

THE POLICE ARE SUMMONED...
NOTHING STOLEN, THE MAN HAD NO ENEMIES, YET HE WAS MURDERED! IT ISN'T RIGHT!
THE FINGER-PRINTS ON THE KNIFE DON'T CHECK WITH ANY ON FILE! IT'S A TOUGH ONE!

THIS IS GOING DOWN ON THE BOOK AS "MURDER BY PERSON OR PERSONS UNKNOWN!"
YOU WON'T NEED ME ANY LONGER SO I'LL BE TODDLING ALONG!

AT HIS HOME, BRUCE TELLS HIS YOUNG WARD, DICK GRAYSON, OF THE CASE.
THIS SORT OF LOOKS LIKE A PERFECT CRIME, EH, BRUCE? NO CLUES...
AH, BUT YOU'RE WRONG. THERE IS A CLUE, AND ONLY I AND THOMAS KNOW ABOUT IT ... BUT ONLY I KNOW IT'S A CLUE!

A WEIRD, CLOSE-FITTING COSTUME TRANSFORMS BRUCE WAYNE INTO THE MAN THAT IS THE "EYES OF NIGHT"... THE BATMAN!
ONCE AGAIN THE BATMAN TAKES TO HIS LONE PATROL!

SOMETIME LATER, HIS TALL, CLOAKED FIGURE INCHES UP THE VINE THAT CLINGS OUTSIDE THE POTTER HOME....

WHO.. WHAT ARE YOU?
WHO IS BETTER. I'M THE BATMAN! I WANT TO FIND OUT WHO KILLED YOUR MASTER AND WHY. WILL YOU HELP ME?

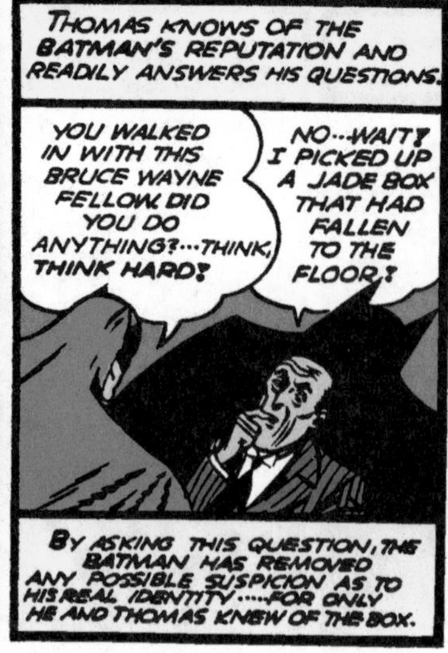
THOMAS KNOWS OF THE BATMAN'S REPUTATION AND READILY ANSWERS HIS QUESTIONS.
YOU WALKED IN WITH THIS BRUCE WAYNE FELLOW. DID YOU DO ANYTHING?...THINK, THINK HARD!
NO...WAIT! I PICKED UP A JADE BOX THAT HAD FALLEN TO THE FLOOR!
BY ASKING THIS QUESTION, THE BATMAN HAS REMOVED ANY POSSIBLE SUSPICION AS TO HIS REAL IDENTITY.....FOR ONLY HE AND THOMAS KNEW OF THE BOX.

THE MASTER HAD ONLY PURCHASED IT THIS MORNING FROM ACHMED, THE CURIO DEALER.
THE POLICE DON'T KNOW OF THIS YET... SO DON'T TELL THEM. DON'T TELL THEM TILL YOU HEAR FROM ME!

OUTSIDE, THE BATMAN EXAMINES THE BOX... AS FATE WOULD HAVE IT, HIS FINGER PRESSES THAT SAME BIT OF CARVING... THERE IS A CLICK!
WHA.... A FALSE BOTTOM. NOW I GET IT. SOMETHING WAS IN THAT BOTTOM. THE KILLER MURDERED POTTER TO GET IT!

THE MURDERER DIDN'T NEED THE BOX ANYMORE, SO HE DROPPED IT.....AND UNWITTINGLY LEFT A PERFECTLY GOOD CLUE.
THE BATMAN'S SURMISE IS CORRECT, FOR AT THAT MOMENT...
BUT THE BOX... IT WAS NO LONGER OF ANY USE!
IMBECILE! IT MIGHT LEAD THE POLICE HERE. FIND THE BOX AND BRING IT TO ME!

SOMETIME AFTER---
..AND WHERE DID THE BATMAN GO WITH THE JADE BOX? TELL ME-OR I...
NO! HE...HE WENT TO ACHMED'S CURIO SHOP!

COME! WE WILL FIND THE BATMAN ...AND WE WILL DEAL WITH HIM! TO ACHMED'S!

MEANWHILE...
AN ORIENTAL SOLD YOU THIS BOX AMONG SOME OTHER GOODS THIS MORNING AND THEN CAME BACK AGAIN LATER??
HE WANTED THE JADE BOX BACK. WHEN I TOLD HIM IT WAS SOLD, HE GOT VERY EXCITED. HE DEMANDED THE NAME AND ADDRESS OF THE BUYER.... AND I GAVE IT TO HIM.

THE BATMAN WALKS OUT THE CURIO SHOP DOOR. SUDDENLY, HE STOPS AND STARES AT THE SIDEWALK...
OH-OH. SOMEONE'S WAITING FOR ME! HE'S GOT A KNIFE!

WHISTLING NONCHALANTLY, THE BATMAN CONTINUES TO WALK...WHILE DEATH HOVERS ABOVE HIM!

ABRUPTLY, THE BATMAN WHIPS INTO ACTION!

UMMPH!
HYA, FELLA? WHAT'S NEW?

THE BATMAN DROPS TO THE GROUND AND SWERVES INSTANTLY AS A KNIFE HISSES PAST HIS EAR....
AH...ENTER THE VILLAINS!

♫ ARE THE STARS OUT TONIGHT ♫
C-R-A-C-K!

GUNS? KNIVES? WALKING ARSENALS?

THANKS... YOU CAME IN HANDY!

A FIST LIKE A CHUNK OF STEEL SLAMS AGAINST THE ORIENTAL'S JAW!
ALL THIS ENTERTAINMENT YOU'VE PROVIDED ME HAS BEEN VERY LOVELY, BUT I'M GETTING RATHER TIRED OF IT!

HEY WHAT'S GOING ON AROUND HERE?
ENTER THE LAW!

THE POLICEMAN GIVES CHASE. HE RACES DOWN A DARK ALLEY.... AND SUDDENLY HALTS....
GONE!

...AND WHEN THE POLICEMAN RACES TO WHERE THE FALLEN ORIENTALS WERE....
THEY'RE GONE, TOO! WONDER WHAT IT WAS ALL ABOUT ANYWAY?

DAYS PASS. THEN, STRANGE THINGS HAPPEN IN THE ORIENTAL QUARTER, IN TEA SHOPS, CHOP SUEY PLACES, LAUNDRIES....
YOU WANT TO PROTECT MY LAUNDRY FROM DANGER? BUT WHAT POSSIBLE DANGER CAN THERE BE?
THE WINDOW CAN BE SMASHED...THE CLOTHES TORN. ALL THIS MAY HAPPEN UNLESS YOU PAY US!

YOU....YOU ARE GANGSTERS! I WILL NOT.... WHAT...
BUZZzzz...

UPON HEARING THE WORDS WHISPERED IN HIS EAR, THE ORIENTAL'S EYES GROW WIDE WITH FRIGHT. HE PROTESTS NO LONGER!
YES...YES. I WILL TAKE YOUR PROTECTION. I WILL DO SO AT ONCE!
WE ARE GRATIFIED AT YOUR SUDDEN HASTE. IT IS MOST WISE... MOST WISE!
AND SO IT IS THE LENGTH AND BREADTH OF CHINATOWN. INNOCENT STORE-KEEPERS PAY FOR "PROTECTION" UPON A FEW WORDS WHISPERED IN THEIR EARS!

THE SITUATION BECOMES A GRAVE ONE.....SO GRAVE, A COMMITTEE CALLS ON THE HONORABLE UNOFFICIAL MAYOR OF THE ORIENTAL QUARTER.... LOO CHUNG.
MY HUMBLE HOUSE IS GREATLY HONORED BY YOUR PRESENCE. BUT WHAT BUSINESS CAN YOU HAVE WITH CHUNG?
THIS "PROTECTION" WE ARE FORCED TO PAY. WE COME TO YOU WITH A PLAN TO FIGHT THIS MENACE.

THE POLICE CANNOT HELP SO WE MUST TURN TO ONE WHO HAS AIDED US BEFORE.
IT IS HE OF THE DARK CLOTHING AND WINGS OF THE FLYING BAT...HE WHO IS CALLED.... BATMAN!

DID I HEAR MY NAME SPOKEN?
IT.. IT IS HE.. THE BATMAN!

I CAME TO SEE CHUNG ON ANOTHER MATTER, BUT NOW THAT I'M HERE LET'S HAVE THE DETAILS OF THIS "PROTECTION" RACKET.
ONE MUST GO BACK TO 1203 WHEN THE GREAT MONGOL CONQUEROR, GHENGIS KHAN, RULED ALL ASIA.

"HE WAS A CRUEL MAN AND RULED WITH AN IRON HAND.... AND ON THAT HAND WAS A RING!"
THIS IS THE RING OF GHENGIS KHAN. WHEN I DIE, MY SON SHALL WEAR IT AND BECOME A RULER AS SHALL HIS SONS AND THEIR SONS.....TO THE END OF TIME!

THE RING.
"LATER, THE KHAN RULE WAS ENDED, BUT STILL MEN FLOCKED TO HIS DESCENDANTS WHO WORE THE RING.."
LISTEN TO ME. THE PEOPLE OF THIS VILLAGE MUST PAY TRIBUTE AS THEY DID TO MY GREAT FOREFATHERS
AI! TRULY IT SHALL BE SO!

"AND SO DOWN THE AGES A KHAN GATHERED 'ROUND HIM A GROUP OF CUT-THROATS AND BANDITS WHO PLAGUED THE PEOPLE OF SMALL TOWNS!"

FOR A LONG TIME, OUR PEOPLE HAVE NOT BEEN BOTHERED BY KHAN BANDITS, BUT NOW...
NOW WE HAVE HEARD THAT A KHAN WEARS THE RING HERE IN AMERICA!
I SEE...A KHAN HAS STARTED THIS "TRIBUTE" RACKET HERE. TIMES HAVEN'T CHANGED MUCH, IT SEEMS!

YOU MAY BE SURE I'LL DO EVERYTHING I CAN TO STOP THIS NEW KHAN AND HIS MOB!
WE KNOW WHAT THE BATMAN PROMISES... HE WILL DO!

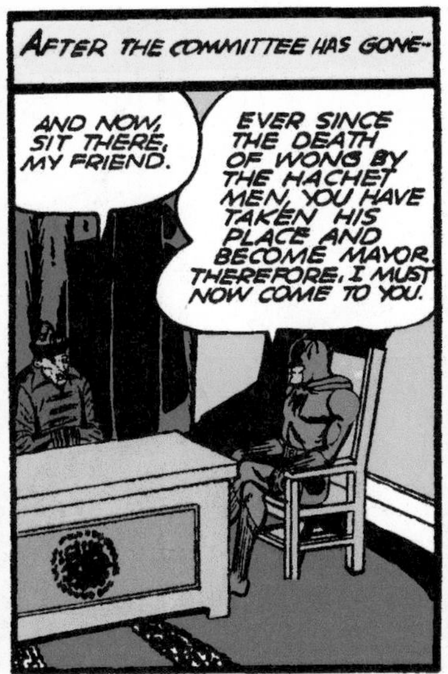
AFTER THE COMMITTEE HAS GONE--
AND NOW, SIT THERE, MY FRIEND.
EVER SINCE THE DEATH OF WONG BY THE HACHET MEN, YOU HAVE TAKEN HIS PLACE AND BECOME MAYOR. THEREFORE, I MUST NOW COME TO YOU.

THIS BOX CAUSED A MAN'S DEATH. IT IS OF ASIATIC ORIGIN. CAN YOU TELL ME ANYTHING ABOUT IT?
CERTAINLY! I CAN EVEN TELL YOU WHAT WAS IN IT....

I THOUGHT SURELY YOU MUST HAVE GUESSED BY NOW. IT WAS THIS.... THE RING OF GHENGIS KHAN!

WITH A HOARSE CRY, THE BATMAN LEAPS TO HIS FEET WHEN SUDDENLY THE FLOOR SEEMS TO OPEN UP. DOWN HE PLUNGES, WITH THE LAUGH OF LOO CHUNG RINGING IN HIS EARS!
HA HA HA HA!

THE BATMAN HITS THE HARD CEMENT BOTTOM AND LIES DAZED. A GIANT SHAPE MOVES TOWARD HIM FROM THE SHADOWS....

AS THE BATMAN RAISES HIS HAND, THE BEAST LEAPS!
A WILD DOG

THE BATMAN SWERVES, BUT AS THE BEAST CHARGES PAST, ONE CLAW-LIKE PAW RAKES HIS SIDE....

THAT DOG CAN TEAR ME TO PIECES!
GRRRRRR!

BEAST AND MAN LOCK IN A FURIOUS STRUGGLE....SHARP TEETH SNAP AT THE BATMAN'S THROAT.

GRRRRR!!

SUDDENLY, THE DESPERATE BATMAN MANAGES TO BLAST A FIST TO THE MAD DOG'S HEAD....
THERE! HOPE THIS STOPS HIM FOR A MINUTE AT LEAST! CAN'T HOLD OUT MUCH LONGER!

I'M FREE! HERE IT COMES AGAIN! GOTTA PUT EVERYTHING I'VE GOT IN THIS ONE!

THE BATMAN'S FIST MOVES OUT WITH BLURRED SPEED...THE WHOLE WEIGHT OF HIS BODY BEHIND THE BLOW. CRACK! AND IT CRASHES AGAINST THE BEAST'S JAW...

FOR A MOMENT THE BEAST SEEMS SUSPENDED IN THE AIR....THEN DROPS TO THE FLOOR!
GOSH.... THAT WAS CLOSE! MY LEGS FEEL LIKE JELLY.

A FEW MINUTES LATER..
AND NOW A LITTLE ACID ON THE LOCK FROM A VIAL OF MY UTILITY BELT

ABRUPTLY, A FLASHLIGHT PICKS OUT HIS FORM....
WHA--? THE BATMAN IS FREE-ROUSE THE OTHERS!

A HUGE GONG RESOUNDS TO SLEDGE-HAMMER BLOWS
BONG!
BONG!
BONG!

AS THE GONG SUMMONS CHUNG'S MEN, THE BATMAN RACES DOWN THE PASSAGE. SUDDENLY, HE STOPS AS HE SEES.....
OH-OH!

CRACK!

THE BATMAN'S HANDS SHOOT OUT..... CLOSES ABOUT THE END OF THE WHIP.... AND HE JERKS HARD!
I'LL TAKE THIS, IF YOU DON'T MIND!
?

ENRAGED, THE MONGOL PULLS A KNIFE...
I CUT YOU TO PIECES!
NOT TODAY, BROTHER!

USING THE MONGOL'S OWN PIG-TAIL, THE BATMAN CHOKES HIM INTO UNCONSCIOUSNESS.
THAT DOES IT!

NOW I'LL LET YOU DOWN, POP. I---
THAT WON'T BE NECESSARY!

YOU ARE VERY STRONG AND QUICK-- BUT I DON'T THINK THAT THOSE AMAZING QUALITIES WILL HELP MUCH AGAINST BULLETS.

AS THE CHUNG'S TRIGGER FINGER TIGHTENS, A STRANGE LOOKING FIGURE ENTERS!
PREPARE TO DIE, BATMAN!

I HAVE COME FOR YOU, O WICKED MEN!
AIEE! LOOK!

HERE I GO AGAIN!
AS THE MEN TURN THEIR ATTENTION FROM THE BATMAN, HE LEAPS INTO ACTION!

SUDDENLY, THE WEIRD FIGURE WHIPS OFF ITS HEAD....AND REVEALS....ROBIN, THE BOY WONDER!
ROBIN! I THOUGHT IT WAS YOU!
I GOT TIRED OF WAITING FOR YOU OUTSIDE, SO I DECIDED TO SEE WHAT WAS UP. GOOD THING I DID, TOO!

As his men fall beneath flailing fists, Chung flees in terror...
You won't get very far, Chung!

A quick flip... the whip snakes out... and whips around Chung's body...
ULP!
S-N-A-P...

I thought you'd see it my way!

Chung's men disposed of, the Batman frees the old man... who tells him what he knows.
Now, perhaps, you can clear up the rest of the mystery for me.
I was the last mayor's father. Wong, your friend--was really a Khan descendant! He had the ring, but refused to use it... too honorable!

"Only he and I knew of the ring, but one day after Wong's death, Chung stumbled upon it...."
The Khan ring!
"I saw the glitter of greed in his eyes. I knew I must act to save the liberty of our people"--

"That night as he slept, I stole the ring from his pocket and placed it in the box with the double bottom. Immediately, Chung knew I had stolen it... I was searched by his men...."
Ho... no ring, but a very valuable jade box.
Let us sell it to Achmed, the dealer. We will receive much money for it!
"That's how it fell into Achmed's, and finally Porter's hands."
12

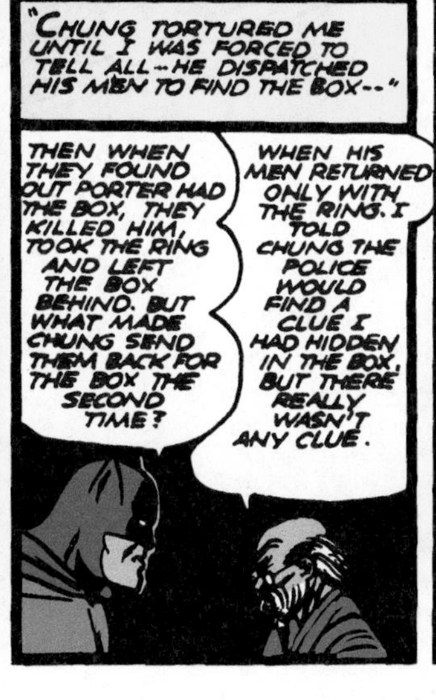
"Chung tortured me until I was forced to tell all--he dispatched his men to find the box--"
Then when they found out Porter had the box, they killed him, took the ring and left the box behind. But what made Chung send them back for the box the second time?
When his men returned only with the ring, I told Chung the police would find a clue I had hidden in the box, but there really wasn't any clue.

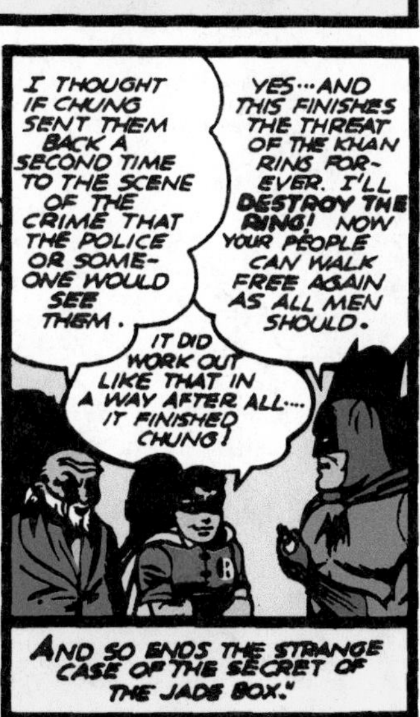
I thought if Chung sent them back a second time to the scene of the crime that the police or someone would see them.
Yes... and this finishes the threat of the Khan ring forever. I'll destroy the ring! Now your people can walk free again as all men should.
It did work out like that in a way after all... it finished Chung!
And so ends the strange case of the secret of the jade box.

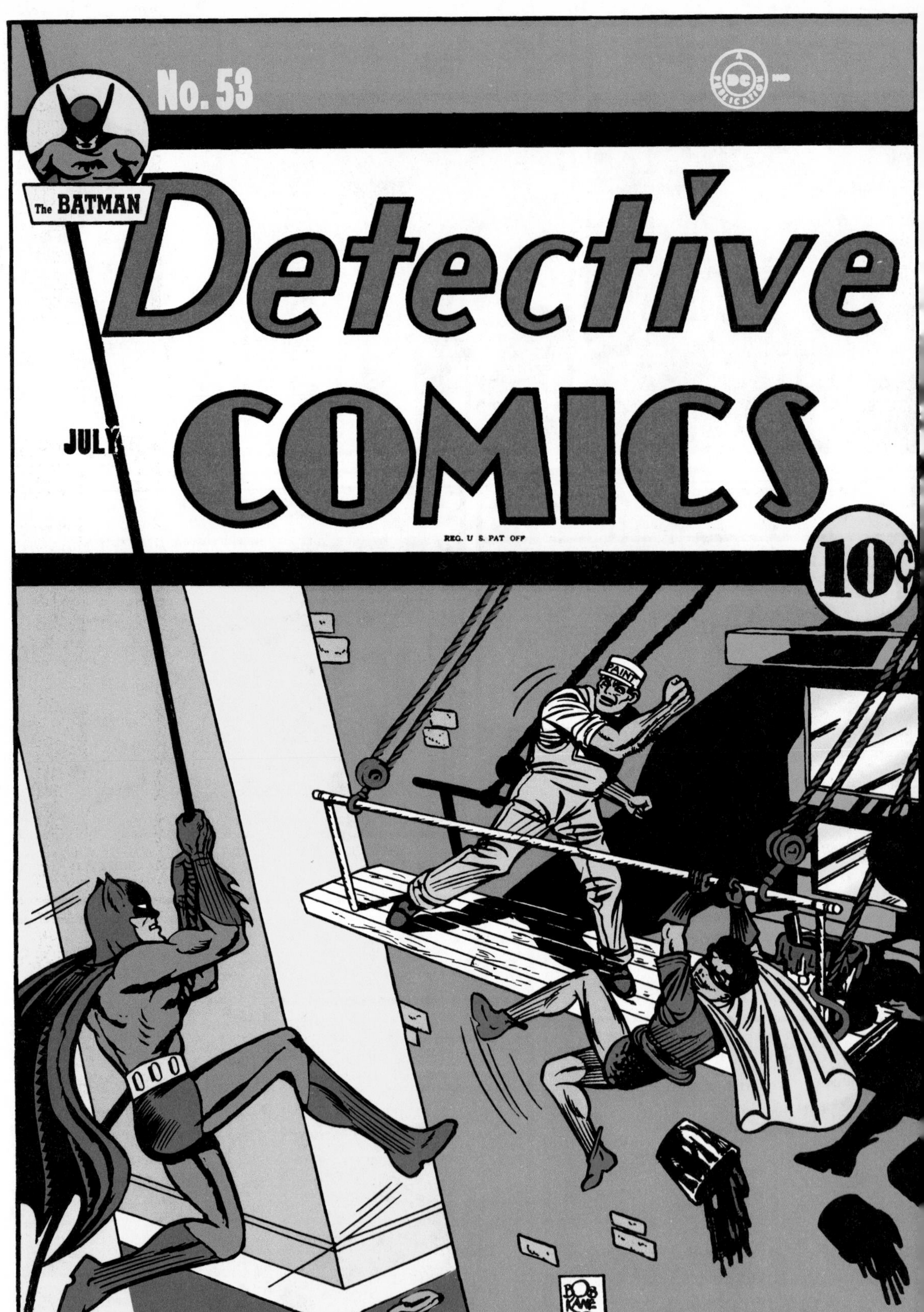
No. 53
A DC PUBLICATION
The BATMAN
Detective
JULY
COMICS
REG. U S. PAT OFF
10¢
PAINT
BOB KANE

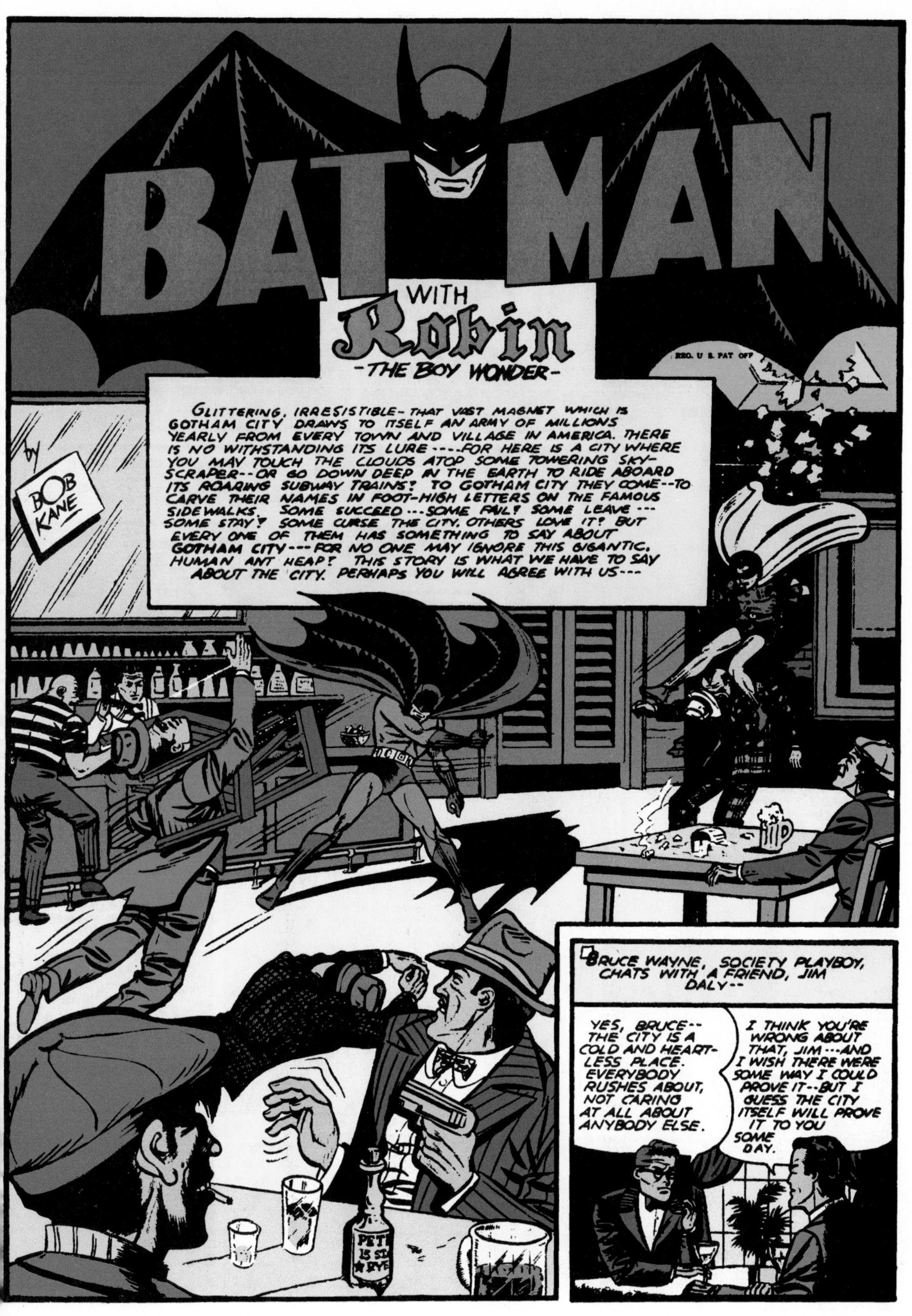
BATMAN
WITH Robin -THE BOY WONDER-
REG. U.S. PAT OFF
by BOB KANE
GLITTERING, IRRESISTIBLE- THAT VAST MAGNET WHICH IS GOTHAM CITY DRAWS TO ITSELF AN ARMY OF MILLIONS YEARLY FROM EVERY TOWN AND VILLAGE IN AMERICA. THERE IS NO WITHSTANDING ITS LURE----FOR HERE IS A CITY WHERE YOU MAY TOUCH THE CLOUDS ATOP SOME TOWERING SKY-SCRAPER--OR GO DOWN DEEP IN THE EARTH TO RIDE ABOARD ITS ROARING SUBWAY TRAINS! TO GOTHAM CITY THEY COME--TO CARVE THEIR NAMES IN FOOT-HIGH LETTERS ON THE FAMOUS SIDEWALKS. SOME SUCCEED---SOME FAIL! SOME LEAVE---SOME STAY! SOME CURSE THE CITY, OTHERS LOVE IT! BUT EVERY ONE OF THEM HAS SOMETHING TO SAY ABOUT GOTHAM CITY---FOR NO ONE MAY IGNORE THIS GIGANTIC, HUMAN ANT HEAP! THIS STORY IS WHAT WE HAVE TO SAY ABOUT THE CITY. PERHAPS YOU WILL AGREE WITH US---
BRUCE WAYNE, SOCIETY PLAYBOY, CHATS WITH A FRIEND, JIM DALY--
YES, BRUCE-- THE CITY IS A COLD AND HEART-LESS PLACE. EVERYBODY RUSHES ABOUT, NOT CARING AT ALL ABOUT ANYBODY ELSE.
I THINK YOU'RE WRONG ABOUT THAT, JIM---AND I WISH THERE WERE SOME WAY I COULD PROVE IT--BUT I GUESS THE CITY ITSELF WILL PROVE IT TO YOU SOME DAY.

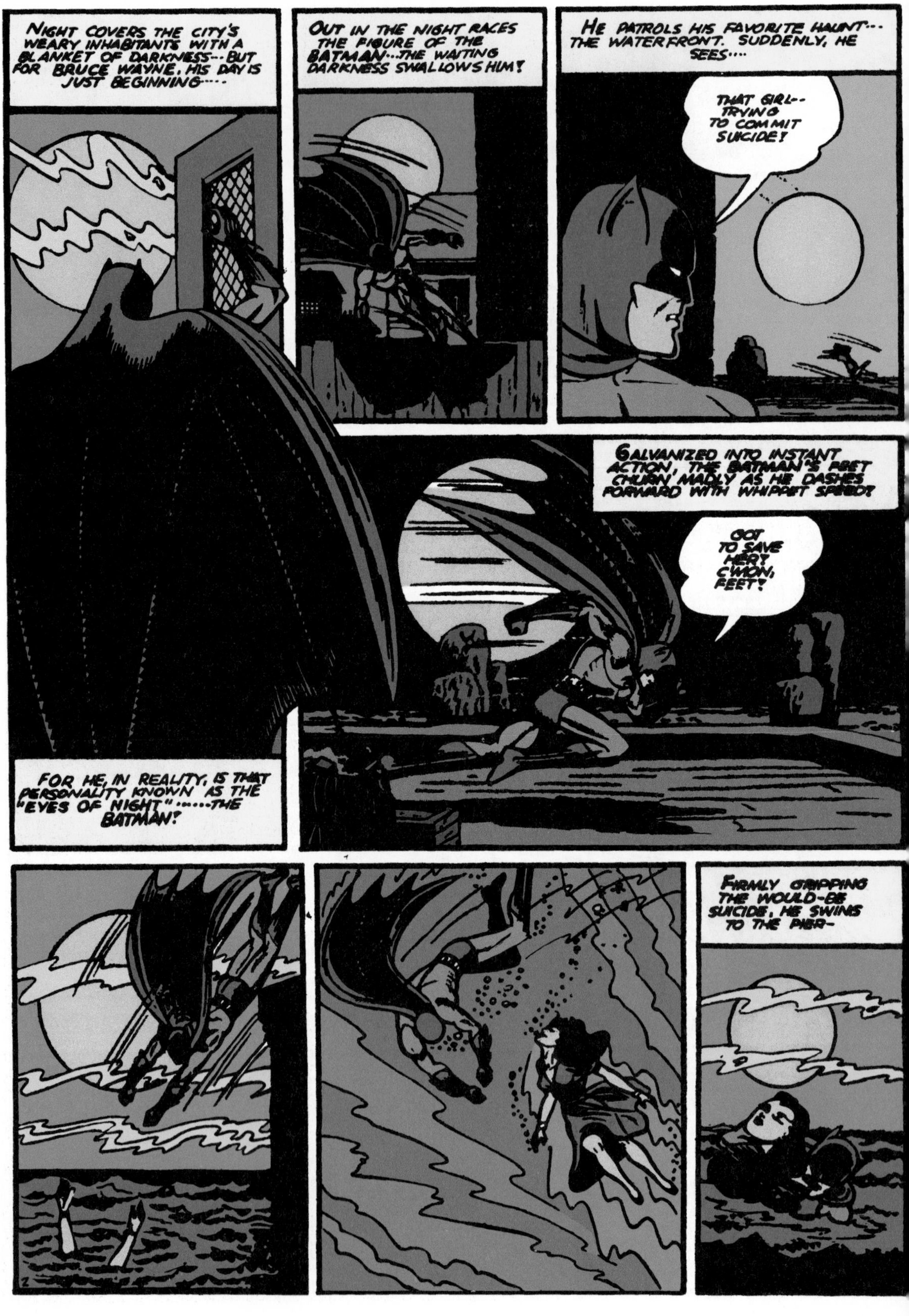

NIGHT COVERS THE CITY'S WEARY INHABITANTS WITH A BLANKET OF DARKNESS--BUT FOR BRUCE WAYNE, HIS DAY IS JUST BEGINNING----

OUT IN THE NIGHT RACES THE FIGURE OF THE BATMAN...THE WAITING DARKNESS SWALLOWS HIM!

HE PATROLS HIS FAVORITE HAUNT--- THE WATERFRONT. SUDDENLY, HE SEES....

THAT GIRL-- TRYING TO COMMIT SUICIDE!

GALVANIZED INTO INSTANT ACTION, THE BATMAN'S FEET CHURN MADLY AS HE DASHES FORWARD WITH WHIPPET SPEED!

GOT TO SAVE HER! C'MON, FEET!

FOR HE, IN REALITY, IS THAT PERSONALITY KNOWN AS THE "EYES OF NIGHT"......THE BATMAN!

FIRMLY GRIPPING THE WOULD-BE SUICIDE, HE SWINS TO THE PIER-

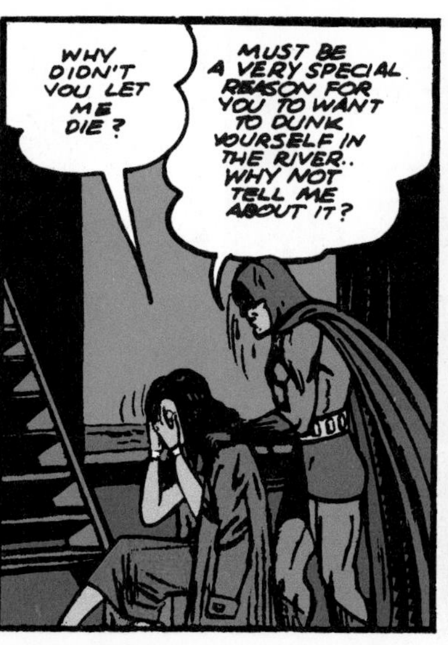
WHY DIDN'T YOU LET ME DIE?
MUST BE A VERY SPECIAL REASON FOR YOU TO WANT TO DUNK YOURSELF IN THE RIVER.. WHY NOT TELL ME ABOUT IT?

CALMED BY THE BATMAN'S MASTERFUL MANNER, THE GIRL TELLS HER STORY... REVEALS HER NAME IS VIOLA VANE.... THAT SHE'S FROM A SMALL TOWN.
I'M AN ACTRESS. I THOUGHT I'D COME HERE AND SET THE TOWN AFIRE WITH MY ACTING. I DIDN'T MAKE ENOUGH FIRE TO LIGHT A CANDLE. ALL I AM NOW IS AN UNDERSTUDY TO A STAR!

MY MOTHER AND DAD DON'T KNOW THAT. I-I KEPT SENDING THEM LETTERS SAYING I WAS A GREAT STAGE STAR AND THEY BELIEVED ME!
THAT'S NO REASON TO COMMIT SUICIDE-

I RECEIVED A TELEGRAM THIS MORNING. MOTHER AND DAD ARE ALREADY ON THEIR WAY HERE--- GOING TO PAY ME A VISIT FOR A FEW DAYS!
OH---AND YOU'RE ASHAMED TO FACE THEM BECAUSE THEY'RE SURE TO FIND OUT THE TRUTH. HMM, YOU'RE ON A SPOT!

IT WOULD BREAK THEIR HEARTS. I CAN'T FACE THEM. I JUST CAN'T!
PERHAPS IT ISN'T AS BAD AS ALL THAT---

NOW---IF YOU'LL GIVE ME YOUR WORD YOU WON'T TRY ANYMORE BATHS IN THE RIVER, I MAY HELP YOU. PROMISE?
I PROMISE-- BUT I DON'T POSSIBLY SEE HOW YOU CAN HELP ME...

AFTER THE GIRL HAS GONE--
THIS IS MY CHANCE TO HELP THAT POOR KID AND ALSO PROVE TO JIM DALY THAT THE CITY DOES HAVE A HEART! I HOPE I'M NOT WRONG!

LATER IN THE NIGHTCLUB---
AND NOW A LITTLE SURPRISE, CUSTOMERS. WE PRESENT FOR THE FIRST TIME---

THANKS FOR THE INTRODUCTION! I REALLY DIDN'T EXPECT IT!
LOOK! THE BATMAN!
DON'T TELL ME HE'S PART OF THE FLOOR SHOW-

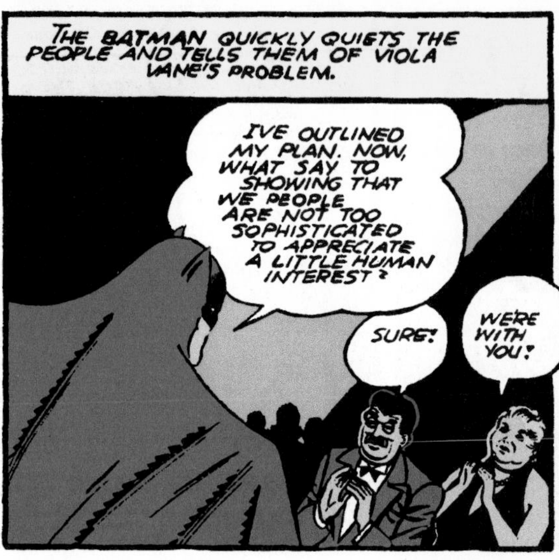
THE BATMAN QUICKLY QUIETS THE PEOPLE AND TELLS THEM OF VIOLA VANE'S PROBLEM.
I'VE OUTLINED MY PLAN. NOW, WHAT SAY TO SHOWING THAT WE PEOPLE ARE NOT TOO SOPHISTICATED TO APPRECIATE A LITTLE HUMAN INTEREST?
SURE!
WE'RE WITH YOU!

THE GIRL WILL NEED AN ESCORT, SOMEONE HANDSOME, WEALTHY, AND GOOD-NATURED ENOUGH TO PLAY ALONG WITH OUR PLAN.
I KNOW JUST THE FELLOW! HE'S A BIT LAZY, BUT WEALTHY AND GOOD LOOKING.

HIS NAME IS BRUCE WAYNE!
GULP-THAT'S ME!

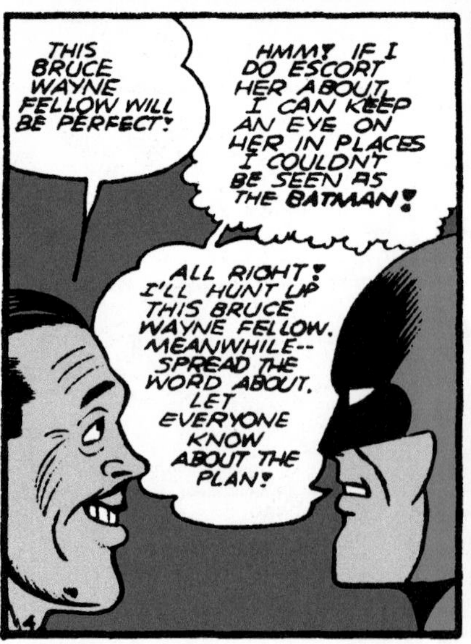
THIS BRUCE WAYNE FELLOW WILL BE PERFECT!
HMM! IF I DO ESCORT HER ABOUT, I CAN KEEP AN EYE ON HER IN PLACES I COULDNT BE SEEN AS THE BATMAN!
ALL RIGHT! I'LL HUNT UP THIS BRUCE WAYNE FELLOW. MEANWHILE-- SPREAD THE WORD ABOUT. LET EVERYONE KNOW ABOUT THE PLAN!

THE BATMAN GOES FROM NIGHTSPOT TO NIGHTSPOT TELLING EVERYONE OF VIOLA VANE. THEN HE CALLS ON THE RADIO NETWORKS.
THE WHOLE TOWN WILL SOON KNOW ABOUT IT, BUT IF YOU BROADCAST IT ON THE RADIO, THE GIRL'S PARENTS MIGHT HEAR IT AND---
I UNDERSTAND. YOU MAY REST ASSURED WE WILL NOT BROADCAST ANYTHING PERTAINING TO THE GIRL.

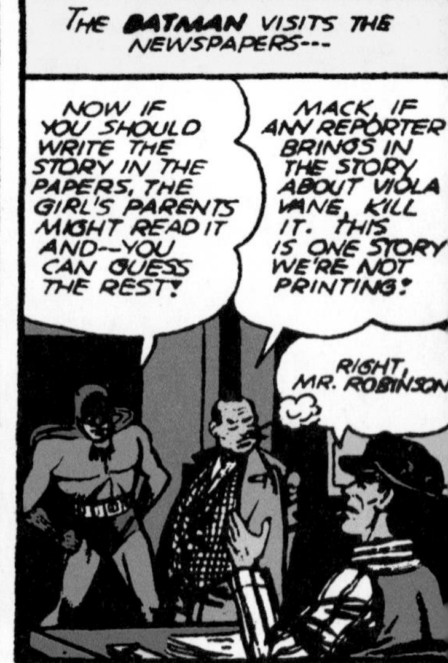
THE BATMAN VISITS THE NEWSPAPERS---
NOW IF YOU SHOULD WRITE THE STORY IN THE PAPERS, THE GIRL'S PARENTS MIGHT READ IT AND--YOU CAN GUESS THE REST!
MACK, IF ANY REPORTER BRINGS IN THE STORY ABOUT VIOLA VANE, KILL IT. THIS IS ONE STORY WE'RE NOT PRINTING!
RIGHT, MR. ROBINSON

BUT, OF COURSE, THERE IS ALWAYS ONE PERSON WHO DOESN'T UNDERSTAND. IN THE OFFICE OF THE DAILY STAR...
WHAT DO I CARE IF SOMEBODY GETS HURT. I'LL DO WHAT I WANT! NOW GET OUT-- GET OUT!
NASTY FELLOW, AREN'T YOU?

THE BATMAN'S HAND MOVES WITH ALMOST UNBELIEVABLE SPEED---
SORRY! I'M ALLERGIC TO GUNS!

LISTEN, LITTLE MAN---IF YOUR ROTTEN, YELLOW SCANDAL SHEET PRINTS A LINE OF THAT STORY, I'LL TAKE A PERSONAL INTEREST IN YOUR PAST HISTORY-

I WARN YOU! PRINT A LINE AND I'LL EXAMINE YOUR PAPER AND YOUR PAST---- AND I'LL BET I COME UP WITH ENOUGH FACTS FOR A SENATE INVESTIGATION!
HEH-HEH! I--I WAS ONLY FOOLING- HEH-HEH! I'LL BE GLAD TO COOPERATE WITH YOU. BE ONLY TOO GLAD TO!

AS THE NEWS SPREADS AROUND TOWN, THE BATMAN CALLS UPON VIOLA VANE ---AS BRUCE WAYNE!
BUT MR. WAYNE, I--I DON'T UNDERSTAND!
THE NAME IS BRUCE---AND THERE'S NO NEED FOR YOU TO UNDERSTAND. THE BATMAN TOLD ME WHAT YOU'RE TO DO! NOW PUT ON YOUR BONNET AND LETS TODDLE ALONG!

IN A BEAUTY PARLOR--
THIS IS VIOLA VANE. GIVE HER THE WORKS!
AH, MISS VANE. WE'VE HEARD ALL ABOUT YOU. COME THIS WAY, PLEASE!
YOU-- YOU HEARD ALL ABOUT ME?

LATER---SHE IS TAKEN TO THE PENTHOUSE SUITE OF A FAMOUS HOTEL!
THE KEYS TO YOUR SUITE, MISS VANE!
YOUR FROCKS, MISS VANE!
YOUR FURS FROM KNOX FURRIERS, MISS VANE!
YOUR JEWELRY FROM MARTIERS, MISS VANE!
HATS

AFTER THEY HAVE GONE, BRUCE EXPLAINS--
YOU SEE, THIS BATMAN CHAP HAS BEEN SCOUTING AROUND TOWN TELLING EVERYBODY ABOUT YOU- SO-O-O EVERYBODY IS CONTRIBUTING TO YOUR CAUSE. YOU'LL BE A STAR--AT LEAST WHILE YOUR PARENTS ARE HERE! HEY---WHAT ARE YOU BAWLING ABOUT?
EVERYONE HAS BEEN SO NICE TO ME! I'M SO HA-P-PY!

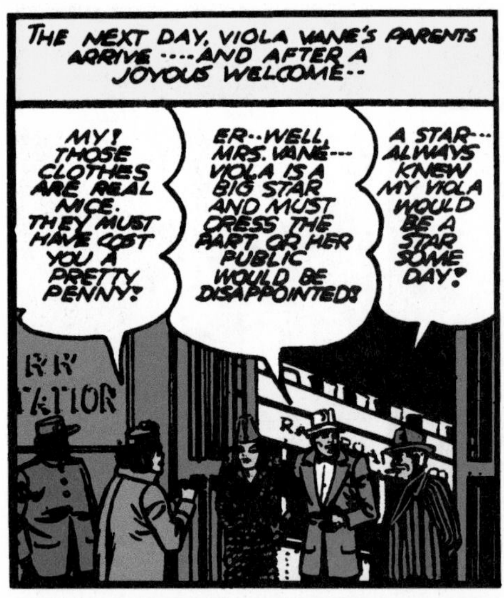
THE NEXT DAY, VIOLA VANE'S PARENTS ARRIVE ----AND AFTER A JOYOUS WELCOME--
MY! THOSE CLOTHES ARE REAL NICE. THEY MUST HAVE COST YOU A PRETTY PENNY!
ER--WELL, MRS. VANE--- VIOLA IS A BIG STAR AND MUST DRESS THE PART OR HER PUBLIC WOULD BE DISAPPOINTED!
A STAR--- ALWAYS KNEW MY VIOLA WOULD BE A STAR SOME DAY!

LET'S NOT WASTE TIME. I WANT TO SHOW YOU EVERYTHING THERE IS TO SEE IN GOTHAM CITY.
ALWAYS DID WANT TO GO TO THE TOP OF THE STATE BUILDING! IS IT REALLY 102 STORIES HIGH?
AND I'VE ALWAYS DREAMED OF SHOPPING IN A FIFTH AVENUE STORE.

THAT EVENING, AFTER A SWIFT AND EXCITING TOUR OF THE TOWN, THEY TAKE THE OLD COUPLE TO A NIGHTCLUB.
SO THIS IS A NIGHTCLUB! GOSH-- WAIT TILL I TELL THE BOYS BACK HOME.
IT'S JUST LIKE THE PICTURES I'VE SEEN OF THEM IN THE MOVIES!

SUDDENLY, A SPOTLIGHT SHIFTS TO THEIR TABLE----
---AND WE ARE PARTICULARLY FORTUNATE TO HAVE WITH US THE GREAT DRAMATIC ACTRESS, VIOLA VANE, WHO IS HERE WITH HER PARENTS!
VIOLA--- LOOK--- THEY'RE APPLAUDING YOU!
YOU MUST BE A VERY POPULAR ACTRESS!

--AND AS FOR THE APPLAUDERS---
LET'S MAKE IT LOOK GOOD FOR THE OLD FOLKS!
THE BATMAN CERTAINLY MUST BE REGULAR, THINKING UP AN IDEA LIKE THIS.
STOP TALKING-- AND APPLAUD!

THE STORY OF VIOLA VANE HAS TRAVELED BY WORD OF MOUTH AROUND THE CITY AND THE PEOPLE EAGERLY JOIN IN THE NOBLE DECEPTION. NIGHTSPOT AFTER NIGHTSPOT APPLAUDS THE "STAR" AND HER PARENTS---

LATER---AFTER THEY REACH THE PENTHOUSE "HOME"---
WELL, GOOD NIGHT, SON. WE SURE DID HAVE A FINE TIME!
MR. WAYNE IS AN EXCEPTIONAL ESCORT, ISN'T HE, VIOLA?
HE CERTAINLY IS. (YOU DON'T KNOW THE HALF OF IT!)

UPON REACHING HOME, BRUCE WAYNE DISCARDS HIS PLAYBOY CLOTHES FOR THAT OF ----THE BATMAN!
BETTER RELIEVE ROBIN----LEFT HIM GUARDING THOSE FURS AND JEWELS SENT BY KNOX AND MARTIERS! CAN'T LEAVE THEM LYING AROUND LOOSE!

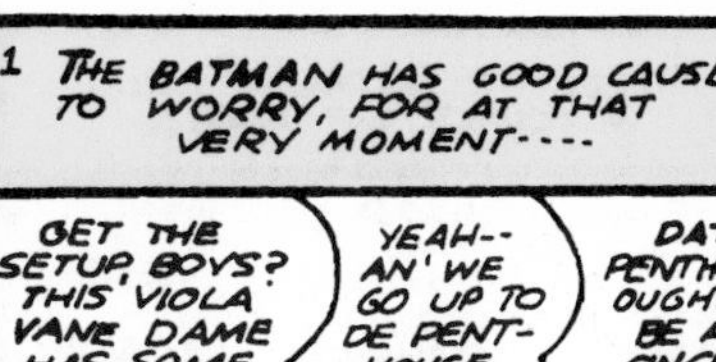
1 THE BATMAN HAS GOOD CAUSE TO WORRY, FOR AT THAT VERY MOMENT----
GET THE SETUP, BOYS? THIS VIOLA VANE DAME HAS SOME FURS AND JEWELRY GIVEN HER TO USE WHILE HER OLD FOLKS ARE HERE!
YEAH-- AN' WE GO UP TO DE PENT-HOUSE AND TAKE 'EM-
DAT PENTHOUSE OUGHTA BE A CINCH WHAT WITH DAT OTHER CONSTRUCTION JOB BEIN' PUT UP NEAR IT!
2
DE BATMAN THOUGHT UP THE IDEA FOR DIS VANE DAME'S ACT, EH, TOOTHY?
YEAH...AND AFTER WE TAKE THE STUFF, HE'LL HAVE TA TAKE THE BLAME FOR THE ROBBERY, TOO! HAW HAW!
MAYBE DE COPS WILL THINK HE PULLED DIS JOB HIMSELF! AIN'T DAT A LAUGH! HAW!

3
A SHORT TIME AFTER--- UNKNOWN TO VIOLA VANE, ROBIN SECRETLY PATROLS THE PENTHOUSE WALK.
I DON'T KNOW WHY THE BATMAN TOLD ME TO KEEP WATCH AROUND HERE. GOSH, NOTHING IS GOING TO HAPPEN-

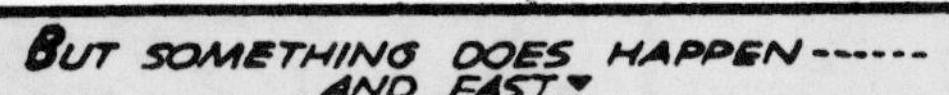
4 BUT SOMETHING DOES HAPPEN------ AND FAST!

5 THE GUNBUTT AND BLACK-NESS SWOOP DOWN ON ROBIN!
THERE-- THAT SHOULD HOLD YOU!

6
SAY--- THAT'S THE ROBIN KID THAT HELPS THE BATMAN. BETTER LET ME PLUG 'IM, TOOTHY.
YEAH-- AND BRING EVERY COP IN THE CITY UP HERE! C'MON-- LET'S GET THE STUFF AND SCRAM!

7 MOMENTS PASS. THE CURTAIN OF DARKNESS LIFTS FROM ROBIN'S EYES. A COWLED FIGURE SHAKES HIM...THE BATMAN!
ROBIN! ARE YOU ALL RIGHT? WHAT HAPPENED?
FEELS LIKE THE BUILDING FELL ON ME ---WHA-- BATMAN--THREE GUYS---- ONE CLUBBED ME---

THE BATMAN SWIFTLY DARTS INTO THE PENTHOUSE BUILDING---
THIEVES-- THEY STOLE THE FURS AND THE JEWELS--.
I WAS AFRAID OF THAT! DO YOUR MOTHER AND DAD KNOW ABOUT IT?

NO--- THEY'RE IN THE NEXT ROOM. YOU'D BETTER CALL THE POLICE! MAYBE THEY CAN STILL CATCH THE THIEVES!
NO...THAT WOULD MEAN PUBLICITY-- EXPOSURE FOR YOU! ROBIN AND I WILL HANDLE THIS IN OUR OWN QUIET WAY!

ROBIN AND BATMAN HOLD A "COUNCIL OF WAR!
I GOT A GOOD LOOK AT THE FELLOW WHO CLOUTED ME. BOY, DID HE HAVE A MOUTHFUL OF TEETH!
TEETH, EH? THERE'S ONLY ONE FELLOW WHO ANSWERS THAT DESCRIPTION- TOOTHY HARE- C'MON! WE'RE GOING TO WORK.

MOMENTS LATER FIND THE DYNAMIC DUO CLAMBERING UP THE ROOFTOP OF A ONE-STORY BUILDING-

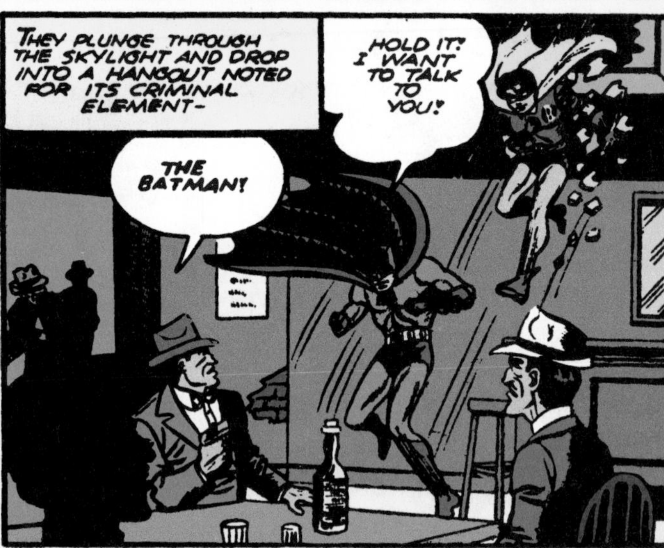
THEY PLUNGE THROUGH THE SKYLIGHT AND DROP INTO A HANGOUT NOTED FOR ITS CRIMINAL ELEMENT-
HOLD IT! I WANT TO TALK TO YOU!
THE BATMAN!

TAKE IT EASY!

I DIDN'T COME HERE TO START A FIGHT!
8

FOR GOSH SAKES, DON'T YOU FELLOWS---

UNDERSTAND ENGLISH?

THE BATMAN FIGHTS WITH THE WILD FURY OF AN UNLEASHED TORNADO!
BY HEAVEN, I'LL MAKE YOU LISTEN TO ME, OR I'LL BREAK A COUPLE OF JAWS IN THE ATTEMPT!
CRACK!

AFTER A FEW MOMENTS OF THE BATMAN AND ROBIN, THE CRIMINALS ARE ONLY TOO ANXIOUS TO LISTEN-
NOW THAT EVERYTHING IS QUIET AND PEACEFUL, I CAN TALK!

THE BATMAN TELLS OF TOOTHY'S LOOTINGS OF THE VIOLA VANE PENTHOUSE--
SO YOU SEE WHAT A ROTTEN TRICK IT IS ON THIS VIOLA VANE GIRL! I WANT TO FIND TOOTHY. HAVE ANY OF YOU ANY IDEA WHERE HE MIGHT BE HIDING OUT?
ER--NAW--WE DON'T KNOW NOTHIN'
YEAH--WE AIN'T TALKIN'!

SEEING HE CAN'T SECURE ANY INFORMATION, THE BATMAN LEAVES. AS HE DOES SO A FUGITIVE FIGURE SIDLES UP TO HIM---
PSSST--- I MAY BE A CROOK, BUT I NEVER PULLED A DOITY STUNT LIKE TOOTHY DONE-- HE USUALLY HIDES OUT IN THE SHACKS AFTER A JOB! ROOM 31!
THANKS!

THE SHACKS! A CROOKED ROW OF WEATHER-BEATEN OLD HOUSES THAT SERVE AS A CRIMINAL HIDEOUT ON THE EDGE OF THE WATERFRONT!
NOT EXACTLY CHEERFUL-LOOKING, ARE THEY?
THEY'RE DANGEROUS RATHOLES FILLED WITH HUMAN RODENTS! ONCE WE WALK IN THERE, WE WALK INTO TROUBLE!

THE BATMAN! THE WHOLE HOUSE COMES TO LIFE AS THAT DREADED NAME SWEEPS THROUGH THE HALLS LIKE A PRAIRIE FIRE!

THE BATMAN IS HERE!

THE BATMAN!

UP THOSE STAIRS, ROBIN!

FIGURES HURTLE AT THEM, BUT THE BATMAN AND ROBIN TWIST ASIDE, ELUDING THEM!

EVERY TRICK OF THEIR CAREER IS BROUGHT INTO PLAY AS THE BATMAN AND ROBIN BATTLE THEIR WAY FORWARD!

UP AND AT 'EM, ROBIN!

BATMAN WE CAN'T KEEP THEM OFF FOREVER!

YOU'RE RIGHT! I'LL TAKE CARE OF THAT SITUATION!

THE BATMAN EXTRACTS A GLASS VIAL FROM HIS UTILITY BELT----AND HURLS IT AT THE THUGS MASSED AT THE BOTTOM OF THE STAIRS!

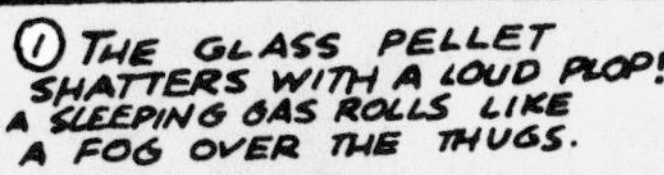
1 THE GLASS PELLET SHATTERS WITH A LOUD PLOP! A SLEEPING GAS ROLLS LIKE A FOG OVER THE THUGS.

GAS? MY THROAT!
CAN'T SEE!

2 A SECOND LATER, THE HOODLUMS LIE UNCONSCIOUS ON THE FLOOR!
THEY'RE SLEEPING LIKE BABIES? WHAT NOW?
ROOM NO. 31-- TOOTHY'S ROOM!

3 THE BATMAN PUSHES THE DOOR OPEN. HE AND ROBIN FLING THEMSELVES TO THE SIDE AS BULLETS BLAST PAST THEM!
WE DARE YA TA! HAW!
COME AND GET US, BATMAN-- IF YOU CAN! HAW HAW!

4 WITH THE SWIFTNESS OF CHAIN-LIGHTNING, THE BOY WONDER CHARGES INTO THE ROOM!

A BAG OF WIND-- I THOUGHT SO!

5
NOTHING I LIKE BETTER THAN A GOOD DARE!

6
OVER YOU GO, SONNY!
HEY-- TOOTHY'S RUN OUT ON US!

7
WENT DOWN THE FIRE ESCAPE, THE YELLOW MUTT, AND HE'S THE GUY THAT CLOUTED ME--

...I CAN'T LET HIM GET AWAY WITH THAT!

THE BOY WONDER DROPS LIKE A PLUMMET TO THE SPEEDING CAR!
YOU LITTLE BRAT...I SHOULDA PLUGGED YOU THE LAST TIME!
YOUR MISTAKE, TOOTHY--BUT IT'S TOO LATE NOW!

AS THE STRUGGLING FIGURES SWAY TO AND FRO, THE CAR CAREENS MADLY---AND PLUNGES OFF THE PIER!

WITH FEAR IN HIS HEART, THE BATMAN RACES TO THE PIER'S EDGE!
ROBIN! ROBIN! ARE YOU ALL RIGHT?

I'M ALL RIGHT--- BUT TOOTHY ISN'T..... ONLY I THINK FROM NOW ON WE OUGHT TO CALL HIM TOOTHLESS!!

SOMETIME AFTER--
WELL, WE GOT YOUR FURS AND JEWELS BACK, NOW WE ---SAY- WHAT'S WRONG?
EVERYTHING! MOTHER AND DAD WANT TO SEE ME ACT IN THE PLAY I'M SUPPOSED TO BE STARRING IN. NOW THEY'LL FIND OUT I'M ONLY THE UNDERSTUDY!

THE BATMAN LEAVES AND SEEKS OUT THE STAR OF THE PLAY
YOU SEE THE SPOT THE POOR KID IS ON. LET HER TAKE YOUR PART IN THE PLAY TOMORROW NIGHT. HOW ABOUT IT?
OF COURSE. BESIDES, IT WOULD BE MY LAST PERFORMANCE, ANYWAY.
SURE -SHE HAS TO LEAVE FOR HOLLYWOOD AFTER THE SHOW--GOING TO DO A PICTURE.

BUT---
BUT---
NO BUTS! YOU'RE GOING TO STAR IN THE PLAY! EVEN YOUR NAME WILL BE IN BRIGHT LIGHTS ON THE MARQUEE!

THE NEXT NIGHT, AS BRUCE WAYNE ONCE MORE, HE ESCORTS THE OLD COUPLE TO THE THEATRE
THERE THEY ARE. THEY'VE COME TO SEE THE UNDERSTUDY PLAY THE STARRING ROLE-- NOT REALIZING SHE ISN'T THE STAR!
THE OLD DEARS MUST BE SO THRILLED!

THE HOUSELIGHTS DIM-- THE CURTAINS PART-- THE PLAY BEGINS--AND VIOLA VANE ACTS AS SHE'S NEVER ACTED BEFORE!
I WISH THERE WERE A JUMPING OFF PLACE WHERE I---

AND WHEN THE CURTAIN COMES DOWN UPON THE LAST ACT----
I NEVER KNEW SHE COULD ACT LIKE THAT! JUST LISTEN TO THAT APPLAUSE. THAT'S HER FIFTH CURTAIN CALL!

BUT NOW VIOLA VANE IS ACTING FOR TWO PEOPLE AN OLD MAN AND AN OLD WOMAN... HER PARENTS!
VIOLA---YOU'RE TAKING OVER THE ROLE WHEN THE STAR GOES TO HOLLYWOOD. I WAS GOING TO GET A BIG-NAME ACTRESS-- BUT I'VE CHANGED MY MIND. YOU'RE GOING TO BE MY NEW STAR!
A STAR! I'M A STAR AT LAST!

AND THE NEXT DAY AS VIOLA'S PARENTS TAKE THEIR LEAVE---
VIOLA, MOTHER AND I WILL NEVER FORGET THIS LITTLE TRIP!
YOU'RE A FINE ACTRESS, VIOLA---A FINE ACTRESS! THAT WAS A GREAT ROLE YOU PLAYED ON THE STAGE.
DEAR MOTHER AND FATHER, IF YOU ONLY KNEW THE ROLE I PLAYED OFF STAGE. THAT WAS WHEN I DID MY BEST ACTING!

......LATER AS THE OLD PEOPLE SIT IN THE TRAIN---
MY! WEREN'T THE PEOPLE NICE TO VIOLA! YOU KNOW, MOTHER, I HAD A FUNNY FEELING ALL THE TIME THAT PEOPLE WERE LOOKING AT US IT WAS AS IF--- AS IF---
AS IF THEY WERE SHARING SOME SORT OF BIG SECRET WITH EACH OTHER-BUT I GUESS IT WAS ONLY OUR IMAGIN-ATION.

AND AS BRUCE WAYNE ONCE AGAIN CHATS WITH HIS FRIEND, JIM DALY---
BRUCE, I GUESS I MUST APOLO-GIZE TO YOU! NOW I CAN SEE THE CITY DOES HAVE A HEART AFTER ALL!
YES--ONLY ONE MUST TEAR AWAY THE FALSE PRETENSE AND SHAM TO FIND IT-BUT IT'S THERE--IT'S THERE FOR US TO FIND IF WE CARE TO LOOK DEEP ENOUGH!
BOB KANE

No. 2

A DC PUBLICATION IND

WORLD'S FINEST COMICS

96 PAGES

15¢

FORMERLY WORLD'S BEST COMICS

SUPERMAN • ZATARA

BATMAN AND ROBIN

RED, WHITE AND BLUE

BATMAN
REG. U.S. PAT. OFF.
WITH Robin -THE BOY WONDER-
by BOB KANE
IN GREAT CITIES ALL OVER THE WORLD...... FROM THE FLOURISHING CAPITALS OF THE WESTERN WORLD TO THE ARID DESERTS OF THE FAR EAST, ONE NAME HAS BECOME A SYMBOL OF JUSTICE.....ONE NAME HAS STRUCK FEAR INTO THE HEARTS OF MEN OF CRIME---- THAT IS THE NAME OF THE BATMAN! MASTER OF DARKNESS...FOE OF ALL EVIL, THE BATMAN, WITH HIS YOUNG AIDE, ROBIN THE BOY WONDER, HAS WAGED UNCEASING WAR AGAINST THE DENIZENS OF THE UNDERWORLD AND DELIVERED A MORTAL BLOW TO ORGANIZED CRIME. LET US PICK UP THEIR TRAIL NOW AS THEY LEAD US INTO THE MEMORABLE CASE OF... "THE MAN WHO COULDN'T REMEMBER!"
FOR THE PAST TWO MONTHS, GOTHAM CITY HAS SEEN THE FLARE-UP BETWEEN TWO RIVAL GANGS. THE RESULT IS-----
GOTHAM GAZETTE 12¢
GANG WAR!

ON A SUNNY AFTERNOON, AS EAGER SHOPPERS CROWD THE STREETS, A CAR SCREECHES 'ROUND A CORNER, THE SNOUT OF A MACHINE GUN FLAMING SUDDEN DEATH.
SO LONG, FRANKIE!
NO! NO! AAAH---
ROBIN & SON

THE CAR WHIPS OUT OF SIGHT, LEAVING BEHIND TWO SPRAWLED FIGURES-- A RIVAL GANGSTER--- AND AN INNOCENT, OLD MAN!
THE OLD GUY'S HURT BAD. SOMEBODY CALL AN AMBULANCE.
THOSE ROTTEN KILLERS! SOMETHING OUGHT TO BE DONE ABOUT THEM.
NOT WITH THE CROOKED D.A. WE'VE GOT!

LETTERS FROM INDIGNANT CITIZENS POUR IN TO NEWSPAPER OFFICES. RADIO BROADCASTS ARE MADE. FINALLY, THE GOVERNOR HIMSELF INTERVENES, HE APPOINTS A SPECIAL PROCECUTOR TO TAKE CHARGE--- A BRAVE, COURAGEOUS MAN NAMED WILLIAM KENDRICK.
I'M GOING AFTER THE RACKETEERS IN THIS TOWN! I DON'T CARE HOW IMPORTANT THEY ARE- I'M GOING AFTER THEM!
WOW! I WONDER WHAT BIG TIM BANNON WILL SAY TO THIS!

AND WHEN INTERVIEWED, BIG TIM BANNON, POLITICAL BOSS OF THE CITY, SAYS....
THIS GUY KENDRICK TALKS BIG. NOW LET'S SEE HIM ACT BIG!

AND OUSTED DISTRICT ATTORNEY GRAVES SAYS....
HE'S GOING TO FIND THAT GETTING RID OF RACKETS IN THIS TOWN ISN'T SO EASY. I OUGHT TO KNOW!
BUT, OF COURSE, WE KNOW THE FORMER D.A. IS AND WAS IN BANNON'S PAY!

-AND SAYS MITCH MASON, OF THE WEST SIDE MOBSTERS.....
WHO...KENDRICK? NAW--WE AIN'T WORRYIN' ABOUT HIM. HE'S THE GUY THAT SHOULD WORRY!
...AND TRIG COOLER, HEAD OF THE RIVAL EAST SIDE MOB--
ALL I GOTTA SAY IS KENDRICK SHOULDN'T OUGHTA WORK TOO HARD- IT AIN'T HEALTHY!

IN RETALIATION TO THESE THREATS, A CITIZENS' COMMITTEE IS FORMED, WITH WEALTHY BUSINESSMAN AMBROSE TAYLOR AT ITS HEAD.
WE CITIZENS ARE BEHIND KENDRICK. WE INTEND TO GIVE HIM EVERY SUPPORT, IN SPITE OF PRESSURE BY CERTAIN POLITICAL GROUPS!

KENDRICK GOES TO WORK WITH A VENGEANCE. INSIDE A WEEK, MOST OF THE MINOR RACKETEERS ARE IMPRISONED.
...AND NOW I'M AFTER THE BIG-SHOT RACKETEERS. I KNOW THEM AND THEIR CONNECTIONS...AND HAVE EVERY FACT WRITTEN DOWN IN WHAT I CALL MY "LITTLE BLACK BOOK!"
NEWS OF THE LITTLE BLACK BOOK TRAVELS THROUGH THE TOWN LIKE WILDFIRE---

A DAY LATER, KENDRICK CHATS WITH A SOCIETY FRIEND, BRUCE WAYNE.
WHEN YOU MENTIONED THAT LITTLE BLACK BOOK, YOU WERE SORT OF SIGNING YOUR OWN DEATH WARRANT... OR DIDN'T YOU KNOW?
I'VE HAD NOTES THREATENING DEATH SENT ME ALREADY, BUT THAT ISN'T GOING TO STOP ME ONE BIT!

SO YOU HAVE HAD DEATH THREATS SENT YOU..? THESE MOBSTERS DON'T LOSE ANY TIME.
FORGET IT! IF YOU'RE NOT DOING ANYTHING TONIGHT, WHY NOT COME UP FOR DINNER? IT'S THE SERVANTS' NIGHT OFF. I'LL BE ALL ALONE!

LATER THAT DAY....
..YES-- THE WAITER HEARD KENDRICK SAY HE'D BE ALL ALONE TONIGHT.
YEAH? WELL--- MAYBE WE OUGHTA GO UP AND KEEP HIM COMPANY.

....AND IN A CERTAIN MOBSTER'S HEADQUARTERS----
I JUST GOT THE TIP-OFF THAT KENDRICK IS GONNA BE BY HIS LONESOME TONIGHT.
THIS IS JUST THE BREAK WE BEEN WAITIN' FOR. CALL A COUPLA THE BOYS IN! THIS IS PERFECT!

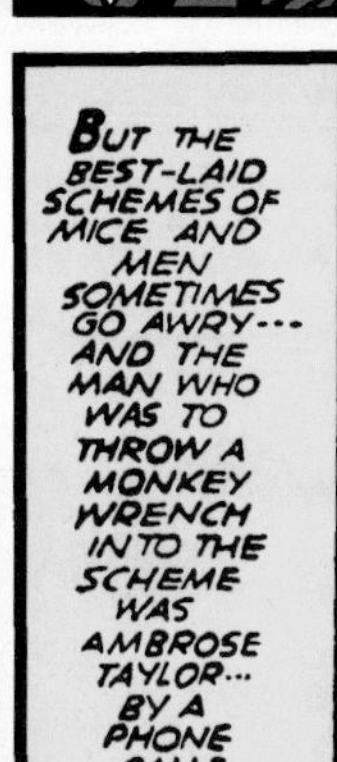
BUT THE BEST-LAID SCHEMES OF MICE AND MEN SOMETIMES GO AWRY--- AND THE MAN WHO WAS TO THROW A MONKEY WRENCH INTO THE SCHEME WAS AMBROSE TAYLOR... BY A PHONE CALL!

IS IT POSSIBLE TO SEE YOU THIS EVENING? I HAVE SOME SPECIAL NEWS FROM THE CITIZENS' COMMITTEE.
BY ALL MEANS, I'LL BE QUITE ALONE, AND NO ONE WILL DISTURB US AS WE TALK.

NIGHT CLOAKS THE CITY, BRINGING WITH IT THE BEGINNING OF A STRANGE ADVENTURE. IN HIS APARTMENT, BRUCE WAYNE SPEAKS WITH HIS YOUNG WARD, DICK GRAYSON.
I DON'T LIKE THE IDEA OF KENDRICK BEING ALL ALONE TONIGHT!...I THINK I'LL KEEP AN EYE ON HIM!
I DON'T BLAME YOU. HE SURE LEFT HIMSELF WIDE OPEN FOR TROUBLE BY MENTIONING THAT LITTLE BLACK BOOK!

INSTEAD OF BRUCE WAYNE, SOCIETY PLAYBOY--THE BATMAN! SILENTLY, A BLOTTED SHAPE IN THE GLOOM, THE BATMAN RACES THROUGH THE NIGHT!

AS HE REACHES KENDRICK'S LODGINGS, HE NOTICES A CAR IDLING NEARBY.....
THAT CAR.... FROM THE LICENSE NUMBER, I CAN TELL IT'S BANNON'S! SOMETHING'S UP!

NOISELESSLY AS A JUNGLE CAT, HE MOVES UP THE FIRE ESCAPE---

-AND BURSTS IN KENDRICK'S ROOM UPON A HORRIBLE SCENE!

THE BATMAN!

WHAT...? KENDRICK... TAYLOR!

THE BATMAN BECOMES A THUNDERBOLT OF FURY!!!

YOU ROTTEN MURDERERS!

THAT'S IT! HOLD HIM SO I CAN PLUG HIM!

HE'S ALIVE JUST HAD HIS SCALP CREASED BY A BULLET! NOW FOR KENDRICK!

THE BATMAN PROPS UP KENDRICK JUST IN TIME TO HEAR HIS LAST WORDS!
BATMAN-- HOME-- BLACK BOOK-- DEVIL'S DUNGEON-- AAAAH--

THE BLACK BOOK-HOME-- DEVIL'S DUNGEON! WHERE CAN THAT BE! I---A FACE AT THE WINDOW!

I KNOW THAT FACE. THAT WAS GRAVES-- NOW WHAT WAS HE DOING HERE? MMM!

THIS ROOM MUST BE SOUNDPROOF OR ELSE THE POLICE WOULD BE HERE BY NOW. BETTER GET TAYLOR SOME MEDICAL ATTENTION. HE'S A VERY VALUABLE MAN NOW!

YES, SIR. TAYLOR IS THE ONLY WITNESS TO KENDRICK'S MURDER. HE CAN PICK OUT THE MAN WHO SHOT HIM---AND MAYBE IT WASN'T THOSE THUGS, EITHER!

WHY WAS BANNON'S CAR PARKED NEARBY? WHY DID GRAVES PEER IN THE WINDOW? MAYBE ONE OF THOSE TWO SHOT KENDRICK. I'LL KNOW SOON ENOUGH WHEN TAYLOR COMES TO!

AS THE BATMAN REACHES THE STREET WITH HIS PRECIOUS BURDEN, BULLETS WHINE THICKLY ABOUT HIM, SPATTERING THE WALL BEHIND
OH-OH! TROUBLE!
5

IN ONE LIGHTNING MOVE, THE BATMAN FLATTENS HIMSELF AND TAYLOR AGAINST THE GROUND--- AND NONE TOO SOON.
THEY MUST HAVE BEEN WAITING. IF I CAN JUST REACH THAT BRICK--
TAT-TAT-TAT
RAT-TAT-TAT
RAT-TAT-TAT
RAT-TAT-TAT
RAT-TAT-TAT

THE BATMAN HURLS THE BRICK INTO THE FACE OF THE MACHINE-GUNNER---

WITH A CLASH OF GEARS, THE CAR LEAPS AWAY.
EVIDENTLY, SOMEONE DOESN'T WANT TAYLOR TO LIVE TO TESTIFY WHO MURDERED KENDRICK----THUGS--- BANNON'S CAR-- DRIVEN AWAY BY GRAVES. THIS GROWS INTERESTING!

MINUTES LATER--THE APARTMENT OF LINDA PAGE, A SOCIETY GIRL WHO HAS BECOME A NURSE IN ORDER TO MAKE SOMETHING OF HERSELF.
BATMAN! WHAT-- WHO--?
THIS MAN'S BEEN HURT! HE NEEDS ATTENTION QUICKLY!

UNDER LINDA'S EXPERT NURSING, TAYLOR SOON REGAINS CONSCIOUSNESS-
YOU'RE ALL RIGHT NOW, TAYLOR. NOW TELL ME. YOU SAW KENDRICK SHOT. WHO DID IT?
SHOT----? YES-- SHOTS! I HEARD THEM!

YES--I KNOW. BUT YOU KNOW WHO SHOT KENDRICK AND YOURSELF? WHO WAS IT?
I-I-- DON'T REMEMBER-- I DON'T REMEMBER ANYTHING!
6

WHAT? BUT---
BATMAN, I'VE SEEN THIS TYPE OF CASE BEFORE. THIS MAN HAS AMNESIA!! THE BULLET THAT HIT THE TOP OF HIS HEAD HAS CAUSED HIM TO TEMPORARILY LOSE HIS MEMORY!

WH-AT? AMNESIA? OF ALL THE... TELL ME, HOW LONG WILL IT BE BEFORE HE REGAINS HIS MEMORY?
IT VARIES, MAYBE TODAY--MAYBE TOMORROW-MAYBE NEXT MONTH -MAYBE NEXT YEAR ONE NEVER KNOWS!

OF ALL THE BREAKS! HERE I HAVE A WITNESS TO A MURDER---AND HE LOSES HIS MEMORY! AND THAT ISN'T ALL! KENDRICK DIES SAYING-- "HOME.... BLACK BOOK.... DEVIL'S DUNGEON!"

DEVIL'S DUNGEON! UGH! I CAN'T QUITE PICTURE A BLACK BOOK IN-
PICTURE! I'VE GOT IT! BUT WAIT--GRAVES WAS AT THE WINDOW WHEN KENDRICK TALKED--BUT I DON'T IMAGINE HE HEARD KENDRICK.

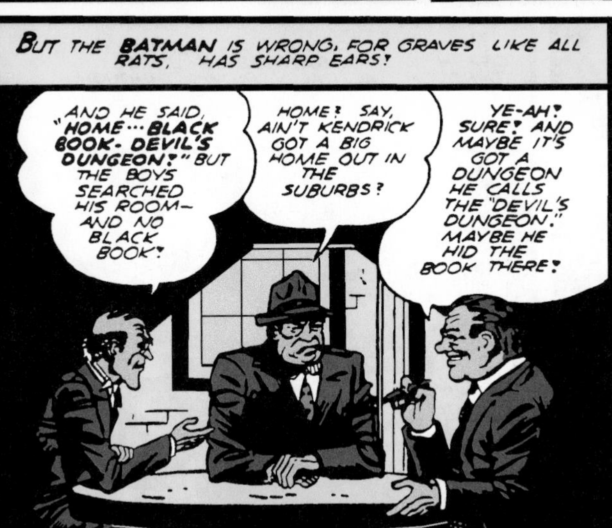
BUT THE BATMAN IS WRONG, FOR GRAVES LIKE ALL RATS, HAS SHARP EARS!
"AND HE SAID, "HOME...BLACK BOOK- DEVIL'S DUNGEON!" BUT THE BOYS SEARCHED HIS ROOM-AND NO BLACK BOOK!
HOME? SAY, AIN'T KENDRICK GOT A BIG HOME OUT IN THE SUBURBS?
YE-AH! SURE! AND MAYBE IT'S GOT A DUNGEON HE CALLS THE "DEVIL'S DUNGEON." MAYBE HE HID THE BOOK THERE!

WE BETTER GET THAT BOOK BEFORE THE BATMAN GETS IT, OR WE'RE COOKED!
YE-AH GET ALL THE BOYS TOGETHER, WE'LL RIDE UP THERE IN TWO CARS! AND AFTER WE GET THE BLACK BOOK..
— I'LL GET THE BOYS TO FINISH THE JOB THEY STARTED ON TAYLOR!

AND AT THAT MOMENT-
I'LL TELL ROBIN TO FETCH THE BATMOBILE WE'RE GOING TO KENDRICK'S HOME AND I'M TAKING TAYLOR WITH ME IN CASE HE SUDDENLY REMEMBERS.
I'M COMING WITH YOU THEN. HE'S STILL A SICK MAN AND MAY HAVE A RELAPSE, AND DON'T ARGUE WITH ME I'M A NURSE.

A SHORT TIME LATER, A CAR STREAKS LIKE A BULLET UP THE ROAD LEADING TO THE SUBURBS IT IS THE BATMOBILE!

IT WHIZZES PAST TWO SLOWER MOVING CARS TRAVELING THE SAME ROAD----THE CARS CONTAINING BANNON AND THE MOBSTERS!
WOW! DID YOU SEE THAT? THE BAT-MOBILE--- GOING LIKE A SHOT!
C'MON, I KNOW THESE ROADS THERE'S A SHORT-CUT THAT WILL GIVE US A CHANCE TO BEAT HIM TO THE HOUSE!

BANNON'S KNOWLEDGE OF THE SHORT-CUT ENABLES THE MOBSTERS TO BEAT THE BATMOBILE TO A TURN IN THE ROAD NEAR THE HOUSE-
WHAT'S THE IDEA OF PUTTING THE CARS LIKE THAT?
LOOK—THE BATMAN WILL COME AROUND THAT TURN FAST---SO FAST HE WON'T BE ABLE TO STOP. HE'LL CRASH AND THAT WILL BE HIS FINISH!

AND A SCANT FEW MOMENTS LATER--
LOOK OUT! WE'RE GOING TO CRASH!
CAN'T STOP IN TIME -- CAN'T TURN —HIT TREES-- ONLY ONE THING TO DO--

---STEP ON THE GAS AND GO---

THERE IS A DEAFENING, RENDING CRASH AS THE BATMOBILE BORES THROUGH, ACTUALLY PLOWS THROUGH THE CARS, TOSSING THEM ASIDE LIKE FLIMSY, WOODEN BOXES!!
--THROUGH!!

WOW! DID YOU SEE THAT? I STILL CAN'T BELIEVE IT!
YEAH! C'MON! THERES NO TIME TO WASTE! THE HOUSE IS NOT FAR FROM HERE!

OH MY-- AREN'T THE ROADS BUMPY!
GOOD GIRL-- SHE'S GOT NERVE! WHEW! GOOD THING THIS CAR IS MADE OF A SPECIAL REINFORCED GLASS AND STEEL! THAT MUST HAVE BEEN BANNON AND HIS MOB!

A FEW MINUTES LATER, THE BATMOBILE APPROACHES A SOLITARY HOUSE THAT LOOMS SULLEN AGAINST THE FROWNING SKY---

THE BATMAN FORCES HIS ENTRY WITH A PASS-KEY. THE DOOR CREAKS SLOWLY INWARD AND THE LARGE, EMPTY HOUSE STRETCHES BEFORE THEM LIKE THE YAWNING JAWS OF A COLOSSAL MONSTER!
CHEERFUL-LOOKING PLACE... I DON'T THINK!
NO LIGHTS! ELECTRICITY MUST HAVE BEEN SHUT OFF!

TREADING SOFTLY, AS IF NOT TO AWAKEN THE GHOSTS OF THOSE LONG DEAD, THE GROUP MOUNTS THE STAIRCASE.
IT'S A LUCKY THING YOU FOUND THAT CANDLE!
SHH! FOLLOW ME!

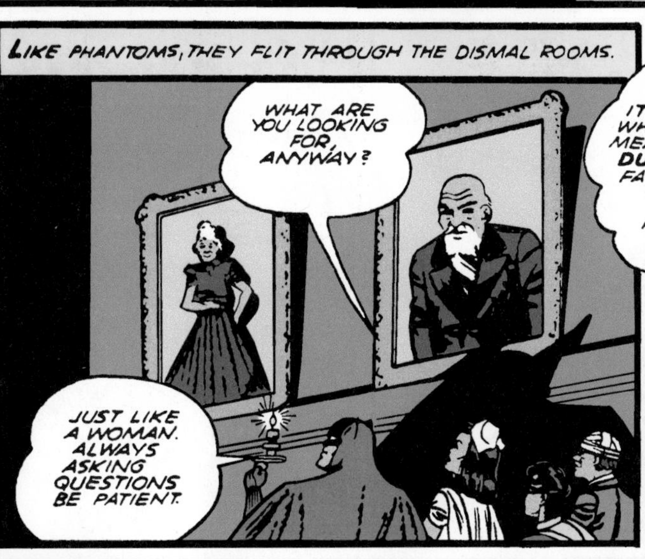
LIKE PHANTOMS, THEY FLIT THROUGH THE DISMAL ROOMS.
WHAT ARE YOU LOOKING FOR, ANYWAY?
JUST LIKE A WOMAN. ALWAYS ASKING QUESTIONS BE PATIENT.

THIS IS IT! THIS IS WHAT KENDRICK MEANT. "DEVIL'S DUNGEON!" A FAMOUS PAINTING BY THE ARTIST ROUSSAL!

...AND BEHIND THE PICTURE, WHERE KENDRICK HID IT... IS THE BLACK BOOK!
9

THAT'S ONE POINT SETTLED! NOW, TAYLOR... DO YOU REMEMBER NOW WHO SHOT KENDRICK AND YOURSELF? THINK, MAN... THINK!!
I...I--I'M TRYING... BUT I CAN'T REMEMBER!

SUDDENLY, THEY HEAR THE DOOR BURST OPEN DOWN-STAIRS. VOICES ARE RAISED IN ANGRY SHOUTS!
THAT WOULD BE BANNON AND HIS MEN.
THEY DON'T KNOW TAYLOR IS HERE. THEY'LL KILL HIM IF THEY FIND HIM. QUICK! IN HERE! ROBIN AND I WILL STAND THEM OFF!

As Robin advances to the head of the stairs, Bannon lets out a shout!
This table is just what I need!
There's that Robin kid. Let's get him!
Just like going sleigh riding!
Huh?... Look out!
He's going to hit us!

Wheeee... some fun.

The dazed men pick themselves up at the bottom of the stairs---
We'll split up. Half of you get that kid. We others will go up and get the Batman!

But as the men chase after the nimble Robin, the boy leaps---
There he goes! C'mon!

And then swings back --- with amazing results!
Tch-tch! You should look where you're going!

MEANWHILE, BANNON AND GRAVES LOSE THEIR WAY IN THE CLOSE-PRESSING DARKNESS.
WE'RE SEPARATED FROM THE MEN!
ANYBODY COULD LOSE HIMSELF IN THIS DARK PLACE. CAN'T SEE A THING!
I CAN'T SEE THEM, BUT THOSE VOICES TELL ME BANNON AND GRAVES ARE HERE!

FROM A POUCH, ESPECIALLY BUILT IN HIS BELT, THE BATMAN TAKES A QUEER-LOOKING PAIR OF GLASSES
NOW I'LL HAVE SOME FUN!

THOUGH HE HIMSELF CANNOT BE SEEN, WITH THESE ESPECIALLY PREPARED GLASSES, THE BATMAN CAN SEE IN THE DARK---AS WOULD A REAL BAT!
I WOULDN'T STRIKE THAT MATCH IF I WERE YOU, BANNON!
THE BATMAN! BUT HOW DID HE KNOW--?IT'S PITCH BLACK IN HERE!

THE BATMAN, THROUGH A THOROUGH STUDY OF VENTRILOQUISM, CAN THROW HIS VOICE IN ANY DIRECTION HE PLEASES.
AND YOU HAD BETTER LEAVE THAT GUN IN YOUR POCKET, GRAVES!
HOW--?

THE MEN SHUDDER IN TERROR AT THE "SUPERNATURAL" POWER OF THE BATMAN!
BANNON! HE CAN SEE! HE CAN SEE IN THE DARK!
IT'S UNCANNY! THAT GUY SEES IN THE DARK LIKE A REAL BAT! LET'S GET OUT OF HERE!
11

IT'S JUST THAT I DON'T WANT TO SOIL MY HANDS ON YOU TWO!

SUDDENLY, A SCREAM RINGS THROUGH THE HOUSE. THE FEW REMAINING THUGS HAVE FOUND LINDA AND TAYLOR!
LOOK! A DAME... AND TAYLOR!
WELL! BOY, ARE WE GLAD TO SEE YOU!
A GUN BUTT CRASHES DOWN ON TAYLOR'S HEAD!
LET GO OF ME, YOU BEASTS!
THIS FOR YOU, CHUM!
DIS DAME IS A WILD CAT!

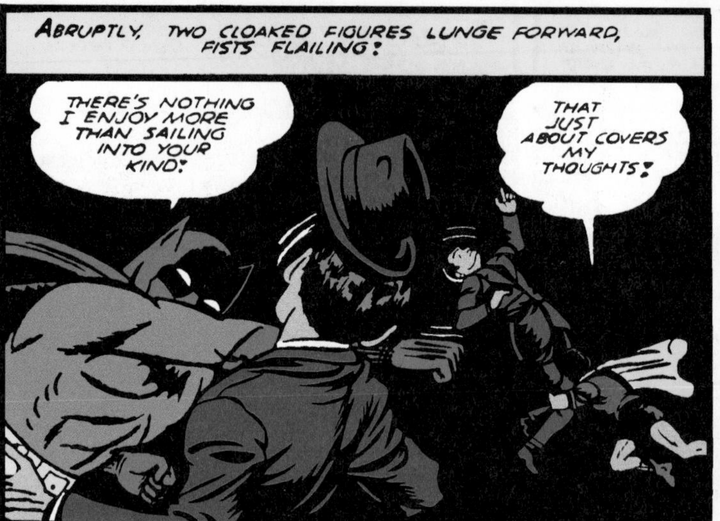
ABRUPTLY, TWO CLOAKED FIGURES LUNGE FORWARD, FISTS FLAILING!
THERE'S NOTHING I ENJOY MORE THAN SAILING INTO YOUR KIND!
THAT JUST ABOUT COVERS MY THOUGHTS!

IN A FEW, FLYING MOMENTS, THE THUGS HAVE BEEN FLATTENED AND TRUSSED UP WITH THE OTHERS!
HE'S COMING ROUND NOW.
I...I... WAIT.. IT'S COMING BACK TO ME! I REMEMBER NOW!
WHA..! THE BLOW ON THE HEAD DID IT!

I REMEMBER! I KILLED KENDRICK! THEN TRIG COOLER'S BOYS CAME IN AND SHOT ME!

SUDDENLY, TAYLOR CUTS OFF HIS WORDS AS HE REALIZES WHAT HE HAS SAID IN HIS EXCITEMENT HIS HAND FLASHES TO A POCKET...
YES.. I KILLED HIM...WITH THIS VERY GUN! A FAT LOT OF GOOD IT WILL DO YOU TO KNOW!
THE AMAZING CONFESSION HAS SO ASTOUNDED THE BATMAN THAT FOR ONCE HE HAS BEEN CAUGHT FLATFOOTED...

....BUT NOT FOR LONG! A SHOT BUZZES OVER HIS HEAD AS HE LEAPS!

THE TWO LOCK GRIPS! BACK AND FORTH THEY SWAY ONTO THE HALL BALCONY IN A WILD DERVISH OF DEATH!

WITH A TITANIC EFFORT, THE BATMAN TEARS A HAND FREE, WINDS IT INTO A FIST--- AND CRASHES IT AGAINST TAYLOR'S CHIN!

A SUDDEN SPLINTERING OF WOOD, AND TAYLOR PLUNGES THROUGH THE BALCONY RAILING!

TAYLOR--- THE MURDERER! IT DOESN'T MAKE SENSE!
SURE IT DOES. TAYLOR WAS THE REAL LEADER OF THE WEST SIDE MOBSTERS! MITCH MASON WAS ONLY HIS LIEUTENANT!
THEN HE SHOT KENDRICK BECAUSE HE THOUGHT HE KNEW--- AND HAD THE INFORMATION IN THE LITTLE BLACK BOOK!

WHEN MY BOYS WENT INTO THE ROOM TO FORCE KENDRICK TO GIVE UP THE BLACK BOOK, THEY SAW THAT TAYLOR SHOT HIM. THEY TRIED TO GET TAYLOR 'CAUSE HE WAS FROM THE RIVAL MOB.
HMM! YOU WERE WORKING WITH BANNON-- GIVING HIM A CUT FOR POLITICAL PROTECTION! BUT WHY DIDN'T YOU JUST TELL THE POLICE TAYLOR WAS THE MURDERER? YOU'D HAVE RID YOURSELF OF HIM THAT WAY.
BOB KANE

IF WE SQUEALED ON TAYLOR, TAYLOR WOULD TALK HE KNOWS THINGS ABOUT A LOT OF US THAT MIGHT GET US IN PRISON CELLS, TOO!
A CASE OF SELF-PROTECTION WELL, NOW ALL THAT'S LEFT TO DO IS GIVE THE BLACK BOOK TO THE POLICE AND LET THEM TAKE OVER.

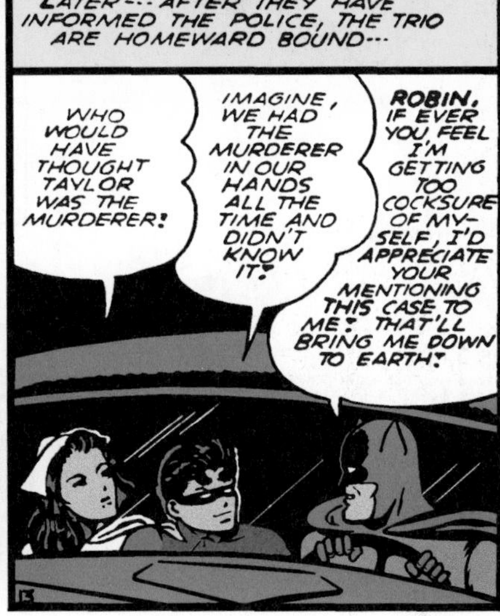
LATER--- AFTER THEY HAVE INFORMED THE POLICE, THE TRIO ARE HOMEWARD BOUND---
WHO WOULD HAVE THOUGHT TAYLOR WAS THE MURDERER!
IMAGINE, WE HAD THE MURDERER IN OUR HANDS ALL THE TIME AND DIDN'T KNOW IT!
ROBIN, IF EVER YOU FEEL I'M GETTING TOO COCKSURE OF MY-SELF, I'D APPRECIATE YOUR MENTIONING THIS CASE TO ME! THAT'LL BRING ME DOWN TO EARTH!
13

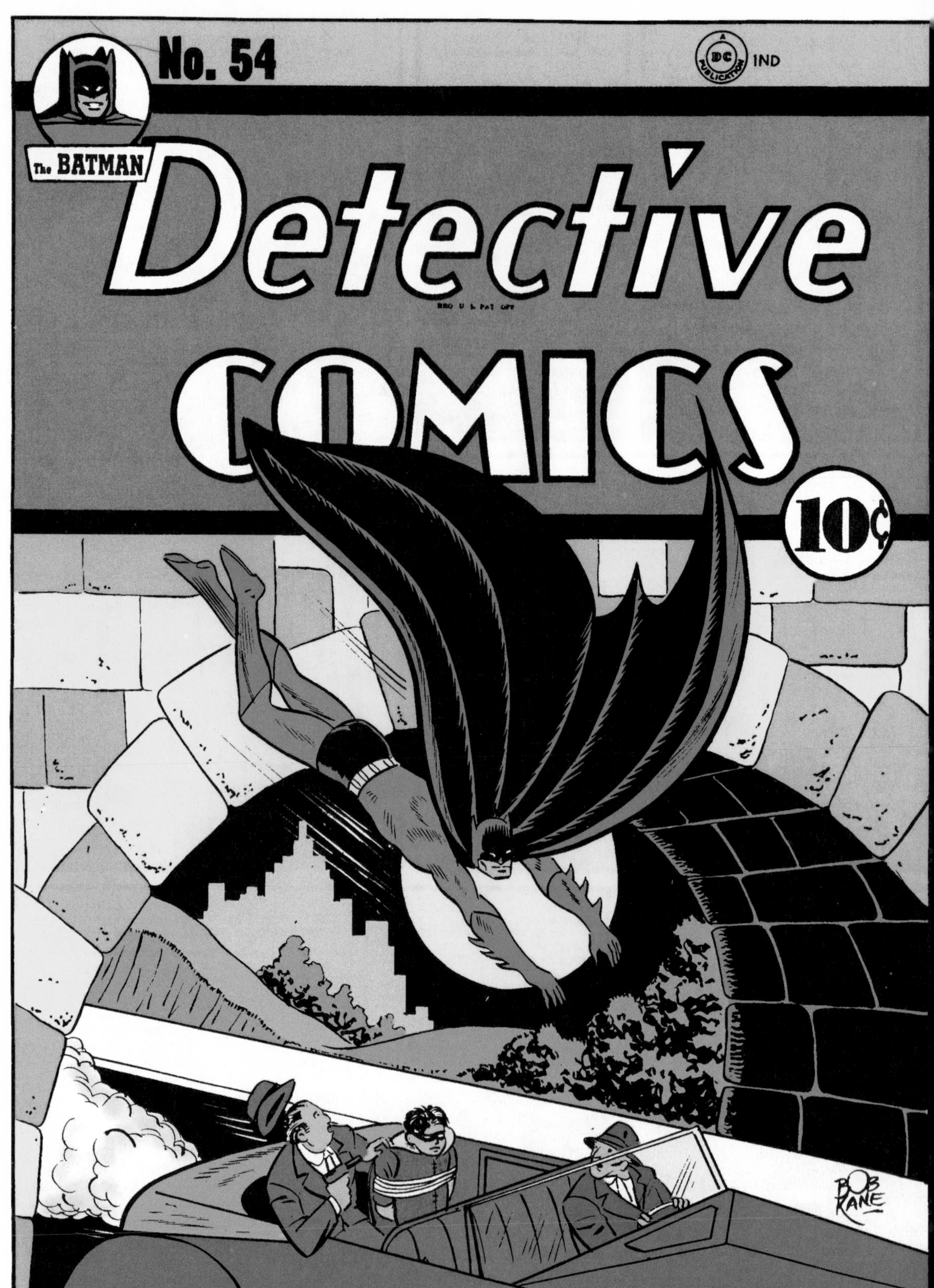
No. 54
A DC PUBLICATION
IND
The BATMAN
Detective
COMICS
10¢
BOB KANE

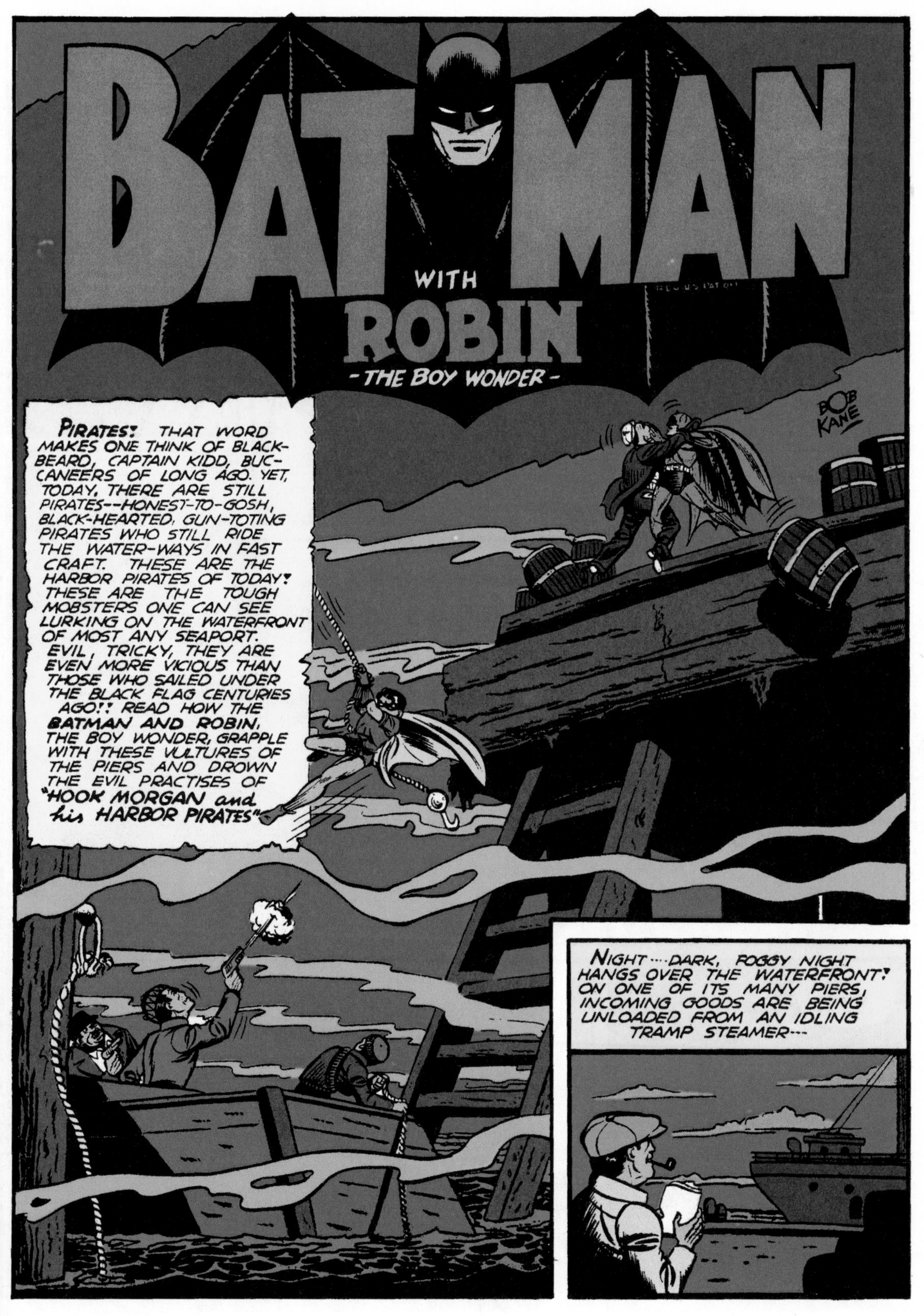
BATMAN
WITH
ROBIN
-THE BOY WONDER-
BOB KANE
PIRATES! THAT WORD MAKES ONE THINK OF BLACK-BEARD, CAPTAIN KIDD, BUC-CANEERS OF LONG AGO. YET, TODAY, THERE ARE STILL PIRATES--HONEST-TO-GOSH, BLACK-HEARTED, GUN-TOTING PIRATES WHO STILL RIDE THE WATER-WAYS IN FAST CRAFT. THESE ARE THE HARBOR PIRATES OF TODAY! THESE ARE THE TOUGH MOBSTERS ONE CAN SEE LURKING ON THE WATERFRONT OF MOST ANY SEAPORT. EVIL, TRICKY, THEY ARE EVEN MORE VICIOUS THAN THOSE WHO SAILED UNDER THE BLACK FLAG CENTURIES AGO!! READ HOW THE BATMAN AND ROBIN, THE BOY WONDER, GRAPPLE WITH THESE VULTURES OF THE PIERS AND DROWN THE EVIL PRACTISES OF "HOOK MORGAN and his HARBOR PIRATES"
NIGHT....DARK, FOGGY NIGHT HANGS OVER THE WATERFRONT! ON ONE OF ITS MANY PIERS, INCOMING GOODS ARE BEING UNLOADED FROM AN IDLING TRAMP STEAMER---

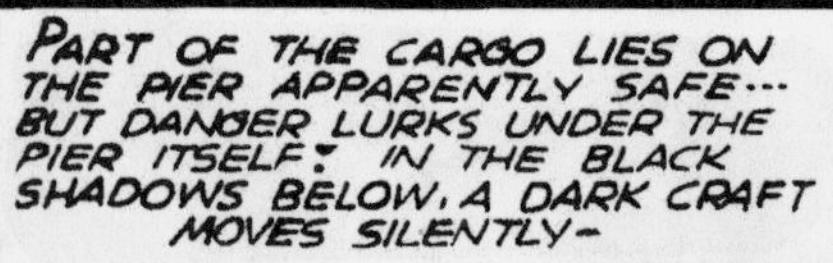

LIKE EVIL TERMITES, THE MEN BORE THROUGH THE WOODEN PIER--

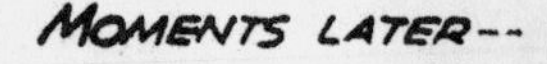

AS THE WHINING SNARL OF THE POLICE SIREN BREAKS OUT FROM THE CRAFT, AN ANSWER COMES INSTANTLY – RED FLAMES STAB THROUGH THE BLACK NIGHT!
HARBOR PIRATES!
THEY'RE FIRING BACK AT US! THAT CAN MEAN ONLY ONE THING!

THE POLICE BOAT CLEAVES THROUGH THE SWIRLING WATERS, RAPIDLY CLOSING THE GAP BETWEEN THE TWO BOATS
OPEN FIRE!

GET THAT LIGHT, SOMEBODY! THAT SEARCH-LIGHT! CAN'T SEE!

A HAIL OF LEAD SPRAYS THE POLICE SEARCHLIGHT!
LOOK OUT!

WHILE THE POLICE REPLACE THE LIGHT WITH A NEW BULB, THE PIRATE LAUNCH ROARS AWAY!
5

THE POLICE DOGGEDLY PURSUE THE SPEEDING PIRATE LAUNCH--BUT WHEN THE THE NEW SEARCHLIGHT COVERS THE WATERS WITH DAYLIGHT BRILLIANCE, THE POLICE FIND--
IT'S GONE! THE PIRATE BOAT IS GONE!

THE DAZZLING WHITE EYE OF THE SEARCHLIGHT LOOKS DOWN ON EMPTY WATERS!!
WE WERE RIGHT BEHIND IT! WHERE COULD IT HAVE GONE?
BLAMED IF I KNOW! ALL I KNOW IS IT'S GONE! THAT BOAT SEEMS TO HAVE VANISHED AS IF IT WERE PLUCKED OUT OF THE WATERS BY A GIANT HAND!

BUT LINDA IS WRONG...BRUCE WAYNE DOES MAKE USE OF THE NIGHT. IT IS NIGHT...DARK, MYSTERIOUS NIGHT THAT SHROUDS THE PERSONALITY OF THE BATMAN-

I'M GOING TO FIND OUT JUST HOW THAT STOLEN, EXCLUSIVE CLOTH GOT INTO THAT STORE I LOOKED AT TODAY. I'LL BET THE ANSWER WILL BE INTERESTING!

BATLIKE, HE FLITS THRU THE GLOOMY STREETS!

HOW'S BUSINESS?
FINE--- FINE---- OH-OH OH!

NOW TALK FAST OR I'M LIKELY TO GET VERY IMPATIENT! WHO SOLD YOU THAT CLOTH YOU FEATURE IN YOUR WINDOW--- AND WHAT'S THE FIRM'S ADDRESS?
S-SURE--- A MAN FROM THE CONROY MERCHANDISE COMPANY SOLD IT TO ME THIS AFTERNOON. THEY HAVE A WAREHOUSE ON THE EAST PIER ON 46 STREET!

AFTER THE BATMAN LEAVES-
DEAR---DEAR! A MASKED MAN- AND SUCH A QUEER COSTUME! PERHAPS HE'S A THIEF AND MEANS TO DO HARM TO MR. CONROY! I'D BETTER WARN HIM!

YES.... HE WAS MASKED! HAD A CAPE THAT LOOKED LIKE BATWINGS!
BATWINGS! THE BATMAN!
THANK YOU---AND I WOULDN'T CALL THE POLICE IF I WERE YOU! I'LL TAKE CARE OF THIS CRIMINAL!

HOOK, THE BATMAN! HE'S ON HIS WAY OVER! WHAT WILL WE DO?
THE BATMAN, EH? LET HIM SHOW HIS FACE IN HERE. MAYBE WE'LL MUSS IT UP A LITTLE FOR 'IM. YE-AH?

MINUTES LATER---
HELLO, MR. CONROY! WHAT'S NEW IN IMPORTED CLOTHS?
EH? WHO--- WHAT DO YOU WANT?

INSTANTLY, MANY FORMS LUNGE AT HIM FROM BEHIND THE STACKED BARRELS AND BALES
WHA... A TRAP!
OKAY, BOYS-- TAKE HIM!

YOU'LL HAVE TO BUILD A BETTER MOUSE TRAP TO CATCH ME!

THE BATMAN'S FISTS STRIKE WITH THE FURY OF TWIN THUNDERBOLTS!

TOUGH GUY, AIN'T CHA? THIS'LL SOFTEN YA UP!

BEFORE THE DAZED BATMAN CAN SHAKE OFF THE EFFECTS OF THE CRUEL BLOW, A ROPE IS PASSED ABOUT HIS WRISTS-
TIE THAT WILDCAT UP BEFORE HE STARTS ALL OVER AGAIN!
WOW! THAT GUY'S GOT A PUNCH LIKE THE KICK OF A MISSOURI MULE!
6

A BLAST OF COLD AIR STRIKES THE BATMAN AS HE IS THRUST INTO A THICK-WALLED REFRIGERATOR ROOM, USED TO STOCK STOLEN GOODS!
THIS OUGHTA COOL YOU OFF-PERMANENT! THE TEMPERATURE IS BELOW ZERO IN HERE! INSIDE OF A HALF HOUR YOU'RE GONNA BE NOTHING BUT ONE BIG CHUNK OF ICE!

TOO LATE THE BATMAN HURLS HIS BODY FORWARD! THE HEAVY REFRIGERATOR DOOR SLAMS SHUT!

AGAIN THE BATMAN'S MUSCULAR FRAME POUNDS, BATTERS AT THE STEEL DOOR IN A FUTILE ATTEMPT TO ESCAPE FROM THE MANTLE OF COLD THAT WRAPS ABOUT HIM!

THE BATMAN GROWS NUMB WITH COLD AS INVISIBLE ICE FINGERS TOUCH HIS SHIVERING BODY!

THE BATMAN BUTTS HIS HEAD AGAINST THE DANGLING LIGHT BULB---

---THE BULB SWINGS OUT IN A WIDE ARC!

AGAIN HE BUTTS AT IT--HARDER THIS TIME! IT SWINGS OUT FARTHER IN A WIDER SWEEPING ARC!

ONE MORE JAB OF THE BATMAN'S HEAD AND THE BULB SWINGS OUT---OUT TILL IT SHATTERS AGAINST A REFRIGERATOR WALL!

THE BATMAN LIES ON THE FLOOR, HIS HANDS PROBING FOR A JAGGED PIECE OF THE SMASHED GLASS BULB!

WITH THE RAZOR-SHARP SLIVER BETWEEN FINGERS ALMOST NUMB WITH COLD, HE SAWS AWAY AT HIS BONDS--

FREE! NOW THE BATMAN BRINGS FORTH A VIAL FROM HIS UTILITY BELT--

NOW, CONROY, BEFORE I EXERCISE MY KNUCKLES ON YOUR FACE... **TALK!** WHERE DID HOOK AND HIS PIRATE DEVILS GO? TALK OR I'LL--

NO--NO! HE-- THEY'RE GOING TO GET ON THE INCOMING LINER, THE **DOLPHIN**, AND ARE GOING TO LOOT THE SHIP! NOW YOU'RE NOT GOING TO HIT ME, ARE YOU---ARE YOU?

AFTER TRUSSING CONROY UP, THE **BATMAN** UNSCREWS THE HEELS OF HIS BOOTS, REVEALING THEIR HOLLOWS, FILLED WITH AN APPARATUS FOR A SMALL WIRELESS.

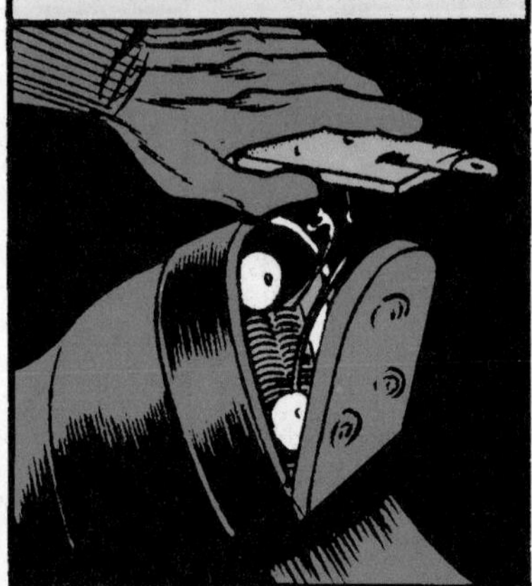

A MOMENT LATER, THE BATMAN'S CALL FLASHES TO ROBIN'S WAITING EARS!

AT THAT VERY INSTANT-- ON THE BLACK WATERS A CURIOUS SCENE IS BEING PLAYED.

OKAY, GUYS--YOU ALL GOT YOUR ORDERS! THE DOLPHIN OUGHT TO BE ALONG ANY MINUTE NOW! LET'S GET STARTED!

YOU SAY YOUR FREIGHTER WAS TORPEDOED BY A SUBMARINE?
YES--- WE'VE BEEN DRIFTING FOR HOURS! GOOD THING YOU CAME ALONG!

BUT ONCE UPON THE DECK, THE "SURVIVORS" SUDDENLY WHIP EAGER HANDS INTO THEIR DUFFLE BAGS AND---
WHY-WHAT IS THIS?
THIS IS A STICKUP! NOW BE NICE OR ELSE THERE'S GONNA BE A LOT O' STIFFS LAYIN' AROUND!

WHY, YOU-- OH-H!
GET BACK IN LINE BEFORE I RIP YOUR HEAD OFF!
R-R-RIP

ANYBODY ELSE THAT TRIES ANYTHING GETS THE SAME KIND O' MEDICINE! OKAY, BOYS---TAKE WHAT'S IN THEIR POCKETS AND WHAT YOU SEE ON THIS TUB THAT'S WORTH ANYTHING!
OH, MY FACE-- MY FACE.

WHILE THE PIRATES TAKE OVER THE SHIP, A WEIRD CRAFT SWOOPS DOWN FROM THE BLACK SKY. IT IS THE BATPLANE!

IT GLIDES NOISELESSLY OVER THE LINER AND HANGS THERE MOTIONLESS. TWO MANTLED FIGURES SLIP DOWN A DANGLING ROPE LADDER---
I SET THE ROBOT CONTROLS!
GOOD! NOW LET'S GET 'EM!

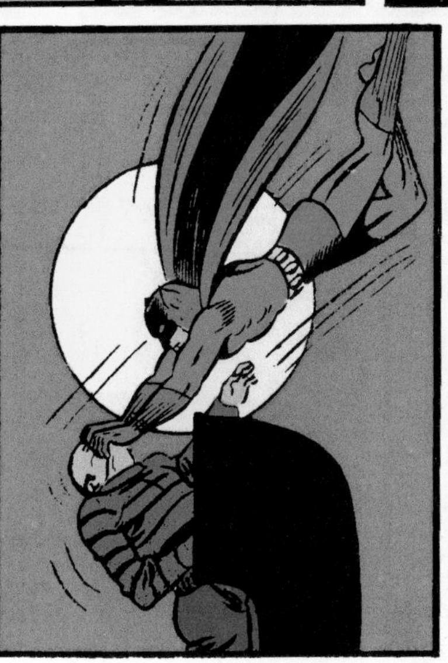

THOSE PIRATES MUST BE ALL OVER THE SHIP-- SO WE'LL HAVE TO SEPARATE! YOU TAKE THE LOWER DECK!
RIGHT! HERE'S WHERE WE SEE SOME ACTION!

HELP! BOYS! IT'S THE BATMAN! B....UGH!

OH-OH! THE KID'S IN TROUBLE AGAIN! LOOKS LIKE I'LL HAVE TO SAVE HIS LIFE!
ROUSED BY THE CRY AND THE SHOT, THE PIRATES SWARM FORWARD--

...A LIFE SAVER!
?
LIFE

AH! HELLO!
THERE HE IS, THE BATMAN! C'MON, LETS GET HIM!

AMAZING HOW I ALWAYS FIND TIME TO ENJOY MYSELF, EVEN IN THE TIGHTEST SCRAPES!

HELLO, ROBIN-- WHAT'S THE SCORE?
PERFECT STRIKE!

AS THE PIRATES SPILL DOWN IN A TANGLE OF WAVING ARMS AND LEGS, THE BATMAN LEAPS OVER THEM. HIS EYES FASTEN UPON A FALLEN DECK HOSE
THAT'S WHAT I WANT! TURN IT ON, ROBIN!

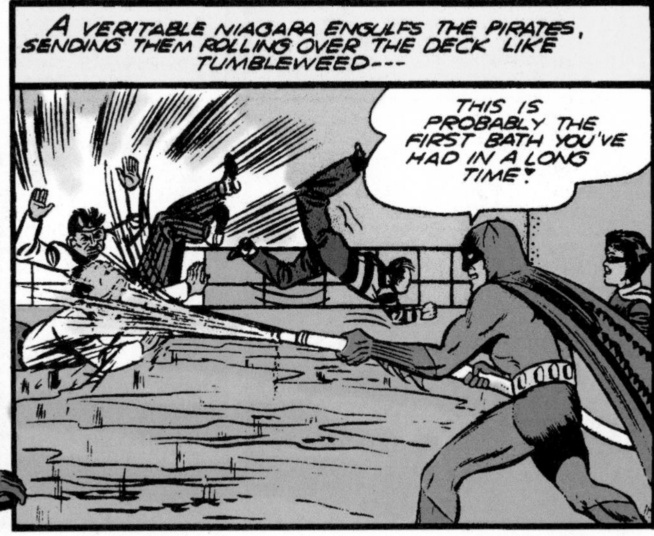
A VERITABLE NIAGARA ENGULFS THE PIRATES, SENDING THEM ROLLING OVER THE DECK LIKE TUMBLEWEED---
THIS IS PROBABLY THE FIRST BATH YOU'VE HAD IN A LONG TIME!

THE NOW HELPLESS PIRATES ARE HERDED TOGETHER BY THE SHIP'S CREW!
I DON'T SEE HOOK! HE MUST HAVE RUN OUT ON HIS MEN!
LOOK! THERE HE IS...SWIMMING TO THAT LAUNCH!

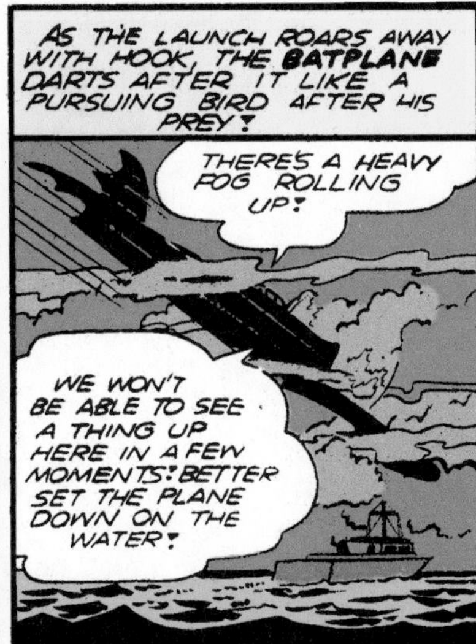
AS THE LAUNCH ROARS AWAY WITH HOOK, THE BATPLANE DARTS AFTER IT LIKE A PURSUING BIRD AFTER HIS PREY!
THERE'S A HEAVY FOG ROLLING UP!
WE WON'T BE ABLE TO SEE A THING UP HERE IN A FEW MOMENTS! BETTER SET THE PLANE DOWN ON THE WATER!

AS THE BATPLANE HITS THE WATER, THE BATMAN PUSHES A BUTTON. MIRACULOUSLY, THE WHEELS ARE DRAWN IN... THE WINGS FOLD AGAINST THE SIDES--
THE BATPLANE HAS BEEN TRANSFORMED INTO A SPEEDBOAT!!

THE SHORE LINE BECOMES A BLUR AS THE BOATS FLASH PAST AT AMAZING SPEED! MILE AFTER MILE WHIPS BY--
THAT BOAT IS A FAST ONE!
...AND WE CAN'T SEE SO CLEARLY NOW WITH THIS HEAVY FOG!

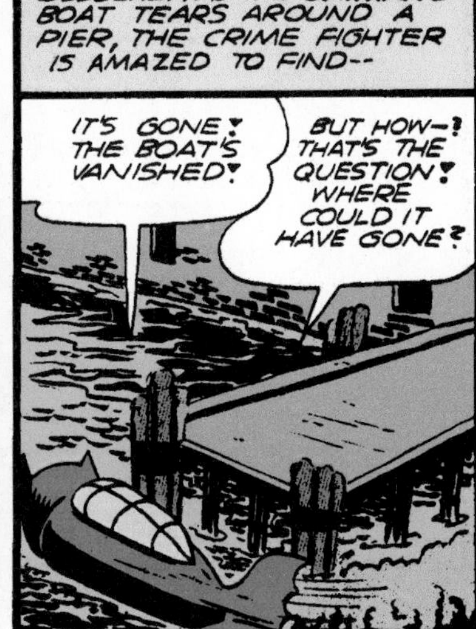
SUDDENLY, AS THE BATMAN'S BOAT TEARS AROUND A PIER, THE CRIME FIGHTER IS AMAZED TO FIND--
IT'S GONE! THE BOAT'S VANISHED!
BUT HOW-? THAT'S THE QUESTION! WHERE COULD IT HAVE GONE?

THE BATMAN GUIDES HIS CRAFT TO A CONCRETE WALL OF A WAREHOUSE ON THE RIVER FRONT NEARBY---
WHAT'S THE IDEA OF BRINGING THE BOAT OVER HERE?
THAT PIRATE LAUNCH DIDN'T GO UNDER THE WATER, SO THERE MUST BE A LOGICAL EXPLANATION FOR ITS DISAPPEARANCE! NOW...WHY SHOULD THIS BRICK BE OF A DIFFERENT COLOR THAN THE OTHERS, EH?

THERE IS A SUDDEN CLICK AND THE WALL MOVES UP! A YAWNING CHAMBER IS REVEALED!
GOSH! THE WALL MOVES UP, A SECRET HIDEOUT!
I SUSPECTED AS MUCH! THIS IS WHY THE POLICE WERE ALWAYS MYSTIFIED BY THE UNCANNY DISAPPEARANCE OF THE PIRATE LAUNCHES

NOW FOR MY FRIEND, HOOK MORGAN!

YAHOO!
I'M GOING TO TEAR YOUR HEAD OFF, BATMAN!
MAYBE - BUT FIRST I'M GOING TO PAY YOU BACK FOR THAT LITTLE REFRIGERATION INCIDENT!

SEE WHAT I MEAN?
GIVE IT TO HIM, BATMAN!
12

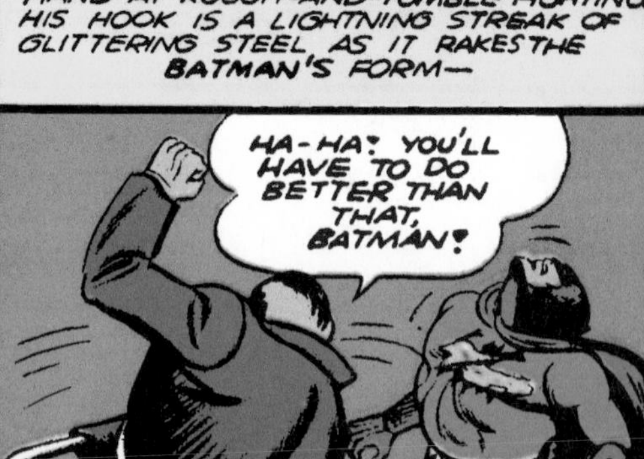
BUT THE PIRATE LEADER IS AN OLD HAND AT ROUGH-AND-TUMBLE FIGHTING HIS HOOK IS A LIGHTNING STREAK OF GLITTERING STEEL AS IT RAKES THE BATMAN'S FORM—
HA-HA! YOU'LL HAVE TO DO BETTER THAN THAT, BATMAN!

THE HOOK DIGS IN BACK OF THE BATMAN'S SHOULDER, AND HE IS DRAWN TOWARD THE LEERING PIRATE!
C'MERE!

HA-HA! HOW DO YOU LIKE THAT, BATMAN? HA!
I'D LIKE TO HELP THE BATMAN -- BUT HE'D GET SORE-THIS IS HIS FIGHT!

AS THE PIRATE TUGS AT THE HOOK THE BATMAN TEARS HIMSELF FREE FROM HIS IRON GRIP AND---
AND HOW DO YOU LIKE THAT, HOOK?

THE BATMAN BOUNDS FORWARD WITH THE EASY GRACE OF A GREAT CAT! HIS FIST WHISTLES THRU THE AIR ----- CRACK! AND THE HARBOR PIRATE FLIES BACK INTO A SPRAWLING UNCONSCIOUS MASS UPON THE FLOOR---

WOW! THAT WAS A FIGHT!
DON'T I KNOW IT! WHEW! JUST LET ME CATCH MY BREATH A MINUTE AND WE'LL BE ON OUR WAY! THE COPS WILL BE PLENTY INTERESTED IN KNOWING THAT THIS IS THE END OF THE HARBOR PIRATES!
THE END

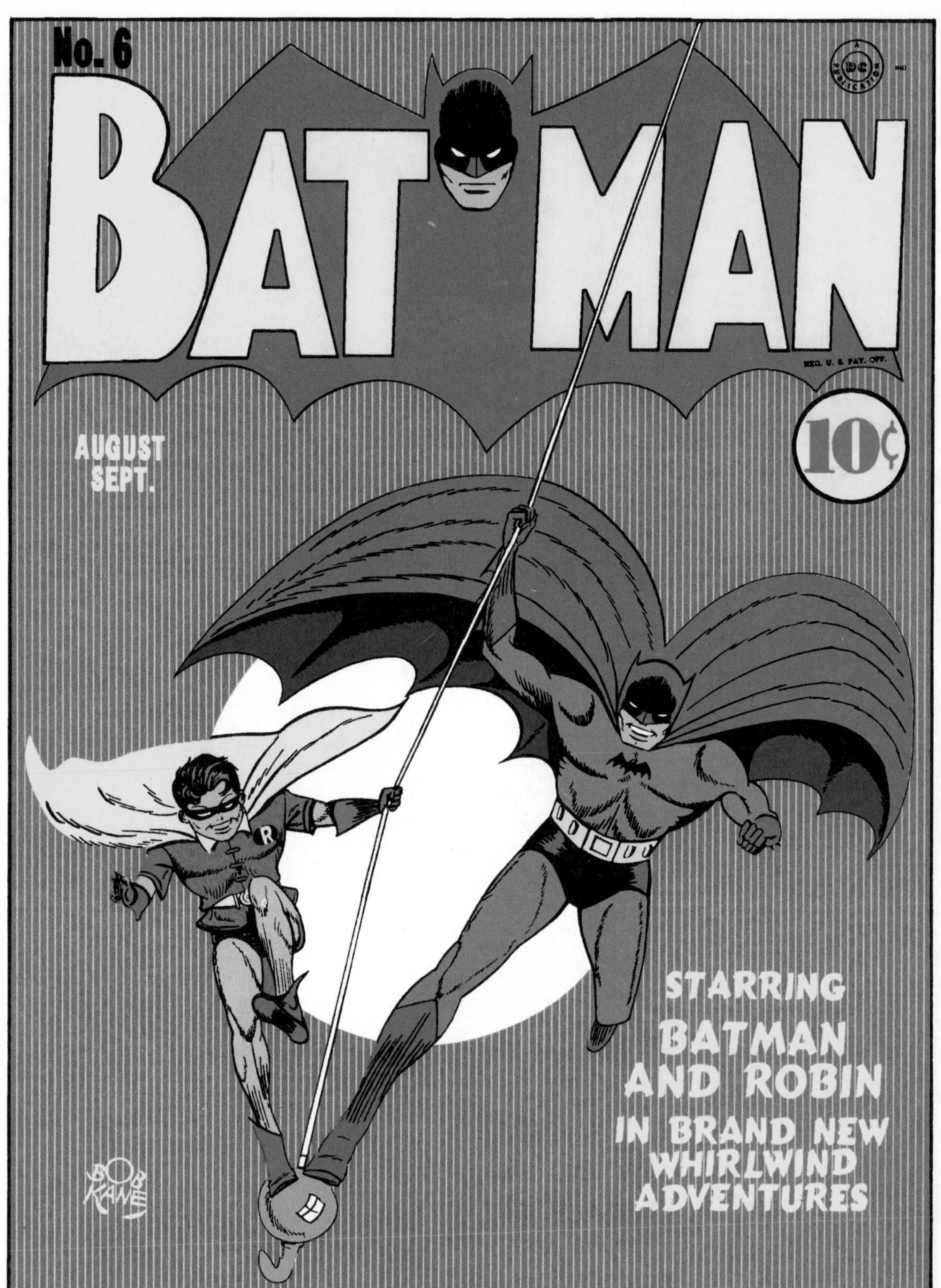
No. 6
A DC PUBLICATION
BATMAN
REG. U. S. PAT. OFF.
10¢
AUGUST SEPT.
STARRING
BATMAN
AND ROBIN
IN BRAND NEW
WHIRLWIND
ADVENTURES
BOB KANE

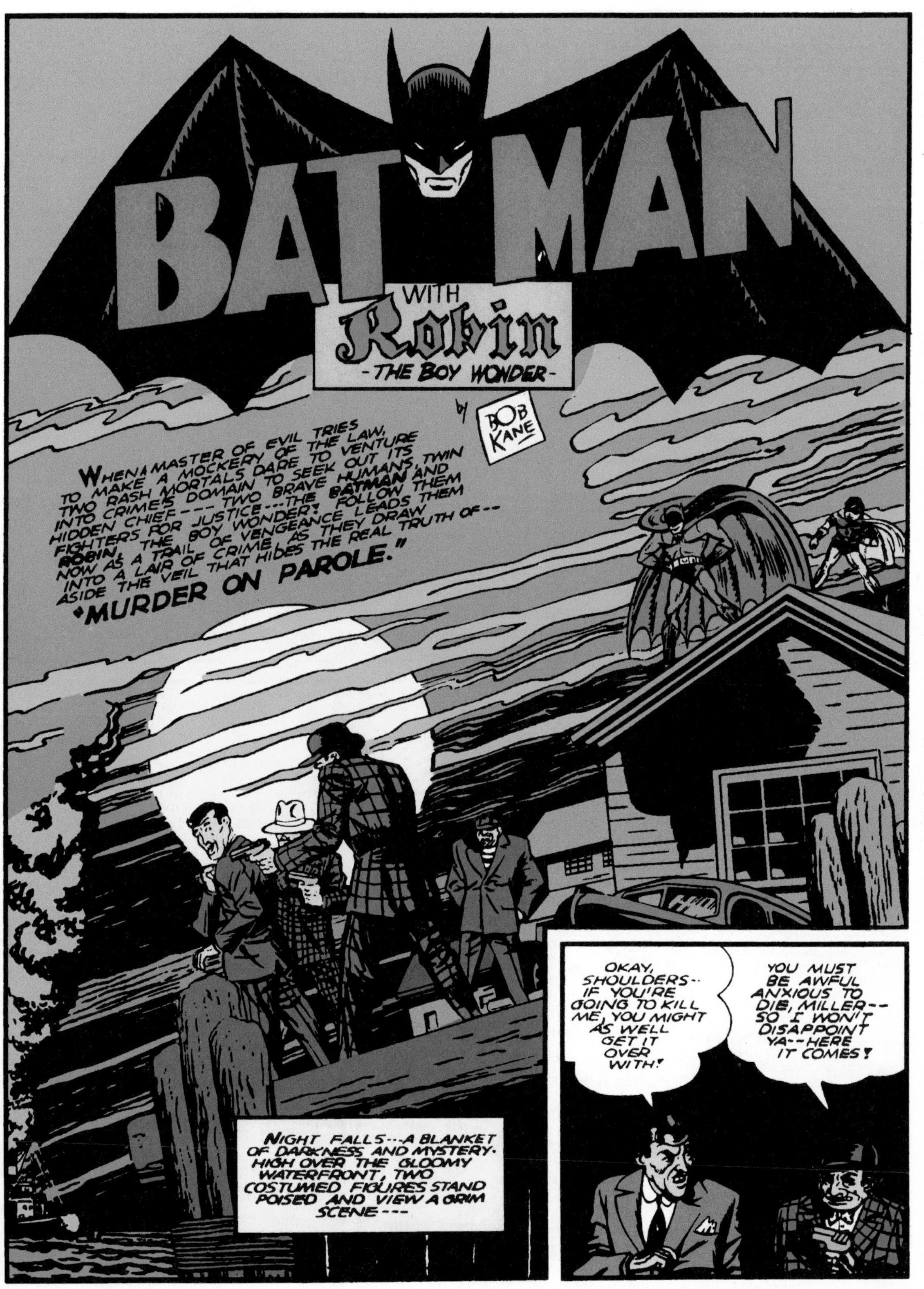
BATMAN
WITH Robin -THE BOY WONDER-
by BOB KANE
WHEN A MASTER OF EVIL TRIES TO MAKE A MOCKERY OF THE LAW, TWO RASH MORTALS DARE TO VENTURE INTO CRIME'S DOMAIN TO SEEK OUT ITS HIDDEN CHIEF--- TWO BRAVE HUMANS, TWIN FIGHTERS FOR JUSTICE---THE BATMAN AND ROBIN, THE BOY WONDER! FOLLOW THEM NOW AS A TRAIL OF VENGEANCE LEADS THEM INTO A LAIR OF CRIME, AS THEY DRAW ASIDE THE VEIL THAT HIDES THE REAL TRUTH OF--
"MURDER ON PAROLE."
NIGHT FALLS---A BLANKET OF DARKNESS AND MYSTERY. HIGH OVER THE GLOOMY WATERFRONT, TWO COSTUMED FIGURES STAND POISED AND VIEW A GRIM SCENE---
OKAY, SHOULDERS-- IF YOU'RE GOING TO KILL ME, YOU MIGHT AS WELL GET IT OVER WITH!
YOU MUST BE AWFUL ANXIOUS TO DIE, MILLER-- SO I WON'T DISAPPOINT YA--HERE IT COMES!

SUDDENLY, THE TWO GRIM FIGURES, UP ON HIGH, LEAP!
C'MON, ROBIN-- THIS LOOKS LIKE OUR FIGHT, TOO!
I'M RIGHT WITH YOU!

GREETINGS AND SALUTATIONS AND SUCH!
HELLO!

THE BATMAN'S FIST SNAKES OUT---
WHENEVER I SEE A FACE LIKE YOURS, MY KNUCKLES JUST ITCH TO GET TO WORK ON IT!

I NEVER DISAPPOINT MY KNUCKLES EITHER!

WHEW!
NOW— NOW, IS THAT NICE? SHOOTING PEOPLE IN THE BACK!

NEXT TIME I'LL DRIVE YOUR HEAD DOWN SO FAR YOU'LL BE ABLE TO CHEW ON YOUR SHOES!

A SUDDEN TURN OF EVENTS!
OKAY-- RELAX, BATMAN. THIS BABY TELLS YOU TO!

GET IN THE CAR, BOYS--- WHILE I STITCH MY NAME ON THEIR CHESTS!

ROBIN SUDDENLY KICKS THE HAT INTO THE THUG'S FACE AS HIS MACHINE-GUN FIRES WILDLY
A GOAL FOR OUR SIDE!
ULP!

THE THUGS PULL AWAY IN THEIR CAR - LEAVING A TRAIL OF BLAZING LEAD!
DOWN-- HUG THE GROUND!

HA! I GOT MILLER ANYWAY! SO LONG!
OH-H-H

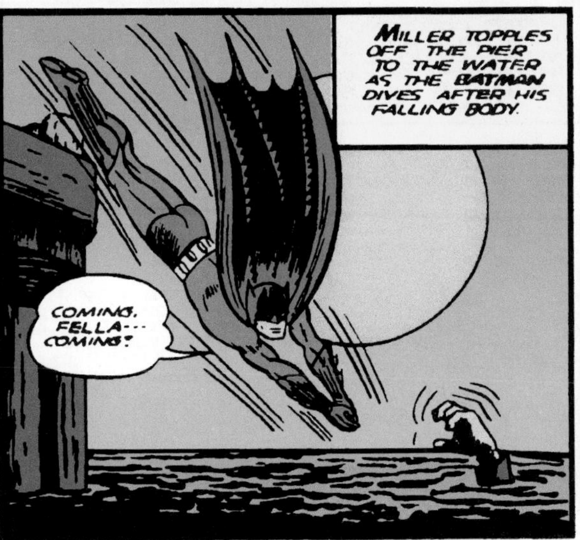
MILLER TOPPLES OFF THE PIER TO THE WATER AS THE BATMAN DIVES AFTER HIS FALLING BODY.
COMING, FELLA--- COMING!

GRAB HIM, ROBIN. HE'S BEEN SHOT!
HE ALMOST HAD COMPANY!

BATMAN-- GOT TO TELL YOU ABOUT SOMETHING-- SOMETHING BIG---
HERE---TAKE IT EASY. YOU CAN TELL ME LATER ON, AFTER A LITTLE MEDICAL TREATMENT.

NO---NO-- GOT TO TELL YOU NOW--- BEFORE I PASS OUT--

MILLER'S STORY--
"MY NAME IS CHICK MILLER. I WAS A CONVICT IN THE STATE PRISON, SENTENCED TO FIVE YEARS. I WAS SERVING MY THIRD YEAR WHEN IT GOT ME---"
STIR CRAZY! I'LL GO STIR CRAZY IF I DON'T GET OUT OF HERE SOON! I'VE GOT TO GET OUT!

IF YOU WANT TO GET OUT, CHICK-- I CAN ARRANGE IT-- A PAROLE!
PAROLE-- YOU--- HOW?

WHY DON'T YOU GET YOURSELF OUT, SLINK---WHO DO YOU THINK YOU'RE KIDDIN'?
LISSEN---I GET GOOD DOUGH FROM THE BIG SHOT FOR GETTIN' GUYS LIKE YOU OUT----WHEN I GET MY PILE, I'M GETTING OUT, TOO! NOW YOU LEAVE EVERYTHING TO ME--

"SURE ENOUGH, A FEW DAYS LATER, I WAS CALLED BEFORE THE PAROLE BOARD---"
ARRUMPH---. MR. MILLER, YOU HAVE BEEN THOUGHT OF AS ELIGIBLE FOR PAROLE!
PAROLE MIGHT BE ARRANGED, IF WE FEEL YOU'LL GO STRAIGHT.
MY-- YOU DON'T LOOK LIKE A CRIMINAL!

"AFTER DISCUSSING MY CASE WITH ME, THEY MADE ME GO OUTSIDE WHILE THEY TALKED---AND WHEN THEY CALLED ME BACK AGAIN---!"
ARRUMPH-- MR. MILLER, WE HAVE DECIDED IN YOUR FAVOR FOR PAROLE!
PAROLE- I---I DON'T KNOW HOW TO THANK YOU-- I--
TUT-TUT, MY BOY. WE FEEL YOU DESERVE IT!
"WHEN I WAS READY TO LEAVE THE PRISON, I WENT BACK TO THANK MY CELL-MATE, SLINK DANIELS. HE SAID SOMETHING. I DIDN'T KNOW WHAT HE MEANT THEN, BUT FOUND OUT SOON ENOUGH!"
I WISH THERE WAS SOME WAY I COULD MAKE IT UP TO YOU FOR WHAT YOU DID!
DON'T WORRY. YOU WILL.. YOU WILL!

"THE BIG DAY FINALLY CAME--THE PRISON GATE CLANGED BE-HIND ME. IT WAS SPRING--- THE AIR WAS CLEAN AND FRESH. BIRDS WERE AROUND. THEY WERE LIKE ME -- FREE!"
NO MORE PRISON FOR ME! FROM NOW ON I'M GOING STRAIGHT! ANYBODY WHO THINKS A LIFE OF CRIME PAYS, IS A SUCKER!
PRISON

"THEN TWO MEN APPROACHED ME--"
HELLO, MILLER!
WHO ARE YOU?
WE'RE FRIENDS OF SLINK DANIELS. HE TOLD US ABOUT YOU. WE'RE GONNA TAKE CARE O' YOU-- GET YOU A JOB!

"A JOB SOUNDED SWELL TO ME! THEY TOOK ME TO A SWANKY HOTEL TO SEE THEIR BOSS. YOU COULD HAVE KNOCKED ME OVER WITH A FEATHER WHEN I SAW WHO IT WAS--
YOU.... FROM THE PAROLE BOARD!
HELLO, MILLER!

YOU HAVE A JOB FOR ME, SIR?
YES--I HAVE. I WANT YOU TO HELP SOME OF MY BOYS CRACK THE NATIONAL BANK!!

"FOR A MINUTE, I COULDN'T BELIEVE MY EARS, BUT THE BOSS KEPT ON TALKING AND I LEARNED THE TRUTH!"
SURE-- I MANAGED TO GET YOU PAROLED JUST LIKE MY OTHER BOYS---SO YOU COULD WORK FOR ME! THAT'S HOW YOU PAY FOR YOUR PAROLE. STAY WITH ME AND YOU'LL MAKE BIG MONEY! HOW ABOUT IT?

NOT ME! I'M THROUGH WITH CRIME. I'M GOING STRAIGHT. I'M NOT GOING BACK TO JAIL AGAIN!
MMM! BY THE WAY-- EVER SEE THIS BEFORE? HERE--- LOOK AT IT!

"I HELD THE CASE AND EXAMINED IT---"
NO... I NEVER SAW THIS BEFORE!
I KNOW YOU DIDN'T. AS A MATTER OF FACT, IT'S PART OF A HOLDUP JOB THAT WAS JUST PULLED ABOUT A HALF HOUR AGO!

WH-AT!
I'VE GOT YOUR FINGERPRINTS ON THIS CASE! ALL I HAVE TO DO IS SHOW THIS TO THE POLICE AND THEY'D HAVE YOU BACK IN JAIL SO FAST, IT WOULD MAKE YOUR HEAD SWIM!

OKAY--SEND ME BACK. SEND ME BACK AND I'LL TELL THEM WHO YOU ARE -- AND WHAT YOU REALLY ARE- I'LL--
YOU'VE TALKED QUITE ENOUGH. SHOULDERS, TAKE HIM TO THE CAR AND SHOW HIM THE SIGHTS--MAYBE THE WATERFRONT!
GOTCHA, BOSS!

THEY BROUGHT ME HERE. YOU--YOU KNOW-- THE REST--
QUICK--- TELL ME! WHO IS THE BOSS?

....AND TRUE TO FORM, TOO. IN THE MOVIES AND IN MYSTERY STORIES, THE MAN ALWAYS DIES OR PASSES OUT JUST WHEN HE'S ABOUT TO REVEAL THE MASTER CRIMINAL'S NAME! WELL--- BETTER GET HIM TO A HOSPITAL RIGHT AWAY!
HE'S FAINTED
HE-- HE-- OOH--

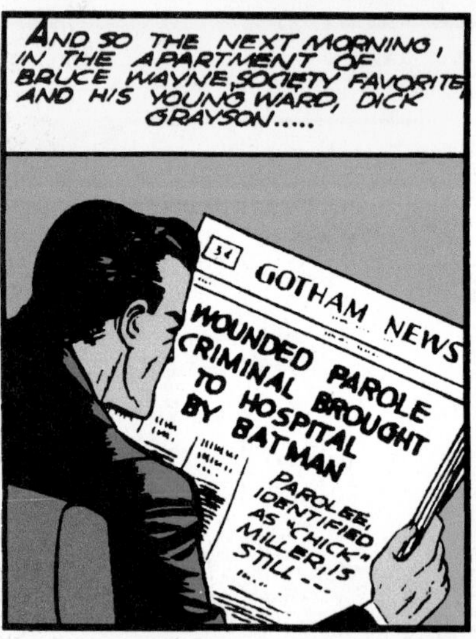
AND SO THE NEXT MORNING, IN THE APARTMENT OF BRUCE WAYNE SOCIETY FAVORITE, AND HIS YOUNG WARD, DICK GRAYSON.....
5¢
GOTHAM NEWS
WOUNDED PAROLE CRIMINAL BROUGHT TO HOSPITAL BY BATMAN
PAROLEE, IDENTIFIED AS "CHICK" MILLER, IS STILL---

YOU KNOW, DICK---I THINK THOSE MEN WHO SHOT MILLER WILL TRY AGAIN TO GET HIM AT THE HOSPITAL BEFORE HE RECOVERS AND TALKS.
HMM! I GUESS THEY WOULD!

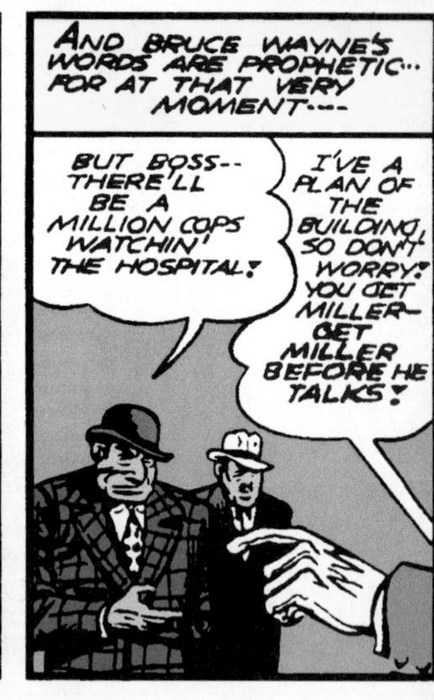
AND BRUCE WAYNE'S WORDS ARE PROPHETIC... FOR AT THAT VERY MOMENT---
BUT BOSS-- THERE'LL BE A MILLION COPS WATCHIN' THE HOSPITAL!
I'VE A PLAN OF THE BUILDING, SO DON'T WORRY! YOU GET MILLER- GET MILLER BEFORE HE TALKS!

THAT VERY NIGHT----THE HOSPITAL WINDOW SLIDES OPEN--
OKAY, GUYS--THIS IS MILLER'S ROOM!

BUT AS THE DOOR PUSHES IN---SOMETHING FLIES OUT--- THE BATMAN'S FIST!

AN AVALANCHE OF FIST DESCENDS UPON THE THUGS!
THE BATMAN!
IN PERSON!
AS THE THUGS SUDDENLY SURGE TOWARD THEIR DREADED NEMESIS, AN OPERATING TABLE BEARS DOWN ON THEM---AND ABOARD IT IS--
ROBIN-- IT'S THAT ROBIN KID!
THOUGHT I'D BRING THE TABLE! YOU'LL NEED IT AFTER I GET THROUGH WITH YOU!
BULL'S-EYE!
REINFORCEMENTS RUSH THE TWIN BATTLERS!
GET THEM!
SLUG 'EM!
DRAWN BY SHOUTS AND SHOTS, POLICE SWARM TOWARD THE MAKESHIFT BATTLE FIELD!
HALT, OR WE'LL FIRE!
COPPERS! LET'S ALL LAM OUTA HERE! DOWN THE FIRE ESCAPE!
AS THE POLICE GIVE FUTILE CHASE TO THE FLEEING THUGS, THE BATMAN AND ROBIN FIND THEM-SELVES IN A TIGHT SPOT!
HOLY CATS! THE BATMAN AND ROBIN!
NOW WE'RE IN FOR IT! THE POLICE AREN'T AS YET EXACTLY TOO FOND OF MY SLIGHTLY DIFFERENT WAY IN FIGHTING CRIME!
SORRY-- BUT THIS IS NECESSARY!

LIKE TWO FLEET DEER, THEY RACE DOWN THE LONG CORRIDOR!
LET'S GO, ROBIN!

LATER--
WELL-- WE GOT AWAY FROM THE POLICE, BUT SO DID THE GUN-MEN!
THEIR MYSTERIOUS BOSS ACTED FIRST, BUT NOW IT'S MY TURN! HERE'S WHERE THE BATMAN GOES TO TOWN!

THAT NIGHT----WINGING SILENTLY OVER THE STATE PRISON IS A CRAFT OF WEIRD DESIGN--THE BATPLANE!
WHA...?

DOWN A DANGLING LADDER SCRAMBLES THE BATMAN. BEFORE THE STARTLED GUARD CAN MAKE AN OUTCRY, SOME-THING PLOPS DOWN BESIDE HIM...AND HE FALLS ASLEEP!
ZZZZ...

THROUGH THE PRISON HE DARTS, HURTLING THE HARMLESS SLEEP-INDUCING CAPSULES.
BATM... BA.... AAAH... SO SLEEPY ZZZZ...

CAPSULES PLOP INTO SLINK'S CELL WHILE HE SLEEPS!
NOW TO TAKE HIS CELL-MATE TO THE BATPLANE!

IN THE BATPLANE, AN AMAZING TRANSFORMATION TAKES PLACE--THE BATMAN BECOMES SLINK'S CELL-MATE
NOW TO APPLY THE MAKEUP WHILE HE'S STILL UNCONSCIOUS!
HEY-- WAKE UP-- THATS IT--
WHAT--? YOU'RE ME...ME EXACTLY-- YOU EVEN TALK LIKE ME!

IT IS THE BATMAN WHO BECOMES SLINK'S CELLMATE AND BEGINS HIS GREAT IMPERSONATION--
THIS CELL IS DRIVIN' ME NUTS! I'M GONNA MAKE A BREAK FOR IT!
I GOT A BETTER WAY TO SPRING YOU, MARTY! HOW ABOUT A PAROLE?

AND SO IT IS NOT LONG AFTER THE BATMAN IS FREED BY THE PAROLE BOARD!
ARRUMPH-- MARTY LODEN, WE HAVE DECIDED IN YOUR FAVOR!
YOU ARE A FREE MAN!
WHICH.... WHICH ONE OF THESE MEN IS THE "BOSS"?

AND THE BOYS MEET "MARTY LODEN" AND TAKE HIM TO THE "BOSS"--
HIM!
SURE--- SURE---YOU GOT ME OUT. SURE I'LL WORK WITH YOUR MOB!
YOU'RE A SENSIBLE FELLOW, MARTY-- YOU CAN START TO WORK!

THE BOSS!
I'M SENDING THE BOYS OUT TO ROB A WAREHOUSE OF SILKS TONIGHT! YOU CAN GO ALONG!

THAT NIGHT, ROBIN TAKES HIS STAND BY THE BOSS'S ROOM....
THE BATMAN TOLD ME TO BE SURE THE BOSS DOESN'T GET ANY IDEAS ABOUT GETTING AWAY--- GOT TO BE CAREFUL-- KEEP MY EYES OPEN-

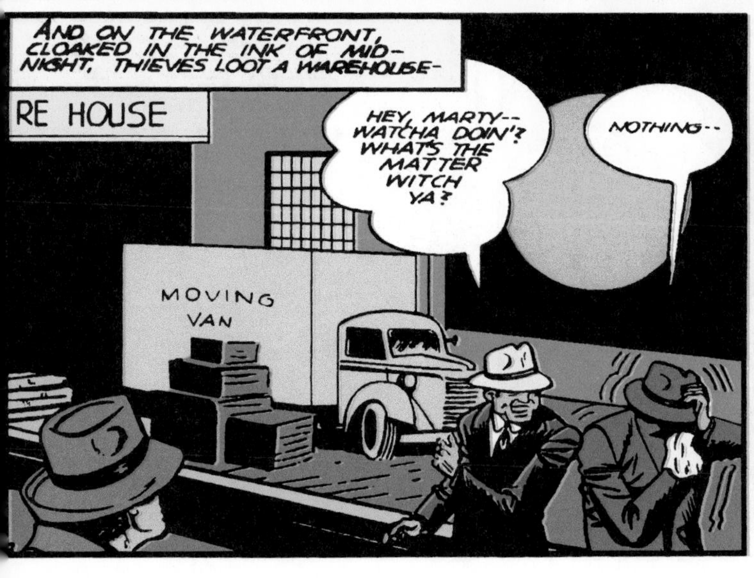
AND ON THE WATERFRONT, CLOAKED IN THE INK OF MID-NIGHT, THIEVES LOOT A WAREHOUSE-
RE HOUSE
HEY, MARTY-- WATCHA DOIN'? WHAT'S THE MATTER WITCH YA?
NOTHING--
MOVING VAN

MARTY, THE GANGSTER, WIPES THE MAKEUP FROM HIS FACE, RIPS OFF HIS CLOTHING AND STANDING IS HIS PLACE IS---
THE BATMAN! UGH!

AT YOUR SERVICE!

THE BATMAN RUSHES INTO THE WARE-HOUSE-- A TREMENDOUS LEAP----
THE SCENE SEEMS PERFECTLY SET FOR THIS PARTICULAR BIT OF ACTION!

THE CAPED FIGURE SWINGS OUT-
PERFECT STRIKE!

A NIAGARA OF SILK ENGULFS THE THIEVES!
MMMPH!

AS THE BATMAN DROPS FROM THE ROPE, OTHER POWERFUL FIGURES LUNGE AT HIM--
WHERE DID THESE BABIES COME FROM? I'VE TAKEN ON MORE OF A JOB THAN I BARGAINED FOR!

THE BATMAN FIGHTS LIKE A CORNERED TIGER AS OTHERS JOIN THE MELEE!
GET HIM! NOW'S OUR CHANCE!

EVEN THE BATMAN CANNOT STAND AGAINST THESE OVERWHELMING ODDS- A SUDDEN BLOW SENDS THE BATMAN REELING---CRASHING THROUGH GLASS--

MINUTES PASS---
HE AIN'T COME UP YET! THAT GUY'S GONE FOR GOOD THIS TIME!
NOW THAT THE BATMAN IS FINISHED, LET'S FINISH UP HERE! GET THE STUFF AWAY AND THEN WE SCRAM BACK TO THE BOSS!

LATER--- AS ROBIN PACES THE HALLWAY, A HAND WHIPS ABOUT HIS MOUTH--
IT'S THAT WISE ROBIN KID THAT WORKS WITH THE BATMAN!
YEAH-- THE BOSS WILL BE GLAD TO SEE HIM!

THE BOSS IS INFORMED OF THE SWIFT-MOVING EVENTS OF THAT NIGHT----
SURE --- THE BATMAN WAS MARTY LODEN!
SO --- WELL--- MAYBE WE OUGHT TO TAKE GOOD CARE OF ROBIN, TOO-- VERY GOOD CARE!

SUDDENLY, THE DOOR CRASHES OPEN -- AND IN WALKS SLINK!
SLINK! WHAT--- WHAT ARE YOU DOING OUT OF JAIL?
I BROKE OUT. I WAS GETTIN' STIR CRAZY LIKE THOSE GUYS YOU GET OUT ON PAROLE!

YOU FOOL! WHY DIDN'T YOU WAIT TILL I GOT YOU OUT ON PAROLE!
WHO YOU KIDDIN'? NOT EVEN YOU CAN GET ME OUT---NO GUYS WITH MURDER RAPS ARE PAROLED-- AN' YOU KNOW IT!

SUDDENLY, THE EERIE WAIL OF A POLICE SIREN CUTS THROUGH THE NIGHT AIR!
COPS--- THEY MUST'VE FOLLOWED YOU HERE!
I'LL FIX THEM!

MEN! SPREAD OUT--- SURROUND THE PLACE-- GET ALL THE PEOPLE FROM THE BUILDING OUT---AND THEN START FIRING!
UGH!

REALIZING THEY MUST THROW IN WITH SLINK, THE PAROLE BOSS' THUGS SEND LEAD SCREAMING AT THE POLICE. THE DUEL BETWEEN THE LAW AND THE LAWLESS HAS BEGUN!

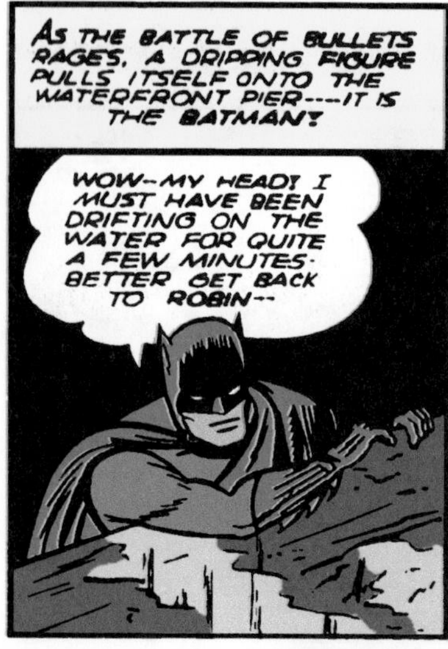
AS THE BATTLE OF BULLETS RAGES, A DRIPPING FIGURE PULLS ITSELF ONTO THE WATERFRONT PIER---IT IS THE BATMAN!
WOW--MY HEAD! I MUST HAVE BEEN DRIFTING ON THE WATER FOR QUITE A FEW MINUTES. BETTER GET BACK TO ROBIN--

MEANWHILE, THE BOSS' THUGS FALL LIKE LEAVES IN A STORM BEFORE THE WITHERING GUNFIRE---
GET MOVING, KID!
THEY'RE CUTTIN' US TO PIECES!
LOOK OUT! THEY'RE SHOOTING... (COUGH-COUGH!) TEAR GAS CARTRIDGES!

IF ANY COP SO MUCH AS MOVES INTO THE BUILDING, THIS BOY DIES!
RUN INSIDE AND SEE IF THERE ARE ANY MORE OF THEM HOLED UP!
HERE COME THE RATS-- RUNNING OUT OF THEIR HOLES!
COUGH!
IT'S YOU, BATMAN! I'VE ALWAYS WANTED TO GET THE GREAT BATMAN--AND NOW I'M GOING TO GET MY WISH! COME ON BATMAN-- HA-HA!
HELLO! I'M COMING FOR ROBIN!
ROBIN! I DON'T WANT TO SEE THAT BOY KILLED! EVEN THOUGH HE DOES WORK OUTSIDE THE LAW, STILL HE DOES FIGHT CRIME! IF---

AND ALONE AND UNAFRAID, THE BATMAN WALKS TOWARD WHAT SEEMS CERTAIN DEATH...
I'M COMING UP THERE TO GET YOU! I'M WALKING UP THE STEPS NOW!
AND THOSE WILL BE THE LAST STEPS YOU'LL EVER WALK! HA-HA!

BETTER GET READY, I'M ALMOST THERE!
HA! I'M READY-- AND WAITING TO SEE YOU DIE!

I'M HERE, FELLA!
OKAY, BATMAN-- YOU ASKED FOR IT!

ABRUPTLY-- ROBIN ACTS WITH THE SPEED OF THOUGHT---
OOF!

THE CRIME-FIGHTER AND CRIME-MASTER CLASH IN A BATTLE TO DEATH.

A SUDDEN BLOW SENDS THE BATMAN OFF BALANCE AND REELING TOWARD AN OPEN ELEVATOR SHAFT--
NOW I'LL FINISH YOU OFF!

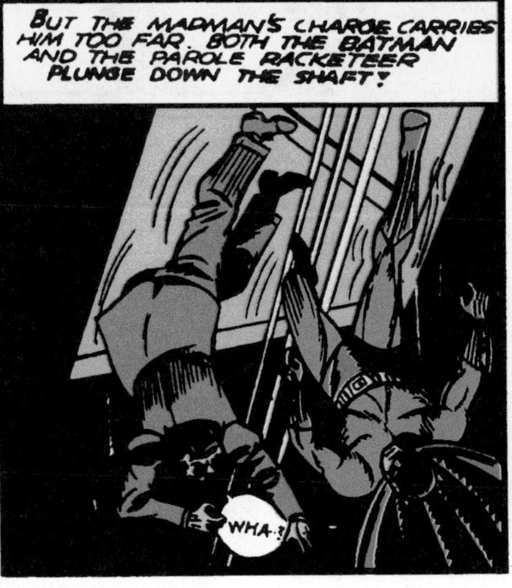
BUT THE MADMAN'S CHARGE CARRIES HIM TOO FAR. BOTH THE BATMAN AND THE PAROLE RACKETEER PLUNGE DOWN THE SHAFT!
WHA-!

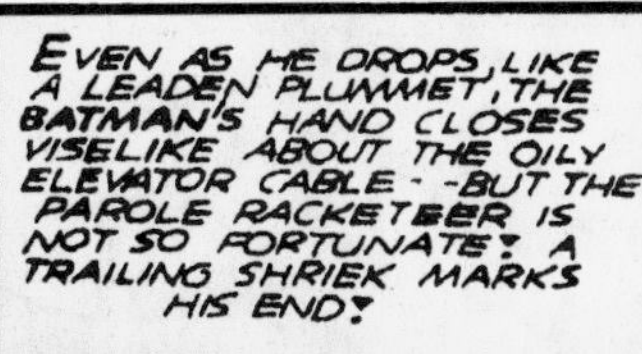
EVEN AS HE DROPS, LIKE A LEADEN PLUMMET, THE BATMAN'S HAND CLOSES VISELIKE ABOUT THE OILY ELEVATOR CABLE--BUT THE PAROLE RACKETEER IS NOT SO FORTUNATE! A TRAILING SHRIEK MARKS HIS END!

AAAA AAA
BOB KANE

LATER-
WELL, I SUPPOSE ALL THOSE MEN PAROLED BY THEIR BOSS WILL GO BACK TO JAIL?
ALL EXCEPT MILLER! HE EARNED HIS PAROLE. YOU KNOW, IT'S EASY FOR MOST PEOPLE TO UNDERSTAND CRIME DOESN'T PAY, BUT WHEN A CRIMINAL SUDDENLY REALIZES IT, AS MILLER DID, WELL THAT'S ABOUT THE BEST MORAL LESSON THERE CAN BE!

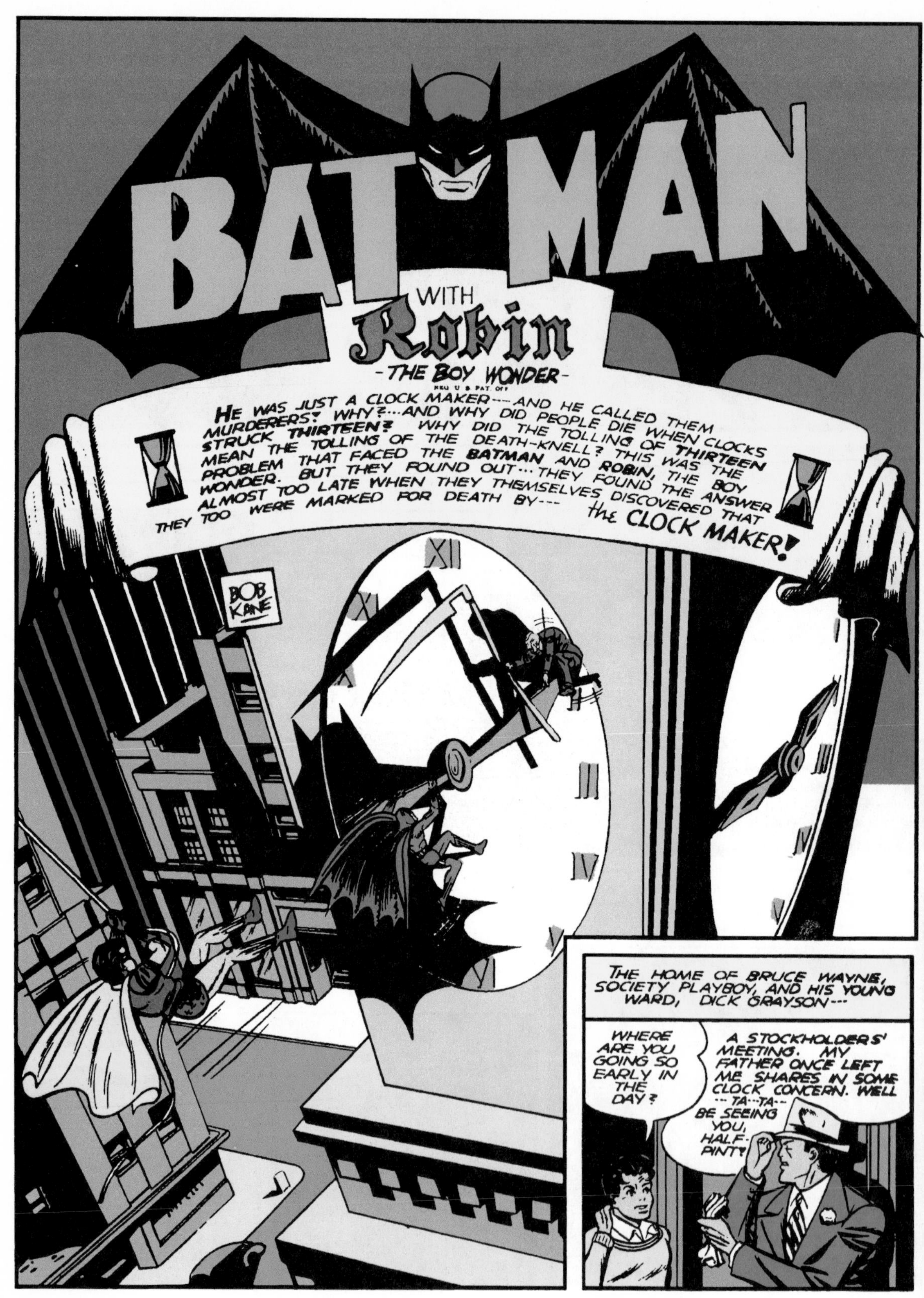
BATMAN
WITH
Robin
-THE BOY WONDER-
HE WAS JUST A CLOCK MAKER--- AND HE CALLED THEM MURDERERS! WHY?...AND WHY DID PEOPLE DIE WHEN CLOCKS STRUCK THIRTEEN? WHY DID THE TOLLING OF THIRTEEN MEAN THE TOLLING OF THE DEATH-KNELL? THIS WAS THE PROBLEM THAT FACED THE BATMAN AND ROBIN, THE BOY WONDER. BUT THEY FOUND OUT... THEY FOUND THE ANSWER ALMOST TOO LATE WHEN THEY THEMSELVES DISCOVERED THAT THEY TOO WERE MARKED FOR DEATH BY--- the CLOCK MAKER!
BOB KANE
THE HOME OF BRUCE WAYNE, SOCIETY PLAYBOY, AND HIS YOUNG WARD, DICK GRAYSON---
WHERE ARE YOU GOING SO EARLY IN THE DAY?
A STOCKHOLDERS' MEETING. MY FATHER ONCE LEFT ME SHARES IN SOME CLOCK CONCERN. WELL --TA--TA-- BE SEEING YOU, HALF-PINT!

THE HOBBS CLOCK BUILDING---
HOBBS
HOBBS
SOME OLD BUILDING-WITH THAT GIGANTIC CLOCK TELLING ALL THAT THE HOBBS CLOCK COMPANY IS THE LARGEST IN THE WORLD! GOOD STUNT!

BRUCE JOINS THE STOCKHOLDERS, WHO LISTEN IN BORED TONES AS THE CHAIRMAN DRONES ON AND ON AND ON....
HO HUM!
ISN'T THAT GUY EVER GOING TO LET US GO HOME?
SHH-HH- THIS IS VERY IMPORTANT, KEATING!
OH-- QUIET, ATKINS! AND YOU TOO, KEATING!

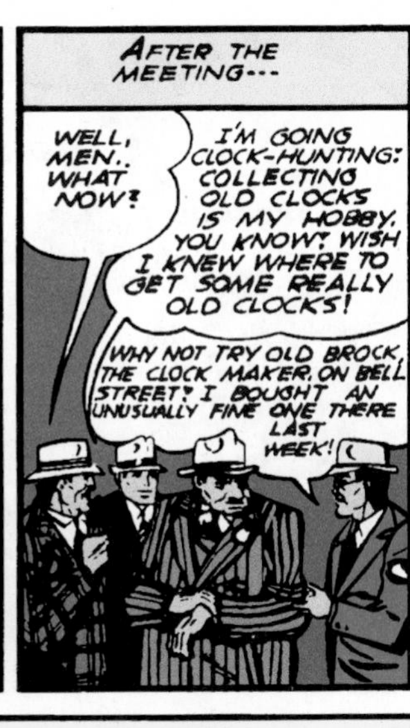
AFTER THE MEETING---
WELL, MEN.. WHAT NOW?
I'M GOING CLOCK-HUNTING! COLLECTING OLD CLOCKS IS MY HOBBY, YOU KNOW! WISH I KNEW WHERE TO GET SOME REALLY OLD CLOCKS!
WHY NOT TRY OLD BROCK, THE CLOCK MAKER, ON BELL STREET! I BOUGHT AN UNUSUALLY FINE ONE THERE LAST WEEK!

QUEER OLD FELLOW, BROCK--- THINKS HE'S FATHER TIME! EVEN WEARS AN HOUR-GLASS AROUND HIS NECK-- HE'S A REGULAR FANATIC ON TIME!
I'D LIKE TO SEE THIS "FATHER TIME" FELLOW! I'LL JOIN YOU, AND I DARE SAY BRUCE WILL, TOO!

SOMETIME LATER---A SMALL SIDE STREET---
SO THIS IS THE PLACE! DOESN'T LOOK LIKE MUCH, DOES IT?
AND THAT'S GOOD! IT'S IN JUST THIS SORT OF PLACE THAT ONE CAN PICK UP THE OLDEST CLOCKS
ELIAS BROCK CLOCKMAKER

INSIDE THE CRAMPED INTERIOR. CLOCKS STAND ON SHELVES AND COUNTERS---CLOCKS, HUNDREDS OF THEM, ALL TICKING WITH PERSISTENT, MONOTONOUS REGULARITY---
MR. BROCK?
I AM BROCK, THE CLOCK MAKER! YOU WISH TO BUY ONE OF MY FRIENDS?

FRIENDS? OH---WHY--- YES----THAT CLOCK OVER THERE-
THAT ONE IS AN OLD FRIEND OF MINE. HE HAS BEEN WITH ME FOR MANY YEARS!

AH---YOU CHAPS DON'T MIND IF I TAKE A LITTLE TIME LOOKING OVER THESE CLOCKS, DO YOU?
DON'T BE SILLY--- I'M JUST KILLING TIME--- I'M NOT DOING ANYTHING THIS AFTERNOON, ANYWAY!
GO AHEAD--- I'VE PLENTY OF TIME, TOO!

THAT--- THAT MAN'S CRAZY! DID YOU HEAR HIM RAVE ON?

HE'S A FANATIC ON TIME IF I EVER SAW ONE!

YES--- ISN'T HE, THIS CLOCK MAKER--- ISN'T HE---

EXACTLY ONE DAY LATER---- BRUCE WAYNE RECEIVES A PHONE CALL FROM KEATING.

BRUCE, I'M WORRIED! FOR THE LAST FEW HOURS I'VE SEEN PROWLERS ABOUT MY HOUSE. I THINK--- I THINK THEY WANT TO KILL ME.

NONSENSE! WHY SHOULD ANYONE WANT TO KILL YOU? GO BACK TO BED! YOU'VE JUST GOT THE JITTERS.

THE BATMOBILE RACES TO THE KEATING HOME IN RECORD TIME!
HELP!
C'MON, ROBIN! LOOKS LIKE WE'RE BEING PAGED!

UP THE STEPS AND INTO THE HOUSE DART THE BATMAN AND ROBIN---TWIN AVENGERS OF EVIL!
GREETINGS--!
THE-THE BATMAN!

---AND SALUTATIONS--
...AND ALL THAT SORT OF THING!

HOLD HIM STILL! GIMME A CHANCE TO PLUG 'IM!

YOU HAD YOUR CHANCE, MUGG---BUT YOU MUFFED IT!
OOF!

BEFORE THE HOODLUMS CAN RECOVER, THE BATMAN IS UPON THEM LIKE A POUNCING TIGER!
VERY NICE! NOW I DONT HAVE TO SOIL MY HANDS ON THE BOTH OF YOU!

OUTSIDE, THE THUGS SCRAMBLE TO THEIR FEET AND RUN TO THEIR CAR!
C'MON! LET'S GET OUTA HERE--- BUT FAST!
WAIT-- MITCH IS INSIDE. HE MIGHT TALK!

HE WON'T GET A CHANCE TO SQUEAL TO THE BATMAN--
OHHH..

THEY'RE GETTING AWAY! LET'S GET THEM!
SOME OTHER TIME! KEATING LOOKS AS IF HE NEEDS SOME MEDICAL ATTENTION!

LATER---
WHAT--- WHO---?
TAKE IT EASY! YOU'RE ALL RIGHT NOW. JUST A BIT BRUISED, THAT'S ALL--

AND STILL LATER, IN THE BATMOBILE.....
I WONDER WHY THOSE KILLERS WERE AFTER KEATING?
I'VE A HUNCH SOMEONE WANTED TO KILL KEATING AND SENT THOSE THUGS THERE TO MAKE IT LOOK LIKE THEY WERE TRYING TO ROB AND THEN KILL HIM! IT WOULD BE A NICE COVER-UP!

AND THAT VERY MOMENT---
...AND THEN THE BATMAN AND THAT ROBIN KID WALKED IN!
WE TOOK CARE OF MITCH BEFORE WE SCRAMMED. HE WON'T SAY NOTHIN' ANYMORE
ALL RIGHT... LEAVE ME ALONE NOW. I WANT TO THINK!

THE BATMAN, EH? I'LL HAVE TO BE SUBTLE NOW WITH HIM AROUND! THE TICKING OF THOSE CLOCKS DISTURBS MY THOUGHTS.... CLOCKS... THERE'S A THOUGHT! I WONDER-- I WONDER--
TICK
TICK
TOCK

TWO NIGHTS LATER, IN THE KEATING HOME. A CLAW-LIKE HAND DEPOSITS A SUBSTITUTE CLOCK WHERE ANOTHER ONCE STOOD!

LATER THAT NIGHT, AS KEATING SITS AT HIS DESK----

THE CLOCK TOLLS ON---

...SIX....SEVEN...EIGHT.... NINE....TEN....

GAS RISES FROM THE CLOCK IN A MALIGNANT CLOUD!

DEATH STRIKES AT THIRTEEN!

THE NEXT DAY, AT NOON TIME...KEATING'S BODY IS DISCOVERED. POLICE SWARM INTO THE DEATH ROOM. ACCOMPANYING HIS FRIEND, POLICE COMMISSIONER GORDON, IS BRUCE WAYNE....

THE CLOCK TOLLS ON.... NINE.... TEN...ELEVEN....

BUT ONLY BRUCE HAS COUNTED THE CLOCK'S STROKES!

AND AT THAT VERY MOMENT IN A MUSTY OLD STORE, THE BENT, LITTLE MAN KNOWN AS BROCK, THE CLOCK MAKER, CACKLES WITH SATISFIED LAUGHTER---

AND THAT VERY NIGHT, IN THE HOME OF HENRY DECKER---A STOCK-HOLDER IN THE HOBBS CLOCK COMPANY ----TWELVE O'CLOCK!

THE CLOCK TOLLS ON!.... NINE....TEN.....ELEVEN.. TWELVE---

DEATH STRIKES AT THIRTEEN!

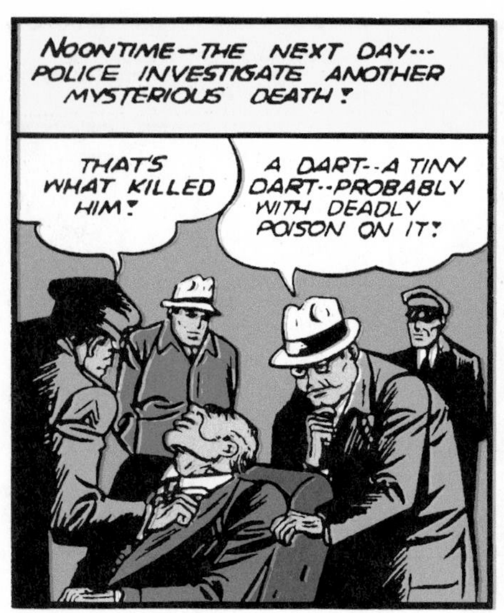
NOONTIME—THE NEXT DAY... POLICE INVESTIGATE ANOTHER MYSTERIOUS DEATH!
THAT'S WHAT KILLED HIM!
A DART--A TINY DART--PROBABLY WITH DEADLY POISON ON IT!

I WONDER WHO BLEW THAT DART? OH—TWELVE O'CLOCK!
THE CLOCK TOLLS ON-- FOUR --- FIVE --- SIX --- SEVEN --- EIGHT!

NINE ... TEN ... ELEVEN... TWELVE ---
THIRTEEN... LIKE THE OTHER ONE ...
WHA-- YOU'RE CRAZY!
LOOK! THERE'S YOUR MURDERER! THAT LITTLE BUGLER!

CRAZY, AM I? HERE--THIS BUGLER BLEW THE DART WHEN THE CLOCK READ MIDNIGHT! DECKER HAD A HABIT OF READING IN THIS CHAIR TILL LATE AT NIGHT!
OF COURSE, AND OUR MURDERER KNEW THAT! HE KNEW DECKER'S HEAD WOULD BE IN LINE WITH THE CLOCK! WHY--OUR MURDERER MUST BE A CLEVER DEVIL!

AND IN HIS DINGY STORE, THE CLOCK MAKER LAUGHS GLEEFULLY AS HUNDRED OF CLOCKS CHIME AT ONCE.
HEE--HEE! THAT'S RIGHT-- THAT'S RIGHT! THIS CLOCK IS FOR A MAN WHO KILLS TIME- THIS CLOCK IS FOR BRUCE WAYNE! HEE--HEE-- HEE--
AND BRUCE WAYNE IS THE BATMAN!

THAT VERY NIGHT AS THE MIDNIGHT HOUR DRAWS CLOSE, THE LOUD DANGLE OF A DOOR-BELL BRINGS DICK GRAYSON TO THE DOOR OF THE WAYNE HOME.
PACKAGE FOR YA!
THANK YOU!

IT'S A CLOCK! NOW WHY SHOULD ANYONE SEND US A CLOCK?

THE CLOCK TOLLS THE HOUR --- MIDNIGHT!
BONG!
BONG
BONG
FOUR-- FIVE --- SIX --- SEVEN --- EIGHT---

SUDDENLY, A FIGURE HURTLES INTO THE ROOM—PICKS UP THE CLOCK—AND---
BONG
BONG
?

NINE---TEN--ELEVEN-TWELVE---THIRTEEN--- THEN---A THUNDEROUS BLAST DEAFENS THE NIGHT!
BOOM!
WHAT A FIRE-CRACKER THAT WAS!
WHEW!

GOOD THING I HEARD THAT CLOCK START TO CHIME. I KNEW WE HAD NO CLOCKS LIKE THAT! LOOKS LIKE SOME-BODY DOESN'T LIKE US, EH, KID?

THE VERY NEXT NIGHT! ONCE AGAIN BRUCE WAYNE DONS THE INK-HUED GARB OF THE BATMAN!
NOW REMEMBER-- IF I'M NOT BACK WITHIN THE HOUR, COME AND GET ME!
CHECK!

SOMETIME LATER - THE BATMAN'S CAPED FIGURE BENDS OVER A FILING CABNET!
HOBBS CLOCK COMPANY
JUST AS I THOUGHT! BOTH KEATING AND DECKER WERE BOTH STOCKHOLDERS IN THE HOBBS CLOCK COMPANY. THINGS TIE UP! I'D BETTER MAKE A PHONE CALL!

THE BATMAN PHONES THE BANKER, SELBY--
HELLO, SELBY- ARE YOU ALL RIGHT?
CLICK!
OF COURSE I'M ALL RIGHT! WHO IS THIS SPEAKING-- WHA?--THE MAN HUNG UP!

AND IN THE CRAMPED INTERIOR OF HIS LITTLE SHOP, THE CLOCK MAKER LISTENS INTENTLY TO A MAN WHO SPEAKS TO HIM--
BRUCE WAYNE IS STILL ALIVE! SOMETHING WENT WRONG, BUT WE'LL GET HIM THE NEXT TIME! NOW, I'VE ANOTHER KILLER OF TIME FOR YOU-- PETER SELBY, THE BANKER!
YES I'VE SEEN HIM! HE SITS IN HIS OFFICE, IDLY WATCHING TIME PASS BY WHILE HIS STAFF MAKES MONEY FOR HIM. THE MURDERER!

QUICK! GIVE ME THE ADDRESS OF THIS MAN SO I MAY LET ONE OF MY FRIENDS. A CLOCK, AVENGE THE DEATH OF TIME!
SURE--- SURE--- HIS ADDRESS IS---
WHY DON'T YOU GIVE HIM YOUR ADDRESS...

--ATKINS?
WHO? -THAT COSTUME- YOU'RE THE BATMAN!

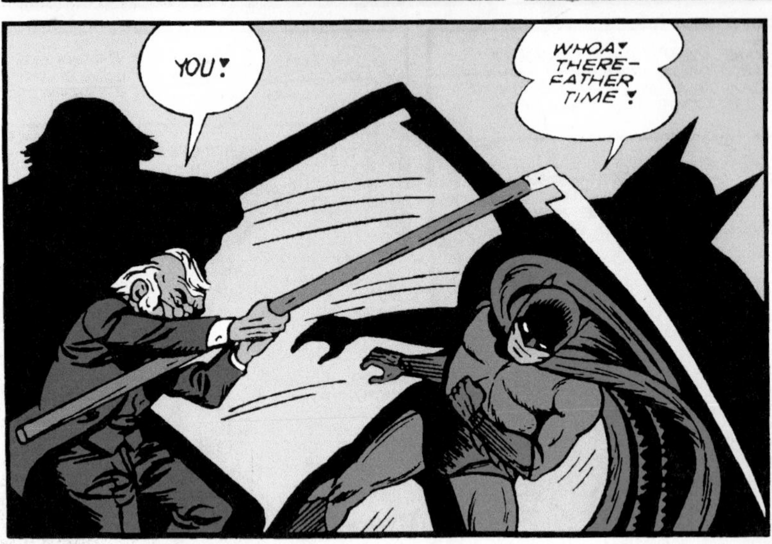
YOU!
WHOA! THERE- FATHER TIME!

I HATE TO HIT AN OLDER MAN---BUT I'M AFRAID THIS TIME IT'S NECESSARY!

THAT GUN WON'T DO YOU ANY GOOD, ATKINS! I KNOW WHY YOU KILLED THOSE STOCK-HOLDERS, KEATING, AND DECKER! YOU WANTED TO CONTROL HOBBS CLOCK COMPANY BY YOURSELF!
THAT'S RIGHT! WHEN OLD HOBBS, THE FOUNDER OF THE COMPANY, DIED, HE LEFT A WILL STATING HIS PERSONAL STOCKS WERE TO BE DIVIDED AMONG THE OTHER MEMBERS!..

...AND THAT EACH TIME ANOTHER STOCKHOLDER DIED, HOBBS' PERSONAL STOCK WAS TO BE DIVIDED AMONG THE SURVIVING MEMBERS! I HAD MORE STOCK THAN ANY-ONE ELSE TO BEGIN WITH---
AND SO YOU FIGURED IF YOU HAD THE OTHERS KILLED OFF, YOU ALONE WOULD SOON OWN THE CONTROLLING SHARES OF STOCK! A CLEVER MAN, BUT A MAD ONE!

MAD? HA---IT WAS CLEVER! I EVEN PLAYED ON THE FANATICAL OLD CLOCK MAKER'S WARPED SENSES---MADE HIM THINK THE OTHERS WERE "MURDERERS OF TIME" AND SHOULD BE KILLED -- JUST AS I'M GOING TO KILL YOU RIGHT NOW!
9

WITH ONE CAT-LIKE BOUND, THE BATMAN IS UPON ATKINS!

THE GUN GOES OFF---AND THE BULLET FINDS ITS MARK!

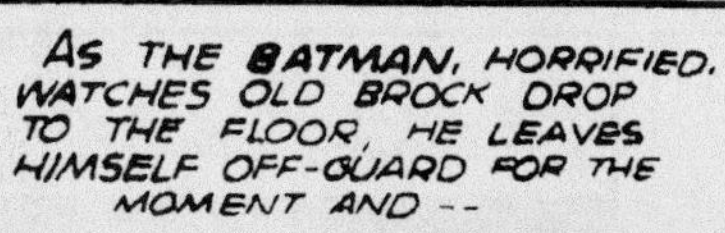
AS THE BATMAN, HORRIFIED, WATCHES OLD BROCK DROP TO THE FLOOR, HE LEAVES HIMSELF OFF-GUARD FOR THE MOMENT AND --

ATKINS BINDS THE BATMAN WITH ROPE!

SUDDENLY, A VOICE WHIRLS ATKINS ABOUT!

A SHRIEK IS SUDDENLY CUT OFF: DEATH HAS COME TO ATKINS!

AS THE MADMAN RAVES ON - THE BATMAN REGAINS CONSCIOUSNESS

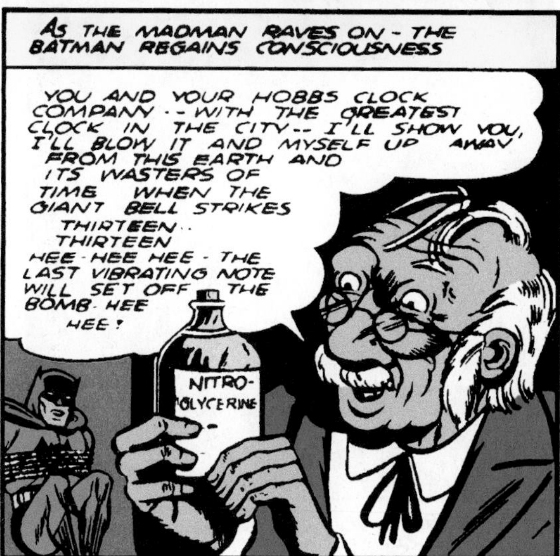

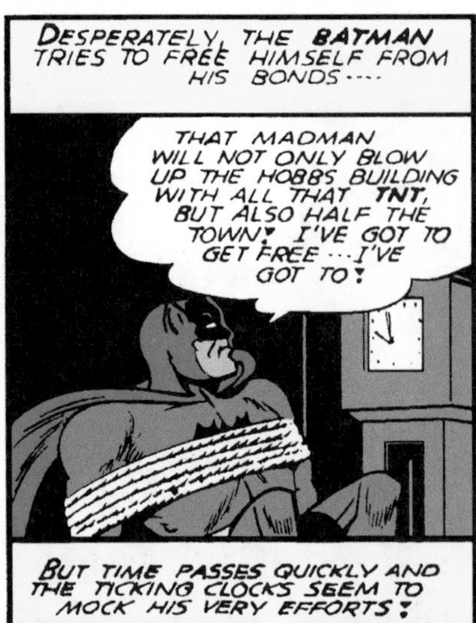

AND NOW IT IS A FIGHT AGAINST THE INEXORABLE ADVANCE OF TIME ITSELF, AS BELOW, TWO MEN BATTLE, AND ABOVE, THE PONDEROUS BELL CLANGS .... FOUR!

NOW I'VE NO SCRUPLES ABOUT SOCKING YOU, MR. CLOCK MAKER!

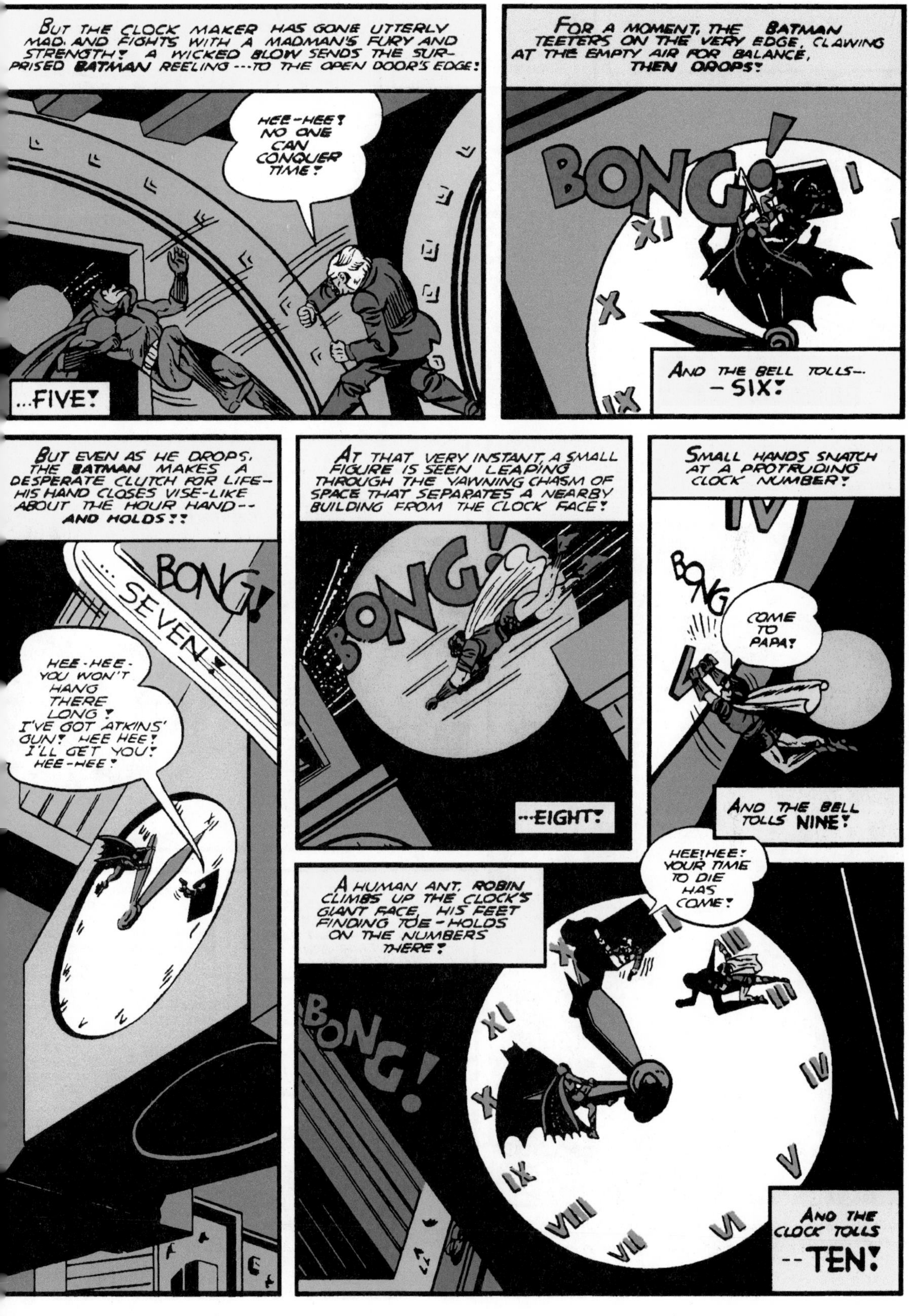

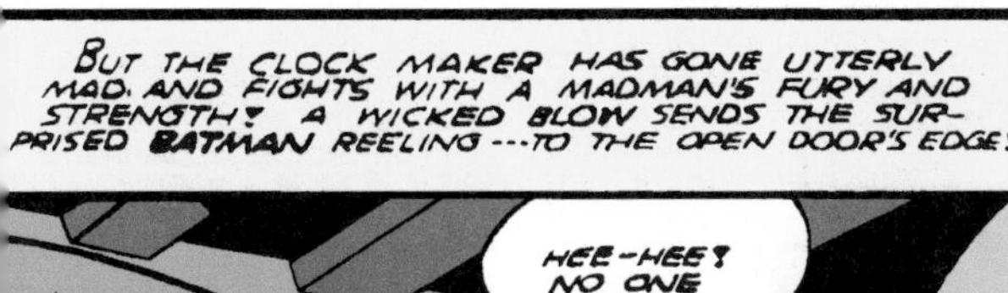

AT THAT VERY INSTANT, A SMALL FIGURE IS SEEN LEAPING THROUGH THE YAWNING CHASM OF SPACE THAT SEPARATES A NEARBY BUILDING FROM THE CLOCK FACE!

BONG!

---EIGHT!

SMALL HANDS SNATCH AT A PROTRUDING CLOCK NUMBER!

BONG

COME TO PAPA!

AND THE BELL TOLLS NINE!

A HUMAN ANT, ROBIN CLIMBS UP THE CLOCK'S GIANT FACE, HIS FEET FINDING TOE-HOLDS ON THE NUMBERS THERE!

HEE! HEE! YOUR TIME TO DIE HAS COME!

BONG!

AND THE CLOCK TOLLS --TEN!

1 REACHING OUT, HIS HANDS CLOSE ON THE CLOCK MAKER---

AND THE CLOCK TOLLS ELEVEN!

2 WHO FALLS WITH A TRAILING SHRIEK AS THE BELL TOLLS-- TWELVE--

3 AND NOW THE TWIN BATTLERS OF CRIME RACE UP TO THE BELFRY ITSELF AS THE GIANT BELL SWINGS PONDEROUSLY... ITS HUGE CLAPPER READY TO CRASH FOR A FINAL CLANG- AND SHATTERING DEATH!

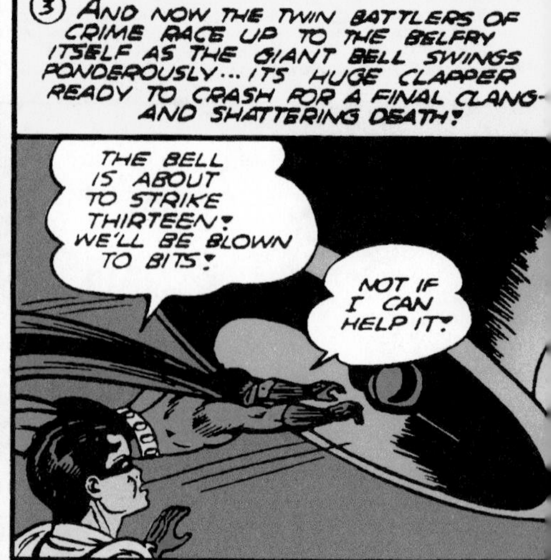

4 AND THE BATMAN'S BODY WINDS ABOUT THE GIANT CLAPPER AS IT CRASHES WITH SICKENING FORCE AGAINST THE GREAT BELL---

THE BATMAN'S BODY ACTS AS A BUFFER! THE DEAFENING VIBRATION THAT IS TO SET OFF THE DEADLY T.N.T. DOES NOT COME!

5 BACK AND FORTH SWAYS THE GIANT CLAPPER CRASHING THE BATMAN'S BRUISED FORM AGAINST THE BELL AS IF TO DISLODGE HIM-- BUT HE HOLDS FAST, LIKE GRIM DEATH!

UGH! GOT TO HOLD ON--GOT TO, OR THIS WHOLE TOWN WILL BE BLOWN UP---

AT LAST, THE CLAPPER SWAYS NO MORE. ROBIN HAS FOUND THE MECHANISM THAT STOPS THE BELL'S GIANT SWING!

LATER, A SLEEK, VEHICLE BEARS AWAY TWO HEROIC FIGURES-- BATMAN AND ROBIN, THE BOY WONDER!

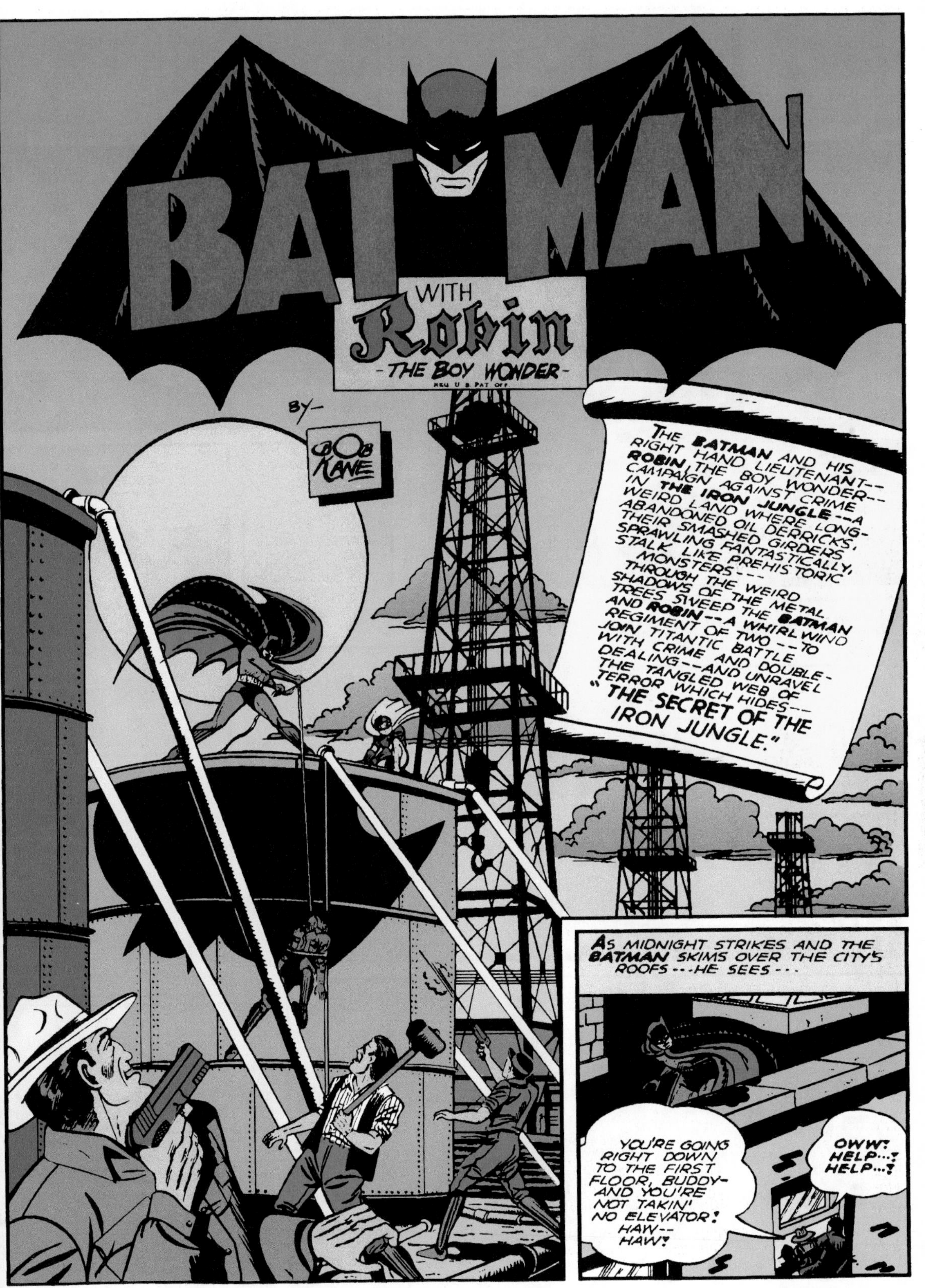
BATMAN
WITH Robin
-THE BOY WONDER-
REG U.S. PAT OFF
BY-
BOB KANE
THE BATMAN AND HIS RIGHT HAND LIEUTENANT-- ROBIN, THE BOY WONDER-- CAMPAIGN AGAINST CRIME IN THE IRON JUNGLE--A WEIRD LAND WHERE LONG-ABANDONED OIL DERRICKS, THEIR SMASHED GIRDERS SPRAWLING FANTASTICALLY, STALK LIKE PREHISTORIC MONSTERS--- THROUGH THE WEIRD SHADOWS OF THE METAL TREES SWEEP THE BATMAN AND ROBIN--A WHIRLWIND REGIMENT OF TWO--TO JOIN TITANIC BATTLE WITH CRIME AND DOUBLE-DEALING--AND UNRAVEL THE TANGLED WEB OF TERROR WHICH HIDES--- "THE SECRET OF THE IRON JUNGLE."
AS MIDNIGHT STRIKES AND THE BATMAN SKIMS OVER THE CITY'S ROOFS---HE SEES---
YOU'RE GOING RIGHT DOWN TO THE FIRST FLOOR, BUDDY-AND YOU'RE NOT TAKIN' NO ELEVATOR! HAW--HAW!
OWW! HELP...! HELP...!

YOU CAN'T DO THIS TO ME!
--AND THEY'RE NOT GOING TO!
WELL, HE'S A GONER. LET'S SCRAM!
EASY, MISTER-YOU'RE OKAY NOW.
SAFELY INSIDE THE OFFICE, THE BATMAN LISTENS TO A TALE OF CRIME AND TERROR!
THEY'RE OUT TO GET ME. YOU SEE, THEY'RE TRYING TO WRECK PAGE OIL COMPANY-- I'M THE NEW YORK REPRESENTATIVE.
WELL, YOU'D BETTER KEEP OUT OF SIGHT NOW-- THERE'S NO TELLING WHAT MAY HAPPEN.
NEXT MORNING, BRUCE WAYNE- SOCIETY PLAYBOY TO THE WORLD, BUT THE BATMAN ONLY TO DICK GRAYSON, ALIAS ROBIN THE BOY WONDER -SITS IN HIS STUDY WHEN THE TRIM FIGURE OF LINDA PAGE ENTERS.
WHY, LINDA-QUITTING WORK?
BRUCE, PLEASE BE SERIOUS. I HEARD DAD'S HAVING TROUBLE DOWN AT HIS TEXAS OIL FIELDS-
---IF HE NEEDS MONEY--
NO. HIS LIFE IS IN DANGER! EVER SINCE THAT GUSHER WAS EXPECTED--
NOTE A GUSHER IS A MONSTER SPOUT OF OIL THAT OFTEN BRINGS UNTOLD WEALTH--SHOOTING THOUSANDS OF FEET FROM BELOW THE EARTH, HUNDREDS OF FEET INTO THE AIR. GUSHERS HAVE BEEN KNOWN TO POUR OUT OIL AT THE RATE OF TWO MILLION GALLONS A DAY.
...GRAHAM MASTERS, DAD'S PARTNER, THREATENS TO PUSH MY FATHER OUT BEFORE THE GUSHER SENDS STOCKS SOARING!
MEANWHILE, AT TOM PAGE'S HEADQUARTERS AT THE PAGE OIL COMPANY-
YOU'RE OLD--IT'S MY TURN NOW, I TELL YOU! SO GET OUT WHILE THE GOING IS STILL GOOD!
I'VE GOT BIG PLANS FOR MYSELF-- AND THIS OLD GUY'S NOT GOING TO STAND IN MY WAY!

AT THAT VERY MOMENT, LINDA IS TELLING BRUCE WHAT HAS BEEN GOING ON--
---AND ALL KINDS OF STRANGE ACCIDENTS HAVE BEEN HAPPENING---

CHATTING CASUALLY THROUGH THE LIPS OF BRUCE WAYNE-- OUR PLAYBOY PLANS RAPIDLY WITH THE SUREFIRE BRAIN OF THE BATMAN!
OH! THINK I'D LIKE TO SEE TEXAS AGAIN--I NEED A VACATION.
WELL, WATCH OUT FOR THOSE BIG, HUSKY TEXANS! I'LL BE DOWN LATER TO SEE NOTHING HAPPENS TO YOU.

NO SOONER HAS LINDA LEFT THAN DICK GRAYSON, ALIAS ROBIN THE BOY WONDER, DARTS INTO THE ROOM---
I OVER-HEARD EVERYTHING.
LISTEN TO ME, THEN--WE'VE GOT TO GET TO TEXAS BEFORE SOME-THING HAPPENS TO LINDA'S FATHER.

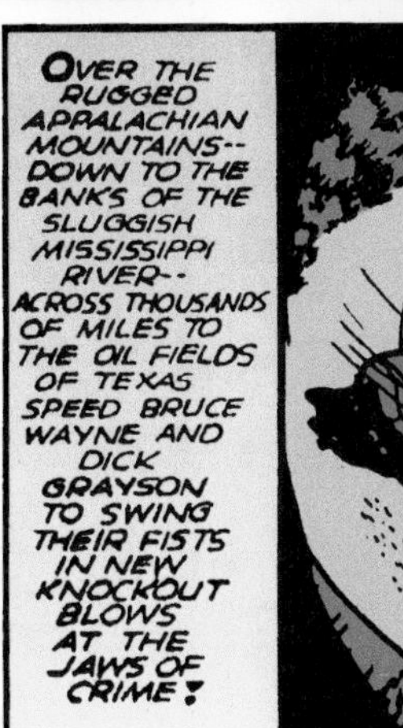
OVER THE RUGGED APPALACHIAN MOUNTAINS--DOWN TO THE BANKS OF THE SLUGGISH MISSISSIPPI RIVER--ACROSS THOUSANDS OF MILES TO THE OIL FIELDS OF TEXAS SPEED BRUCE WAYNE AND DICK GRAYSON TO SWING THEIR FISTS IN NEW KNOCKOUT BLOWS AT THE JAWS OF CRIME!

GEE, I'VE ALWAYS WANTED TO SEE THE MISSISSIPPI!
YOU'D BETTER GET BACK IN THE TRUNK NOW. NO ONE MUST SEE YOU.

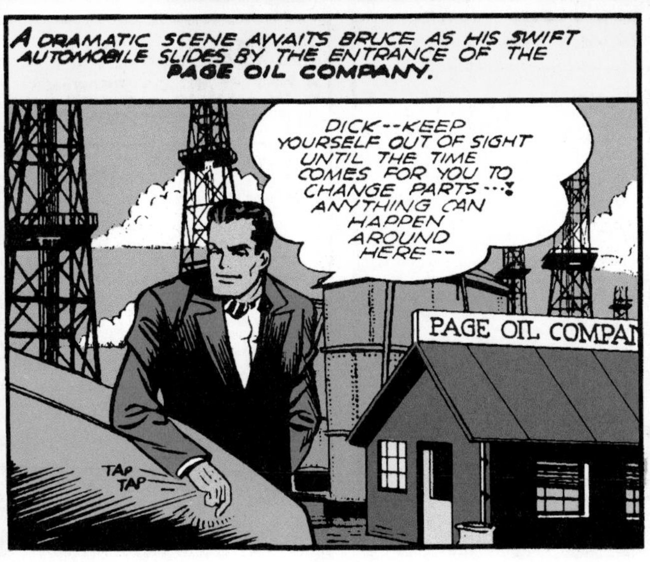
A DRAMATIC SCENE AWAITS BRUCE AS HIS SWIFT AUTOMOBILE SLIDES BY THE ENTRANCE OF THE PAGE OIL COMPANY.
DICK--KEEP YOURSELF OUT OF SIGHT UNTIL THE TIME COMES FOR YOU TO CHANGE PARTS--! ANYTHING CAN HAPPEN AROUND HERE--
PAGE OIL COMPAN
TAP TAP

....AND ANYTHING DOES!
IT'S YOUR LAST CHANCE.
--AND YOURS, TOO!

WHO INVITED YOU IN HERE, PRETTY BOY?
I MIGHT ASK THE SAME OF YOU!

WISE GUY, EH--?

YOU...
SHOULDN'T STRAIN YOURSELF, YOU KNOW--

PARDON ME, SIR. I DIDN'T MEAN TO KICK YOU!
OUCH!

OH! I'M SO SORRY-- BUT ACCIDENTS WILL HAPPEN--
4

AFTER MASTERS LEAVES--
THAT WAS MY PARTNER, BRUCE! HE JUST WARNED ME THAT, IF I DIDNT SELL OUT BY MIDNIGHT, MY LIFES IN DANGER!
DON'T WORRY, MR. PAGE— THAT KIND OF THING ONLY HAPPENS IN STORY BOOKS!

AS THEY TALK, TOM'S TRAITOROUS PARTNER HOLDS A WHISPERED CONFERENCE WITH CHUCK, HIS CHIEF STRONG-ARM MAN--
WHEN THAT WISE GUY COMES OUT-- START A FIGHT WITH HIM! AND MAKE IT GOOD!
I GETCHA, BOSS! YOU AND THE BOYS'LL SNATCH OLD GRANDPOP WHILE ITS GOING ON. SMART STUFF, CHIEF--

A FEW MINUTES LATER, BRUCE, DRESSED IN A SPOTLESS, WHITE SUIT, GOES OUTSIDE TO LOOK THINGS OVER -
WELL-- SO THE RECEPTION COMMITTEE IS WAITING.

LOOKS LIKE CHUCK AND HIS GANG ARE GETTING READY FOR SOME DIRTY WORK.
IF HE STARTS ANY-THING, WE'LL CLEAN THEM ALL UP--THOSE TROUBLE-MAKERS DESERVE A GOOD BEATING!

AS BRUCE WALKS FORWARD--A NO-MAN'S LAND IS FORMED BETWEEN THE TWO SIDES-
WELL-- HERE'S MY CHANCE TO MIX WITH REAL SOCIETY--
YOU ARE-- BUT NOT IN THE WAY YOU THINK-

WHEN CHUCK GIVES US THE EYE, START SWINGING!
I GOT SOME BRASS KNUCKLES THAT NEED BREAKING IN!

GEE-- AIN'T THAT A SWEET, LITTLE, WHITE SUIT HE'S WEARING--! HAW! HAW!

I DON'T LIKE YOUR FACE- MUCH RATHER YOU KEPT IT COVERED!
OOF!
5

PLEASE, KEEP YOUR DISTANCE!

CHUCK IS MADE TO LOOK RIDICULOUS BEFORE HIS OWN MEN–
DON'T TAKE IT LYING DOWN, CHUCK. HAW HAW--!

BRUCE'S STRATAGEM WORKS--CHUCK, INFURIATED, WADES INTO HIS OWN MEN!
LAUGH AT ME, WILL YA--!
WELL, THEY'RE DOING OUR JOB FOR US VERY NICELY!
CERTAINLY SAVED US A LOT OF TROUBLE. LET'S GET BACK TO WORK.

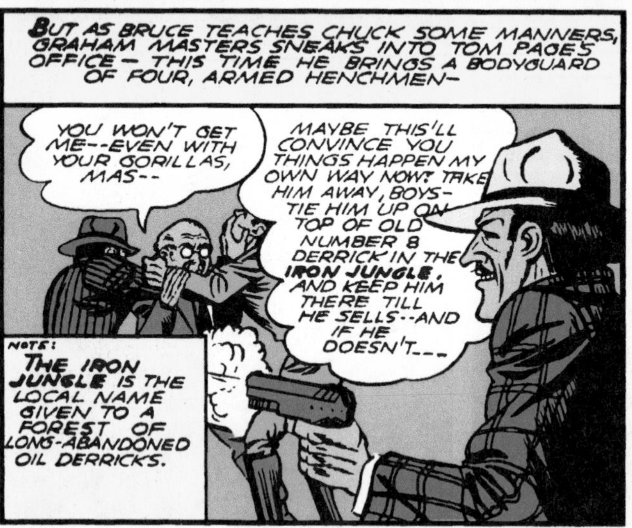
BUT AS BRUCE TEACHES CHUCK SOME MANNERS, GRAHAM MASTERS SNEAKS INTO TOM PAGE'S OFFICE– THIS TIME HE BRINGS A BODYGUARD OF FOUR, ARMED HENCHMEN–
YOU WON'T GET ME--EVEN WITH YOUR GORILLAS, MAS--
MAYBE THIS'LL CONVINCE YOU THINGS HAPPEN MY OWN WAY NOW! TAKE HIM AWAY, BOYS– TIE HIM UP ON TOP OF OLD NUMBER 8 DERRICK IN THE IRON JUNGLE, AND KEEP HIM THERE TILL HE SELLS--AND IF HE DOESN'T---
NOTE: THE IRON JUNGLE IS THE LOCAL NAME GIVEN TO A FOREST OF LONG-ABANDONED OIL DERRICKS.

HE'S SHOT– BOSS!
THE IRON JUNGLE! HE'S NOT HURT BAD. GET HIM OUT OF THE BACK DOOR AND HURRY IT UP.

BUT OUTSIDE, NIGHT IS FALLING, AND BRUCE SLIPS AWAY TO THE OLD BUNK-HOUSE WHERE HE HAD AGREED TO MEET DICK--
COME ON, ROBIN--INTO YOUR WORK CLOTHES!
---I'VE A HUNCH THERE ARE GOING TO BE BIG DOINGS TONIGHT!

MEANWHILE, A YELLOW ROADSTER PULLS UP-- AT THE VERY MOMENT MASTERS SNEAKS OUT OF THE OFFICE. LINDA PAGE HAS ARRIVED EARLIER THAN SHE PLANNED.
CHUCK– C'MERE– QUICK--LOOK WHO'S HERE? PAGE'S DAUGHTER–
GET OFF MY CAR AT ONCE!

GEE, BOSS! SHE'S WORSE THAN A BUCKING BRONCO!
WE'VE GOT TO GET HER OUT OF HERE BEFORE THEY SEE US!

BUT AS THEY MAKE GOOD THEIR ESCAPE--TWO MASKED FIGURES SHOOT FROM THE DOOR OF THE OLD BUNKHOUSE!
I'VE NEVER DRIVEN ONE OF THESE BEFORE!
THERE'S NO TIME LIKE NOW TO BEGIN! LINDA'S IN THAT CAR AND WE'VE GOT TO GET HER OUT!

SHE'S OUT-- WHAT WE GONNA DO WIT'DE DAME?
THAT DEPENDS ON WHAT HER OLD MAN DOES. WE'LL TURN AROUND AT THE LEON BEND AND MAKE FOR THE IRON JUNGLE BY THE OLD ROAD!
PAGE
PAGE

IN HOT PURSUIT THE HEAVY OIL TRUCK THUNDERS DOWN THE ROAD!

THE BATMAN! BUT WHERE - HOW??
UGGH!

INTO THE LAST LAP SPEEDS THE TRUCK--- A MONSTER BON FIRE LASHING OUT WITH SCARLET OIL FOR WHIPS! AS IT SCREECHES TO A HALT ROBIN AND THE BATMAN, LINDA UNDER THE LATTER'S ARM, LEAP—AND NONE TOO SOON—

BOOM

WE HAVEN'T A SECOND TO LOSE-TAKE CARE OF LINDA-I'M GOING AFTER CHUCK AND MASTERS!

WITH PANTHER-LIKE MOVEMENT, THE BATMAN TRAILS HIS QUARRY INTO THE DENSE SEMI-TROPICAL UNDERGROWTH THAT SWARMS ALL OVER THE IRON JUNGLE!
THIS TIME YOU'RE NOT GETTING AWAY!
THE BATMAN SCOUTS THRU THE THICKETS. IN THE GLARE OF THE COMING STORM'S FIRST FLASH OF LIGHTNING, HE SEES TOM PAGE LASHED TO THE TOPMOST GIRDER OF A DESERTED DERRICK!
INSTANTLY, THE BATMAN SCALES THE VERY NEXT DERRICK. LIGHTNING FLARES WEIRDLY ON THE UNCANNY SCENE---
REACHING THE TOWER'S TOP, THE BATMAN GRASPS A GIANT CREEPER--MAKING READY FOR A DEATH-DEFYING GLIDE!
I HOPE THIS CREEPER HOLDS!
LIGHTNING RENDS THE SKY, ILUMINATING THE BATMAN AS HE LEAPS....
9
THE GUNMEN'S WEAPONS HURL SUDDEN DEATH!
WHA...? THE BATMAN-ALIVE!
GET THAT GUY--AND MAKE SURE THIS TIME!
THE STREAM OF BULLETS SEVER THE CREEPER-- THE BATMAN'S SOLE LINK WITH THE WORLD!

THE THING'S FALLING APART!

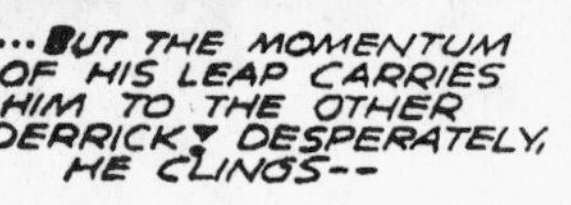
...BUT THE MOMENTUM OF HIS LEAP CARRIES HIM TO THE OTHER DERRICK! DESPERATELY, HE CLINGS--

YOU'RE IN FER A DROP, BUDDY!
DON'T BE TOO SURE--

YOU NEED A LESSON, TOO--

--SEE WHAT I MEAN?

MEANWHILE, ROBIN SIGHTS THE BATMAN'S LONE STRUGGLE AGAINST OVERWHELMING ODDS--
LOOKS AS THOUGH BATMAN NEEDS ME-

WHA--! IT'S ONLY A KID!

-WITH A BIG PUNCH!

1
GOTCHA!

2
THAT'LL TEACH YOU, FRESH KID!

3 LED BY CHUCK, THE THUGS BUNDLE ROBIN INTO THE HAND LIFT. THEY PLAN TO LEAVE THEIR VICTIMS AT THE TOP TO BURN!
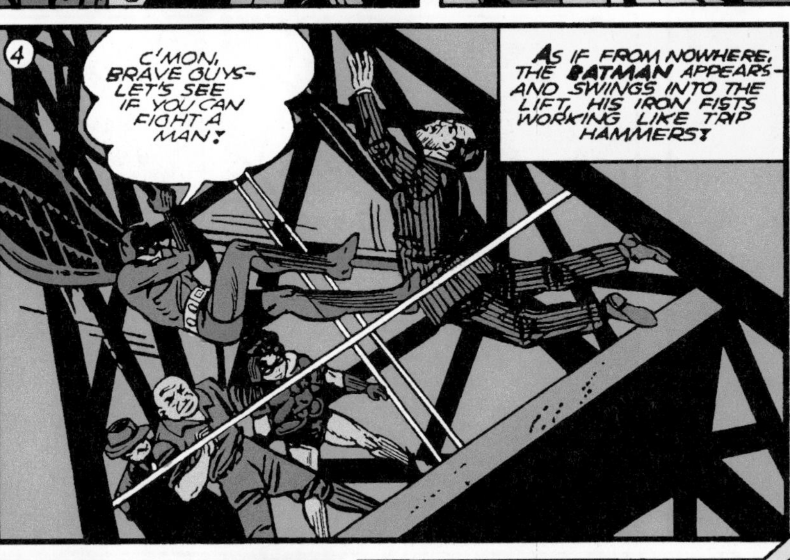
4
AS IF FROM NOWHERE, THE BATMAN APPEARS-- AND SWINGS INTO THE LIFT, HIS IRON FISTS WORKING LIKE TRIP HAMMERS!
C'MON, BRAVE GUYS-- LET'S SEE IF YOU CAN FIGHT A MAN!

5
I'LL FINISH THEM ALL-- NOW!

6 THE SHAFT GIVES WAY AND THE MEN TOPPLE TO THEIR DOOM!
THAT'S JUSTICE FOR YOU-- GUNMEN KILLED BY THEIR OWN LEADER.

7 DEPOSITING ROBIN ON THE GROUND, THE BATMAN TAKES AFTER MASTERS---
OH, YEAH?
I'M COMING FOR YOU, MASTERS. PLEASE DON'T BE IMPATIENT!

HIGH ON THE CRUMBLING DERRICK, THEY LOCK IN A DEATH STRUGGLE---
1
GET HIM, BATMAN!
LET'S SEE HOW WELL YOU FIGHT WITHOUT A GUN!
JUST AS THE BATMAN FREES OLD TOM FROM HIS BONDS- THE OLD DERRICK CRUMBLES EARTHWARD!
HELP!
STRAIGHTEN YOUR BODY, MR. PAGE!
2

3
ONLY THE SPONGY AND INNUMERABLE LAKES OF OIL SAVE THEM-- ABSORBING THE FALL!
WE'VE GOT TO GET TO OIL WELL NUMBER THREE--THEY'LL BE BLASTING IN FIVE MINUTES-- AND IT MAY BE THE GUSHER!
WHEW-THAT WAS A CLOSE SHAVE! MASTERS MUST BE TRAPPED IN THE WRECKAGE!

4
THEY'VE KILLED JOE! ANOTHER TWO MINUTES AND THE RAIN WILL RUIN THE NITRO CHARGE! THE MEN ARE AFRAID!
I'LL DO THE JOB!
5
I'LL GET THAT BATMAN AND OLD PAGE IF IT'S THE LAST THING I DO!

6
NOW...!

SUDDENLY--
NOT SO FAST, RAT--

MASTERS FREES HIS GUN-ARM TO TAKE A SHOT AT ROBIN, BUT IN THE ENSUING STRUGGLE, HIS ARM IS FORCED BACK-

1
....THE GUN FLAMES-
THE BATMAN IS CERTAINLY RIGHT-- CRIME DOES NOT PAY--

2
MEANWHILE, THE BATMAN PUSHES THE PLUNGER-- THOUSANDS OF FEET BELOW THE EARTH THERE IS A TREMENDOUS EXPLOSION--AS THE OIL IS UN-LEASHED BY THE NITRO'S POWERFUL KICK—
HEADS UP--HERE SHE GOES-

3
MY WORK'S DONE—YOU FINISH THE REST. GOODBYE!
WAIT A MOMENT-YOU SAVED MY LIFE-AND I WANT TO THANK YOU!

4
LOOK AT THAT DARN GUSHER---GOING TO BRING MILLIONS OF GALLONS OF OIL--WHEE--HARRAH!
THE OIL COMPANY'S SAFE AT LAST-

5
WHY, HELLO, LINDA--WHAT BRINGS YOU HERE? I HEARD A LOT OF NOISE AND WONDERED WHAT WAS HAPPENING--
I'M SORRY IT SPOILED YOUR BEAUTY SLEEP.

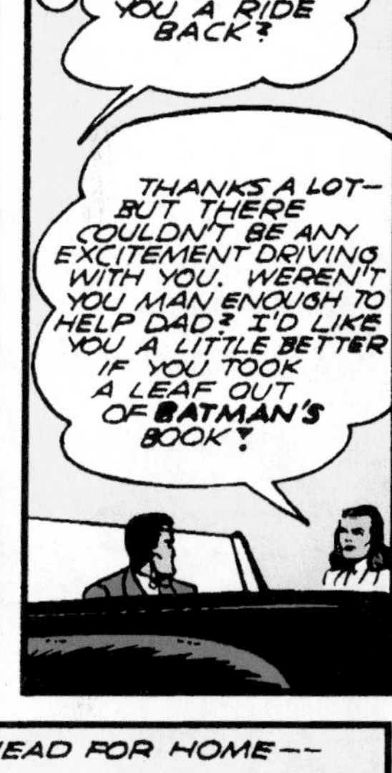
6
CAN I GIVE YOU A RIDE BACK?
THANKS A LOT-BUT THERE COULDN'T BE ANY EXCITEMENT DRIVING WITH YOU. WEREN'T YOU MAN ENOUGH TO HELP DAD? I'D LIKE YOU A LITTLE BETTER IF YOU TOOK A LEAF OUT OF BATMAN'S BOOK!

7
BRUCE AND DICK HEAD FOR HOME--
POOR LINDA--SHE'LL NEVER KNOW! SOMETIMES I KIND OF WISH SHE COULD KNOW
AW GEE! THE BATMAN'S JOB IS TO HUNT CRIMINALS!
BOB KANE
13

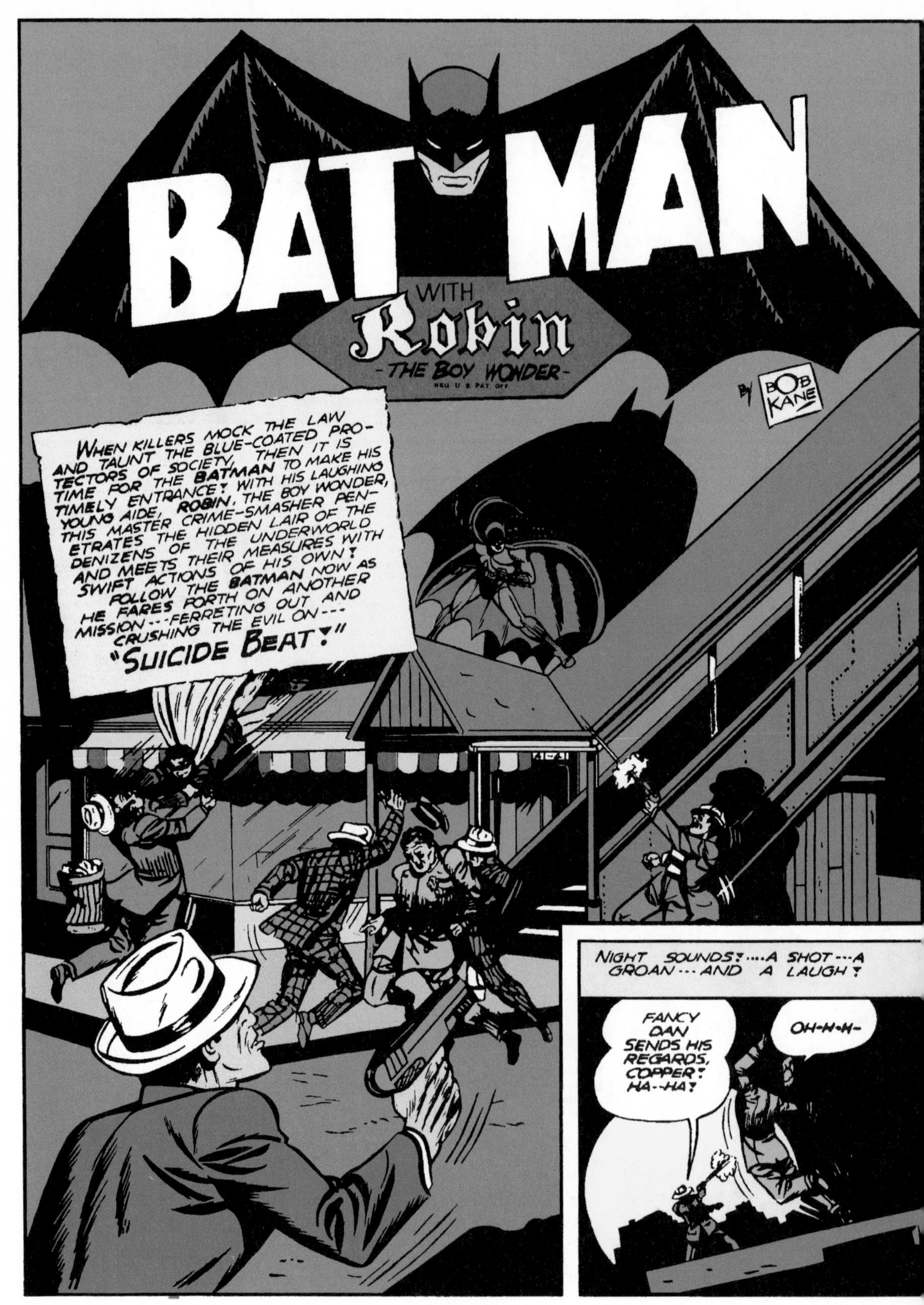
BATMAN
WITH
Robin
-THE BOY WONDER-
REG U.S. PAT OFF
BY BOB KANE
WHEN KILLERS MOCK THE LAW AND TAUNT THE BLUE-COATED PROTECTORS OF SOCIETY, THEN IT IS TIME FOR THE BATMAN TO MAKE HIS TIMELY ENTRANCE! WITH HIS LAUGHING YOUNG AIDE, ROBIN, THE BOY WONDER, THIS MASTER CRIME-SMASHER PENETRATES THE HIDDEN LAIR OF THE DENIZENS OF THE UNDERWORLD AND MEETS THEIR MEASURES WITH SWIFT ACTIONS OF HIS OWN! FOLLOW THE BATMAN NOW AS HE FARES FORTH ON ANOTHER MISSION---FERRETING OUT AND CRUSHING THE EVIL ON---
"SUICIDE BEAT!"
NIGHT SOUNDS!....A SHOT---A GROAN---AND A LAUGH!
FANCY DAN SENDS HIS REGARDS, COPPER! HA--HA!
OH-H-H-

LATER---
IT'S GROGAN. HE DIDN'T HAVE A CHANCE!
HE MUST HAVE BEEN CROWDING FANCY DAN! THEY DON'T LIVE LONG WHEN THEY DO THAT!

NO WONDER THEY CALL THIS "SUICIDE BEAT"! ANY COP THAT GETS THIS BEAT PRACTICALLY COMMITS SUICIDE! FANCY DAN SEES TO THAT!

GROGAN IS THE THIRD COP TO BE FOUND DEAD HERE! I PITY THE POOR GUY THAT GETS THIS BEAT NEXT!
SO DO I!

KELLY, YOU HEARD ABOUT GROGAN LAST NIGHT. I WANT AN EXPERIENCED MAN TO TAKE OVER HIS BEAT. I'M APPOINTING YOU.
YES, SIR!

KELLY, YOU LOOK MIGHTY CHEERFUL FOR A MAN WHO HAS TO TAKE OVER SUICIDE BEAT!
WHY SHOULDN'T KELLY BE SMILING? DIDN'T YOU HEAR THAT HIS SON, JIMMY, GETS HIS BADGE TODAY!
'TIS THE WEARIN' OF THE GREEN-

SURE--AND WHAT MAN WOULDN'T BE PROUD OF A SON LIKE ME BOY, JIMMY! 'TIS THE BLESSED DAY THAT HE BECOMES A ROOKIE POLICEMAN! TWO GENERATIONS OF KELLYS POLICEMEN!

WELL, I HOPE HE'S A BETTER COP THAN HIS OLD MAN!
HA-HA!
QUIET--OR I'LL HAVE ME JIMMY LOCK THE BOTH OF YE UP IN A CELL!

MIDNIGHT---KELLY'S CHEERFUL WHISTLE IS HEARD ON GRIM SUICIDE BEAT!
DID YER MOTHER COME FROM IRELAND-- SURE THERE'S---

HEY, COPPER!

THAT'LL TEACH YOU COPPERS TO STAY OUTTA FANCY DAN'S TERRITORY!!

MINUTES LATER---
EASY SON-- EASY!
DAD-- DAD--

WHO SHOT HIM? WHO KILLED MY FATHER?
PROBABLY ONE OF FANCY DAN'S BOYS!

WELL---WHAT ARE YOU WAITING FOR? WHY DON'T WE ARREST HIM!
TAKE IT EASY, JIMMY, EVEN IF WE DID ARREST FANCY DAN OR HIS MOBSTERS WE COULDN'T PROVE ANYTHING! YOU SEE, SON---

FANCY DAN RUNS THIS NEIGHBORHOOD---HAS FOR A LONG TIME--WHENEVER WE DO PIN A LITTLE SOMETHING ON HIM, HE MANAGES TO WIGGLE OUT OF IT! HE'S GOT PROTECTION! THE ROTTEN POLITICAL BOSS OF THIS WARD IS HIS "SILENT" PARTNER!

AS SOON AS A POLICEMAN STARTS TO GET ANYTHING ON HIM, HE GETS SHOT! THAT'S WHY YOUR FATHER WAS KILLED--HE HAD A REPUTATION AS A GOOD COP. FANCY DAN WAS AFRAID OF HIM!
INSPECTOR-- I WANT TO TAKE OVER SUICIDE BEAT!

WHAT'S THAT! SUICIDE BEAT--WHY I'D BE SENDING YOU TO YOUR DEATH!
I WANT SUICIDE BEAT-- FANCY DAN KILLED MY FATHER. I'M GOING TO GET FANCY DAN---I'M GOING TO GET HIM IF IT'S THE LAST THING I DO!

THE NEXT MORNING --- BRUCE WAYNE, SOCIETY PLAYBOY, SITS IN THE OFFICES OF HIS FRIEND, POLICE COMMISSIONER GORDON---
I KNOW I GAVE THE ROOKIE A TOUGH BEAT, BUT I'VE GOT A HUNCH HE'LL PIN SOMETHING ON FANCY DAN!
IF HE DOESN'T, WE'LL BE PINNING SOMETHING ON HIM -- A WREATH!

AT LEAST, THE BOY WILL GET THE COOPERATION OF THE PEOPLE ON THOSE STREETS, WON'T HE?
A CROOKED POLITICIAN RUNS THAT STREET-- AND HE'S A SMART POLITICIAN. HE LENDS THE POOR PEOPLE MONEY, BUYS THEM FOOD ON CHRISTMAS-
FINDS MEN JOBS, ETC., AND ASKS IN RETURN THAT THEY VOTE FOR HIM AND PROTECT HIS JACKALS- NATURALLY, THE PEOPLE DO JUST AS HE SAYS-AND HATE COPS! JIMMY WON'T GET ANY HELP FROM THEM!
VERY INTERESTING! WELL-I-I'LL BE TODDLING ALONG NOW! SEE YOU IN JAIL, GORDON!
SEE YOU IN A NIGHT CLUB IS MORE LIKE IT- I THINK YOU SPEND YOUR LIFE THERE!

THAT AFTERNOON -- ALL OF THE PEOPLE OF SUICIDE BEAT TURN OUT TO WATCH ROOKIE JIMMY KELLY. THOUGH GRIM AND SILENT, THEIR HATRED OF HIM IS LIKE LOUD THUNDER..

THEN, WITHOUT WARNING --
SQUASH!

PETE'S BAR
WHY, YOU LITTLE--
HAW-HAW!

A LITTLE KID RAN IN HERE. WHERE DID HE GO?
I DIDN'T SEE NO KID!

I DIDN'T SEE NO KID!
BUT YOU MUST HAVE SEEN HIM. HE RAN RIGHT IN HERE!
IF HE DIDN'T SEE NO KID, HE DIDN'T SEE NO KID ... COPPER!

FANCY DAN!
SO YOU'RE THE NEW CHEESE AROUND HERE! ME...I DON'T LIKE COPPERS! AND THAT'S A GOOD TIP, KID! SEE WHAT I MEAN!

C'MON, BOYS! ME ---- I DON'T LIKE THE ATMOSPHERE O' THE PLACE NOW!
YEAH--- I GUESS **BLUE UNIFORMS** DON'T AGREE WIT' YA!
MY FATHER'S MURDERER! I COULD KILL HIM NOW-- SO EASY! BUT THAT'S NOT A COP'S WAY! I'LL GET HIM THE WAY POP WOULD HAVE---AND I'LL GET HIM!

LATER, AS TWILIGHT FALLS, A CAR WHIPS ABOUT A CORNER AT INSANE SPEED!
WHEE-- MORE SPEED-- I'LL OPEN THIS BUGGY UP TO THE LIMIT!
THAT LITTLE GIRL ---- IN FRONT OF THAT CAR! SHE'LL BE KILLED!

AS IF SHOT FROM A CANNON, JIMMY'S BODY HURTLES DIRECTLY ACROSS THE PATH OF THE ONCOMING CAR --

...AND MISSES CRUSHING DEATH BY SCANT INCHES!
MY LITTLE GIRL! MY LITTLE ANNA! THANK HEAVENS SHE'S ALL RIGHT!
THE DIRTY RAT IS GETTING AWAY!

SUDDENLY, AS IF FROM NOWHERE, TWO MANTLED FIGURES RACE FORWARD -- THE BATMAN AND ROBIN.
AFTER HIM, **ROBIN**! LET'S BORROW THIS CAR!
RIGHT!
5

A SURGING ROAR OF POWER AND THE CAR LEAPS AWAY IN PURSUIT!

ON SCREAMING TIRES, THEY DRAW ABREAST OF THE DRUNKEN DRIVER'S RACING CAR---
A GUN, TOO! THAT COMPLETES THE PICTURE!
I'LL PLUG YA FULLA HOLES!

A DARING LEAP--

WHAT YOU NEED IS SOMETHING TO PUT YOU ASLEEP...AND THIS IS IT!

MINUTES LATER---
HERE, TAKE CARE OF THIS RAT! ADIOS!
THE BATMAN! HOW?...

JIMMY DRAGS THE DRUNK TO JAIL---BUT THE NEXT DAY, ALDERMAN SKIGG APPEARS---
AND, HENRY---I MEAN, JUDGE, YOU UNDERSTAND HOW THIS POOR, HAPPY MAN DECIDED TO CELEBRATE HIS FINDING A JOB AND IF HE TOOK---
HUH!

AND A LITTLE LATER---
SO YA GOT HIM OUT, EH, SKIGG?
DON'T I ALWAYS GET YOUR BOYS OUT?
NOW WHAT DO WE DO--PLUG THE COPPER?
6

NO! GET RID OF HIM, BUT NO SHOOTING-- THREE DEAD COPS IN A ROW MIGHT BRING DOWN THE GOVERNOR!
SKIGG IS RIGHT! WE'LL JUST MUSS HIM UP ENOUGH SO THAT HE GOES TO THE HOSPITAL! ME---I GOT AN IDEA!

THAT VERY NIGHT---SUICIDE BEAT LIES CLOAKED IN SILENCE AND DARKNESS. SUDDENLY---THE SOUND OF A SCUFFLE---
YA DOITY HEEL!
WHY, I'LL PULVERIZE YA!
A FIGHT!

BUT AS JIMMY TRIES TO SEPARATE THE TWO, THEY SUDDENLY TURN ON HIM.....AND OUT OF THE SHADOWS LEAP MORE THUGS!
A TRAP!
SOCK THAT COPPER! LET'S GET HIM!

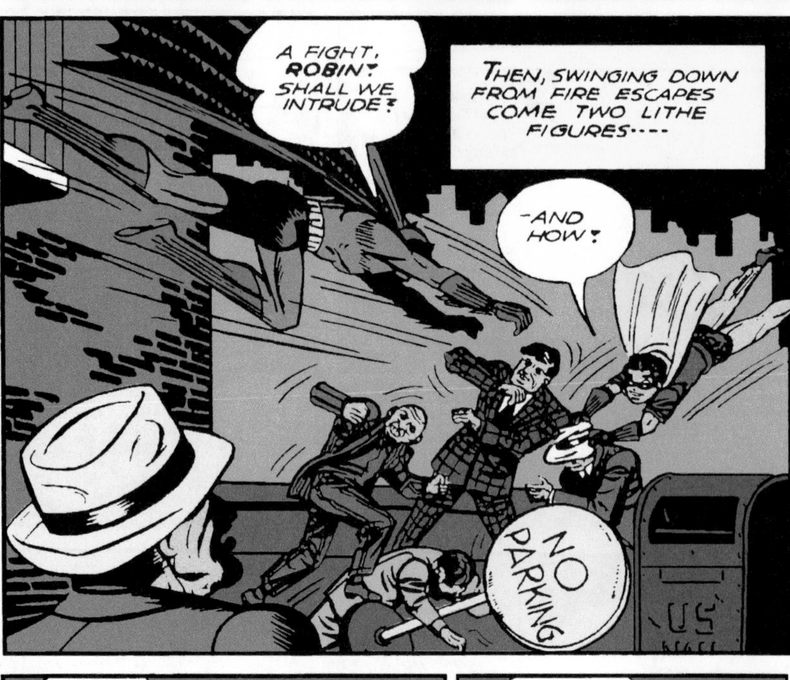
THEN, SWINGING DOWN FROM FIRE ESCAPES COME TWO LITHE FIGURES----
A FIGHT, ROBIN! SHALL WE INTRUDE?
-AND HOW!
NO PARKING
US

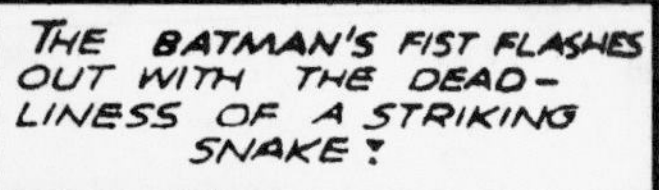
THE BATMAN'S FIST FLASHES OUT WITH THE DEADLINESS OF A STRIKING SNAKE!

MY...YOU MUST SEE YOUR DENTIST MORE OFTEN!

I'LL MOIDER YA!
TSK! TSK!

ASHES TO ASHES!

AND NOW, JIMMY HAS RECOVERED.....
NOW--- THIS IS MORE LIKE IT!

SUDDENLY, A CAR SHOOTS FROM BEHIND A CORNER---STOPS LONG ENOUGH TO PICK UP THE HOODLUMS, AND THEN SPEEDS AWAY-----

NO USE TRYING TO GET THOSE RATS!
WELL--WHAT'S THIS? THEY MUST HAVE DROPPED THIS IN THE SCUFFLE!

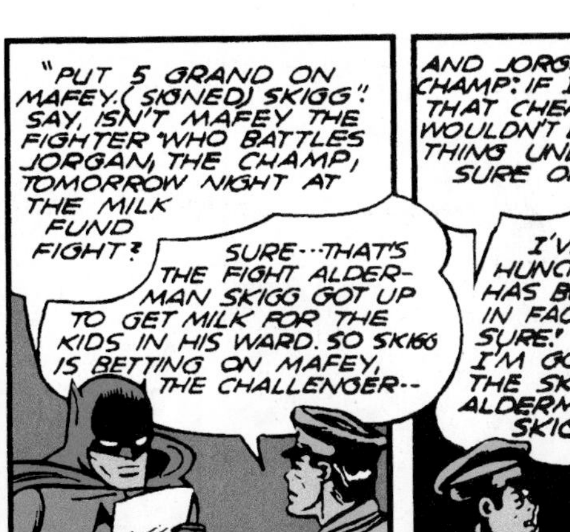
"PUT 5 GRAND ON MAFEY.(SIGNED) SKIGG". SAY, ISN'T MAFEY THE FIGHTER WHO BATTLES JORGAN, THE CHAMP, TOMORROW NIGHT AT THE MILK FUND FIGHT?
SURE---THAT'S THE FIGHT ALDERMAN SKIGG GOT UP TO GET MILK FOR THE KIDS IN HIS WARD. SO SKIGG IS BETTING ON MAFEY, THE CHALLENGER--

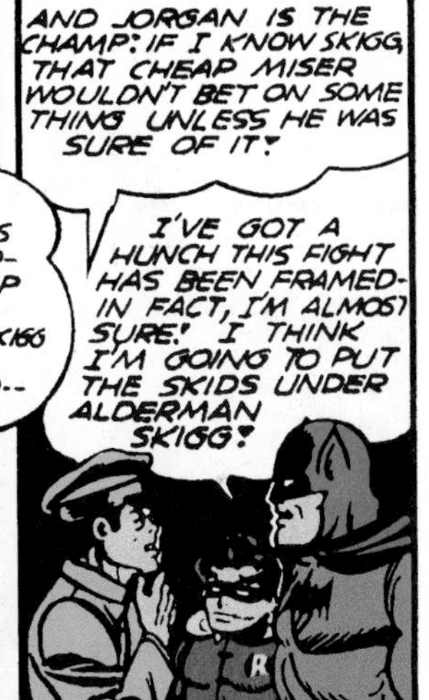
AND JORGAN IS THE CHAMP: IF I KNOW SKIGG, THAT CHEAP MISER WOULDN'T BET ON SOMETHING UNLESS HE WAS SURE OF IT!
I'VE GOT A HUNCH THIS FIGHT HAS BEEN FRAMED-IN FACT, I'M ALMOST SURE! I THINK I'M GOING TO PUT THE SKIDS UNDER ALDERMAN SKIGG!

THE NEXT NIGHT---ALDERMAN SKIGG ADDRESSES THE HUGE CROWD IN THE STADIUM....
AND SO, LADIES AND GENTLEMEN, ARUMPH--I'VE ARRANGED SO THAT THE PROCEEDS WILL BUY GOOD MILK FOR STARVING BABIES---BLAH--BLAH--

AND IN THE CHAMP'S DRESSING ROOM, A SHADOW MOVES ACROSS THE WALL--
WHA---? OH--H-H-H!

IN THE RING ---- THE CHALLENGER, BIFF MAFEY, ACKNOWLEDGES THE PLAUDITS OF THE CROWD.
WHERE'S THE CHAMP? HE SHOULD BE HERE!

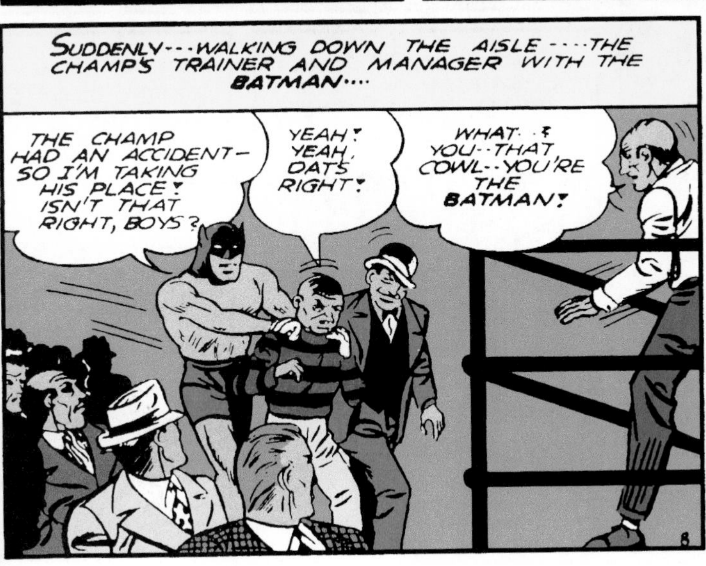
SUDDENLY---WALKING DOWN THE AISLE----THE CHAMP'S TRAINER AND MANAGER WITH THE BATMAN....
THE CHAMP HAD AN ACCIDENT-SO I'M TAKING HIS PLACE! ISN'T THAT RIGHT, BOYS?
YEAH! YEAH, DATS RIGHT!
WHAT--? YOU--THAT COWL--YOU'RE THE BATMAN!
8

BUT YOU CAN'T TAKE HIS PLACE. IT ISN'T--I MEAN--THE CROWD DON'T WANT A SUBSTITUTE!
HOW ABOUT IT, FOLKS? WANT ME TO FIGHT IN THE CHAMP'S PLACE?

THE CROWD COMES TO A UNANIMOUS DECISION---
YES! WE WANT THE BATMAN!
WE WANT THE BATMAN!

THE BELL CLANGS FOR THE FIRST ROUND--- THE FIGHT IS ON--
THE BATMAN, EH? WELL, HERE'S WHERE I MAKE YOU LOOK LIKE A PUNK!
STOP TALKING, AND FIGHT--

THE BATMAN EASILY SLIPS UNDER A ROUND-HOUSE RIGHT---
JUST A BIG BAG OF WIND!
I'LL--- WHOOSH!!

AND FOLLOWS UP WITH A TERRIFIC UPPERCUT!
9

ONE-- TWO--- TH---
I'LL FIX DAT GUY--
THE CHALLENGER RUBS HIS GLOVE INTO THE CANVAS THAT BEARS THE RESIN FROM THEIR SHOE SOLES----

AS HE RISES, HE SPEARS THE BATMAN IN THE FACE, RUBBING THE RESIN-DABBED GLOVE INTO THE BATMAN'S EYES---

FOR THE MOMENT, THE BATMAN'S EYES ARE BLINDED...HE FACES EASY PREY TO FISTS THAT SNEAK PAST HIS GUARD
HOW DO YOU LIKE THEM ONIONS, BATMAN?

THROUGH BLURRED VISION, HE SEES MAFEY RUSH AT HIM FOR THE KILL....
GET READY TO KISS THAT CANVAS, CHUM!

BUT THE BATMAN IS READY! HIS FIST SHOOTS OUT AND LANDS WITH THE FORCE OF A BASEBALL BAT!

THERE IS NO NEED FOR A COUNT. MAFEY IS OUT---BUT DEFINITELY!
THE WINNAH... THE BATMAN!
BATMAN!
BATMAN!

SUDDENLY, LIGHTS WINK OUT OVER THE STADIUM---
WHO TURNED OUT THE LIGHTS?
WHAT'S HAPPENED?

AND WHEN THEY FLASH ON AGAIN AFTER A FEW MOMENTS---
HUH! HE'S GONE! THE BATMAN'S GONE!

OUTSIDE THE STADIUM--
NICE WORK, KID! YOU TURNED OUT THOSE LIGHTS JUST IN TIME. I DON'T SEE HOW I COULD HAVE GOTTEN THROUGH THE CROWD ANY OTHER WAY!
IT WAS EASY. THERE WAS NO ONE BY THE LIGHT SWITCH!
10

ABRUPTLY, THERE IS THE BLAST OF GUN-FIRE---A VOICE RAISES IN A SHOUT---AS FANCY DAN AND HIS MOBSTERS GET AWAY WITH THE GATE RECEIPTS!
ENTRANC

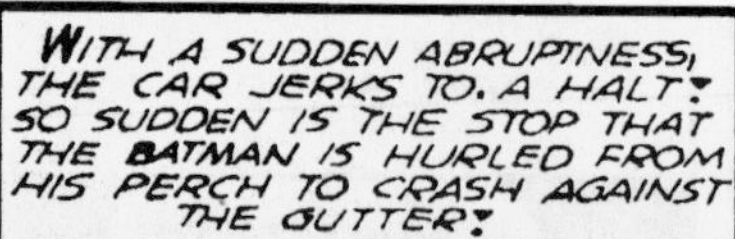

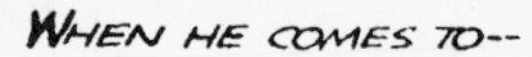

YOU SAVED MY LITTLE GIRL ANNA'S LIFE! THE LEAST I CAN DO IS REPAY YOU THIS WAY! I SAW FANCY DAN AND HIS MOB TAKE THE BATMAN INTO NO. 14 ON THE NEXT STREET!

SOMEONE ON SUICIDE BEAT HELPING A COP-- I CAN'T BELIEVE IT!

THAT ROOKIE COPPER! PLUG 'EM!
THERE HE IS!

DROP THOSE GUNS!
DROP IT! YOU'RE NO EXCEPTION!

AT THE SOUND OF THE SHOTS, A CROWD GATHERS AROUND THE GROUP---
LOOK! THE BUILDING'S ON FIRE!
THE BATMAN- HE MUST BE INSIDE. I'M GOING IN AFTER HIM!
MY BABY!! SHE'S IN THERE, TOO!

LOOK! THE BATMAN!
AND HE'S GOT MY BABY!
HE'S TRAPPED! I'VE GOT TO HELP HIM! SOMEBODY HOLD THIS ROBIN KID BACK. THIS IS MY JOB!

EVEN AS JIMMY DARTS FORWARD INTO THE HOUSE NEXT DOOR, THE ANCIENT, FLIMSY DWELLING GOES UP IN FLAMES---

FIGHTING HIS WAY THROUGH YELLOW, LEAPING TENDRILS HE GAINS THE ROOF WHICH HAS NOT YET CAUGHT FIRE!
CAN YOU JUMP IT?
NO-- CAN'T TAKE A CHANCE WITH THE KID IN MY ARMS! THIS ROOF WILL CAVE IN ANY MOMENT---ONLY ONE THING TO DO! GET READY--

CATCH!
DESPERATE CAST FOR LIFE!

WHEW! GOT HER!

AT THAT INSTANT, FIRE-MEN ARRIVE ---SPREAD A WIDE NET--AND JIMMY LEAPS TO SAFETY WITH HIS PRECIOUS BURDEN---

AND JUST AS THE BUILDING CRASHES INWARD, THE BATMAN MAKES HIS LEAP THROUGH SPACE TO THAT NET THAT SEEMS SO SMALL BELOW!
JUST IN TIME!

IT'S YOU, SKIGG! WELL--JUST IN TIME FOR ME TO TAKE YOU IN!
WHA-- WHAT IS THAT?
MY BABY!

IT'S JUST THAT YOU NOT ONLY RIGGED UP A PHONEY CHARITY FIGHT, BUT YOU ALSO FIXED IT SO FANCY DAN WOULD STEAL THE GATE RECEIPTS!
...AND THOSE GATE RECEIPTS WOULD HAVE BOUGHT MILK FOR THE KIDS OF THIS NEIGHBOR-HOOD!

WELL, JIMMY, I GUESS YOU WON'T HAVE ANY MORE TROUBLE ON SUICIDE BEAT!
YES, AND IF I KNOW MY CROOKS, FANCY DAN AND HIS MEN WILL TALK PLENTY DOWN AT HEAD-QUARTERS.. THANKS TO YOU!

LATER--
BUT HOW DID YOU GET FREE?
I MANAGED TO REACH A STEEL BLADE I HAD HIDDEN IN THE HEEL OF MY BOOT! CLOSE CALL THOUGH! SAY, WONDER WHAT THE PEOPLE THINK OF JIMMY NOW?

THE NEXT DAY-- THE ANSWER TO THE BATMAN'S QUESTION!
HELLO, JIMMY!
IT CERTAINLY IS ---- IT CERTAINLY IS A FINE DAY!
FINE DAY!
BOB KANE

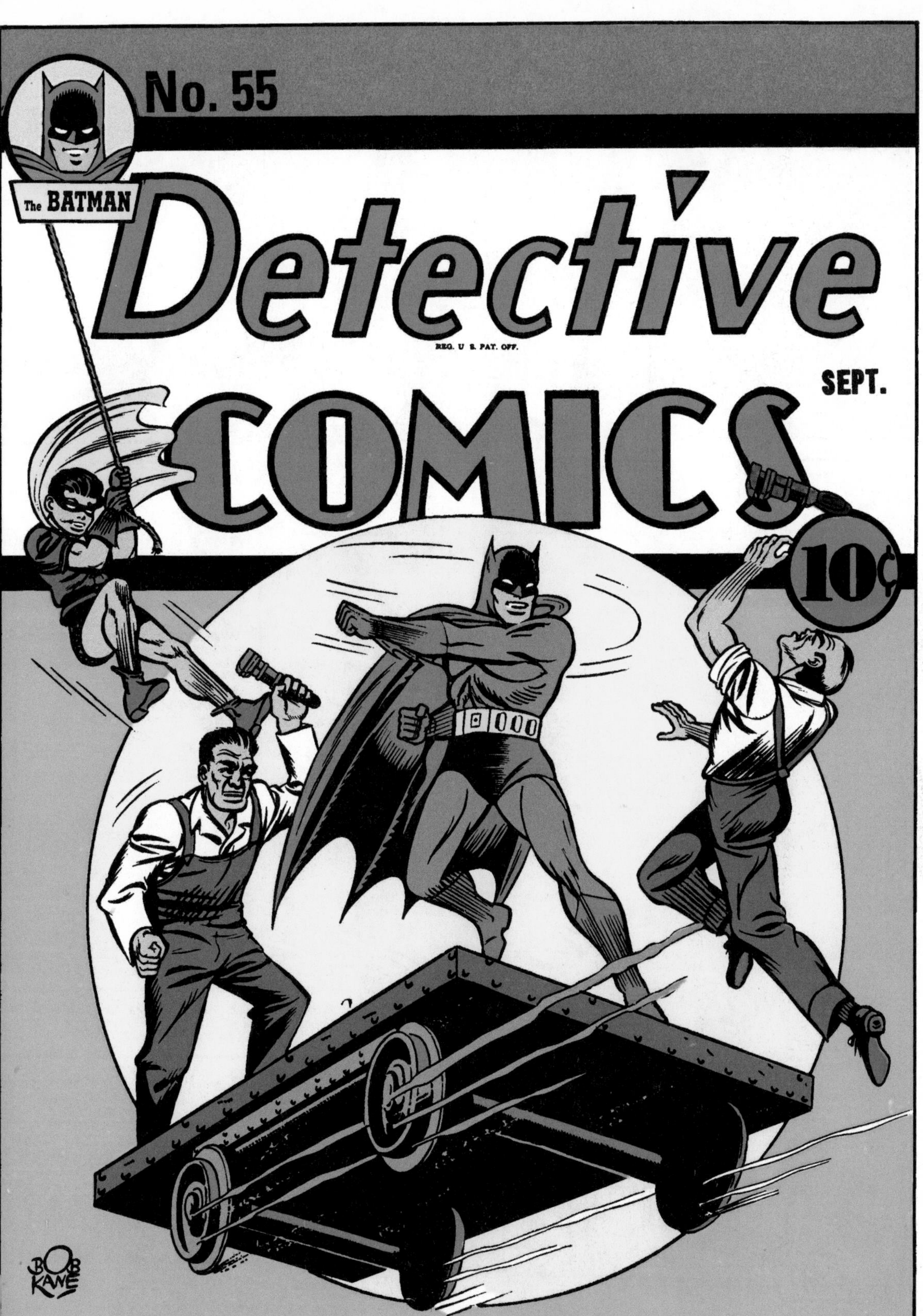
No. 55
The BATMAN
Detective
REG. U. S. PAT. OFF.
SEPT.
COMICS
10¢
BOB KANE

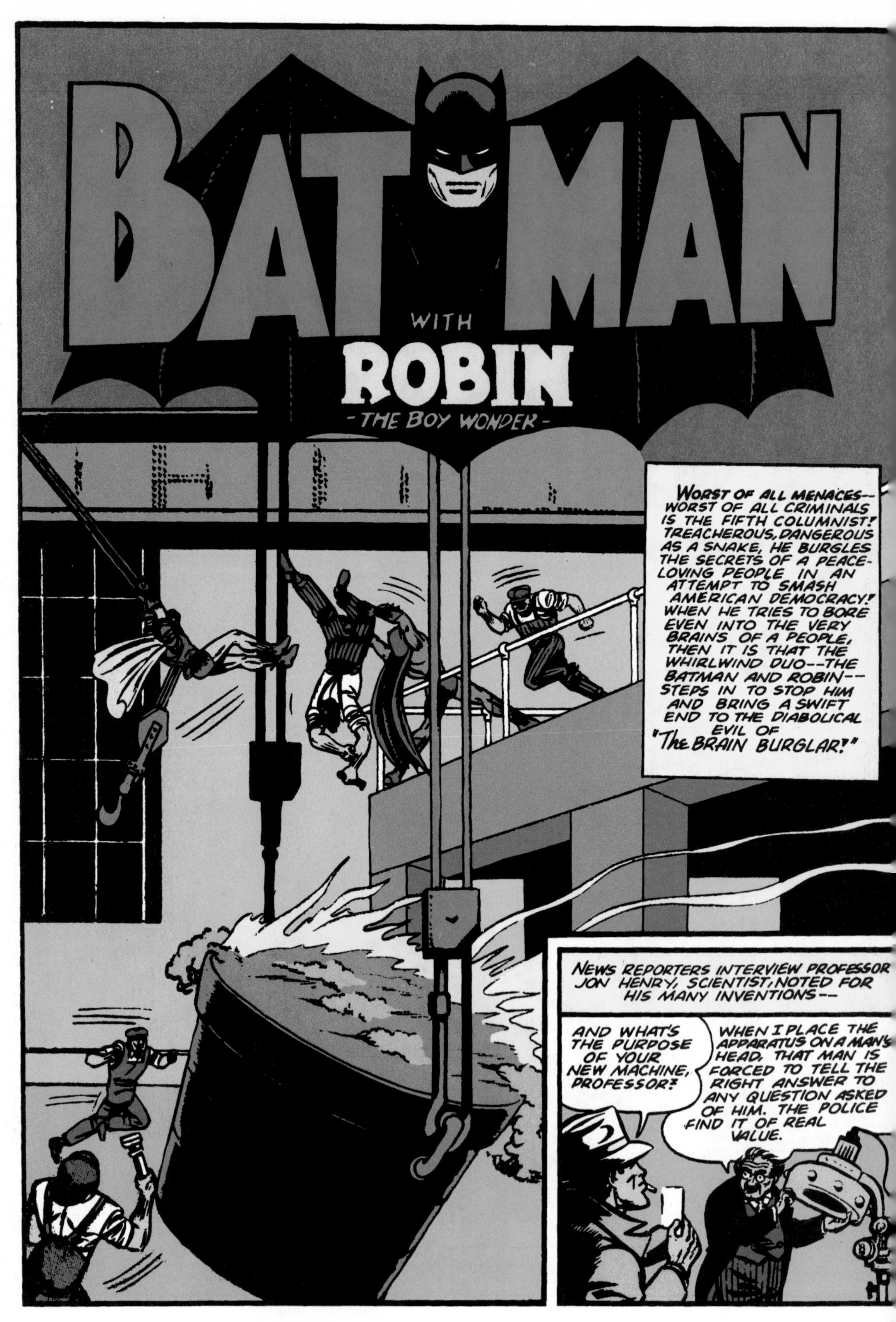
BATMAN
WITH
ROBIN
-THE BOY WONDER-
WORST OF ALL MENACES-- WORST OF ALL CRIMINALS IS THE FIFTH COLUMNIST! TREACHEROUS, DANGEROUS AS A SNAKE, HE BURGLES THE SECRETS OF A PEACE-LOVING PEOPLE IN AN ATTEMPT TO SMASH AMERICAN DEMOCRACY! WHEN HE TRIES TO BORE EVEN INTO THE VERY BRAINS OF A PEOPLE, THEN IT IS THAT THE WHIRLWIND DUO--THE BATMAN AND ROBIN-- STEPS IN TO STOP HIM AND BRING A SWIFT END TO THE DIABOLICAL EVIL OF "The BRAIN BURGLAR!"
NEWS REPORTERS INTERVIEW PROFESSOR JON HENRY, SCIENTIST, NOTED FOR HIS MANY INVENTIONS--
AND WHAT'S THE PURPOSE OF YOUR NEW MACHINE, PROFESSOR?
WHEN I PLACE THE APPARATUS ON A MAN'S HEAD, THAT MAN IS FORCED TO TELL THE RIGHT ANSWER TO ANY QUESTION ASKED OF HIM. THE POLICE FIND IT OF REAL VALUE.

A TRUTH MACHINE, EH? WHEN IS THE DEMONSTRATION OF THE MACHINE TO BE HELD?
TOMORROW AFTERNOON- I THINK I TOLD YOU ENOUGH- THE REST IS A SECRET-

THAT NIGHT...A FUGITIVE FIGURE CREEPS BEHIND THE SCIENTIST AND--
UGH!

WHEN HENRY AWAKENS-
W-WHAT? MY BRAIN MACHINE! WHO ARE YOU? WHAT DO YOU WANT?
I'M DOCTOR DEKER, AND I WANT TO KNOW HOW YOUR BRAIN MACHINE OPERATES!

BRAIN MACHINE OPERATES?-- NEVER!...I'LL NEVER TELL YOU!
HM- PERHAPS WE CAN MAKE YOU! PERSUADE THE PROFESSOR, GENTLEMEN-

OH-H-H--ALL RIGHT--ALL RIGHT--I'LL TELL--
NOW YOU'RE BEING SENSIBLE!

AFTER THE PROFESSOR TALKS--
SO THAT'S HOW IT WORKS! VERY INTERESTING- NOW TO PUT THE MACHINE ON YOU, PROFESSOR! I MAY LEARN SOMETHING!
ME?
2

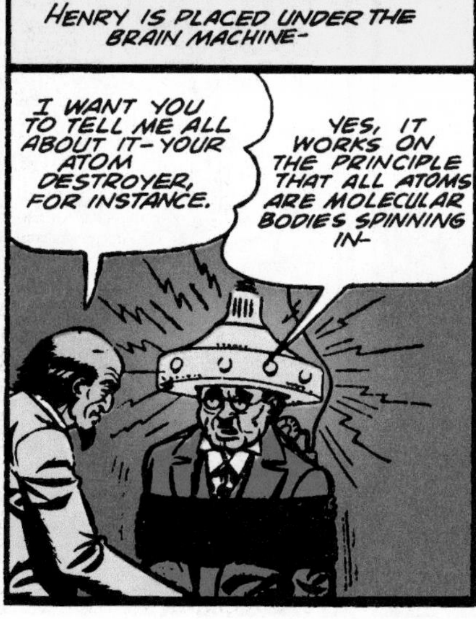
HENRY IS PLACED UNDER THE BRAIN MACHINE-
I WANT YOU TO TELL ME ALL ABOUT IT- YOUR ATOM DESTROYER, FOR INSTANCE.
YES, IT WORKS ON THE PRINCIPLE THAT ALL ATOMS ARE MOLECULAR BODIES SPINNING IN-

WHAT NEW IDEA ARE YOU WORKING ON BESIDES YOUR BRAIN MACHINE?
NEW IDEA? I HAVE ONE! IT'S A TREMENDOUS DISCOVERY-

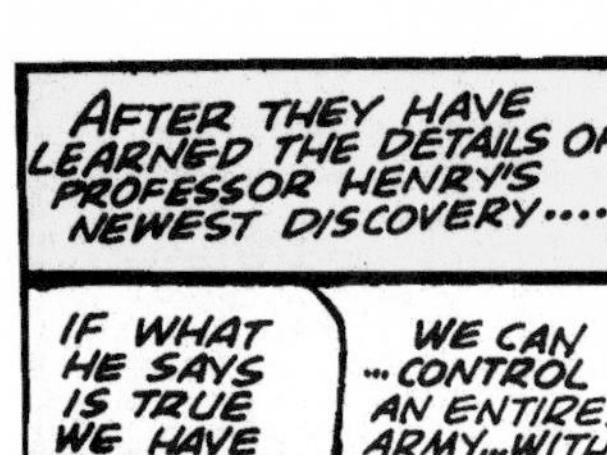
AFTER THEY HAVE LEARNED THE DETAILS OF PROFESSOR HENRY'S NEWEST DISCOVERY....
IF WHAT HE SAYS IS TRUE WE HAVE STUMBLED ONTO SOMETHING THAT IS INDEED TREMENDOUS!
WE CAN ...CONTROL AN ENTIRE ARMY...WITH IT... CALL IN OUR AGENTS. I WANT TO SPEAK TO THEM!

THE ROOM IS FILLED WITH ENEMY AGENTS--
SO, MY COMRADES, I HAVE TOLD YOU EVERYTHING? ARE YOU WILLING TO SUBMIT TO THIS OPERATION?
GLADLY-- WE KNOW WHAT WILL HAPPEN TO US, BUT NO SACRIFICE IS TOO GREAT FOR THE FATHERLAND!

AND SO, THAT NIGHT, MEN SIT AND AWAIT THEIR TURN AS ONE BY ONE THEIR FANATICAL COMRADES SUBMIT TO A MYSTERIOUS OPERATION--

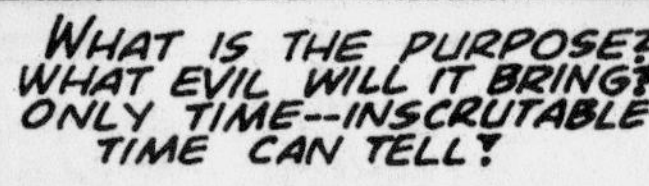
WHAT IS THE PURPOSE? WHAT EVIL WILL IT BRING? ONLY TIME--INSCRUTABLE TIME CAN TELL!

NEXT DAY--
3¢ GOTHAM GAZETTE
PROFESSOR JON HENRY AND BRAIN MACHINE DISAPPEAR!!
THE PRESS WAS AMAZED TO LEARN THIS MORNING OF MYSTIFYING DISAPPEARANCE OF THE NOTED SCIENTIST
PROFESSOR JON HENRY

AND THAT IS ONLY THE BEGINNING-- FAMOUS SCIENTISTS, KEY MEN IN NATIONAL DEFENSE, INVENTIVE CIRCLES AND OTHERS VANISH, SEEMINGLY PLUCKED AWAY BY INVISIBLE, GHOSTLY HANDS--

I THOUGHT YOU HAD A DATE TODAY WITH LINDA PAGE
THAT'S RIGHT! I HAVE-- BUT THIS LATEST DISAPPEARANCE MADE ME LOSE TRACK OF THE TIME!

WHERE ARE YOU GOING WITH HER, ANYWAY?
TO HER UNCLE'S AVIATION PLANT WHERE THEY'RE MAKING A BOMBER FOR THE ARMY!

MINUTES LATER, BRUCE AND LINDA WALK TOWARD THE GREAT AVIATION PLANT!
BRUCE-- IT'S REALLY INSPIRING!
I SEE YOU WANT ME TO GET INTERESTED IN AVIATION SO I'LL FIND MYSELF SOME SORT OF OCCUPATION! SORRY--

I DON'T KNOW WHY I BOTHER TO TRY TO MAKE SOMETHING OF YOU!
MAYBE IT'S BECAUSE YOU LIKE ME, HUH?

QUIET, YOU! LOOK-- JUST LOOK AT THAT PLANE! IT'S A NEW TYPE BOMBER!
HMM- A SLEEK-LOOKING JOB!

SUDDENLY, ONE OF THE WORKERS PUTS HIS HAND TO HIS HEAD AS IF IN INTENSE PAIN!
OH-H-H-
HE MUST HAVE A NASTY HEADACHE--

THEN, WITHOUT WARNING, THE WORKMAN RUNS AMOK---
BRUCE! BRUCE!

SOME OTHER WORKERS ALSO GO BERSERK AND START TO SMASH EVERYTHING BEFORE THEM!
UNCLE! BRUCE, HE'S BEEN HURT!
IF WE DON'T GET OUT OF HERE, HE'S GOING TO HAVE COMPANY!

IT LOOKS LIKE I'M GOING TO BE NEEDED AROUND HERE!
BEHIND THE CRATES, AN AMAZING TRANSFORMATION TAKES PLACE! FROM DISCARDED CLOTHING RISES THE PERSONALITY OF THE BATMAN-

LIKE A HORIZONTAL METEOR, THE BATMAN LUNGES FORWARD!
NOW THERE'S A FELLOW WHO IS JUST ASKING FOR TROUBLE--

AND, BY GOLLY, HE'S GOT IT!

THE BATMAN'S BALLED FIST CONNECTS SOLIDLY WITH THE MAN'S JAW!

AS OTHER MEN RUSH TOWARD HIM, THE BATMAN STOOPS, HIS HAND REACHING FOR A LENGTH OF HOSE---

HELLO! MORE COMPANY!

AND SNAPS IT AT THE CRAZED WORKERS LIKE A WHIP!
I KIND OF THOUGHT THAT WOULD WORK!

THAT HELPS EVEN UP THINGS!

A HUMAN WHIRL-WIND, THE BATMAN STREAKS TOWARD A WORKER TRYING TO DAMAGE THE NOSE OF THE PLANE--

NOW ONE MORE LITTLE BIT OF STRATEGY AND MY WORK IS DONE!
THE BATMAN SLIDES DOWN THE TOP OF THE SLIPPERY PLANE--

HE SENDS A LARGE TIRE WHEEL TOWARD THE REMAINING GROUP OF MADDENED WORKERS!

THE HUGE TIRE LITERALLY MOWS THEM DOWN!

NOW, THE BATMAN SWEEPS FORWARD, HIS TWO FISTS DROPPING THE MAD-MEN LIKE FELLED TREES!
NOTHING LIKE THE OLD ONE-TWO TO MAKE SOMEONE LISTEN TO REASON!

NOW IT'S TIME FOR ME TO GO. THERE'LL BE QUESTIONS AND THAT MIGHT MEAN THE END OF THE BATMAN'S SECRET IDENTITY!
6

LATER, IT IS BRUCE WAYNE WHO STUMBLES OUT FROM BEHIND THE PACKING CASES!
BRUCE! ARE YOU ALL RIGHT?
OH, MY JAW! WHAT HIT ME? WHAT HAPPENED?
WHAT HAPPENED? ONLY SOME MEN WENT CRAZY AND THE BATMAN CAME OUT OF NOWHERE AND STOPPED THEM-THAT'S ALL-

THE BATMAN-THAT GUY AGAIN?
"THAT GUY" PROBABLY SAVED YOUR LIFE AND MY UNCLE'S PLANT FROM BEING RUINED! WHICH IS MORE THAN YOU DID!

I'VE JUST COME FROM THE AIRPLANE FACTORY. OUR OPERATION IS A SUCCESS!
NEXT TIME WE SHALL INCREASE THE POWER- THE MEN WILL BECOME EVEN MORE VICIOUS! AND NOW LET'S TALK ABOUT THIS MAN MASON-.
SOME OF THESE MEN STARTED TO GO CRAZY AND SMASH EVERYTHING IN SIGHT-- WHY?
SABOTAGE, EVIDENTLY. THE MEDICAL REPORT SAID THAT THESE MEN ARE PERMANENTLY INSANE AND HAVE BEEN SENT TO AN ASYLUM!
DO YOU MEAN THEY WENT INSANE!
I'M POSITIVE THIS TIES UP WITH THE MISSING INVENTORS- THAT GIVES ME A THOUGHT!
NOTICE THE STORY ABOUT THE SCIENTIST MASON WHO INVENTED A NEW GUNPOWDER? THE MAN CLAIMS HE'S SEEN SUSPICIOUS LOOKING PEOPLE FOLLOWING HIM LATELY! NOW...SUPPOSE I--
THAT NIGHT--A CLOAKED FIGURE MOVES FLY-LIKE UP A BUILDING WALL---
SORRY, MASON-- BUT BELIEVE IT OR NOT, THIS PUNCH IS PROBABLY GOING TO SAVE YOUR LIFE!
W-WHAT?
STEALTHILY, TIME CREEPS BY ON PADDED FEET—THEN, AFTER WHAT SEEMS HOURS LATER, A DOOR SWINGS OPEN--
YOU'RE COMING WITH US- AND KEEP YOUR MOUTH SHUT OR--
I'LL BE QUIET- DON'T SHOOT!
AND AFTER A WILD RIDE TO A PRIVATE HOSPITAL ON THE EDGE OF TOWN....ONCE AGAIN THAT CERTAIN ROOM--
PROFESSOR HENRY AND DODGE AND--
THESE ARE THE MISSING INVENTORS! THEY HAVE REVEALED ALL THEIR SECRETS UNDER THE BRAIN MACHINE AS YOU SHALL DO IN A MOMENT-
7

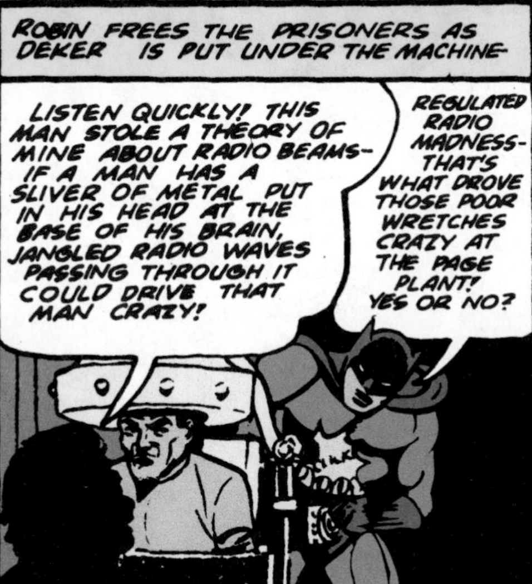

WHEN YOU HIT ME BEFORE, I FELL AGAINST THE LEVER THAT SETS OFF THE JANGLED RADIO BEAMS AND DIRECTED IT AT OUR AGENTS IN THE STEEL FACTORY NEARBY! IN A FEW MINUTES THESE MEN WILL GO MAD, DESTROY, AND DURING THE EXCITEMENT, OTHER SANE AGENTS WILL KIDNAP THE FOREMEN SO WE MAY GAIN THE NEW TYPE STEEL FORMULA YOUR COUNTRY HAS DEVELOPED!

I HEARD THEM TALKING ABOUT A DIRIGIBLE! BETTER QUESTION HIM ABOUT THAT, TOO!
WHAT ABOUT THE DIRIGIBLE?
SOMETIME TONIGHT A GIANT DIRIGIBLE FROM THE FATHERLAND WILL LAND HERE AT THE EDGE OF TOWN AND DISCHARGE MORE AGENTS INTO YOUR COUNTRY-

MAD SABOTEURS--DIRIGIBLES--C'MON, ROBIN! WE'VE GOT WORK TO DO! WE'RE GOING TO THAT STEEL MILL FIRST!
THE BATPLANE IS READY-LET'S GO!

AND ALREADY AT THE STEEL PLANT THE MADMAN-MAKING RADIO WAVES BEGIN THEIR DESTRUCTIVE WORK!

THEN INTO THE HUMAN TIDE RACES THAT TWO-MAN ARMY-THE BATMAN AND ROBIN, THE BOY WONDER!
UP AND AT THEM, ROBIN!
RIGHT BEHIND YOU-FELLA!

COOL OFF, BROTHER--YOU LOOK KIND OF HOT AROUND THE COLLAR!

A LITHE SPRING CARRIES THE BOY WONDER ONTO A MOVING FLATCAR.
GIVE ME THAT! I CAN PUT IT TO BETTER USE!

NICE STUNT! SORTA LIKE IT MYSELF!
9

UP ON THE CATWALK, THE BATMAN COMES TO GRIPS WITH A CRAZED AGENT!
HOLY SMOKE! THAT SOCK DIDN'T EVEN FAZE HIM! THAT GUY'S SO CRAZY, HE DOESN'T EVEN FEEL IT!
WITH THE FRENZIED STRENGTH OF A MADMAN, THE AGENT HURLS HIMSELF AT THE BATMAN, FORCING HIM TO THE CATWALK RAILING!--
KILL--KILL!
BELOW, A CAULDRON OF WHITE-HOT, MOLTEN STEEL WAITS TO CLAIM THE BATMAN-
GOT TO DO SOMETHING--FAST!
WITH A TITANIC EFFORT BORN OF DESPERATION, THE BATMAN TEARS HIMSELF FREE--
HIS BALLED FIST CRASHES AGAINST THE MADMAN'S JAW, AND--
10
RIDE 'EM, COWBOY!
MEANWHILE, ROBIN HANDLES HIS END OF THE JOB. RIDING A HOIST CHAIN, HE TWIRLS HIS SILKEN ROPE--

BREATHLESS MOMENTS FLY PAST THEM, AND THEY SEE--
LOOK! WE'RE TOO LATE! THOSE MEN LOOK LIKE FOREIGN AGENTS SHE HAD TO DROP OFF!
NOT TOO LATE YET- MY SLEEPING GAS PELLETS SHOULD TAKE CARE OF THEM VERY NICELY!

HI, BOYS!
SURPRISE! SURPRISE!
HUH?

ALL YOURS, BUD!
PFFHT!

FRIGHTENED, TWO COWARDLY AGENTS FLEE INTO THE ZEPPELIN'S INTERIOR, WITH THE BATMAN IN FULL PURSUIT!
THOSE TWO FIGHT LIKE DEVILS!
BETTER RUN-- HE'S AFTER US!

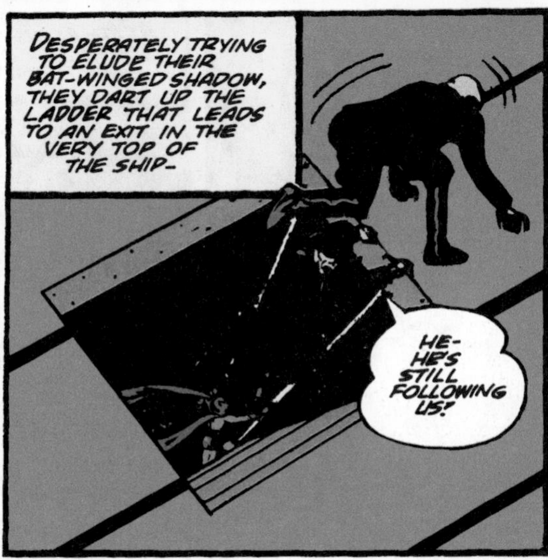
DESPERATELY TRYING TO ELUDE THEIR BAT-WINGED SHADOW, THEY DART UP THE LADDER THAT LEADS TO AN EXIT IN THE VERY TOP OF THE SHIP-
HE-HE'S STILL FOLLOWING US!

IT IS TWO AGAINST ONE ON THE SLICK, SLOPING DIRIGIBLE TOP!

CAUGHT OFF GUARD FOR AN INSTANT, A SUDDEN BLOW SENDS THE BATMAN STAGGERING BACK--
12

OFF BALANCE, THE BATMAN DIGS HIS FINGERS INTO THE DIRIGIBLE'S SURFACE, WHEN--
NOW IS OUR CHANCE!

SUDDENLY, THE BATMAN FINDS THE GRIP HE NEEDS AND CATAPULTS FORWARD, SMASHING INTO THE AGENTS!

THAT WAS CLOSE!

AT THAT INSTANT, THE ZEPPELIN COMMANDER'S GUN BLASTS A SHOT!

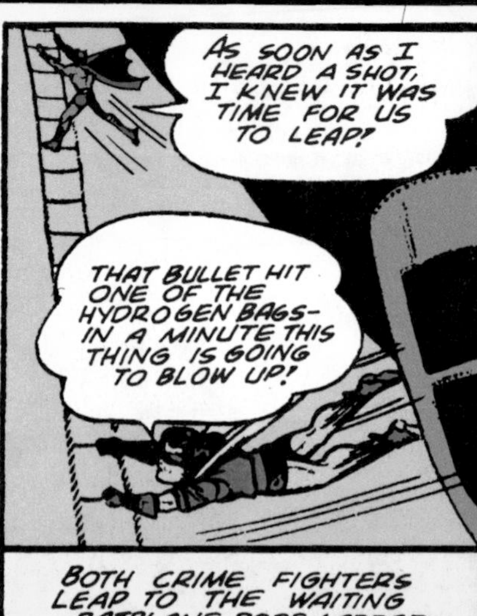
AS SOON AS I HEARD A SHOT, I KNEW IT WAS TIME FOR US TO LEAP!
THAT BULLET HIT ONE OF THE HYDROGEN BAGS- IN A MINUTE THIS THING IS GOING TO BLOW UP!
BOTH CRIME FIGHTERS LEAP TO THE WAITING BATPLANE ROPE LADDER-

SWIFTLY, THE BATPLANE WHIPS AWAY- A THUNDEROUS EXPLOSION DEAFENS THEIR EARS-
BOOM!!
13

A BURNING PYRE MAKES THE DIRIGIBLE'S END!
THERE SHE GOES- AND THE END OF THOSE BIRDS WHO WANTED TO WRECK AMERICAN DEMOCRACY-

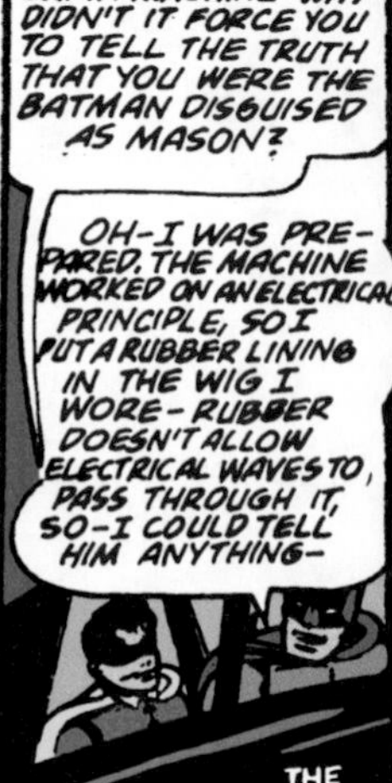
WHEN THAT DOCTOR PUT YOU UNDER THE BRAIN MACHINE- WHY DIDN'T IT FORCE YOU TO TELL THE TRUTH THAT YOU WERE THE BATMAN DISGUISED AS MASON?
OH- I WAS PREPARED. THE MACHINE WORKED ON AN ELECTRICAL PRINCIPLE, SO I PUT A RUBBER LINING IN THE WIG I WORE- RUBBER DOESN'T ALLOW ELECTRICAL WAVES TO, PASS THROUGH IT, SO- I COULD TELL HIM ANYTHING-
THE END-

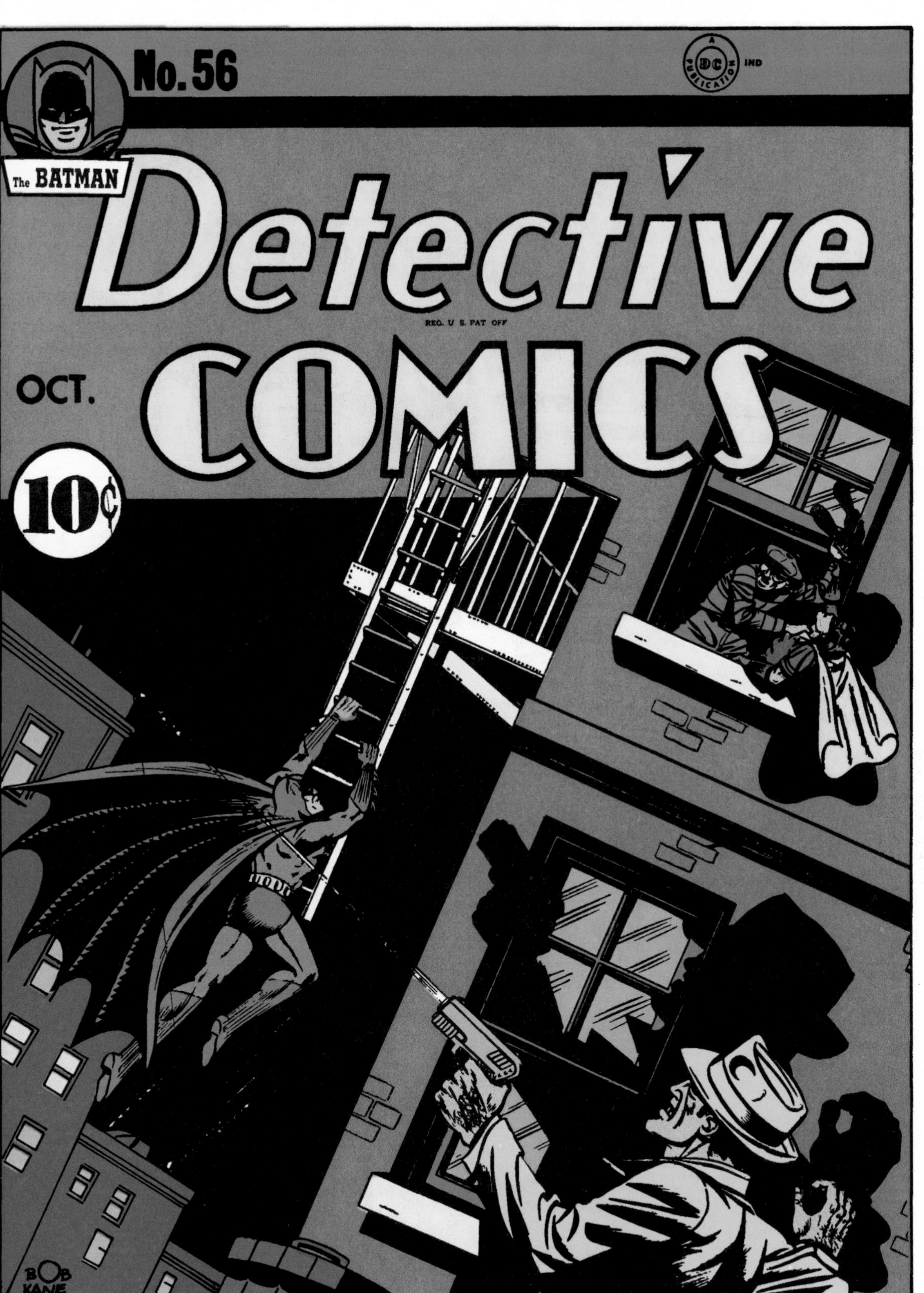
No. 56
A DC PUBLICATION
IND
The BATMAN
Detective
REG. U. S. PAT. OFF.
COMICS
OCT.
10¢
BOB KANE

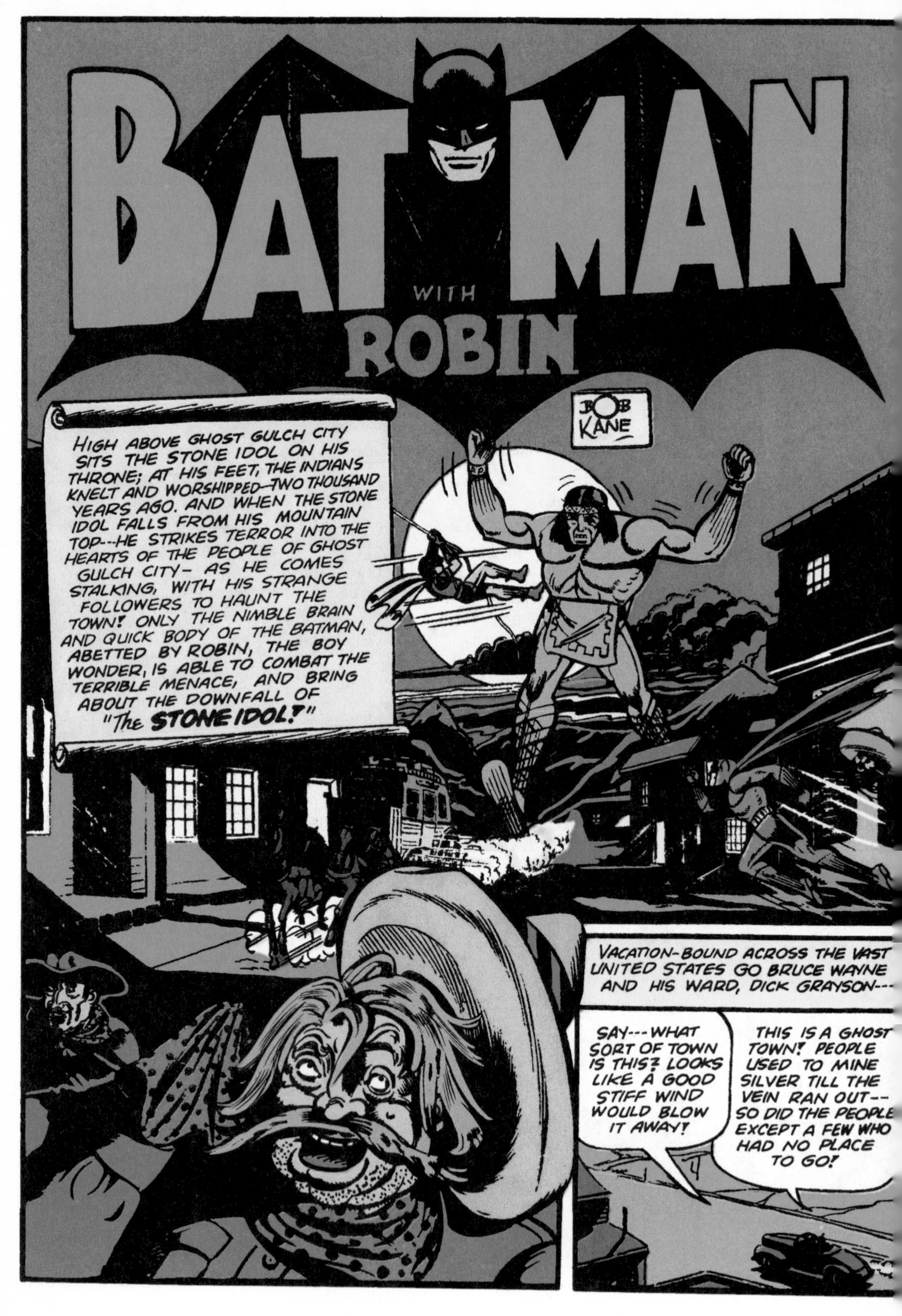
BATMAN
WITH
ROBIN
BOB KANE
HIGH ABOVE GHOST GULCH CITY SITS THE STONE IDOL ON HIS THRONE; AT HIS FEET, THE INDIANS KNELT AND WORSHIPPED--TWO THOUSAND YEARS AGO. AND WHEN THE STONE IDOL FALLS FROM HIS MOUNTAIN TOP--HE STRIKES TERROR INTO THE HEARTS OF THE PEOPLE OF GHOST GULCH CITY- AS HE COMES STALKING, WITH HIS STRANGE FOLLOWERS TO HAUNT THE TOWN! ONLY THE NIMBLE BRAIN AND QUICK BODY OF THE BATMAN, ABETTED BY ROBIN, THE BOY WONDER, IS ABLE TO COMBAT THE TERRIBLE MENACE, AND BRING ABOUT THE DOWNFALL OF "The STONE IDOL!"
VACATION-BOUND ACROSS THE VAST UNITED STATES GO BRUCE WAYNE AND HIS WARD, DICK GRAYSON---
SAY---WHAT SORT OF TOWN IS THIS? LOOKS LIKE A GOOD STIFF WIND WOULD BLOW IT AWAY!
THIS IS A GHOST TOWN! PEOPLE USED TO MINE SILVER TILL THE VEIN RAN OUT--SO DID THE PEOPLE EXCEPT A FEW WHO HAD NO PLACE TO GO!

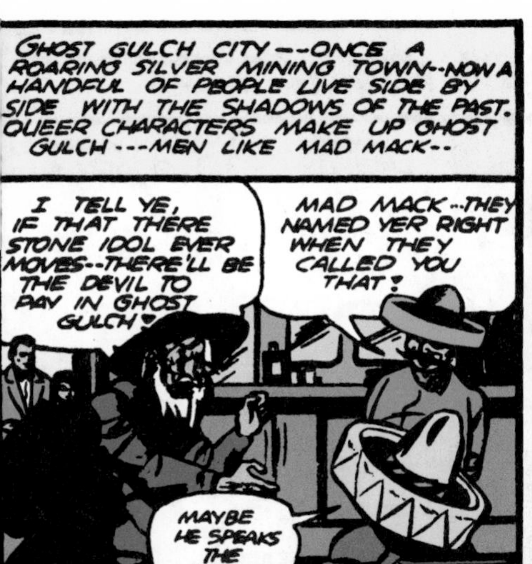
GHOST GULCH CITY--ONCE A ROARING SILVER MINING TOWN--NOW A HANDFUL OF PEOPLE LIVE SIDE BY SIDE WITH THE SHADOWS OF THE PAST. QUEER CHARACTERS MAKE UP GHOST GULCH---MEN LIKE MAD MACK--
I TELL YE, IF THAT THERE STONE IDOL EVER MOVES--THERE'LL BE THE DEVIL TO PAY IN GHOST GULCH!
MAD MACK--THEY NAMED YER RIGHT WHEN THEY CALLED YOU THAT!
MAYBE HE SPEAKS THE TRUTH!

YOU'RE RIGHT-- DON'T FORGET WHAT I WARNED YA-- WATCH OUT FOR THE STONE IDOL! AND WITH THIS STORM COMIN' ON, HE MAY CRASH AT ANY TIME!

WE'D LIKE A ROOM, PLEASE.
YEP--SURE YOU WOULD! LOOKS LIKE A BAD STORM COMIN!

AS THE STORM BREAKS OVER THE TOWN, A LARGE TRUCK CRAWLS UP THE ROAD INTO THE MOUNTAINS--
IT'S A NIGHT FOR THE DEVIL!
SHUT UP AND KEEP YOUR EYES ON THE ROAD!

SUDDENLY THE ROAD STARTS GIVING WAY, AND A GIANT HOLE YAWNS AS THE TRUCK SPEEDS FORWARD--
WATCH OUT! THE ROAD'S GONE!

LIGHTNING BLASTS AT THE VERY FEET OF THE STONE IDOL!

AND AFTER A 2000-YEAR REIGN, THE GOD OF STONE PLUNGES FROM HIS MOUNTAIN!

AS QUICKLY AS IT CAME, THE FURY OF THE STORM CEASES-- AND THE MOON LIGHTS THE STONE IDOL -- STANDING WHERE THE TRUCK HAS DISAPPEARED-
MAD MACK'S PROPHECY HAS COME TRUE--THE STONE IDOL HAS FALLEN!

IN THE MORNING, THE PEOPLE GATHER AROUND THE FALLEN IDOL---
I DON'T LIKE IT--- LEGENDS SAY THERE'LL BE TROUBLE WHEN THE STONE IDOL FALLS!
I'M ASHAMED OF YOU ALL-- SCARED BY AN OLD HUNK OF STONE!

THAT'S NO WAY TO TALK, MR. MAYOR. THE STONE IDOL'S POWERFUL-- LAST NIGHT HE UPPED AND SPOKE TO ME-- ABOUT YOU, MR. MAYOR. HE SAID--

A VIVID, SILVER FLASH SUDDENLY BLINDS THE WATCHERS ON THE MOUNTAIN SIDE--

LIKE A MAGIC WAND, THE LIGHT BRINGS TO LIFE THE STONE LIMBS OF THE OLD IDOL OF THE MOUNTAIN---
THE STONE IDOL'S WALKING!

I, GREAT IDOL OF THE MOUNTAIN, COMMAND YOU TO LEAVE THIS CITY-- ALL WHO DISOBEY-- DIE! LEAVE -- LEAVE ELSE I BRING DESTRUCTION UPON YOU!
3

THE FRIGHTENED PEOPLE KNEEL AT THE FOOT OF THE STONE IDOL--ONLY THE MAYOR REMAINS STANDING--
SAYS WHO? YOU CAN'T CHASE ME OUT OF MY HOME!

AS THE MAYOR APPROACHES, THERE IS ANOTHER BLINDING FLASH---

IT MOVED AND TALKED!
THE OLD LEGEND'S COME TRUE!

MAYOR, YOU'VE GOT TO STOP TALKIN' BACK TO THE IDOL! IF YOU DON'T THE PEOPLE ARE GOIN' TO SUFFER!
I'M NOT AFRAID! HE'S JUST STONE-AND STONE CAN'T MOVE. IT'S A TRICK!

BUT THE PEOPLE BELIEVE. THEY HAVE LIVED HERE TOO LONG AND HEARD TALES OF THE IDOL TOO MANY TIMES..
THIS HOUSE HAS BEEN OUR HOME FOR SUCH A LONG TIME, I HATE TO LEAVE!
MAYBE YOU'D RATHER STAY AND BRING DOWN THE WRATH OF THE STONE IDOL!

AS THE TOWNSPEOPLE MAKE READY TO LEAVE, THEY STOP LONG ENOUGH TO HEAR THE MAYOR.
ARE YOU ALL FRIGHTENED BY A PIECE OF ROCK? YOU'VE GOT TO STAY AND FIGHT FOR YOUR HOMES!

THE STONE IDOL IS COMIN' WITH HIS SERVANTS!

THE STONE IDOL! HE'S COMING! THE STONE IDOL'S COMING!

PEOPLE OF GULCH CITY, YOU HAVE BROUGHT THIS DOOM UPON YOURSELVES! SERVANTS--- DRIVE THESE PEOPLE OUT OF TOWN! DRIVE THEM OUT!
HO
FFF
4

BUT RACING SWIFTLY TOWARD THE IDOL'S STRANGE SERVANTS ARE TWO MANTLED FIGURES.... THE BATMAN AND ROBIN-
C'MON, ROBIN!
RIGHT!

GET A MOVE, OR I'LL.....
THESE ARE HUMANS YOU'RE ORDERING AROUND, NOT ANIMALS!

ON THE HOUSE, CHUM!

BOY, YOU CERTAINLY PACK A LOT OF MUSH AROUND YOUR MIDDLE!
PHHFFT!
I'LL BASH THAT KID'S BRAINS OUT!
BAR

WATCH OUT FOR THOSE SWINGING DOORS!

A FURY WHIPPED INTO ACTION, THE BATMAN TEARS INTO THE IDOL'S SERVANTS!
GET HIM!
C'MON, YOU RATS! I'M KING O' THE HILL! TRY TO KNOCK ME OFF!
5

YOU'RE NOT GOING TO DO IT THAT WAY!
-Z-I-N-G-

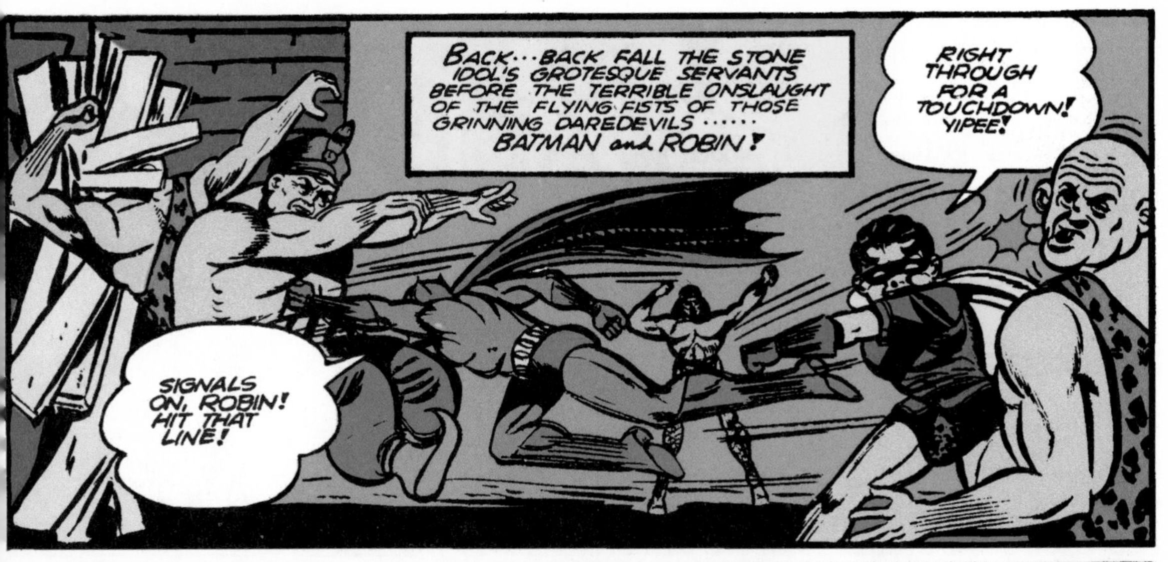
BACK...BACK FALL THE STONE IDOL'S GROTESQUE SERVANTS BEFORE THE TERRIBLE ONSLAUGHT OF THE FLYING FISTS OF THOSE GRINNING DAREDEVILS...... BATMAN and ROBIN!
RIGHT THROUGH FOR A TOUCHDOWN! YIPEE!
SIGNALS ON, ROBIN! HIT THAT LINE!

SUCCESSIVE FLASHES OF SILVER LIGHT SUDDENLY BLIND THE FIGHTING DUO!

WHEN THE LIGHT DIES DOWN, THE BATMAN AND ROBIN SEE THAT THE IDOL IS ONCE MORE ON HIS THRONE AND HIS SERVANTS ARE GONE....
WELL I'LL BE DARNED! HOW DID THEY GET AWAY?
THEY GOT AWAY WHILE WE WERE TEMPORARILY BLINDED--- BUT WHERE THEY WENT IS ANOTHER QUESTION!

THEY WERE MASKED!
WHOEVER THEY WERE, THEY CERTAINLY HAVE MY RESPECT! WHAT FIGHTERS!
WHO WERE THEY?
AS SWIFTLY AS THEY CAME, THE TWO CAPED FIGURES DART BEHIND THE BUILDINGS!

LATER IN THEIR HOTEL---
GOOD THING WE HAPPENED TO LOOK OUT OF OUR HOTEL WINDOW BEFORE AND SAW WHAT HAPPENED! DO YOU THINK THAT STONE IDOL CAN WALK?
THERE ARE LOTS OF STRANGE THINGS THAT MAN HAS BEEN UNABLE TO EXPLAIN IN THE PAST. PERHAPS THE STONE IDOL IS ONE OF THEM....
6

MAD MACK CONFERS WITH THE UNEASY TOWNSMEN AND WORKS THEM UP TILL THEY ARE TERROR CRAZED!
THE MAYOR HAS ANGERED THE STONE IDOL! WE GOTTA SACRIFICE HIM, OR ELSE WE DON'T KNOW WHAT MAY HAPPEN TO US!
YOU'RE RIGHT! HE'S RESPONSIBLE FOR THOSE MASKED FIGHTERS!

THE MAYOR IS SEIZED IN HIS HOME....
WHAT IS THIS?
YOU'RE COMING WITH US, MAYOR!

THE TERRIFIED, SUPERSTITIOUS TOWNSFOLK DRAG THE UNFORTUNATE MAN TOWARD THE HILL WHERE THEY FIND GREAT FIRES BURNING AND THE STONE IDOL WAITING FOR THE SACRIFICE!
LET'S KILL HIM!
YOU FOOLS!
THROW HIM OVER THE CLIFF!

THE SACRIFICE!
HELP! I'M FALLING!

AND HELP DOES COME FROM AN INK-GARBED FIGURE THAT FLASHES THROUGH EMPTY SPACE!

A HAND OF STEEL CLAMPS ABOUT THE FALLING MAN!
GOOD THING I WAS WATCHING NEARBY!

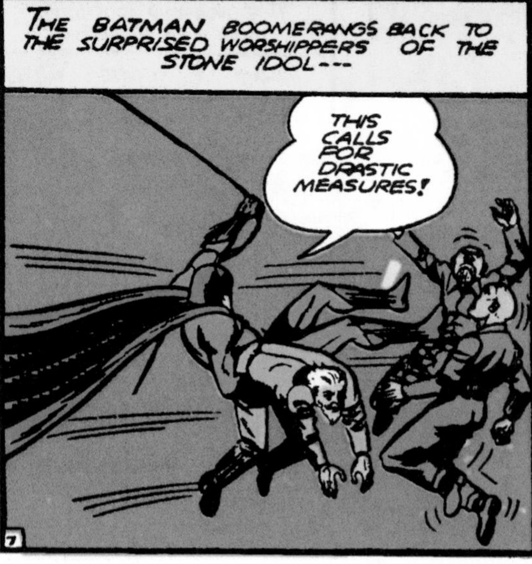
THE BATMAN BOOMERANGS BACK TO THE SURPRISED WORSHIPPERS OF THE STONE IDOL---
THIS CALLS FOR DRASTIC MEASURES!
7

AND NOW, THE BATMAN, JOINED BY ROBIN WHIPS INTO THE SWARMING FANATICS
SOMEONE HAS TO KNOCK A LITTLE SENSE INTO YOUR HEADS!
HOW'S THAT?

SUDDENLY A FLASH OF SILVER LIGHT KNIFES THROUGH THE NIGHT--

HEY! LEGGO!
HE'S GOT ROBIN!

ANOTHER BRILLIANT FLAME OF INTENSE LIGHT BLINDS THE CHARGING BATMAN!
I CAN'T SEE!!

AND WHEN THE LIGHT DIES DOWN AND SIGHT GRADUALLY RETURNS TO THE BATMAN'S TORTURED EYES, HE SEES---
ROBIN IS GONE! WHAT DID YOU DO WITH HIM? SPEAK OR I'LL---

WHAT...? STONE--- IT REALLY IS STONE! STONE THAT MOVES AND SPEAKS?!

IT'S,...IT'S GONE-- CAN'T BE A STONE STATUE THAT GRABBED ROBIN! IT-- IT CAN'T BE--YET-- YET--

WORRIED, CURIOUS BY WHAT HAS HAPPENED, BATMAN AND THE MAYOR COMBINE THEIR STRENGTH TO TOPPLE THE IDOL...
IT'S GOING OVER!
THAT DOES IT!

TO HIS SURPRISE, BATMAN SEES A YAWNING CAVERN BENEATH THE STATUE!
SOMEWHERE DOWN BELOW IS ROBIN! IDOLS, OR WHAT HAVE YOU, I'M GOING IN THERE -ALONE-
GOOD LUCK, SON!

SILENTLY, THE BATMAN DROPS DOWN INTO THE DIM CAVERN BELOW THE GROUND--
A MINE!

WHAT'S THIS CONTRAPTION! LOOKS LIKE A SORT OF CRUDE ELEVATOR-- AND THIS-- IT'S ANOTHER STONE THRONE.

THINGS ARE BEGINNING TO BECOME CLEARER NOW--!

HUH?--- WELL-- WHERE DID YOU TWO DROP FROM?

THAT WILL BE ALL OF YOU!

YOU DON'T THINK I'D NEGLECT YOU, DID YOU?

THEN A VOICE--AND A STARTLING SIGHT---
ONE MOVE AND I'LL SEND A BULLET THROUGH YOUR LITTLE FRIEND!
IF YOU HARM THAT BOY, I'LL SEND YOU DOWN SO DEEP, NO MINER WILL EVER BE ABLE TO FIND YOU!

OOPS! SORRY! MY FOOT MUST HAVE SLIPPED!

SMART KID...EH? HOW D'YA LIKE THIS?
WHACK!

THE BATMAN SPEEDS TO ROBIN'S RESCUE, UNAWARE OF A RUNAWAY, EMPTY ORE CAR WHICH RUMBLES TOWARD HIM...
ROBIN!

CAUGHT UNAWARES, THE BATMAN IS FLUNG INTO THE ORE CAR--

LOOK OUT! HE'S COMING AT US!
WE'LL LET HIM GET RID OF THE KID FOR US!

BUT THE BATMAN SWIFTLY RIGHTS HIMSELF AND--
GOT TO WORK FAST!

BY A MIRACLE OF STRENGTH AND TIMING, THE BATMAN SNATCHES ROBIN FROM UNDER THE CLICKING WHEELS.... AS THE CAR SPEEDS HEAD-ON TOWARD A HEAVY TIMBER DOOR!
WHEW!
10

LOW BRIDGE! THAT STONE WALL... WE'RE HEADED FOR IT. GOT TO....

JUMP!
UGH!

NOW A SEVEN-FOOT GIANT LUMBERS FORWARD TO CONFRONT THE BATMAN!
SO I FINALLY MEET UP WITH THE BIG SHOT!

NOW, MAYBE YOU WILL HAVE RESPECT!
QUITE A PUNCH YOU'VE GOT, FELLA!

WELL- HERE'S A TASTE OF MINE!

LET'S SEE IF YOU HAVE A GLASS JAW!

AGAIN, HIS FIST LASHES OUT, AND THE GIANT STAGGERS BACK UNDER THE TERRIBLE IMPACT!

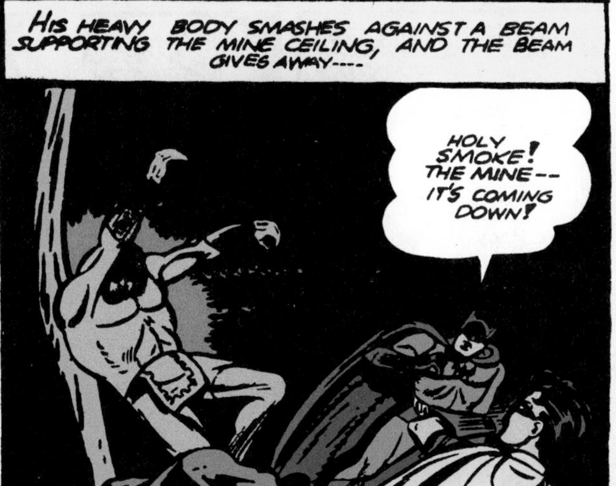
HIS HEAVY BODY SMASHES AGAINST A BEAM SUPPORTING THE MINE CEILING, AND THE BEAM GIVES AWAY----
HOLY SMOKE! THE MINE-- IT'S COMING DOWN!

IN ONE SPLIT-SECOND MOMENT, THE BATMAN AND ROBIN DIVE FOR THE ORE-CAR---
ROBIN! THAT ORE-CAR-- IT'S OUR ONLY CHANCE!

...AND PULL ITS THICK-WALLED PROTECTION OVER THEM AS TONS OF EARTH AND ROCK COLLAPSE!

SOMETIME LATER---TWO HUMAN MOLES DIG THEIR WAY THROUGH THE LOOSE EARTH--BATMAN AND ROBIN-
LOOKS LIKE WE'RE THE ONLY ONES ALIVE!
NOT EXACTLY-THERE'S MAD MACK!

MAD MACK, YOU'RE DYING. BEFORE YOU DO, TELL ME--THIS IS A VALUABLE SILVER MINE, ISN'T IT?
YES---IT IS. THE ORIGINAL OWNER OF THIS MINE NEVER FOUND NOTHIN' SO HE GENEROUSLY LEFT IT TO THE TOWN-I FOUND THE VEIN MYSELF-- BY RIGHT, IT WAS MINE---

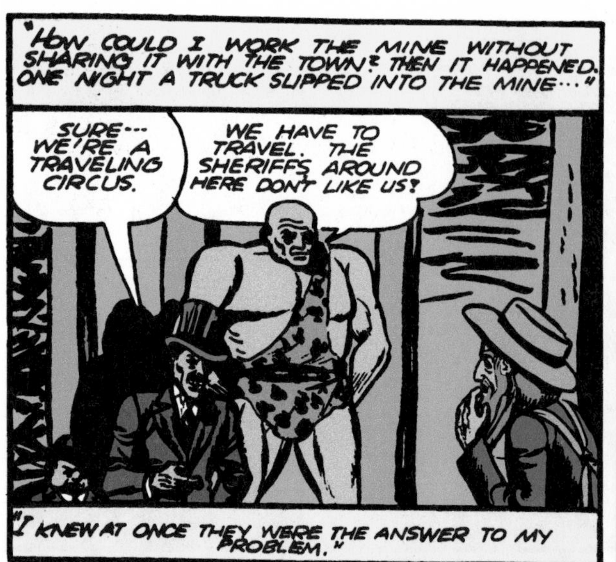
"HOW COULD I WORK THE MINE WITHOUT SHARING IT WITH THE TOWN? THEN IT HAPPENED. ONE NIGHT A TRUCK SLIPPED INTO THE MINE..."
SURE--- WE'RE A TRAVELING CIRCUS.
WE HAVE TO TRAVEL. THE SHERIFFS AROUND HERE DON'T LIKE US?
"I KNEW AT ONCE THEY WERE THE ANSWER TO MY PROBLEM."

"THEY WERE LIKE THE DEVILS THEMSELVES. WHEN I TOLD THEM ABOUT THE MINE- WE QUICKLY THOUGHT UP A PLAN."
SEE? THIS BLACK WIG AND PAINT WILL MAKE OUR STRONG MAN LOOK LIKE THAT STONE IDOL THESE PEOPLE TALK ABOUT SO MUCH!
FINE! WE'LL MAKE THESE OTHERS TO LOOK LIKE HIS SERVANTS. THEN I'LL START TELLING THE PEOPLE THAT THE IDOL HAS COME TO LIFE.
PAINT

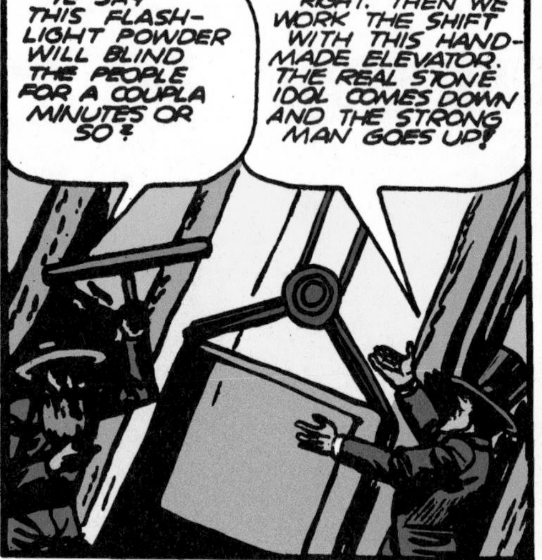
YE SAY THIS FLASH-LIGHT POWDER WILL BLIND THE PEOPLE FOR A COUPLA MINUTES OR SO?
RIGHT. THEN WE WORK THE SHIFT WITH THIS HAND-MADE ELEVATOR. THE REAL STONE IDOL COMES DOWN AND THE STRONG MAN GOES UP!

"WE FIGURED WE SCARE EVERYBODY OUTA TOWN SO WE COULD WORK THE MINE AND SPLIT THE PROFITS!"
IT WOULD'VE WORKED IF IT WASN'T FOR THE MAYOR --- NOW I'M DYING ---- GUESS -- I GOT WHAT'S COMIN' TO ME---

...I'M SORRY I WAS--A GREEDY OLD MAN--- ---I ---

LATER, AFTER EXPLANATIONS--
I THOUGHT I'D NEVER SEE YOU TWO AGAIN WHEN THE EARTH CAVED IN! I THOUGHT YOU WERE GONNERS FOR SURE.
FRANKLY--- FOR A COUPLE OF MINUTES, WE THOUGHT SO, TOO. BUT I GUESS WE WERE LUCKY!

WITH THEIR JOB DONE, THE BATMAN AND ROBIN LEAVE BEHIND A GRATEFUL PEOPLE--
I CERTAINLY HOPE THEY BURIED SUPERSTITION IN THIS TOWN!

QUITE A LITTLE ADVENTURE, WASN'T IT?
AND HOW! AND I THINK WE DESERVE A LITTLE REST AFTER THIS EPISODE!

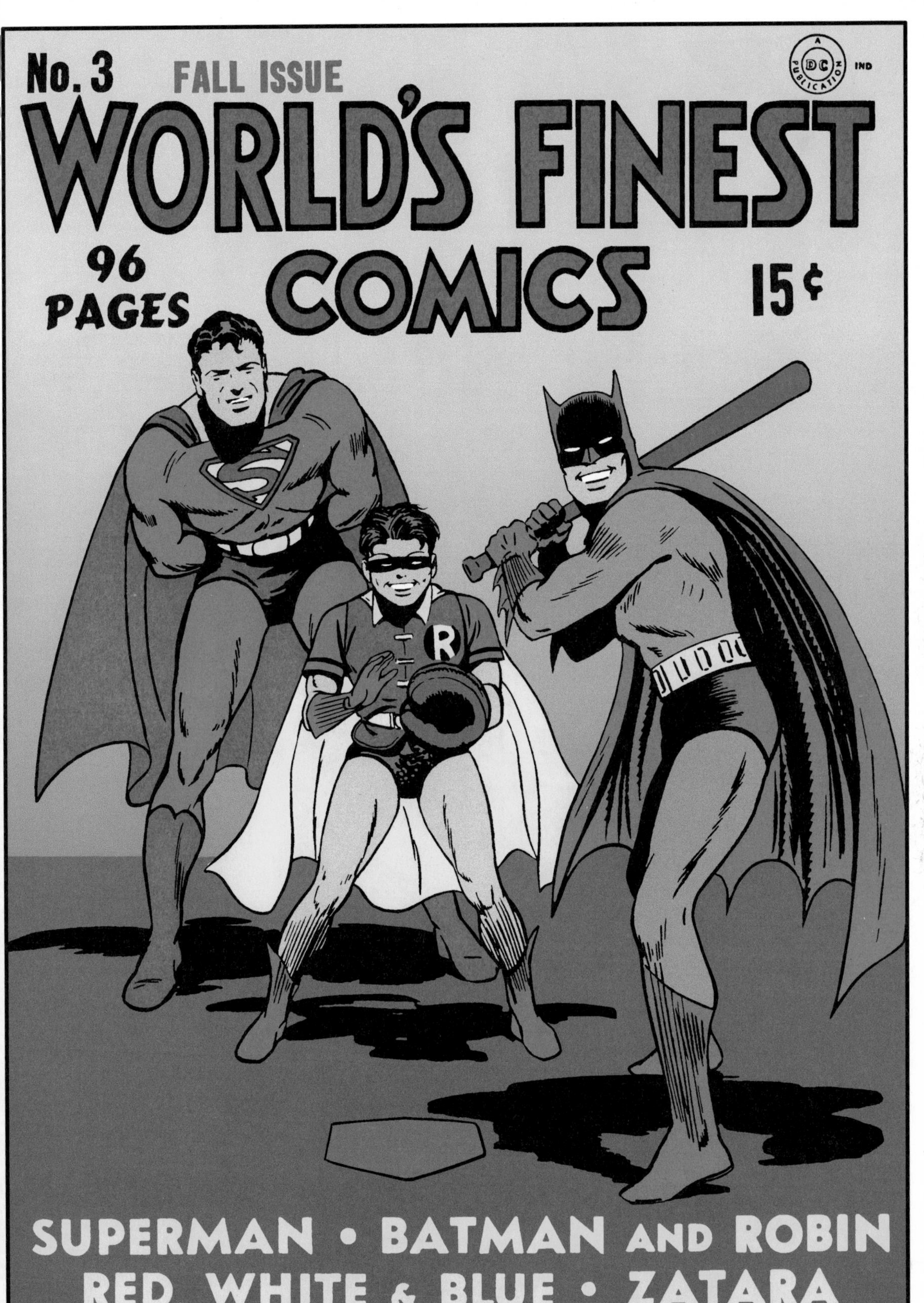
No. 3
FALL ISSUE
A DC PUBLICATION
IND
WORLD'S FINEST COMICS
96 PAGES
15¢
R
SUPERMAN • BATMAN AND ROBIN
RED, WHITE & BLUE • ZATARA

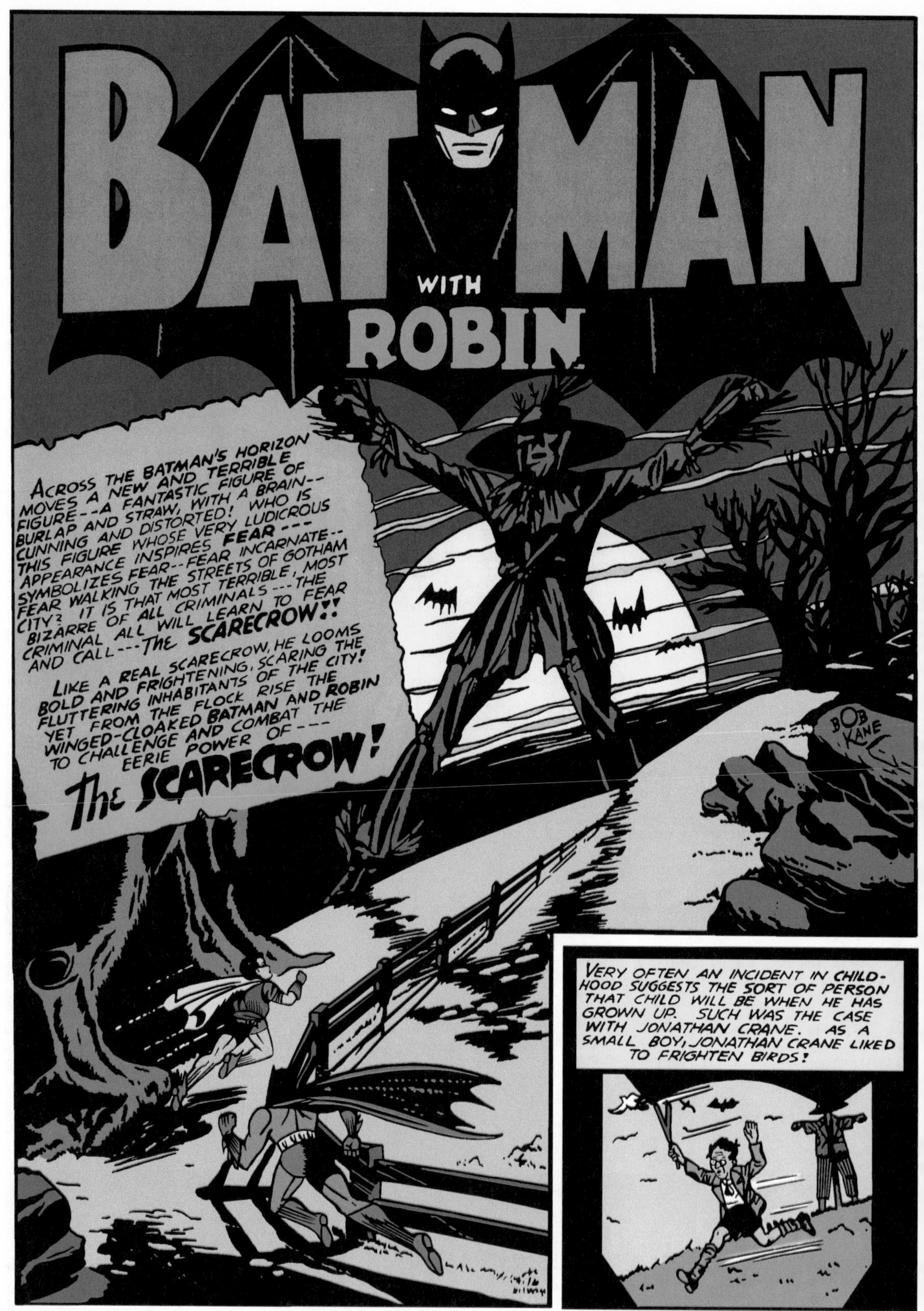
BATMAN
WITH
ROBIN
ACROSS THE BATMAN'S HORIZON MOVES A NEW AND TERRIBLE FIGURE--A FANTASTIC FIGURE OF BURLAP AND STRAW, WITH A BRAIN--CUNNING AND DISTORTED! WHO IS THIS FIGURE WHOSE VERY LUDICROUS APPEARANCE INSPIRES FEAR---SYMBOLIZES FEAR--FEAR INCARNATE--FEAR WALKING THE STREETS OF GOTHAM CITY? IT IS THAT MOST TERRIBLE, MOST BIZARRE OF ALL CRIMINALS---THE CRIMINAL ALL WILL LEARN TO FEAR AND CALL---THE SCARECROW!!
LIKE A REAL SCARECROW, HE LOOMS BOLD AND FRIGHTENING, SCARING THE FLUTTERING INHABITANTS OF THE CITY! YET FROM THE FLOCK RISE THE WINGED-CLOAKED BATMAN AND ROBIN TO CHALLENGE AND COMBAT THE EERIE POWER OF---
The SCARECROW!
BOB KANE
VERY OFTEN AN INCIDENT IN CHILDHOOD SUGGESTS THE SORT OF PERSON THAT CHILD WILL BE WHEN HE HAS GROWN UP. SUCH WAS THE CASE WITH JONATHAN CRANE. AS A SMALL BOY, JONATHAN CRANE LIKED TO FRIGHTEN BIRDS!

WHEN JONATHAN CRANE GREW UP HE BECAME A TEACHER OF PSYCHOLOGY IN A UNIVERSITY--AND THIS IS WHERE WE FIND HIM TODAY--
GENTLEMEN, THIS TERM WE STUDY THE PSYCHOLOGY OF FEAR--FEAR--THAT NAMELESS DREAD THAT GRIPS A PERSON WHEN THOUGHTS OF TERROR RUN THROUGH HIS MIND!

NOTICE THIS GUN! SHOULD I POINT IT AT YOU, YOU WOULD BE AFRAID--BUT YOU WOULD BE MORE AFRAID--

--IF I DID THIS!

NOW YOU SEE WHAT THE GUN CAN DO. IT CAN DESTROY! BEFORE, YOU ONLY GUESSED WHAT IT COULD DO. NOW THAT YOU HAVE SEEN--YOU ARE EVEN MORE AFRAID! SIMPLE PSYCHOLOGY, GENTLEMEN-

AFTER THE CLASS IS OVER--CRANE NEARS SOME OTHER PROFESSORS--
YOU'RE COMING TO THE PARTY I'M GIVING TONIGHT--DON'T FORGET!
ALL EXCEPT ONE, EH? HE LOOKS SO SHABBY IN THOSE OLD CLOTHES-POSITIVELY WEIRD-

HE EARNS THE SAME SALARY WE DO--WHY DOESN'T HE BUY SOME DECENT CLOTHES?
POOR CRANE! HE LOOKS LIKE A SCARECROW IN THOSE CLOTHES-HE CERTAINLY IS A QUEER FELLOW-
HE SPENDS EVERY CENT HE EARNS TO BUY NEW BOOKS-

AND LATER--IN HIS HOME--CRANE PONDERS--
THE FOOLS! DO THEY THINK I WOULD GIVE UP MY PRECIOUS BOOKS JUST TO BUY CLOTHES? BAH! THEY THINK I'M STRANGE AND I LOOK LIKE A SCARECROW--A SCARECROW!

THEY JUDGE HUMAN VALUES BY MONEY--IF I HAD MONEY THEY'D RESPECT ME--AND I COULD BUY MORE BOOKS! YES---IF I ONLY HAD MONEY--LOTS OF MONEY-
2

THE NEXT DAY, AT CLASS---
TAKE THE EXAMPLE OF THE "PROTECTION RACKET" WORKED BY THE GANGSTER! HE WANTS MONEY-- SO HE MAKES PEOPLE PAY HIM! ...AND HOW DOES HE DO IT?

HE MAKES PEOPLE AFRAID--AFRAID SO THAT THEY PAY HIM! YES---HE MAKES THEM AFRAID--AFRAID-- AND HE GETS MONEY-- LOTS OF MONEY-- BECAUSE PEOPLE ARE AFRAID OF HIM!

IN HIS HOME, CRANE'S DISTORTED BRAIN BEGINS THINKING ALONG FANTASTIC LINES--- ALONG CRIMINAL LINES--

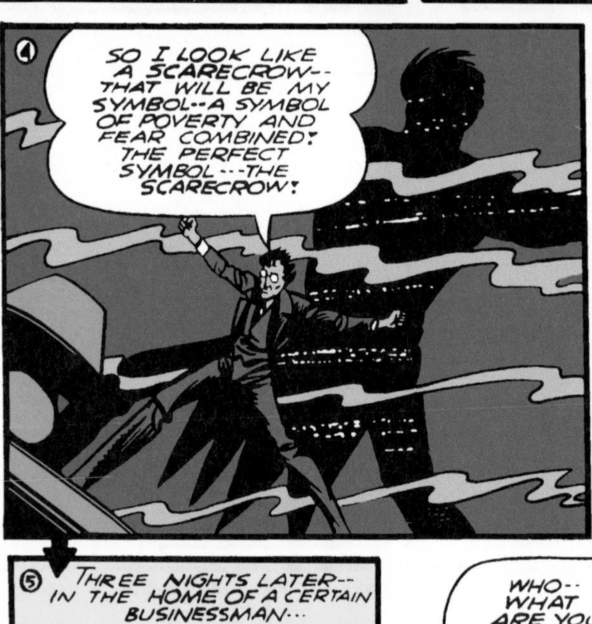
SO I LOOK LIKE A SCARECROW-- THAT WILL BE MY SYMBOL--A SYMBOL OF POVERTY AND FEAR COMBINED! THE PERFECT SYMBOL---THE SCARECROW!

THREE NIGHTS LATER-- IN THE HOME OF A CERTAIN BUSINESSMAN---
WHAT? STRAWS?
YES--MY FRIEND-- STRAWS-- IT IS MY SIGN!

WHO-- WHAT ARE YOU?

I'M THE SCARECROW! I'VE COME TO SELL YOU MY SERVICES--

YOU ARE FRANK KENDRICK! YOUR BUSINESS PARTNER IS SUING YOU BECAUSE YOU STOLE SOME MONEY FROM THE BUSINESS YOU TWO OWN!

FOR A CERTAIN SUM OF MONEY, I WILL SCARE YOUR PARTNER SO THAT HE WILL BE AFRAID TO PROSECUTE YOU--HE WILL DROP THE SUIT! DO YOU WANT TO BUY MY SERVICES?
I... I SUPPOSE SO! WHY NOT? IF YOU CAN STOP MY PARTNER!

THAT VERY NIGHT...
I AM THE SCARECROW! YOU ARE FRANK KENDRICK'S BUSINESS PARTNER! I'VE COME TO TELL YOU, YOU MUST WITHDRAW YOUR SUIT AGAINST HIM!
WHO?

THE NEXT TIME WE MEET IT WILL BE YOUR HEART UNLESS YOU WITHDRAW THE SUIT! YOU HAVE BEEN WARNED BY THE SCARECROW!
AHH! YOU SHOT ME!

THE BATMAN AND ROBIN DART LIGHTLY ACROSS THE ROOF-TOPS--
DID YOU HEAR IT?
YES... A SHOT! SOMETHING'S UP! IT CAME FROM OVER THERE!

WHAT IS IT?
LOOKS LIKE A WALKING SCARECROW-- COME ON, ROBIN!

WITH THE LIGHTNESS OF TRAINED ATHLETES, THE DUO SWINGS TO THE NEARBY BUILDING--
4

DOWN THE FIRE ESCAPE THEY RACE IN PURSUIT OF THE SCARECROW---
COME ON, ROBIN! THAT FELLOW'S FAST ON HIS FEET!

Z-I-N-G--
ABRUPTLY, A BULLET SCREAMS PAST THE BATMAN'S HEAD AND SMACKS INTO THE BRICK BEHIND HIM!

OH-OH! HE'S SPOTTED US! ONLY ONE THING LEFT TO DO!

HI, PAL!

PLEASANT DREAMS!

SLUG THE BATMAN, WILL YOU?

TAKE THAT!
5

THE IS

2 Cents New York

BUSINESSMAN SHOT BY SCARECROW

WALKING SCARECROW WARNS HEROLD

PAUL HEROLD ACCUSES

PROFESSOR JONATHAN CRANE IS CALLED INTO THE PRESIDENT'S OFFICE--
WE HAVE DECIDED TO RELIEVE YOU OF YOUR PROFESSORSHIP HERE! YOUR TEACHINGS ARE ENTIRELY TOO FANATICAL--SUCH AS YOUR SHOOTING A GUN OFF IN CLASS-- WE FEEL---

BAH! WHO CARES WHAT YOU FEEL! I HAVE MONEY NOW. I DON'T NEED YOU ANY MORE!

AND THAT NIGHT IN HIS ROOM, CRANE PONDERS----
THEY FIRED ME! WHO WANTED TO BE A DULL TEACHER ANY-WAY? NOW I CAN HAVE MONEY--MORE MONEY---

AND NOW THE ENSUING DAYS TELL OF THE BEGINNING OF A GREAT CRIME MASTER--OF THE BEGINNING OF DAYS OF TERROR! THE SCARECROW STRIKES AGAIN AND AGAIN!
DAILY
2¢

BRUCE WAYNE MEETS AN OLD FRIEND--THE PRESIDENT OF THE COLLEGE
HELLO, MARTIN! HOW ARE YOU? WHAT'S NEW?
NOTHING MUCH! WE PEOPLE OF COLLEGE USUALLY LEAD A FAIRLY UNEXCITING LIFE-

---THIS "SCARECROW" CRANE, AS WE CALL HIM, WAVED A LARGE ROLL OF BILLS UNDER MY NOSE!
SCARECROW! I WONDER!
AND SPENDS ALL HIS MONEY ON ANCIENT BOOKS, YOU SAY?

AND AT THAT VERY MOMENT, THE SCARECROW PAYS ANOTHER CALL ON A PROSPECTIVE CLIENT!
YES--AND YOU ARE RICHARD DODGE---OWNER OF A FAILING DEPARTMENT STORE-- BEING PUT OUT OF BUSINESS BY A RIVAL-- SOMETHING I CAN REMEDY, IF YOU ARE INTERESTED!
YOU! SCARECROW!

I CAN SCARE AWAY CUSTOMERS--I'LL START A REIGN OF TERROR THAT WILL DRIVE THEM AWAY--
--AND INTO MY STORE! HM! IT'S A BIT UNETHICAL, OF COURSE, BUT IT IS THE OLD LAW OF THE SURVIVAL OF THE FITTEST! YES--YES--

THE NEXT DAY--
SCARECROW! EEEEE

THE BURSTING OF THE SMOKE-BOMB IS A SIGNAL FOR PANIC!
STUPID PACK! PUSHING, CROWDING AGAINST EACH OTHER, LIKE FRIGHTENED ANIMALS!
HELP! SCARECROW!

AND IN THE WAYNE APARTMENT---
"SCARECROW" CRANE--- COULD IT BE A COINCIDENCE?
CALLING ALL CARS-- CALLING ALL CARS-- TO FENTONS' DEPARTMENT STORE-THE SCARECROW IS STARTING RIOT THERE-

C'MON, ROBIN! WE HAVE NO TIME TO LOSE!
RIGHT!

AN INSTANT LATER-- THE BATMOBILE DARTS THROUGH CITY STREETS-

AFTER PARKING THEIR CAR--THEY RACE OVER ROOFTOPS---
IF WE GO IN THIS WAY, BY THE ROOF OF THE STORE, WE WON'T BE SEEN!

TOWARD THE CENTER OF CONFUSION, RACE THE BATMAN AND ROBIN--TO THE SCARECROW!
HI, UGLY!

YOU MISSED! STRIKE ONE!
STUPID CLOD!

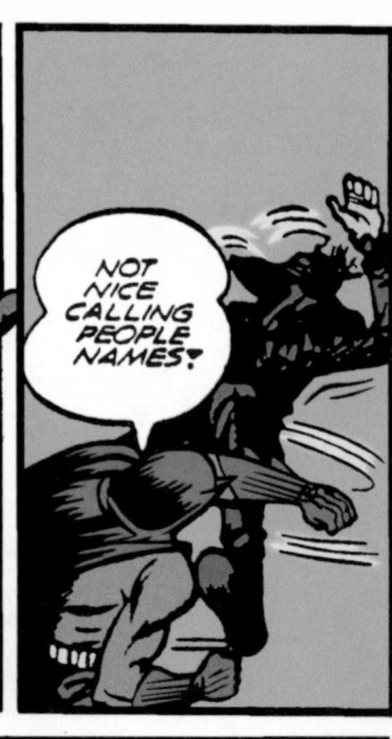
NOT NICE CALLING PEOPLE NAMES!

DOWN THE SLIPPERY LENGTH OF THE COUNTER SPINS THE SCARECROW, THE BATMAN RACING TO MEET HIM---

PLEASED TO MEET YOU!

BLUNDERING FOOL! DO YOU THINK YOU CAN TAKE ME SO EASILY?
9

MEANWHILE, ROBIN FINDS HIMSELF IN TROUBLE-
SORRY-- BUT YOU'RE MAKING A MISTAKE--
STOP HIM!

YOU'RE GOING TO DIE, BATMAN!
SPORTS
HEY! I'VE GOT TO STOP THAT MANIAC!

FROM THE RACK IN THE SPORTS DEPARTMENT, ROBIN SEIZES A BOWLING BALL AND--

UGH!
SET 'EM UP IN THE NEXT ALLEY!

THE SCARECROW RECOVERS SWIFTLY AND SCRAMBLES TO HIS FEET. HIS HAND DIGS INTO A POCKET AND--
I'LL FINISH YOU WITH THIS BOMB!

AGAIN ROBIN MAKES USE OF THE SPORTS DEPARTMENT--
I HOPE MY AIM IS GOOD! IT'D BETTER BE--

BULLS-EYE!!
IT LOOKS LIKE OUR SAWDUST FRIEND HAS GIVEN US THE SLIP AGAIN!
HOLD YOUR FIRE, MEN! IT'S THE BATMAN AND ROBIN!
10

YOU'RE TOO LATE, SARGEANT!
ANYBODY KNOW IF HE STOLE ANYTHING--?
YES, HE TOOK TWO BOOKS FROM THE RARE BOOK DEPARTMENT.

LATER THAT NIGHT--
SO HE STOLE THE RARE BOOKS! THAT TIES IN VERY NEATLY WITH A MAN CALLED SCARECROW CRANE! LEAVE YOUR MASK ON!

WHAT DO YOU WANT?
I BEG YOUR PARDON. MAY I USE YOUR PHONE TO CALL THE GARAGE? MY CAR BROKE DOWN!

AH! RARE BOOKS! QUITE A NICE COLLECTION, TOO! YOU MUST HAVE SPENT A FORTUNE ON THESE!
THAT'S NONE OF YOUR BUSINESS! YOU ASKED FOR A PHONE! THERE IT IS! USE IT AND GET OUT!

BUT ONCE OUTSIDE, THE UNWELCOME VISITOR REMOVES HIS DISGUISE-
THINK HE'S OUR MAN?
I'M POSITIVE! TOMORROW I'M GOING TO CALL ON DODGE, THE DEPARTMENT STORE OWNER! I'LL BET HE HIRED THE SCARECROW TO START THAT RIOT IN FENTON'S STORE!

THE MORON! TO THINK HE WOULD FOOL ME WITH SUCH AN OBVIOUS DISGUISE! TRY TO QUESTION DODGE, WILL HE? HE'LL FIND DODGE DEAD FIRST!

IT'S TIME FOR THE SCARECROW TO WALK AGAIN!
11

AS THE SCARECROW STEPS OUT, A VOICE FLOATS MOCKINGLY TOWARD HIM FROM THE SHADOWS--
NOW FOR-- WHO'S THERE?
THE BATMAN, PAL! I KNEW IF I TALKED LOUD ENOUGH YOU'D MAKE A DUMB MOVE! NOW I HAVE PROOF YOU ARE THE SCARECROW!

TRICK ME, WILL YOU?
DOWN, ROBIN! DOWN!

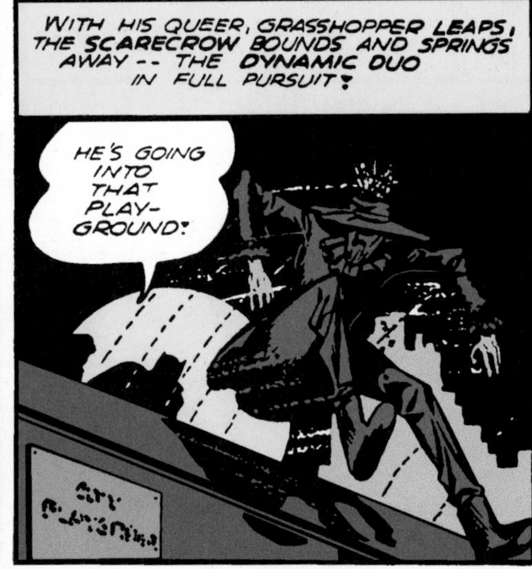
WITH HIS QUEER, GRASSHOPPER LEAPS, THE SCARECROW BOUNDS AND SPRINGS AWAY -- THE DYNAMIC DUO IN FULL PURSUIT!
HE'S GOING INTO THAT PLAY-GROUND!

NOW THIS WILL BE A NICE TRICK IF IT WORKS!

OUT SPRINGS THE BOY WONDER-
IT'S THAT MEDDLESOME BOY AGAIN!

BUT THE SCARECROW'S BONY, KNOTTED FIST SMASHES HIM FULL IN THE FACE ---
YOU HAVE TO BE QUICKER THAN THAT..

DROP THAT GUN!
I'LL FINISH YOU FIRST, THEN YOUR PAL!
BUT THE SCARECROW IS TOO INTENT UPON EVIL TO NOTE THE STILL FLYING SWING ---AND--

12

AS THE SCARECROW REACHES FOR HIS FALLEN GUN---THE BATMAN LEAPS!

A SHOT BLASTS PAST THE BATMAN'S FACE AS THEY LOCK IN A TERRIBLE STRUGGLE!

YOU'LL FIND I'M AS GOOD AT FIGHTING AS YOU ARE, BATMAN!

ONCE AGAIN, THE SCARECROW STOOPS FOR HIS FALLEN GUN WHEN--ROBIN ENTERS THE FRAY!
HOLD THAT POSITION!

BOB KANE

NICE TIMING, KID!
13

WOW! IS HE REALLY OUT AT LAST?
I DON'T KNOW! HE CERTAINLY GAVE ME THE FIGHT OF MY CAREER, BUT FROM NOW ON THE ONLY FIGHTING HE'LL DO IS IN A PRISON CELL!

AND SO THE INFAMOUS, SHORT-LIVED CAREER OF THE SCARECROW COMES TO AN END AT LAST!
THE STUPID FOOLS ACTUALLY THINK THEY'RE GOING TO KEEP ME HERE--
THE End-
WILL THE SCARECROW RETURN? ONLY TIME... ONLY INSCRUTABLE TIME CAN TELL!

No. 7
A DC PUBLICATION
BATMAN
OCT. NOV.
10¢
THE WINNING TEAM!
BOB KANE

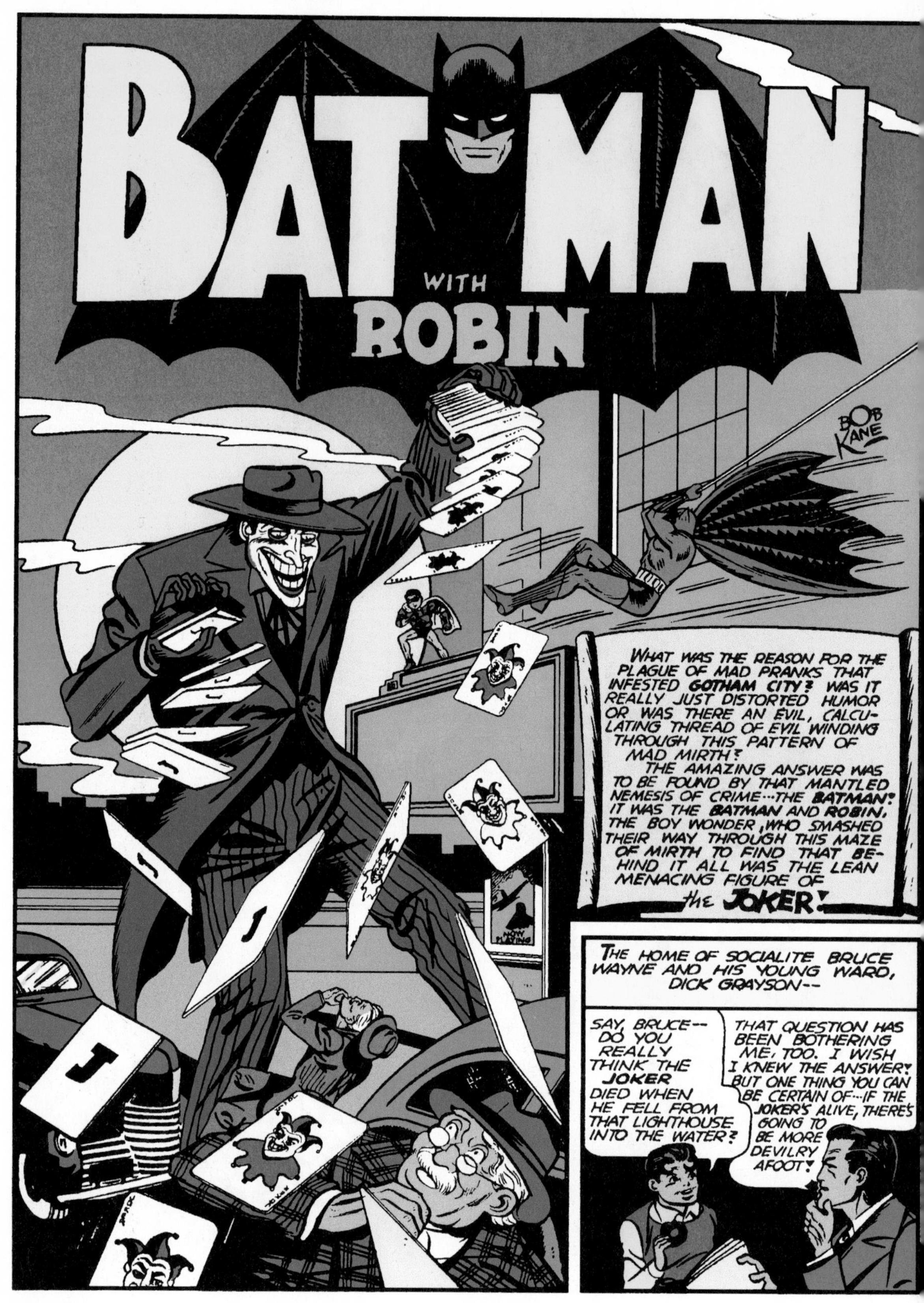
BATMAN
WITH ROBIN
BOB KANE
WHAT WAS THE REASON FOR THE PLAGUE OF MAD PRANKS THAT INFESTED GOTHAM CITY? WAS IT REALLY JUST DISTORTED HUMOR OR WAS THERE AN EVIL, CALCULATING THREAD OF EVIL WINDING THROUGH THIS PATTERN OF MAD MIRTH? THE AMAZING ANSWER WAS TO BE FOUND BY THAT MANTLED NEMESIS OF CRIME...THE BATMAN! IT WAS THE BATMAN AND ROBIN, THE BOY WONDER, WHO SMASHED THEIR WAY THROUGH THIS MAZE OF MIRTH TO FIND THAT BEHIND IT ALL WAS THE LEAN MENACING FIGURE OF the JOKER!
NOW PLAYING
THE HOME OF SOCIALITE BRUCE WAYNE AND HIS YOUNG WARD, DICK GRAYSON--
SAY, BRUCE-- DO YOU REALLY THINK THE JOKER DIED WHEN HE FELL FROM THAT LIGHTHOUSE INTO THE WATER?
THAT QUESTION HAS BEEN BOTHERING ME, TOO. I WISH I KNEW THE ANSWER! BUT ONE THING YOU CAN BE CERTAIN OF...IF THE JOKER'S ALIVE, THERE'S GOING TO BE MORE DEVILRY AFOOT!

AFTER THEY HAVE PICKED UP THE OBJECTS AND LAID THEM DOWN ON THE TABLE AGAIN--

EACH ONE OF THESE OBJECTS HAS BEEN PART OF A MAJOR CRIME! YOUR FINGERPRINTS ARE ON THEM! I COULD HAND YOU OVER TO POLICE... THEY COULD ACCUSE YOU OF BEING INVOLVED IN THOSE CRIMES!

A MAN TAKES A SHOWER ONLY TO FIND THE WATER TAPS ARE NOW SWITCHED! WHAT SHOULD BE COLD WATER IS REALLY SCALDING HOT!

A MAN CAUSES A MINOR RIOT IN A BANK BY THROWING AWAY WHAT IS APPARENTLY MONEY!

BUT A BANK TELLER EXAMINES THE GREEN PAPER AND YELLS OUT--

AND, OF COURSE, ALL THIS PLEASES THE **JOKER** IMMENSELY!

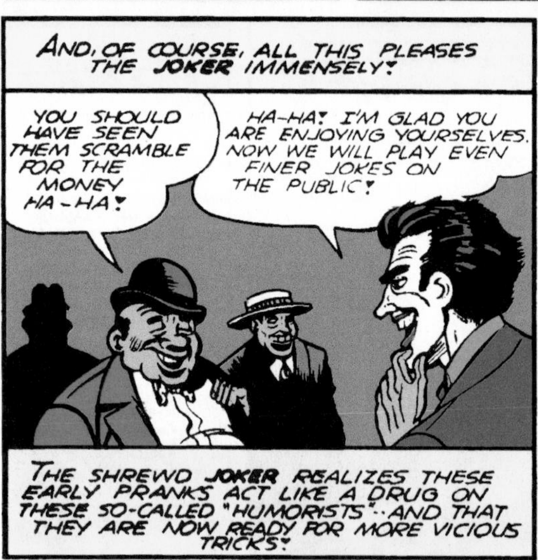

THE SHREWD **JOKER** REALIZES THESE EARLY PRANKS ACT LIKE A DRUG ON THESE SO-CALLED "HUMORISTS"--AND THAT THEY ARE NOW READY FOR MORE VICIOUS TRICKS!

AUTO SIGNS ARE CHANGED ON ROADS, CAUSING TERRIBLE ACCIDENTS--

POISONS ARE PUT IN BOTTLES SUPPOSED TO CONTAIN BENEFICIAL MEDICINES!

ONE "HUMORIST" PULLS A SWITCH THAT SHUNTS A RAILROAD TRAIN ONTO THE WRONG TRACK! RESULT---INSANE LAUGHTER---AND A TRAIN WRECK!

THEN, ONE DAY A PLANE SWOOPS DOWN OVER THE CITY!

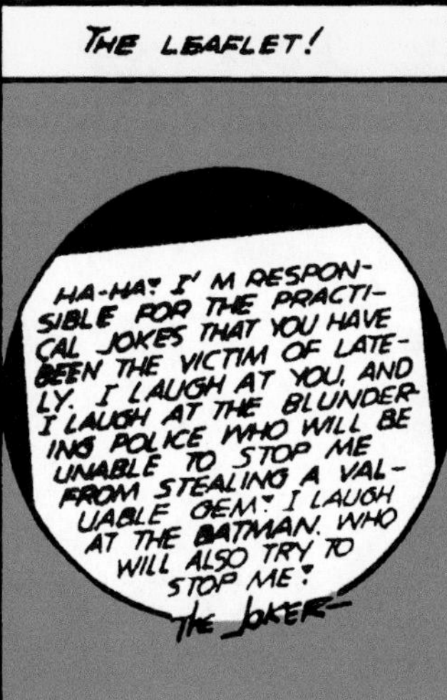
THE LEAFLET!
HA-HA! I'M RESPONSIBLE FOR THE PRACTICAL JOKES THAT YOU HAVE BEEN THE VICTIM OF LATELY. I LAUGH AT YOU, AND I LAUGH AT THE BLUNDERING POLICE WHO WILL BE UNABLE TO STOP ME FROM STEALING A VALUABLE GEM! I LAUGH AT THE BATMAN, WHO WILL ALSO TRY TO STOP ME!
THE JOKER

PUBLIC FEELING NOW RUNS HIGH! NOBODY LIKES TO BE LAUGHED AT -- ESPECIALLY BY A CRIMINAL!
TAKE IT EASY, GORDON! YOU'RE LIKELY TO BURST A BLOOD VESSEL!
HOW CAN I TAKE IT EASY WHILE THE JOKER LAUGHS AT THE WHOLE POLICE FORCE!
POLICE COMMISSIONER GORDON!

MY NAME IS HENRY VERNE! READ THIS NOTE I RECEIVED THIS MORNING!
"TOMORROW NIGHT I WILL ENTER YOUR HOME AND STEAL THE GREAT DIAMOND YOU POSSESS! THE JOKER"

WHAT CAN I DO? THE JOKER WILL SURELY STEAL MY DIAMOND!
NO, HE WON'T! YOU STAY AT HOME! WHEN THE JOKER ENTERS YOUR HOUSE, HE'S GOING TO WALK INTO A TRAP!
YOU HOPE!

AND AT THAT MOMENT--
YOU HAVE DONE WELL! THE PUBLIC AND THE POLICE ARE SO AROUSED AGAINST ME THAT OUR PLANS WILL CATCH THEM OFF-GUARD-

THE NEXT NIGHT --- A STRANGE TENSION GRIPS THE POLICEMEN POSTED ABOUT THE VERNE HOME--
I CAN HEAR VERNE PACING UP AND DOWN INSIDE-BOY, IS HE NERVOUS!
I DON'T BLAME HIM! THIS WAITING AROUND FOR THE JOKER IS GETTING ME, TOO!

AND AT THAT VERY INSTANT, TWO MANTLED FIGURES LOPE SWIFTLY THROUGH GREY CITY STREETS! THEY ARE THE BATMAN AND ROBIN--
C'MON ROBIN, WE'VE GOT A DATE WITH THE JOKER!
LET'S STEP IT UP!
WHEN THEY ARRIVE AT THE VERNE HOME--
LOOK! THEY'RE UNCONSCIOUS!
AND WITH THAT JOKER GRIN ON THEIR FACES! C'MON, LET'S HOPE WE'RE NOT TOO LATE!

H'YA, FUNNYMAN!
WE-LL? THE BATMAN! I WAS WONDERING WHAT HAD KEPT YOU!

NOW YOU DON'T HAVE TO WONDER ANY MORE!
HOLD HIM BATMAN! I'M COMING TO HELP!

DON'T YOU THINK YOU'RE GOING TO NEED A LITTLE HELP YOURSELF?
WHAT?... ANOTHER JOKER!

ROBIN'S COMPLETE SURPRISE LEAVES HIM OPEN FOR A VICIOUS BLOW!
SURPRISES ARE COMING FAST TONIGHT, AREN'T THEY?

ANOTHER GRINNING FIGURE SWEEPS INTO THE ROOM!
HEY..? MY EYES MUST BE GOING BACK ON ME!

FROM THE OPEN DOORWAY POURS AN AVALANCHE OF JOKERS--JOKERS... AND MORE JOKERS! JOKERS OF ALL SIZES AND SHAPES!
HOLY CATS!
EITHER I'VE GONE CRAZY OR I'M HAVING A NIGHT-MARE!

HEY?
IT WAS A FALSE FACE! THEY'RE ALL WEARING FALSE FACES!

AND AT THAT VERY INSTANT, IN ANOTHER PART OF TOWN-
WHO-- WHO ARE YOU? WHAT DO YOU WANT?
I AM CALLED THE JOKER- AND I WANT THAT PRECIOUS DIAMOND YOUR WIFE IS SO FOND OF WEARING SO SHE CAN IMPRESS PEOPLE! THE GEM IS IN THE WALL SAFE! I WANT IT-- NOW-

HOW YOU DOIN', KID?
THEY HAVEN'T GOT ME YET!
AND BACK AT THE VERNE APARTMENT, THE BATMAN AND ROBIN TRY DESPERATELY TO HOLD THEIR OWN AGAINST OVERWHELMING ODDS!

BUT THEY ARE FINALLY OVERCOME BY THE SHEER WEIGHT OF NUMBERS!
WHAT NOW? SHALL WE FINISH THEM FOR GOOD?
NO! HE WANTS THEM ALIVE SO THEY MAY HEAR HIM LAUGH AT THEM! NOW LET'S GO!

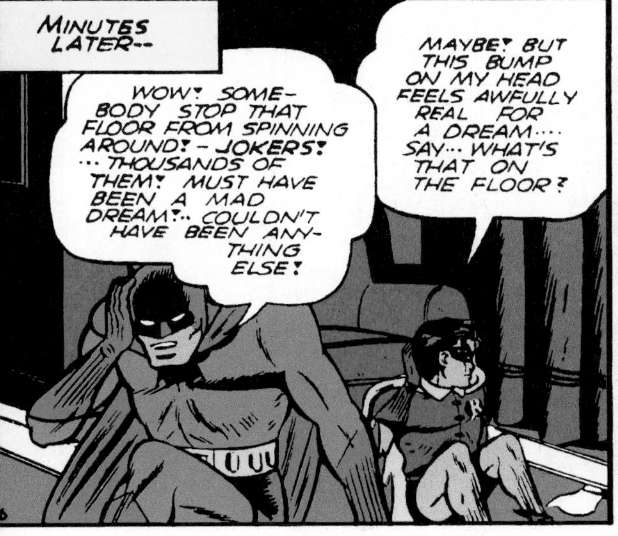
MINUTES LATER--
WOW! SOMEBODY STOP THAT FLOOR FROM SPINNING AROUND! - JOKERS! ... THOUSANDS OF THEM! MUST HAVE BEEN A MAD DREAM!.. COULDN'T HAVE BEEN ANYTHING ELSE!
MAYBE! BUT THIS BUMP ON MY HEAD FEELS AWFULLY REAL FOR A DREAM.... SAY... WHAT'S THAT ON THE FLOOR?

"IF YOU WILL EXAMINE THIS 'DIAMOND' CLOSELY, YOU WILL FIND IT IS ONLY A GLASS DOOR KNOB! IT IS AS PHONEY AS MY NAME.
HENRY VERNE"

AS THE BATMAN AND ROBIN LOOK AT EACH OTHER BLANKLY, A BELL JANGLES RUDELY!
TELEPHONE!
WHO COULD BE CALLING HERE?
R-I-N-G!!

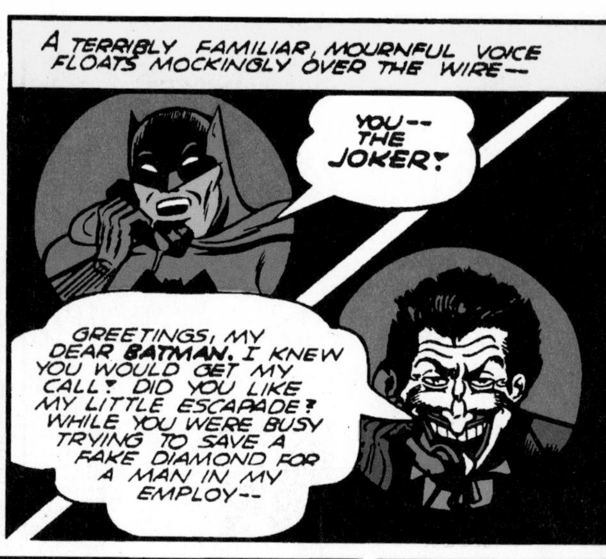
A TERRIBLY FAMILIAR, MOURNFUL VOICE FLOATS MOCKINGLY OVER THE WIRE--
YOU-- THE JOKER!
GREETINGS, MY DEAR BATMAN. I KNEW YOU WOULD GET MY CALL! DID YOU LIKE MY LITTLE ESCAPADE? WHILE YOU WERE BUSY TRYING TO SAVE A FAKE DIAMOND FOR A MAN IN MY EMPLOY--

---I WAS OUT STEALING A REAL GEM! FUNNY, EH? HA HA! WHILE YOU'RE PUZZLING THAT OUT, YOU MIGHT TRY TO SOLVE THIS RIDDLE-- "WHEN IS A DUKE NOT A DUKE?" HA-HA! ADIEU, BATMAN--HA HA! THINK IT OVER BATMAN! HA-HA
YOU LAUGHING HYENA!

THAT GRINNING DEVIL! I'M GOING TO WIPE THAT SMILE OFF HIS FACE IF IT'S THE LAST THING I DO! WE'LL SEE WHO HAS THE LAST LAUGH YET!
HE HAS A SENSE OF HUMOR-- ONLY IT'S DISTORTED!

"WHEN IS A DUKE NOT A DUKE?" I WONDER WHAT HE MEANT BY THAT? HMM-

AND THAT NIGHT---THE JOKER LAUGHS!
HA-HA-HA! WHAT A COMEDY OF ERRORS! AND THE BATMAN WAS THE GOAT! HA-HA! SOON I'LL SHOW HIM ANOTHER GREAT JOKE WHILE HE THINKS ABOUT THAT RIDDLE! HA HA-HA!

A FEW NIGHTS LATER--
"WHEN IS A DUKE NOT A DUKE?" WHAT DOES IT MEAN?
LISTEN TO THIS, BRUCE! "TONIGHT, A DINNER WILL BE GIVEN FOR THE VISITING DUKE MICHEAL, WHO IS HERE COLLECTING FUNDS FOR HIS STARVING PEOPLE!"

"---A VALISE CONTAINING $10,000 WILL BE GIVEN TO DUKE MICHEAL TO AID THE WAR-TORN NATION!"
WHAT? THAT'S IT?... THAT'S IT!

THAT'S WHAT?
DUKE! WHY, HE'S THE JOKER! GET ON YOUR DUDS, DICKEY, MY BOY-- WE'RE GOING TO GET THE JOKER... AND THIS TIME IT'S NO JOKE!

AND AT THAT VERY MOMENT--IN THE HOTEL HOUSING THE DUKE---
JOK... AGGH!

THE TWO POLICEMEN ARE DRAGGED INTO THE DUKE'S ROOM, WHILE THE JOKER---
DUKE MICHEAL AND HIS TWO AIDES, I BELIEVE!
WHO.. AGGH!

THEY'LL SLEEP FOR A FEW HOURS NOW! REMOVE THEIR CLOTHING, WHILE I WORK WITH THE MAKEUP-

A FEW, DEFT MOVEMENTS OF THE SLIM HANDS AND--
IT'S INCREDIBLE!
NOW, PUT ON THEIR CLOTHING AND I'LL GET TO WORK ON YOUR FACES!

AND SO-- MINUTES LATER INTO THE GREAT BANQUET HALL STRIDE THE "DUKE MICHEAL" AND HIS "AIDES!"
HERE COMES THE DUKE NOW!

--AND SO WE GIVE THIS, OUR CONTRIBUTION, FOR THE USE OF FOOD AND CLOTHES TO YOUR PEOPLE!
THANK YOU! THANK YOU! I'M SURE I--- AHEM-- MY PEOPLE WILL PUT IT TO VERY GOOD USES!

PUT DOWN THAT BAG, JOKER!
YOU!
YOU SEE, I SOLVED YOUR RIDDLE!

THE JOKER THINKS FAST!
GUARDS! STOP THAT MAN AND BOY! THEY'RE TRYING TO STEAL THE MONEY!

THE TWIN TORNADOS SWEEP THROUGH THE GUESTS, HURLING THEM ASIDE!
GANGWAY!
SORRY, FELLOWS-- BUT WE'RE COMING THROUGH!

OH-- YOU WANT TO FIGHT, EH?

...WHY DIDN'T YOU TELL ME?

PLEASED TO MEET YOU, BUD!

FROM THE VANTAGE POINTS WHERE THEY HAVE BEEN POSTED SWARM A HORDE OF THE JOKER'S MEN, ANXIOUS TO SAVE THE JOKER AND ESPECIALLY THE $10,000!
C'MON, BOYS! RUSH 'EM!
LOOK, ROBIN-- FOOD AND DISHES!
I GET YOU!

AS THE MEN REACH FOR GUNS, THE BATMAN WHIPS THE TABLE-CLOTH AWAY AND---SLAPS THEM SILLY--
S-W-I-S-H-
NEXT TIME DON'T BE SO IMPETUOUS!

I'VE GOT THE MONEY HIDDEN-- NOW TO BEAT IT--
LOOK! THERE GOES THE JOKER!
C'MON!

HE'S GOING TO GET AWAY IN THAT CAR!
WE'RE GOING TO BORROW THIS ONE AND GET THAT MANIAC--

A WILD CHASE TAKES THE CARS TEARING THRU THE STREETS!
BETTER STEP ON THE GAS! HE'S DRAWING AWAY FROM US!
THIS IS ALL THIS CAR CAN DO! JUST MY LUCK TO PICK A JUNK HEAP!
10

THE JOKER'S CAR SCREAMS TO A HALT!
HE'S STOPPED!
...AND RUNNING INTO THE RAILROAD STATION!

A TRAIN GATE SLAMS SHUT BEHIND THE JOKER--AND IN THE FACES OF BATMAN AND ROBIN!
WE'RE TOO LATE!
NOT YET! C'MON! I'VE GOT A TRICK UP MY SLEEVE, TOO!
HA-HA-HA!

WHERE ARE WE GOING?
TO CATCH A TRAIN! HOLD TIGHT-- I'M GOING TO GIVE THIS BABY ALL SHE'S GOT!

OUT ONTO THE ROAD THEY SPEED UNTIL THEY RACE ALONGSIDE THE RAILROAD TRACKS--
THERE SHE IS, ROBIN! GET READY TO JUMP AT THE CROSSING!

DESPERATION SEEMS TO GIVE WINGS TO THE BATMAN AND ROBIN AS THEY HURL THEIR BODIES AT THE HURTLING TRAIN!
JUMP!

WE MADE IT!
-AND WITH NOT MUCH TO SPARE! NOW LET'S GET THE JOKER!

THERE'S THE JOKER NOW! STOP HIM, SOMEBODY STOP HIM!

THE JOKER IS TRAPPED BETWEEN TWO CARS..
COMING FROM BOTH SIDES-ONLY ONE THING TO DO!

THE MANIAC SCRAMBLES TO THE TOP OF THE LURCHING TRAIN--

BUFFETED BY THE SHRIEKING WIND, THE BATMAN AND ROBIN PICK THEIR WAY ACROSS THE SWAYING CARS THAT TEAR ALONG AT A TERRIFYING CLIP!
LOOK! THE JOKER'S GOING DOWN AGAIN!
WONDER WHAT HE'S UP TO NOW?
US MAIL
JGRR 777

HA-HA-HA HA!
THE MAD JOKER HANGS PERILOUSLY ABOVE THE COUPLINGS BETWEEN TWO CARS...

JUST A LITTLE MORE!
HIS STRONG, LEAN HANDS PLUCK AT THE COUPLINGS, LOOSENING THEM--

JUMP, ROBIN-- JUMP!
JGRR

SO YOU MADE IT, EH? YOU WON'T HANG THERE LONG! I'M SENDING YOU TO BE MANGLED UNDER THE WHEELS!

NOT YET, JOKER... NOT YET... BY A LONG CHANCE!
12

NOW A TITANIC STRUGGLE BEGINS ATOP THE LURCHING CAR! ONE SLIP MEANS--DEATH!
UGH!
HA-HA HA!

A SUDDEN, SAVAGE BLOW SENDS THE BATMAN ON HIS BACK!
A GOOD ONE, EH?

THIS TIME YOU'RE GOING OFF, BATMAN!

COLLECTING ALL HIS STRENGTH, THE BATMAN BOUNCES UP LIKE A RUBBER BALL. HIS FIST CRASHES ON THE JOKER'S JAW!
THIS IS IT, JOKER!

FOR ONE TERRIBLE MOMENT, THE JOKER TEETERS ON THE EDGE OF THE CAR, HIS HANDS CLAWING DESPERATELY AT THE EMPTY AIR--AND THEN--
BOB KANE

I DON'T THINK HE'LL CHEAT DEATH THIS TIME! DO YOU, BATMAN?
MAYBE--HE'S CHEATED DEATH SO OFTEN, YOU JUST CAN'T TRUST THAT GUY! AT LEAST, WE KNOW WE HAD THE LAST LAUGH ON THE JOKER!

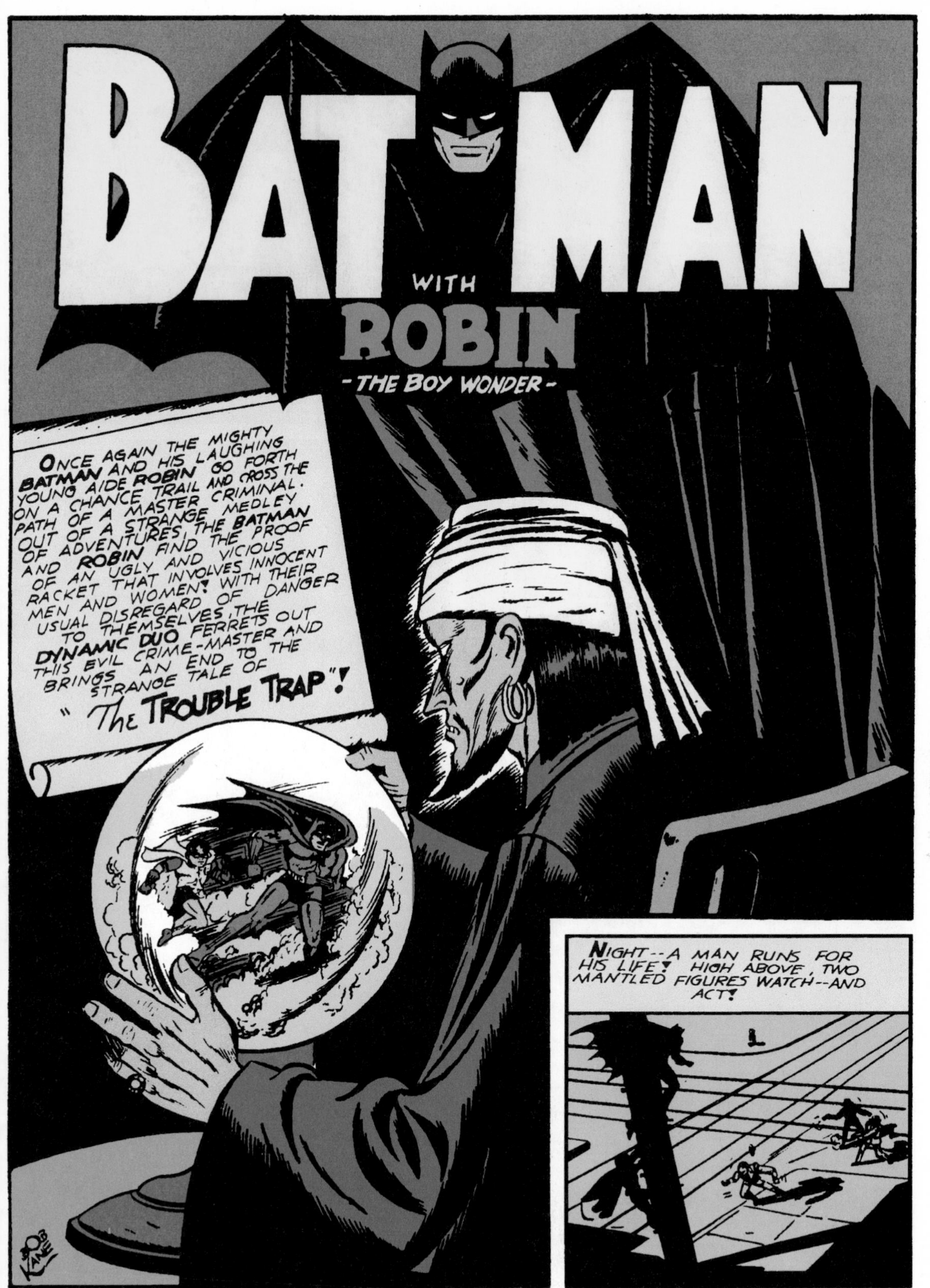
BATMAN
WITH
ROBIN
-THE BOY WONDER-
ONCE AGAIN THE MIGHTY BATMAN AND HIS LAUGHING YOUNG AIDE ROBIN GO FORTH ON A CHANCE TRAIL AND CROSS THE PATH OF A MASTER CRIMINAL. OUT OF A STRANGE MEDLEY OF ADVENTURES, THE BATMAN AND ROBIN FIND THE PROOF OF AN UGLY AND VICIOUS RACKET THAT INVOLVES INNOCENT MEN AND WOMEN! WITH THEIR USUAL DISREGARD OF DANGER TO THEMSELVES, THE DYNAMIC DUO FERRETS OUT THIS EVIL CRIME-MASTER AND BRINGS AN END TO THE STRANGE TALE OF " The TROUBLE TRAP"!
BOB KANE
NIGHT--A MAN RUNS FOR HIS LIFE! HIGH ABOVE, TWO MANTLED FIGURES WATCH--AND ACT!

TOO LATE! A VICIOUS BLAST OF GUNFIRE---AND THE MAN DROPS TO THE GROUND-

OKAY-HE'S THROUGH!
YEAH! WE DID A-LOOK!

YOU ROTTEN KILLERS!

LEMME ALONE! GIMME A CHANCE!
I'LL GIVE YOU A CHANCE!

?
?

WOW!
HOLY CATS!

WHAT WE DO WITH THEM?
CHOKE 'EM! BREAK THEIR NECKS!

SLOWLY, INEXORABLY, THE GIANT HANDS CLOSE TIGHTLY ABOUT THE THROATS OF THE STRUGGLING BATMAN AND ROBIN--

AS THE DESPERATE BATMAN GASPS FOR AIR, HIS FOOT LASHES OUT IN ONE LAST-DITCH EFFORT--

MOMENTARILY STUNNED, THE BRUTE RELEASES HIS DEATH GRIP. THE BATMAN'S HAND REACHES FOR ONE OF THE GLASS PELLETS IN HIS UTILITY BELT--

A FLING OF THE BATMAN'S HAND---AND BLACK SMOKE BILLOWS FORTH--

OKAY, BIG BOY-- DROP HIM!

SUDDENLY, THE EERIE WALL OF A POLICE SIREN FILLS THE NIGHT--
COPPERS-- C'MON!

THE TRUCK WHIPS AWAY FROM THE CURB, AND MAKES THE CORNER ON TWO WHEELS!
HOW'S YOUR THROAT?
IT HURTS! I CAN HARDLY BREATHE!

JUST A SECOND, ROBIN-- LET'S FIND OUT WHO THIS FELLOW IS!

THIS MAN IS HENRY ABBOT-- LOOK! HE'S WITHDRAWN LARGE SUMS OF MONEY FROM HIS BANK AT VARIOUS INTERVALS! VERY CURIOUS!
BETTER LEAVE BEFORE THE POLICE ARRIVE!

I'VE GOT A HUNCH THAT TONIGHT'S EVENTS ARE JUST THE BEGINNING!
RIGHT!

NEXT DAY-
CAN I GO OUT AND PLAY FOR A WHILE?
NOT UNTIL YOU FINISH YOUR HOMEWORK--

HOMEWORK! (GRUMBLE GRUMBLE)
SO LONG NOW!

BRUCE VISITS AN OLD FRIEND--
WHAT'S ON YOUR MIND? YOU LOOK WORRIED!
I ? NOT I-- HA! HA!

NEVER MIND ANNOUNCIN' ME! H'YA--GOT IT FOR ME?
YOU---? ER---NO--- NOT NOW. TONIGHT-- I'LL HAVE IT TONIGHT!
HOLY SMOKE! ONE OF THOSE KILLERS OF LAST NIGHT!

OKAY, I'LL BE BACK AT EIGHT! BETTER HAVE IT OR WE'LL PLAY A COUPLA RECORDS FO' YA!
NO--- I'LL HAVE IT--- I'LL HAVE IT!

WHO WAS THAT BOORISH FELLOW? HE WAS VERY IMPATIENT!
NOBODY IMPORTANT-- NOBODY AT ALL! UH, BRUCE, WOULD YOU MIND RUNNING ALONG NOW? I'M VERY BUSY-

SEE YOU AGAN SOME-TIME!
YOU SAID IT-- I'M COMING HERE AT EIGHT OCLOCK AND FIND OUT YOUR BUSINESS WITH THAT KILLER-
RIGHT, CARL!

THAT NIGHT! EIGHT O'CLOCK! A BLOTTED SHAPE MOVES SILENTLY OVER A WINDOW SILL AND INTO CARL DWYER'S HOME--

AND AT THAT VERY MOMENT CARL DWYER OPENS THE FRONT DOOR--
H'YA! GOT IT NOW?
YES! I HAD TO BORROW IT FROM MY FRIENDS! HERE!

YOU PROMISED TO BRING ME THE RECORD! I PAID YOU!
THE RECORD IS YOURS AFTER THE NEXT MONTH'S PAYMENT- SEE YA NEXT MONTH!

AS THE HOODLUM HURRIES DOWN THE LONELY STREET---
I SWORE I SAW SOMETHIN' FOLLOWIN' ME!

AND THE HOODLUM IS RIGHT! SOMEONE-- SOMETHING IS FOLLOWING HIM--

MINUTES LATER, THE BATMAN SEES THE HOODLUM ENTER A SOLITARY HOUSE. APPROACHING, HE READS ON THE HOUSE NAME-PLATE--
A SWAMI! NOW WHAT CONNECTION CAN THERE BE BETWEEN A SWAMI, A HOODLUM, A MURDERED MAN, TWO GIANT HINDUS AND CARL DWYER?
Granda the Mystic "I know all

AND THIS MONEY PAYMENT FOR RECORDS! -- IT DOESN'T MAKE SENSE! MAYBE IT WILL AFTER I HAVE A CHAT WITH DWYER!

THE DWYER HOME--
DROWNING YOUR TROUBLES?
ULP-- WHO?

WHY DID YOU GIVE MONEY TO THAT THUG? WHAT HAS IT TO DO WITH GRANDA THE MYSTIC?
BLACKMAIL! AT A PARTY SOMEONE SUGGESTED WE VISIT GRANDA THE MYSTIC---

"WE ALL WENT THERE---HE TOOK US INTO HIS ROOM, ONLY ONE AT THE TIME--"
NOW-- LOOK INTO THE CRYSTAL--

LOOK DEEP-- LOOK DEEP-- YOU ARE GROWING SLEEPY--

"IT SEEMED HOURS WHEN I WOKE UP - I THOUGHT NO MORE ABOUT IT UNTIL ONE DAY WHEN
GRANDA! WHAT DO YOU WANT?
I WANT YOU TO LISTEN TO THIS RECORD YOU'LL FIND IT INTERESTING!
6

"THE RECORD BEGAN TO PLAY---IT BEGAN TO TELL ALL ABOUT AN ESCAPADE OF MINE AT COLLEGE-"
IT WAS A HARMLESS PRANK THEN. NEWSPAPERS WOULD PLAY IT UP IF THEY HEARD OF IT!
GRANDA WANTED MONEY FOR THE RECORD OR ELSE- WHEN HE HYPNOTIZED YOU AT HIS STUDIO. HE MADE YOU TALK-

HE PROBABLY HAS A WHOLE GROUP OF FOOLS LIKE MYSELF ON HIS BLACKMAIL LIST!
THERE'S ONLY ONE THING TO DO... CALL THE POLICE-

THE POLICE COMMISSIONER RECEIVES A PHONE CALL-
HELLO, GORDON-- THIS IS THE BATMAN! I SUGGEST YOU RAID THE ESTABLISHMENT OF GRANDA, THE SOCIETY MYSTIC! HE'S RUNNING A BLACKMAIL RACKET! (CLICK!)
WHAT'S THAT? WHO-

THE NEXT DAY...
WHAT'S THE MEANING OF THIS?
SEARCHING FOR BOOKS OR ANYTHING ELSE THAT PERTAINS TO BLACKMAIL!

NOT A THING, COMMISSIONER!
I SEE! AND IF I'M WRONG, I APOLOGIZE.
YOU SEE?
LOOKS LIKE THE BATMAN IS WRONG THIS TIME!

THE NEXT DAY, GRANDA THE MYSTIC RECEIVES A CLIENT--
YES? YOU HAVE TO ASK MY ADVICE?
YEAH! CAN YOU GIVE ME THE LOWDOWN ON THE BATMAN?

THIS BATMAN GUY IS ALWAYS SHOVING MY BOYS AROUND! WANTA TO RUB HIM OUT!
GIVE ME TWO DAYS AND I PROMISE TO DELIVER THE BATMAN IN YOUR HANDS!

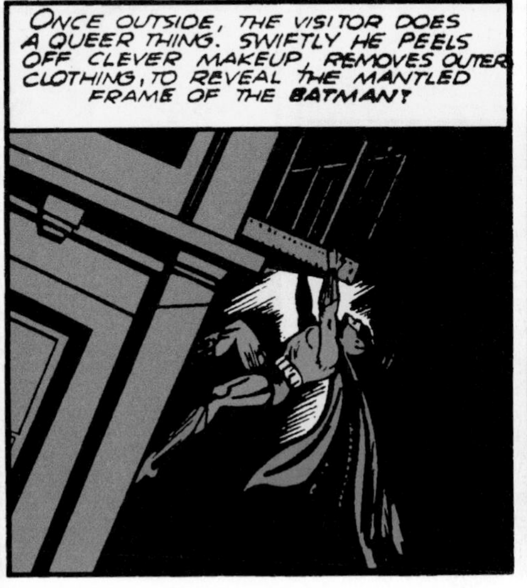
ONCE OUTSIDE, THE VISITOR DOES A QUEER THING. SWIFTLY HE PEELS OFF CLEVER MAKEUP, REMOVES OUTER CLOTHING, TO REVEAL THE MANTLED FRAME OF THE BATMAN!

SO THIS MUGG WANTS TO FIND OUT WHO THE BATMAN IS? EH?
YES! I WILL REVENGE MYSELF ON HIM FOR ATTACKING YOU AND THE GIANTS-

THIS NURSE, LINDA PAGE, HAS BEEN MIXED UP IN THE LAST FEW BATMAN CASES-
I GET IT, BOSS! BRING HER HERE AND MAYBE WE CAN MAKE HER TALK!

THAT NIGHT-- A PROTESTING LINDA PAGE IS LED FROM HER HOME!
I TELL YOU, I DON'T KNOW A THING!
SHUDDUP- AND GET MOVIN'!

AS THE CAR LEAPS AWAY FROM THE CURB, TWO MANTLED FIGURES DROP NOISELESSLY TO THE TOP--

HELLO!
EEEOW!

TERRIFIED AT SIGHTING THE BATMAN, THEY SCRAMBLE OUT OF THE CAR, ONLY---

BLINDFOLDING LINDA SO AS NOT TO REVEAL HIS TRUE IDENTITY, THE BATMAN BECOMES THE KILLER-
HERE'S YOUR MAKEUP!
LINDA IS GOING TO BE KIDNAPPED ALL OVER AGAIN! LISTEN CAREFULLY!

HERE SHE IS, BOSS- AL IS OUTSIDE WITH THE CAR. WHAT NEXT?
PERHAPS TWIST HER ARMS TILL SHE DECIDES TO TALK!

COMMISSIONER, BETTER GET OVER TO GRANDA, THE MYSTIC'S PLACE! HE'S GOT LINDA PAGE KIDNAPPED!
KIDNAPPED? KELLY, GET THE SQUAD CAR READY--!

AND BACK AT GRANDA'S SANCTUM---
SURE, BOSS!
ROBIN HAS PHONED THE POLICE. THEY SHOULD BE HERE IN A LITTLE WHILE!
I WON'T TELL-- I WON'T TELL!...
TWIST HER ARM, JOE!

LOOK OUT FOR THAT CAR!

THE TWO CARS MEET IN A TERRIBLE, HEAD-ON CRASH--
CRASH!!!

I'M ALL RIGHT! HOW IS EVERYONE ELSE?
JUST A BIT SHAKEN UP, SIR-WE'LL HAVE TO GET ANOTHER CAR!

WHAT'S THE MATTER, JOE? LOSING YOUR GRIP?
SOMETHING'S WRONG-THE POLICE SHOULD HAVE BEEN HERE LONG AGO.
9

A SUDDEN CLICK, AND THE LIGHTS WINK OUT-
WHO PUT THE LIGHTS OUT, JOE?

THE LIGHTS FLASH ON AND STANDING, TOWERING IN THE LIGHT---
THE BATMAN! YOU WERE JOE!
YOU'RE GETTING SMARTER BY THE MINUTE!

EVEN AS THE BATMAN CATAPULTS FORWARD, GRANDA'S FOOT FURTIVELY PRESSES A FLOOR BUTTON, AND--

--THE HINDU GIANTS LUMBER INTO THE ROOM...
HOLY SMOKE! THE BIG BOYS AGAIN--

NIMBLE AS A CAT, THE BATMAN SLIPS BENEATH THE SLASHING BLADE!

THE BATMAN CANNOT AVOID THE SECOND GIANT, WHO TOWERS OVER HIM!

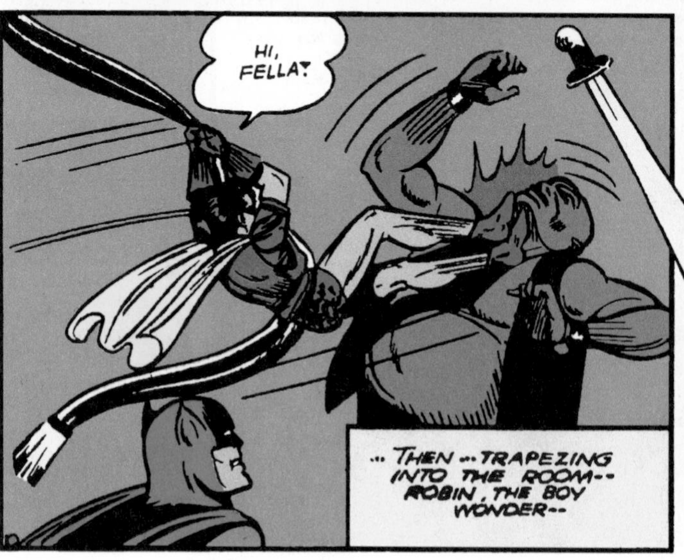
HI, FELLA!
... THEN ... TRAPEZING INTO THE ROOM-- ROBIN, THE BOY WONDER--

JUST IN TIME, ROBIN!
OHH- HERE COMES THE OTHER SHRIMP!

ROBIN TILTS THE CRYSTAL SO THAT IT CATCHES THE LIGHT, AND FLASHES RAYS OF BLINDING RADIANCE AT THE GIANT'S EYES!
NOW'S YOUR CHANCE, BATMAN!

WHAT TEAMWORK!

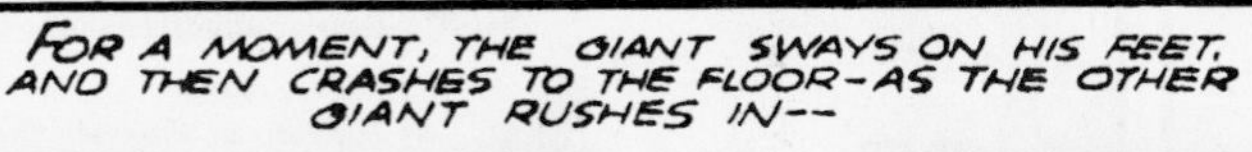
FOR A MOMENT, THE GIANT SWAYS ON HIS FEET, AND THEN CRASHES TO THE FLOOR--AS THE OTHER GIANT RUSHES IN--

THE BIGGER THEY ARE, THE HARDER THEY FALL!

STAND WHERE YOU ARE, BATMAN! A BULLET WILL END YOUR LIFE!

GUNFIRE BLASTS THROUGH THE ROOM! A MAN TOPPLES-- BUT NOT THE BATMAN--

MISS PAGE, ROBIN! BATMAN-- I FIGURED YOU'D FIX GRANDA SOME WAY. WELL, GRANDA-- WE'VE GOT YOU THIS TIME!

LIKE A CORNERED RAT GRANDA MAKES A DESPERATE TRY FOR ESCAPE
NOT YET. YOU HAVEN'T!

A CLASH OF GEARS ---AND GRANDA SPEEDS AWAY AS TWO FIGURES FOLLOW HIS PATH OF FLIGHT!
HE'S GETTING AWAY!
NOT IF I CAN HELP IT! C'MON!

WITH THE BATMAN AT THE WHEEL, THE POLICE CAR WHIPS AWAY AFTER GRANDA!
HOLD ON TO YOUR SEAT BOY!
POLICE

HAIRBREADTH TURNS, SCREAMING TIRES, ALL ARE PART OF THE MAD CHASE THAT FINALLY LEADS TO THE END OF TOWN

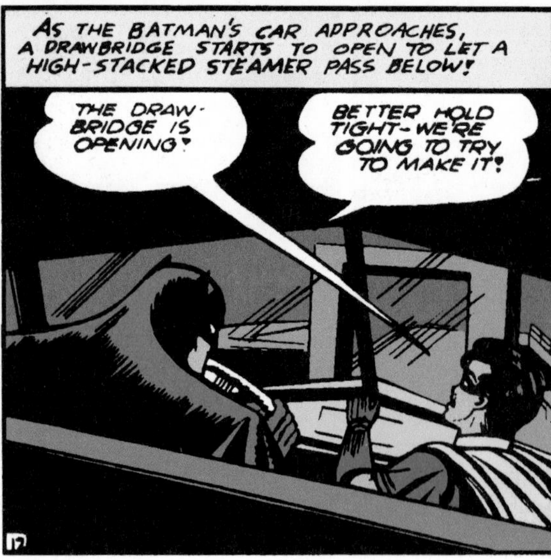
AS THE BATMAN'S CAR APPROACHES, A DRAWBRIDGE STARTS TO OPEN TO LET A HIGH-STACKED STEAMER PASS BELOW!
THE DRAW-BRIDGE IS OPENING!
BETTER HOLD TIGHT- WE'RE GOING TO TRY TO MAKE IT!
17

HERE WE GO-
BUT CAN THEY MAKE IT? OR WILL THE CAR PLUNGE DEEP INTO THE SWIRLING WATERS BELOW?

UP--UP OVER THE YAWNING CHASM HURTLES THE RACING CAR---

MADE IT!

AS THEY DRAW ALONGSIDE GRANDA'S FLASHING AUTOMOBILE, THE BATMAN LEAPS---

THROUGH THE OPEN WINDOW STREAKS THE BATMAN'S BALLED FIST!
BOB KANE

LATER....
HERE'S GRANDA! I SEE YOU FOUND THE BOYS WHERE I LEFT THEM!
YES-- AND THEY'VE BEEN TALKING! THIS ENDS GRANDA'S BLACKMAILING.

HYPNOTIZING PEOPLE AND THEN GETTING RECORDINGS OF THEIR INNERMOST SECRETS. THIS IS THE ROOM WHERE HE HID HIS RECORDS!
NICE WORK, GORDON!

GRANDA'S MEN CONFESSED TO THE MURDER OF HENRY ABBOT! ABBOT WAS GOING TO TELL THE POLICE ABOUT THE BLACKMAIL!
GRANDA KILLED HIM TO PROTECT HIMSELF- GRANDA, YOU'RE GETTING THE CHAIR FOR THIS!
13

THE POLICE DEPARTMENT, THE PEOPLE OF THE CITY THANK YOU AND ROBIN FOR THE SWELL JOB YOU DID!
SEE WHAT I MEAN BY DOING YOUR HOMEWORK AND GAINING THE RESPECT OF YOUR FELLOWMAN?
OKAY- OKAY YOU WIN!
THE END

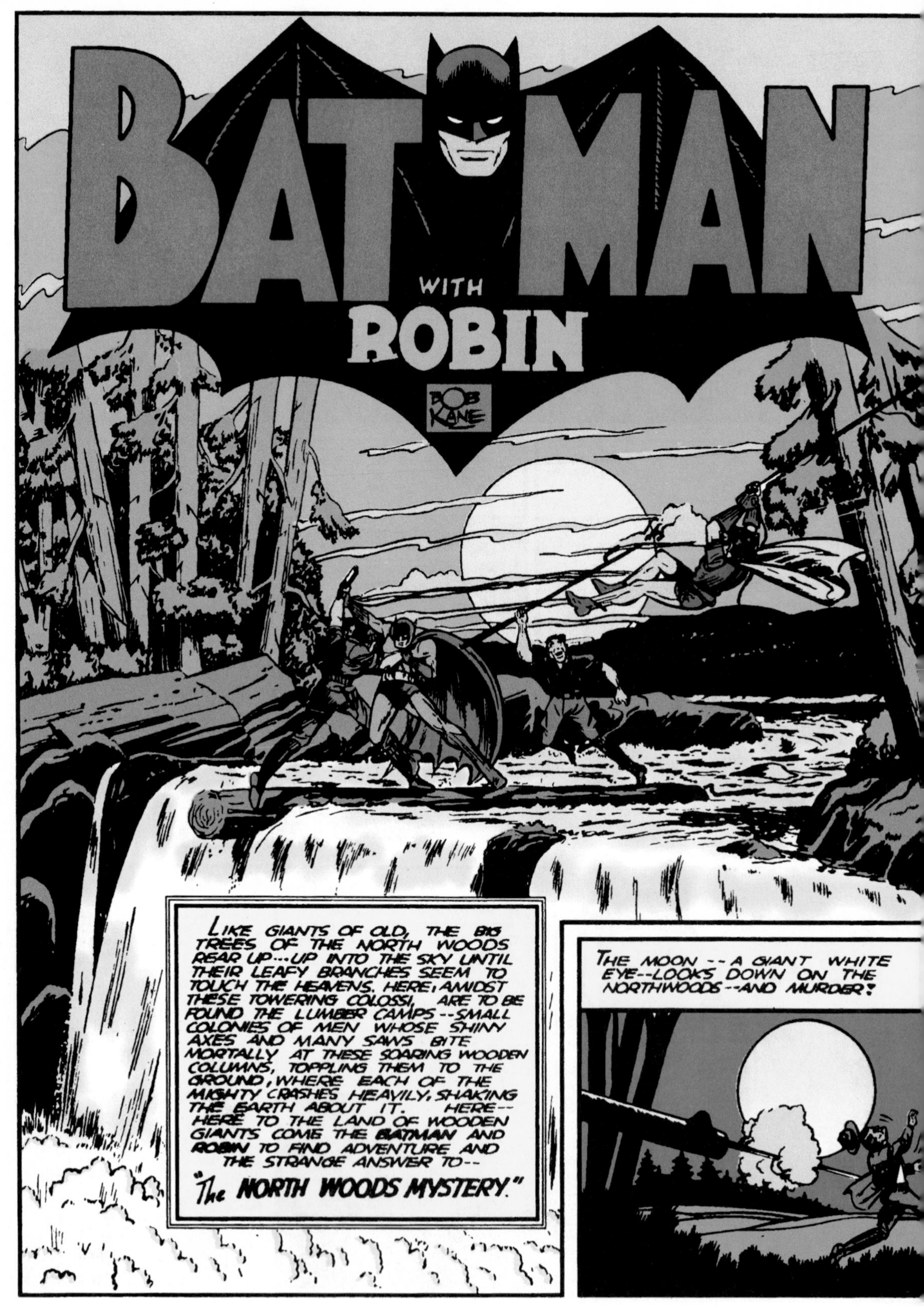
BATMAN
WITH
ROBIN
BOB KANE
LIKE GIANTS OF OLD, THE BIG TREES OF THE NORTH WOODS REAR UP...UP INTO THE SKY UNTIL THEIR LEAFY BRANCHES SEEM TO TOUCH THE HEAVENS. HERE, AMIDST THESE TOWERING COLOSSI, ARE TO BE FOUND THE LUMBER CAMPS--SMALL COLONIES OF MEN WHOSE SHINY AXES AND MANY SAWS BITE MORTALLY AT THESE SOARING WOODEN COLUMNS, TOPPLING THEM TO THE GROUND, WHERE EACH OF THE MIGHTY CRASHES HEAVILY, SHAKING THE EARTH ABOUT IT. HERE-- HERE TO THE LAND OF WOODEN GIANTS COME THE BATMAN AND ROBIN TO FIND ADVENTURE AND THE STRANGE ANSWER TO--
"The NORTH WOODS MYSTERY."
THE MOON --A GIANT WHITE EYE--LOOKS DOWN ON THE NORTHWOODS--AND MURDER!

BRUCE WAYNE CHATS WITH NORA POWELL, SOCIETY FAVORITE--
BRUCE, I STILL SAY THAT MONEY ISN'T EVERY-THING! IT'S--
MISS POWELL-- LOOK AT THIS LATEST PAPER!

"MATTHEW, LUMBER KING, MURDERED!" MY UNCLE-- KILLED!
C'MON, LET'S GET OUT OF HERE!

"LUMBER MAGNATE'S ADOPTED SON, JACK, SUSPECTED OF MURDER, BUT RELEASED FOR LACK OF EVIDENCE. MOTIVE REVEALED IN MURDERED MAGNATE'S WILL THAT LEAVES VAST NUMBER HOLDINGS TO BOTH ADOPTED SON AND NIECE, NORA POWELL!"

WHO IS THIS ADOPTED SON?
JACK CLAYTON, A LUMBERJACK! HE RISKED HIS LIFE TO SAVE UNCLE MAT FROM DEATH IN A LOG JAM!--UNCLE ADOPTED HIM!--I'VE NEVER MET JACK!

HMM! WELL, NORA-- WHAT NOW?
I THINK I'LL CALL JACK UP AND OFFER HIM MY HELP!

A FEW MINUTES LATER ...
HELLO, JACK! THIS IS NORA POWELL. I JUST CALLED TO OFFER MY REGRETS ABOUT UNCLE MAT. IF YOU NEED MY HELP ABOUT ANYTHING, I'LL BE GLAD TO--
THANKS- BUT I DON'T NEED IT! I'LL SEND YOU A CHECK EVERY MONTH FOR YOUR SHARE OF THE LUMBER PROFITS-
2

--SO THAT YOU CAN BUY YOURSELF SOME MORE FUR COATS AND FANCY GOWNS TO WEAR AROUND NIGHT CLUBS- CLICK!

WHO DOES HE THINK HE IS?? I'M GOING TO SHOW HIM I CAN DO THINGS AS WELL AS HE CAN!

BRUCE, HOW WOULD YOU LIKE TO SPEND A VACATION IN THE NORTH WOODS?
POWELL'S MURDER, AND THIS JACK CLAYTON CERTAINLY BEAR INVESTIGATION
SURE- WHY NOT!

THAT NIGHT..
BETTER START PACKING- WE'RE OFF TO THE NORTH WOODS!
HUH?

AND SO, THE NEXT DAY BEARS BRUCE AND NORA ON THEIR JOURNEY TO THE NORTH--
ICE CREAM, CANDY--
HERE, BOY-

AS BRUCE PAYS THE BOY, HE SURREPTITIOUSLY SNEAKS A NOTE INTO HIS HAND--

THE NOTE..
Nice work, Robin - try to get job at the Powell lumber camp when the train stops!

THE NEXT DAY--- THE NORTH WOODS--
JUST LOOK AT THE SIZE OF THOSE TREES!
I'LL SAY! THERE'S THE CAMP!

SUDDENLY- A FALLING TREE LOOMS DIRECTLY OVER THEM-
LOOK OUT!
3

LEAPING FORWARD, BRUCE SLAMS INTO NORA. THE FALLING TREE MISSES THEM BY INCHES-

OH-OH THAT WAS CLOSE!
A LOGGER PROBABLY LEFT FOR A MOMENT, LEAVING THE TREE HALF CUT, NOT REALIZING IT WOULD FALL!

THAT WAS NO ACCIDENT-- SOMEONE WANTED TO KILL HER!

A TALL, YOUNG MAN WITH BLACK HAIR, FLASHING EYES AND LOOKING LIKE A VIOLENT STORM, APPROACHES THEM-
I'M NORA POWELL AND THIS IS MY FRIEND, BRUCE WAYNE- I'M LOOKING FOR--
JACK CLAYTON- SORRY- I DIDN'T WEAR A TUXEDO TO MEET YOU- THIS MAN WILL SHOW YOU TO YOUR SHACK.

WELL-- OF ALL THE NERVE!
EASY NOW--- EASY-
THIS WAY, MISS POWELL!

ABOUT FIVE MINUTES LATER, A YOUNG BOY ENTERS THE CAMP-
I'M KINDA HUNGRY! COULD I SORTA DO ODD JOBS AROUND HERE?
HUNGRY, EH? SURE-- HEY, FRED! GET SOME GRUB FOR THIS KID!

NORA LOOKS ON LUMBER CAMP WORK WITH GREAT INTEREST WHILE BRUCE WAYNE LOOKS ON IN TYPICAL BRUCE WAYNE FASHION-
ISN'T IT JUST THRILLING, BRUCE?
LOOKS AS IF THOSE FELLOWS ACTUALLY ENJOY THEIR WORK!

NORA DOES NOT NOTICE THE LOOK BETWEEN BRUCE AND THE YOUNG BOY-
JUST LOOK AT THE MAGNIFICENCE OF IT ALL! LITTLE MEN CUTTING DOWN THESE WOODEN GIANTS!...
NOTHING BUT TERMITES, THAT'S ALL THEY ARE...

THAT NIGHT---
WISH I KNEW EXACTLY WHY CLAYTON COULD ACT SO HUMAN TO THE BOY AND SO INHUMAN TO US! HE HATES THE GIRL---BUT WHY?

SILENTLY AND SWIFTLY, HE PADS SOFTLY ACROSS THE CAMP GROUNDS TO BE MET BY ANOTHER COSTUMED ROVER--ROBIN, THE BOY WONDER---
C'MON, ROBIN- I WANT TO LOOK AROUND!
NO--WAIT! I SAW TWO FIGURES MOVE INTO THE TOOL SHED-

INSIDE THE TOOL SHED-
A LITTLE ACID ON THESE SAWS AND AXES, AND THEY'LL CRACK UP WHEN THEY TRY TO USE THEM ON TIMBER!
THAT'LL SLOW UP THE LUMBER OUTPUT- AND THAT POWELL DAME WILL BE GLAD TO SELL HER SHARE TO CLAYTON-

NOT QUITE, FELLA, NOT QUITE!
I'LL BATHE YA IN ACID!

SORRY, I PREFER WATER!

OKAY, WISE GUY-- YOU ASKED FOR IT!

BUT IT DOESN'T LOOK LIKE I'M GOING TO GET IT, EH, PAL?

BATMAN, I NEED HELP!
5

AND YOU'RE GETTING IT!

TAKING ADVANTAGE OF THE MELEE, THE OTHER MAKES GOOD HIS ESCAPE!
HE'S GETTING AWAY!
NEVER MIND! WE'VE STILL GOT HIS PAL TO ANSWER A FEW QUESTIONS!

EAGER TO DODGE FURTHER PUNISHMENT, THE REMAINING WRECKER CRINGES BACK BEFORE THE BATMAN, AND IN HIS PANIC, STUMBLES AGAINST A BEAM! A HEAVY HOOK IS LOOSED FROM ITS RACK AND...
FEEL LIKE TALKING, OR...
NO--- NO--- I'LL TALK..

---AND PLUNGING DOWNWARD, SILENCES HIM FOREVER---
GNNGH!
LOOK OUT!

DRAWN TO THE SCENE BY THE DIN OF BATTLE---
LOOK! THE WHOLE CAMP'S COMING THIS WAY!
BETTER SCRAM THROUGH THE BACK WINDOW!

THE TWO-MAN REGIMENT BEAT HASTY RETREAT---

WHY, IT'S WOODY JOE!
THAT HOOK-- MUST HAVE KILLED HIM INSTANTLY!
HOW TERRIBLE-- WHAT WAS HE DOING HERE IN THE MIDDLE OF NIGHT?

HMM! WHAT IS A BOTTLE OF ACID DOING HERE? AS A FRIEND OF POLICE COMMISSIONER GORDON, I'VE LEARNED DETECTIVE PROCEDURE, AND---
YOU--- DETECTIVE WORK! BAH! THIS MAN'S DEATH WAS ACCIDENTAL AND DON'T TRY TO MAKE A POLICE CASE OUT OF IT!

I BELIEVE YOU'RE RIGHT ABOUT IT BEING A MATTER FOR THE POLICE. ALL THESE "ACCIDENTS"... BRUCE--- I'M WORRIED--
NOW--- DON'T START GETTING JITTERY! I'LL BE AROUND TO SEE THAT NOTHING HAPPENS TO YOU!

THE NEXT MORNING...
MISS POWELL-- I'D LIKE YOU TO MEET MR. ASHER--HE OWNS THE ASHER LUMBER COMPANY NEAR BY---
MISS POWELL, I'D LIKE TO BUY YOUR SHARE..... CLAYTON IS WILLING TO SELL HIS-- ISN'T THAT SO, CLAYTON?

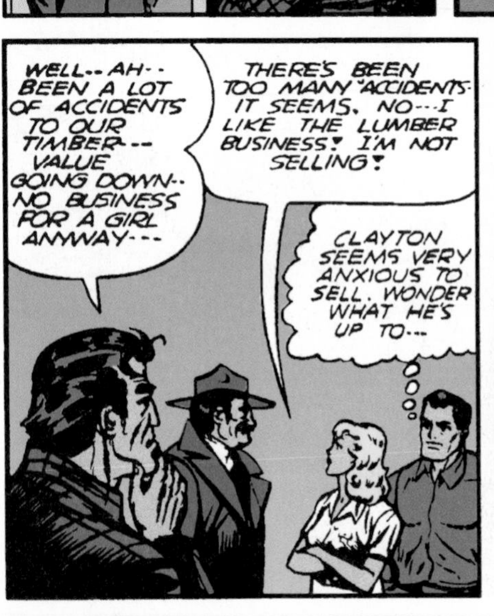
WELL--AH-- BEEN A LOT OF ACCIDENTS TO OUR TIMBER-- VALUE GOING DOWN-- NO BUSINESS FOR A GIRL ANYWAY---
THERE'S BEEN TOO MANY "ACCIDENTS" IT SEEMS. NO---I LIKE THE LUMBER BUSINESS! I'M NOT SELLING!
CLAYTON SEEMS VERY ANXIOUS TO SELL. WONDER WHAT HE'S UP TO---

IN CLAYTON'S CABIN—
YOU'VE GOT TO MAKE HER SELL OUT TO YOU! AND THEN I'LL BUY YOUR COMPLETE HOLDINGS— OR ELSE!
YOU DON'T LEAVE ME MUCH CHOICE! I'LL HAVE TO DO IT!

BUT AS THEY TALK— A SMALL FIGURE LISTENS BY THE WINDOW—

LATER THAT DAY----
I REFUSE TO SELL TO ASHER OR YOU! AND BY THE WAY, WHAT MADE YOU SUDDENLY DECIDE TO BUY MY SHARE? YOU SAID THE VALUE WAS GOING DOWN!
ER---I--I'VE GOT MY REASONS--- EITHER TAKE MY OFFER OR LEAVE IT--- BUT YOU'D BETTER TAKE IT!
NOT THREATENING, ARE YOU, CLAYTON?
7

NOT ME, HE ISN'T! NOW I CAME DOWN HERE TO RIDE ON THE LOGGER TRAIN! WANT TO COME ALONG, BRUCE?
NO-O-O-- THINK I'LL TAKE A LONG NAP!
ANNAND, TAKE MISS POWELL ON THE TRAIN!

NORA RIDES ATOP THE LOGGER TRAIN--
MY-- THIS IS EXCITING!
WAIT TILL THE REAL EXCITEMENT BEGINS, LADY!

--AND IT'S BEGINNIN' RIGHT NOW!

UNSHACKLED BY THE MURDEROUS LOGGER, THE LOG-CAR, NORA LYING UNCONSCIOUS ATOP ITS FREIGHT--- HURTLES BACKWARD DOWN THE TRACK!
IT'LL LOOK LIKE AN ACCIDENT!

AND SWAYING AND ROCKING PERIOUSLY, PLUNGES DOOM-WARD!

--BUT FLASHING FROM A NEARBY THICKET--

--THE BATMAN SWINGS ABOARD THIS AVALANCHE ON WHEELS--
GOT TO WORK FAST-THE CAR'S GOING TO GO OFF ANY MOMENT NOW!
8

LIFTING THE LIMP GIRL UNDER ONE ARM--HE LEAPS DESPERATELY--

--AND GRABS AN OVERHANGING BRANCH WITH THE OTHER----
WOW! NOW THAT'S WHAT I REALLY CALL A "LEAP FOR LIFE!"

LATER ---WHEN NORA COMES BACK TO LIFE--
WHERE AM I--? --AN AWFUL MAN HIT ME ON THE LOG TRAIN-- AND I SWEAR I REMEMBER A MASKED FIGURE--

AT THAT MOMENT---
--AND I HEARD ASHER TELL CLAYTON TO SELL...
MMM SO I WAS RIGHT! AND YET--

SOME TIME LATER--
YOU'RE TRYING TO KILL ME--JUST AS YOU KILLED YOUR FATHER-- YOU CAN'T DENY THAT A HIRED THUG OF YOURS TRIED TO MURDER ME!!
I DID NOT KILL MY FATHER! AND AS FOR THAT LOGGER-- IT'S PURE IMAGINATION ON YOUR PART!

AFTER NORA LEAVES--
I'M DEEP ENOUGH AS IT IS ALREADY-- BUT TO MURDER A GIRL --- AND MY FATHER'S DEATH---- I WONDER NOW IF--

THAT MORNING---
MR WAYNE, MISS POWELL SAYS IF YOU'VE A MIND TO MEET HER OVER DOWN BY THE LOG CHUTE-
THE LOG CHUTE? ALONE? SHE MAY BE IN DANGER

AND BRUCE'S FEARS ARE NO IDLE ONES-- AT THAT VERY MOMENT--

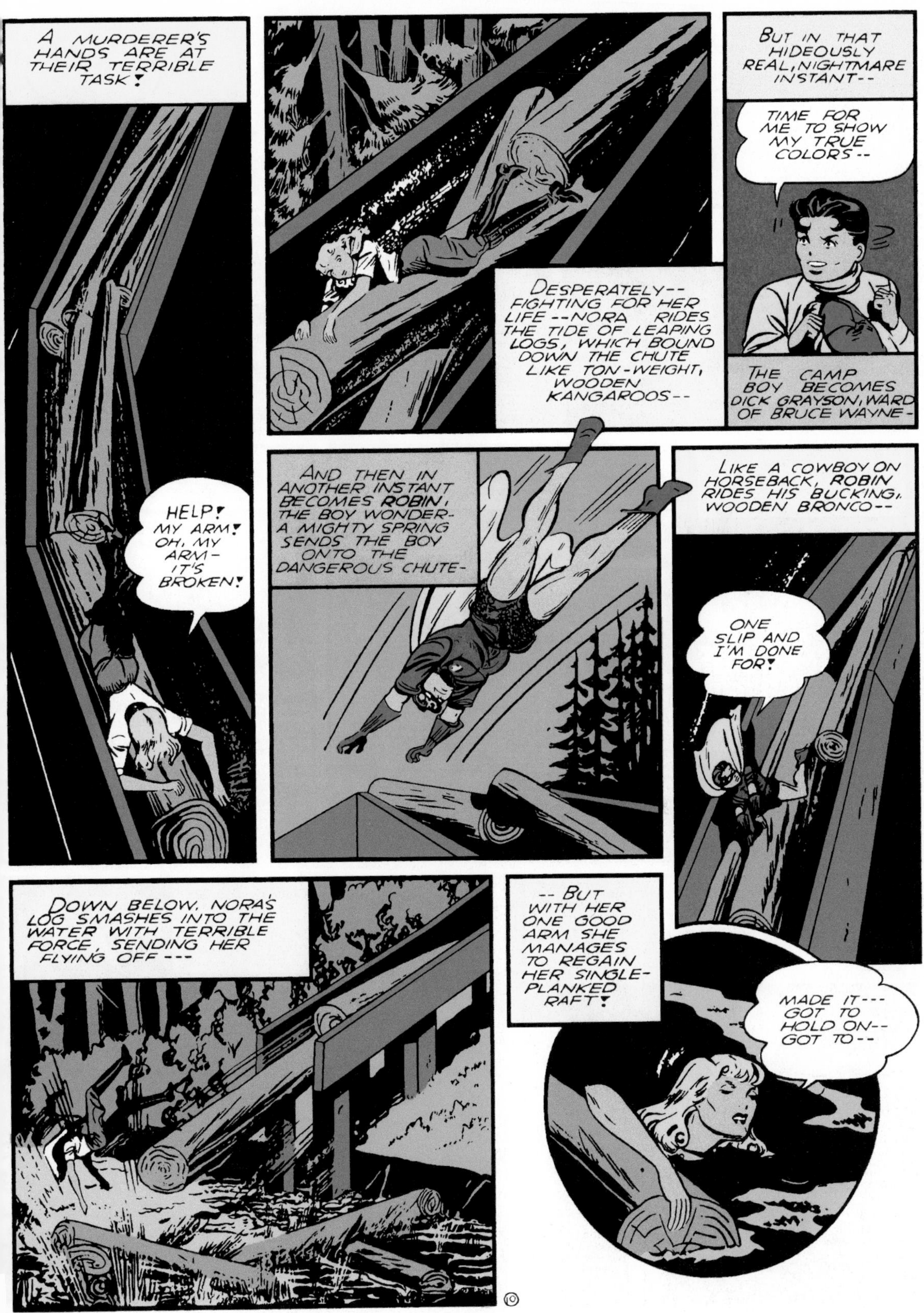
A MURDERER'S HANDS ARE AT THEIR TERRIBLE TASK!
HELP! MY ARM! OH, MY ARM - IT'S BROKEN!
DESPERATELY-- FIGHTING FOR HER LIFE --NORA RIDES THE TIDE OF LEAPING LOGS, WHICH BOUND DOWN THE CHUTE LIKE TON-WEIGHT, WOODEN KANGAROOS--
BUT IN THAT HIDEOUSLY REAL, NIGHTMARE INSTANT--
TIME FOR ME TO SHOW MY TRUE COLORS--
THE CAMP BOY BECOMES DICK GRAYSON, WARD OF BRUCE WAYNE-
AND THEN IN ANOTHER INSTANT BECOMES ROBIN, THE BOY WONDER- A MIGHTY SPRING SENDS THE BOY ONTO THE DANGEROUS CHUTE-
LIKE A COWBOY ON HORSEBACK, ROBIN RIDES HIS BUCKING, WOODEN BRONCO--
ONE SLIP AND I'M DONE FOR!
DOWN BELOW, NORA'S LOG SMASHES INTO THE WATER WITH TERRIBLE FORCE, SENDING HER FLYING OFF ---
-- BUT WITH HER ONE GOOD ARM SHE MANAGES TO REGAIN HER SINGLE-PLANKED RAFT!
MADE IT--- GOT TO HOLD ON-- GOT TO--
(10)

ROBIN SPIES HER AND QUICKLY BOUNDS ACROSS THE SWAYING, ROLLING LOGS AS THEY RIDE DOWN THE SWIFT-MOVING RIVER---
OUGHT TO BE UP TO HER IN ONE SEC!

BUT HE IS ALSO SPIED BY ENEMY LOGGERS, WHO DART AFTER HIM IN SWIFT PURSUIT!
OH-OH! TROUBLE AGAIN!
GET THAT KID!

HAVE A BATH ON ME!

AND DOES "ROLEE RIDING" WITH ANOTHER ON THE SLIPPERY, WAX-SMOOTH TIMBER-
THIS TIME YOU GO IN THE DRINK AND--
MAYBE!

A CLEVER BIT OF FOOTWORK DISPOSES OF HIS SECOND OPPONENT!
SEE WHAT I MEAN?

MEANWHILE, THE PAIN OF HER BROKEN ARM PROVES TOO MUCH FOR NORA! SHE FAINTS DEAD AWAY AS THE LOG IS DRAWN UP INTO THE CONVEYER THAT LEADS TO THE SAWMILL!

BUT ROBIN'S LOG IS CLEVERLY MANEUVERED BY THE THIRD LOGGER, SO THAT IT CLEARS THE LOG JAM -- AND RIDES ON DOWN THE RACING WATERS..
?
HAW! HAW! SO LONG, KID!

..ON...ON...THE LOG RIDES...UNTIL IT TEETERS ON THE VERY EDGE OF THE HIGH FALLS, HEADING FOR THE PLUNGE INTO THE WATERS, CHURNING AND LASHING SO FAR BELOW!
A WATERFALL! -AND I'M GOING OVER!

BUT IN THAT SPLIT-SECOND INSTANT, A CLOAKED FIGURE SWEEPS OUT OVER THE FALLS, DANGLING BY A PRECIOUS STRAND OF SILKEN ROPE, ONE STRONG HAND SNATCHES ROBIN FROM THE VERY BRINK OF DEATH!

BUT ON SHORE LURK TWO SINISTER FIGURES. ONE HACKS AWAY AT THE BATMAN'S SILKEN ROPE!

THIS IS OUR CHANCE TO GET RID OF BOTH MEDDLERS-

BUT THE BATMAN AND ROBIN BOOMERANG BACK JUST IN TIME!
DROP THAT KNIFE!

MEANWHILE, THE CONVEYER CARRIES THE UNCONSCIOUS NORA INTO THE SAWMILL ITSELF--TOWARD A HUGE BUZZSAW, WHOSE JAGGED EDGES HUM A SONG OF DEATH!!

CLOSER..
CLOSER..

BUT STRONG HANDS REACH OUT---AND SNATCH HER FROM DANGER---
IN THE NICK OF TIME!

---AND HE'S RIGHT HERE! YOU INTERFERED ONCE TOO OFTEN!
ASHER!

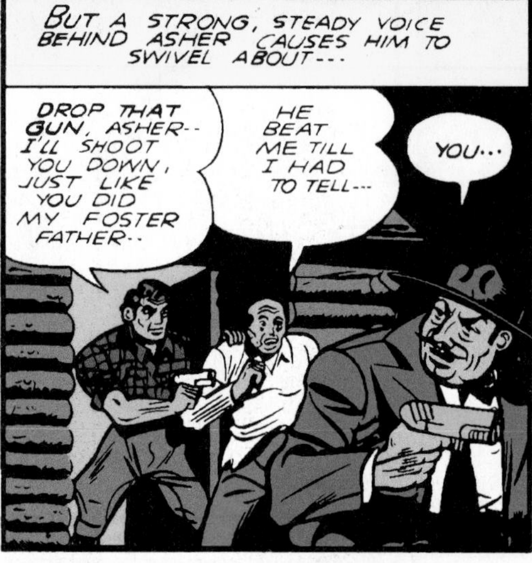
BUT A STRONG, STEADY VOICE BEHIND ASHER CAUSES HIM TO SWIVEL ABOUT---
DROP THAT GUN, ASHER-- I'LL SHOOT YOU DOWN, JUST LIKE YOU DID MY FOSTER FATHER--
HE BEAT ME TILL I HAD TO TELL---
YOU...

RELAX, ASHER-
AND THEN WITHOUT A WORD, THE BATMAN AND ROBIN DISAPPEAR INTO THE WOODS---

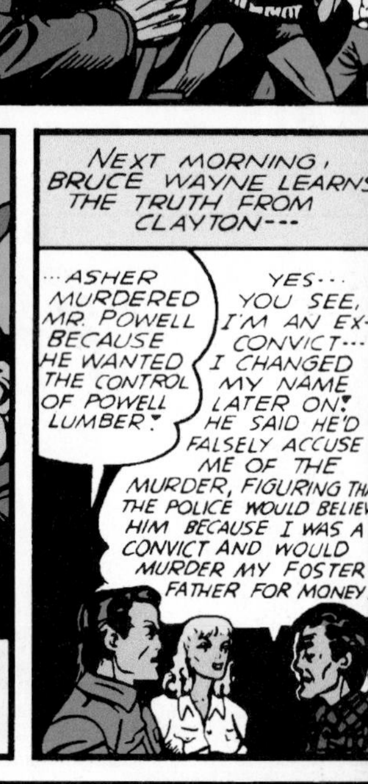
NEXT MORNING, BRUCE WAYNE LEARNS THE TRUTH FROM CLAYTON---
...ASHER MURDERED MR. POWELL BECAUSE HE WANTED THE CONTROL OF POWELL LUMBER!
YES--- YOU SEE, I'M AN EX-CONVICT--- I CHANGED MY NAME LATER ON! HE SAID HE'D FALSELY ACCUSE ME OF THE MURDER, FIGURING THA THE POLICE WOULD BELIEV HIM BECAUSE I WAS A CONVICT AND WOULD MURDER MY FOSTER FATHER FOR MONEY.

THEN HE THOUGHT THESE "ACCIDENTS" TO THE LUMBER WOULD CAUSE MISS POWELL TO SELL OUT HER INTEREST AT A LOW PRICE EITHER TO YOU OR HIM DIRECTLY SO THAT HE WOULD OWN ALL THE POWELL LUMBER COMPANY-
THAT'S RIGHT--HE KNEW I, MYSELF, WOULD SELL HIM OUT-- OR ELSE. HE EVEN BOUGHT OUT SOME OF MY MEN AND HAD THEM TRY TO "ACCIDENTALLY" KILL MISS POWELL WHEN SHE REFUSED TO SELL--
13

YOU HAD SO MUCH MONEY ALREADY, MISS POWELL, THAT I THOUGHT IT WOULDN'T HURT YOU TO SACRIFICE A LITTLE TO SAVE ME FROM BEING FRAMED ON A MURDER CHARGE! BESIDES, I WAS WRONG TO THINK YOU WERE JUST AN EMPTY-HEADED GIRL WHO SAT AROUND IN NIGHTCLUBS--
NOT VERY-- BUT I'M WILLING TO FORGET ABOUT YOUR ONCE BEING A CONVICT, IF YOU'LL FORGET MY FOOLISH PAST, TOO.

BOB KANE
MISS POWELL-- NORA---I LOVED YOU THE MOMENT I SAW YOU--
PLEASE KISS ME AND YOU CAN TELL ME ALL ABOUT IT LATER!
I'D BETTER FIND DICK AND HEAD HOME! IT LOOKS LIKE NORA ISN'T GOING BACK FOR A LONG WHILE- LOVE---AH, LOVE!

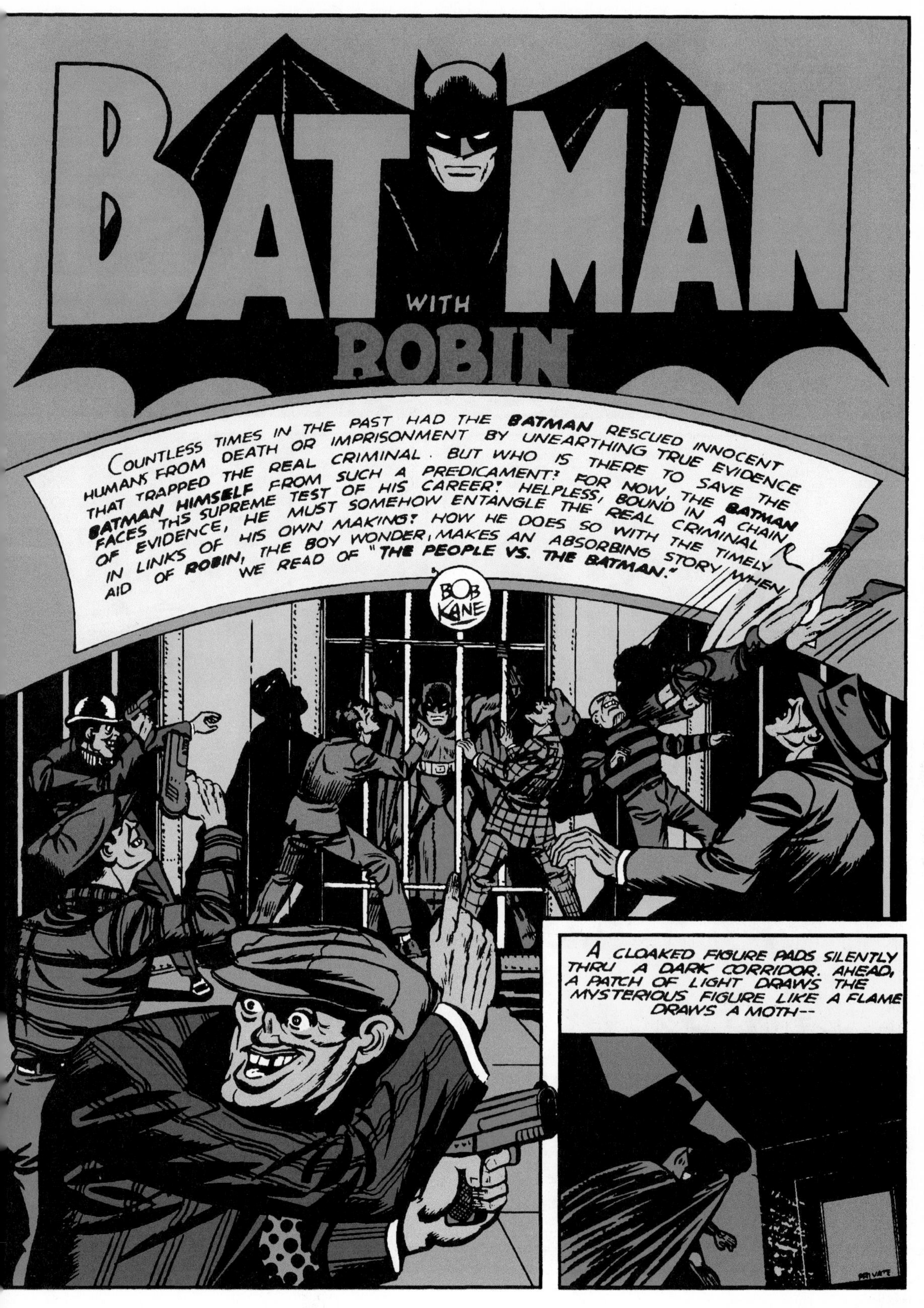
BATMAN
WITH
ROBIN
COUNTLESS TIMES IN THE PAST HAD THE BATMAN RESCUED INNOCENT HUMANS FROM DEATH OR IMPRISONMENT BY UNEARTHING TRUE EVIDENCE THAT TRAPPED THE REAL CRIMINAL. BUT WHO IS THERE TO SAVE THE BATMAN HIMSELF FROM SUCH A PREDICAMENT? FOR NOW, THE BATMAN FACES THS SUPREME TEST OF HIS CAREER! HELPLESS, BOUND IN A CHAIN OF EVIDENCE, HE MUST SOMEHOW ENTANGLE THE REAL CRIMINAL IN LINKS OF HIS OWN MAKING! HOW HE DOES SO WITH THE TIMELY AID OF ROBIN, THE BOY WONDER, MAKES AN ABSORBING STORY WHEN WE READ OF "THE PEOPLE VS. THE BATMAN."
BOB KANE
A CLOAKED FIGURE PADS SILENTLY THRU A DARK CORRIDOR. AHEAD, A PATCH OF LIGHT DRAWS THE MYSTERIOUS FIGURE LIKE A FLAME DRAWS A MOTH--
PRIVATE

LISTEN, HORATIO, ABOUT THAT POULTRY RACKET JOB--

YOU GOTTA GET--- HOLD IT, SOMEONE'S OUTSIDE!

OH, HELLO! I WAS JUST WAITING FOR A STREET CAR!
AWK! IT'S THE BATMAN!

WITH STARTLING SUDDENNESS, THE MANTLED INTRUDER SWEEPS FORWARD!
I ALWAYS BELIEVE IN THE ELEMENT OF SURPRISE TO STEAL A MARCH ON YOUR OPPONENT!

SEE WHAT I MEAN?

NOW---I THINK WE OUGHT TO HAVE A LITTLE TALK!

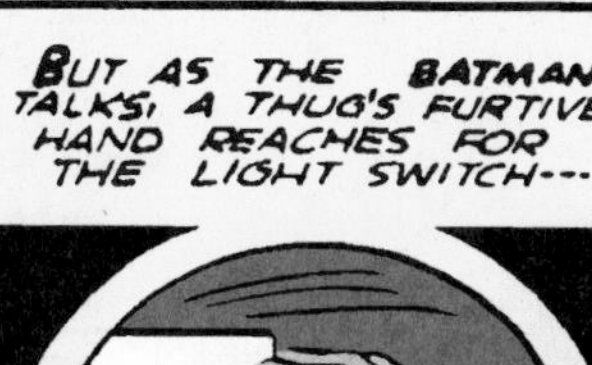
BUT AS THE BATMAN TALKS, A THUG'S FURTIVE HAND REACHES FOR THE LIGHT SWITCH---

AND THE LIGHTS WINK OUT!
OKAY, NOW'S OUR CHANCE! SLUG HIM!
LET'S SCRAM!
BANG
BANG!

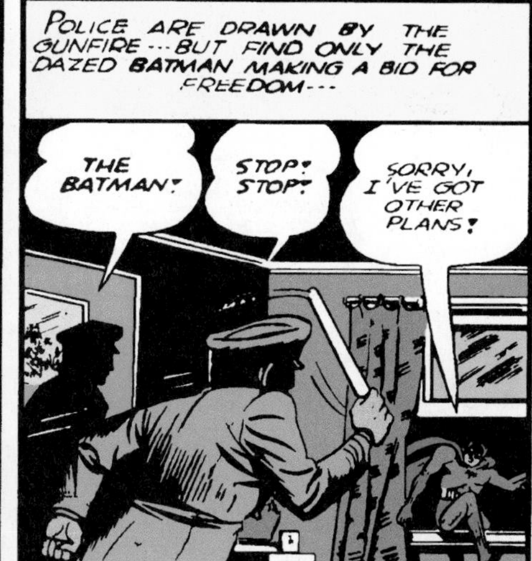
POLICE ARE DRAWN BY THE GUNFIRE---BUT FIND ONLY THE DAZED BATMAN MAKING A BID FOR FREEDOM---
THE BATMAN!
STOP! STOP!
SORRY, I'VE GOT OTHER PLANS!

THE ACROBATIC BATMAN DROPS TO SAFETY!
THERE HE GOES!
I WISH I KNEW WHAT HE WAS DOING HERE!
BECAUSE OF THIS VISIT, THE ENTIRE PHASE OF THE BATMAN'S LIFE IS TO BE AFFECTED!

AND FROM A NEARBY HALLWAY--
THEY'RE GONE NOW!
YEAH!--- BUT IT LOOKS LIKE THE BATMAN IS WISE TO YOU!

LATER...THE HOME OF FREDDIE HILL---
I TELL YA, THE BATMAN'S WISE TO THE FACT THAT DELMAR IS REALLY HEAD OF THE RACKETS IN THIS WARD! SUPPOSE HE MAKES DELMAR TALK-THEN WHAT?
WE GOTTA GET RID OF DELMAR BEFORE THAT HAPPENS! I THINK IT'S TIME I RAN THIS MOB MYSELF-- WEASEL, HERE, IS GONNA BUMP OFF DELMAR-

BUT THE COPS WILL PICK ME UP SURE!
NOT THE WAY I FIGURE IT, CAUSE WE'RE GONNA GET SOMEONE TO TAKE THE RAP FOR YA! NOW LISTEN-YOU GO TO DELMAR'S OFFICE AND WAIT-WAIT FOR A CLIENT---ANY CLIENT TO SHOW UP--- AND THEN YOU--

AT THAT INSTANT---
WHAT'S UP?
I REALLY DISCOVERED SOMETHING BIG-- THINK I'LL INVESTIGATE TOMORROW AS BRUCE WAYNE-HE WOULDN'T AROUSE ANY SUSPICION!

THE NEXT MORNING---
WHAT ARE YOU SO NERVOUS ABOUT, WEASEL? IT--YES, MISS O'DONALD, WHAT IS IT?...
A MR WAYNE TO SEE YOU, SIR!
I BETTER GET OUT BY THE BACK DOOR--WON'T LOOK SO GOOD FOR SOMEBODY TA SEE ME-

MR. DELMAR, I WANT SOME HELP ON MY STOCKS THAT--

OOOH!

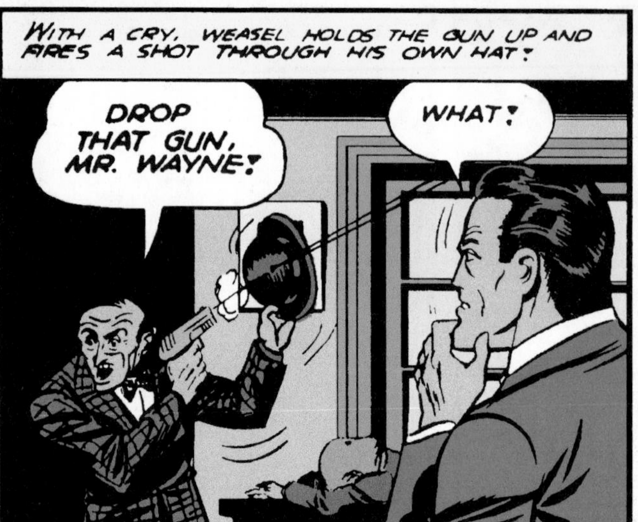
WITH A CRY, WEASEL HOLDS THE GUN UP AND FIRES A SHOT THROUGH HIS OWN HAT!
DROP THAT GUN, MR. WAYNE!
WHAT!

THEN THE MURDERER TOSSES THE SMOKING GUN TO BRUCE--
HERE, CATCH!

INSTINCTIVELY, BRUCE CATCHES THE WEAPON, AS ALL PERSONS WILL DO WHEN OBJECTS ARE TOSSED AT THEM!
MR. WAYNE... YOU KILLED HIM!!

YOU MURDERER!
EEK! HELP! POLICE! MURDER!

AND WHEN THE POLICE ARRIVE ON THE RUN---
WHAT'S HAPPENED?
THAT MAN MURDERED MR DELMAR!
HE KILLED HIM!

POLICE COMMISSIONER GORDON, A CLOSE FRIEND OF BRUCE WAYNE'S --- ARRIVES ----
THIS MURDER IS BAD BUSINESS! WHY DID YOU DO IT?
BUT I DIDN'T! THIS RAT, HERE, DID IT, AND THREW THE GUN AT ME! HE FRAMED ME!

HE'S LYING! LOOK--HE EVEN TOOK A SHOT AT ME! LOOK AT THIS HOLE THE BULLET MADE IN MY HAT!

IT'S TRUE! I HEARD MR. VENNER SHOUT, "DROP THAT GUN, MR. WAYNE!" AND WHEN I OPENED THE DOOR, MR. VENNER WAS HITTING BRUCE WAYNE, WHO HELD THE SMOKING GUN IN HIS HAND- HE MURDERED MR. DELMAR!

AILY PRESS
2¢
SOCIALITE BRUCE WAYNE CHARGED WITH MURDER!

BUT WHAT REASON HAVE I TO KILL HIM? YOU EVEN ADMIT YOURSELF THIS VENNER HAS AN ALIAS AND A PRISON RECORD!
I DON'T BELIEVE YOU DID KILL DELMAR- BUT WHAT CAN I DO? LOOK AT THE EVIDENCE. I HAD TO ARREST YOU!

HOWEVER, YOU'RE NOT LICKED YET. KEEP YOUR COURAGE. HERE'S DICK TO SEE YOU-
BRUCE! BRUCE! GOLLY!

FUNNY, ISN'T IT---THE MAN WHO IS REALLY THE BATMAN--- FRAMED FOR A MURDER RAP!
IT'S THIS LITTLE GUY! I'M GOING TO MAKE HIM TELL THE TRUTH! SOME WAY--SOMEHOW! DON'T WORRY. I'M GOING TO GET YOU OUT OF HERE!
5

THAT NIGHT!
WEASEL VENNER! HE'S GOING TO GET A VISIT FROM ROBIN, THE BOY WONDER!
ROBIN, THE BOY WONDER, TAKES ON A MAN-SIZED JOB TO FREE HIS PAL AND CRIME'S MIGHTIEST FOE FROM A MURDER CHARGE!

THE NEWSPAPERS SAID THIS WAS VENNER'S ADDRESS-

INSIDE VENNER'S APARTMENT--
WELL, HILL, EVERTHING WORKED OKAY! HEY--WHY THE ARTILLERY?
WE WANTA MAKE SURE, IN CASE YOUR CONSCIENCE STARTS TO BOTHER YOU-- SO--WE'RE GONNA FIX IT SO YOU DON'T WORRY ANY MORE!

C'MON, WEASEL, WE'RE TAKIN' YOU FOR A RIDE! THE AIR WILL DO YOU GOOD!
IF THEY KILL HIM, HOW AM I EVER GOING TO GET THE TESTIMONY TO FREE BRUCE?

THINKING ONLY OF BRUCE'S PERIL, ROBIN DISREGARDS PERSONAL DANGER AND DIVES HEADLONG---

IT'S ROBIN-- UGH!
HOW D'YA GUESS IT?

WAIT TILL I TALK TO-- OHH...
OUTA MY WAY! THIS MOB IS AFTER ME-THIS IS MY CHANCE TO BEAT IT-

WEASEL LEAPS DOWN THE STEPS AS HILL AND HIS MOBSTERS RECOVER-
I'M GONNA PLUG THIS BRAT!
FORGET HIM- IT'S WEASEL WE'RE GONNA GET! C'MON!

THERE HE GOES! I'LL--
PUT THAT ROD AWAY! I GOT A BETTER IDEA! GET IN THAT CAR!

AS THE TERRIFIED WEASEL VENNER RACES ACROSS THE GUTTER, HE TURNS A FEAR-STRICKEN FACE UPON A HEAVY CAR THAT BEARS DOWN ON HIM!

----THE CAR LEAPS AWAY IN THE NIGHT, LEAVING BEHIND A SPRAWLED, TWISTED FIGURE!
IT WAS A HIT-AND-RUN DRIVER! I SAW IT!
EEE-- THAT MAN'S BEEN KILLED!

BUT WEASEL IS NOT DEAD---AT LEAST NOT QUITE!
THERE'S NO TELLING HOW MANY DAYS HE'LL BE LIKE THIS! HE'S IN A COMA!
I'LL HAVE TO PUT A POLICE GUARD ABOUT THE ROOM! THIS MAN IS AN IMPORTANT WITNESS IN A MURDER TRIAL!

THE ACCIDENT MAKES INTERESTING HEADLINES--- ESPECIALLY FOR FREDDIE HILL!
"VICTIM STILL ALIVE IN A COMA! DOCTORS GIVE HIM A FIFTY-FIFTY CHANCE TO LIVE! IF WEASEL SHOULD COME TO AND START TO TALK---
WE'LL ALL BE IN THE SOUP! WE GOTTA BUMP THAT GUY OFF!
7

MAYBE THIS ROBIN KID WILL GO TO THE COPPERS AND TELL HOW WE WERE TRYING TO TAKE WEASEL FOR A RIDE!
NOT YET! REMEMBER THAT NIGHT THE COPS SAW THE BATMAN IN DELMAR'S OFFICE? I THINK I GOT AN IDEA HOW TO USE THAT!

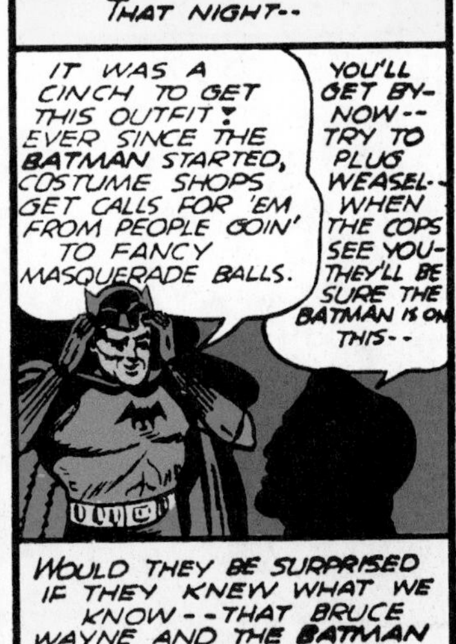
THAT NIGHT--
IT WAS A CINCH TO GET THIS OUTFIT! EVER SINCE THE BATMAN STARTED, COSTUME SHOPS GET CALLS FOR 'EM FROM PEOPLE GOIN' TO FANCY MASQUERADE BALLS.
YOU'LL GET BY-NOW-- TRY TO PLUG WEASEL-- WHEN THE COPS SEE YOU-THEY'LL BE SURE THE BATMAN IS ON THIS--
WOULD THEY BE SURPRISED IF THEY KNEW WHAT WE KNOW--THAT BRUCE WAYNE AND THE BATMAN ARE ONE AND THE SAME.

A BATSHAPED FIGURE MOVES UP THE FIRE ESCAPE OUT-SIDE A HOSPITAL--

HE SWINGS INTO A LIGHTED ROOM, A HAND CLUTCHING A REVOLVER WHEN A NURSE ACCIDENTALLY ENTERS-
EEE-- HELP! POLICE!
WHO--?

POLICE STATIONED OUTSIDE POUR INTO THE ROOM--
THERE HE GOES! IT'S THE BATMAN!
HE TRIED TO KILL VENNER!

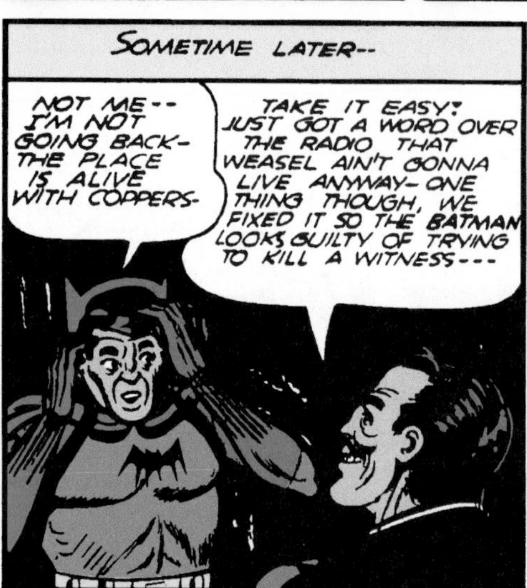
SOMETIME LATER--
NOT ME-- I'M NOT GOING BACK-THE PLACE IS ALIVE WITH COPPERS-
TAKE IT EASY! JUST GOT A WORD OVER THE RADIO THAT WEASEL AIN'T GONNA LIVE ANYWAY- ONE THING THOUGH, WE FIXED IT SO THE BATMAN LOOKS GUILTY OF TRYING TO KILL A WITNESS---

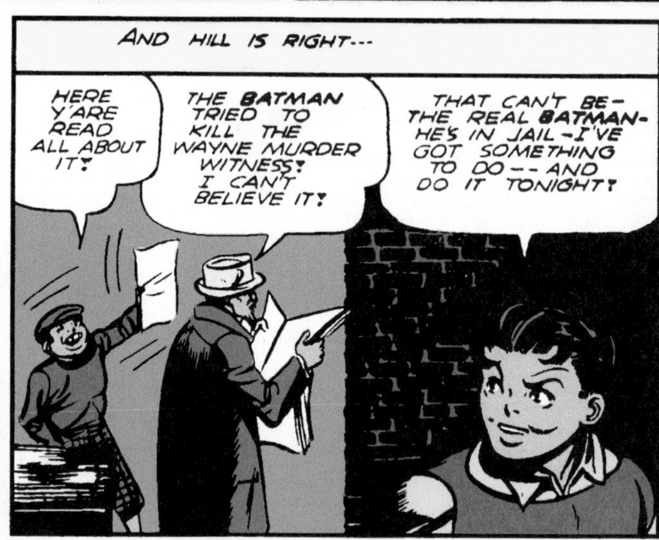
AND HILL IS RIGHT---
HERE Y'ARE READ ALL ABOUT IT!
THE BATMAN TRIED TO KILL THE WAYNE MURDER WITNESS! I CAN'T BELIEVE IT!
THAT CAN'T BE-THE REAL BATMAN-HE'S IN JAIL-I'VE GOT SOMETHING TO DO -- AND DO IT TONIGHT!

DICK SPENDS THE RE-MAINDER OF THE DAY IN THE LIBRARY LOOKING OVER OLD CITY MAPS OF THE CITY-
THAT SHOULD DO IT VERY NICELY---
MAP

BRUCE WAYNE PACES HIS CELL WITH THE RESTLESSNESS OF A CAGED ANIMAL, WHEN--
I'VE GOT TO PROVE I'M INNOCENT--- WHAT'S THAT NOISE THERE?

SUDDENLY A STONE IN THE FLOOR BEGINS TO MOVE-
THE STONE--- SLIDING OUT-----

ROBIN! HOW?
SHHH! I'VE BROUGHT A DUMMY TO TAKE YOUR PLACE--

THE DUMMY IS PLACED ON THE BUNK---
THAT SHOULD KEEP THE GUARDS FOOLED FOR A WHILE- THEY'LL THINK I'M SLEEPING!

WHY, IT'S A SEWER-- HOW DID YOU FIND OUT ABOUT IT?
I READ YOU WERE PLACED IN THE OLD CELL BLOCK HOUSE, BECAUSE THE SEWER BLOCKS WERE BEING REMODELLED. I WENT TO THE LIBRARY AND LOOKED UP SOME OLD MAPS AND FOUND THAT THIS OLD ABANDONED SEWER RAN PARALLEL WITH YOUR CELL. I HAVE YOUR COSTUME WITH ME!

INSTANTS LATER---BRUCE WAYNE BECOMES HIS OTHER DYNAMIC SELF- THE BATMAN!
WHERE TO NOW?
TO DELMAR'S APARTMENT TO LOOK FOR EVIDENCE- THE BATMAN IS GOING TO FIND THE PROOF THAT WILL FREE BRUCE WAYNE!

THIS IS IT! AND FROM THAT CAR OVER THERE, I'D SAY SOMEONE ELSE WAS HERE BEFORE US!

WE CAN'T FIND IT!
THEN KEEP LOOKING! DELMAR HID THOSE RECORDS SOME PLACE! THOSE RECORDS WOULD BLAST ME RIGHT INTO A PRISON CELL, IF THE COPPERS SHOULD FIND THEM!

HILL--YOU'RE LOOKING FOR THE RECORDS, TOO?? COINCIDENCE, ISN'T IT?
THE BATMAN!

THE WINNING TEAM SWEEPS INTO ACTION!
LET'S SEE HOW YOU CAN FIGHT!
HERE'S A LITTLE TREATMENT FOR A HEAD-ACHE!
RIGHT ON THE OLD BUTTON!
THE MISSING RECORDS!
HE HAD IT HIDDEN IN THE TABLE LEG! LOOKS LIKE YOUR NUMBER'S UP, HILL!
NOT YET, IT ISN'T! ONE MOVE, AND I'LL BLOW THIS BRAT'S HEAD OFF!
ACTING SMART, EH BATMAN? JOE, AL-- GET UP!
DON'T WORRY ABOUT ME, BATMAN!
SORRY, ROBIN! YOU'RE WORTH MUCH MORE TO ME THAN THOSE RECORDS-- OKAY, HILL! YOU WIN!
10

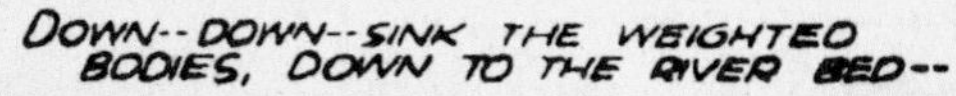

WEASEL HAS JUST COME OUT OF THE COMA, AS HIS NURSE RACES TO CALL THE DOCTOR!

NOW...NOW I REMEMBER--HILL...HILL DOUBLE-CROSSED ME...I REMEMBER...WHAT'S THIS?

OH, YEAH--? WE'LL SEE ABOUT THAT--I'M GONNA DIE ANYWAY-BUT I'LL SHOW HILL WHAT IT MEANS TO DOUBLE-CROSS ME--I GOTTA GET AWAY!

BRUCE WAYNE GOES ON TRIAL FOR THE MURDER OF HORATIO DELMAR

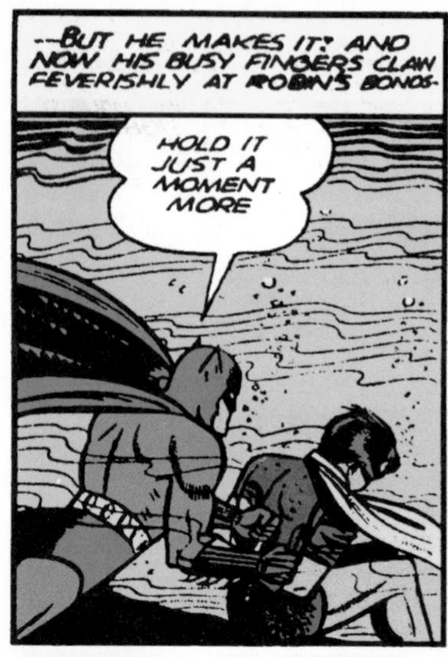

I SAY THAT BRUCE WAYNE PROVED HIS GUILT BY BREAKING JAIL AND--

BRUCE WAYNE IS NOT GUILTY! HERE'S THE MAN WHO CAN TELL YOU WHO KILLED HORATIO DELMAR---HIS GANG CHIEF!

YES-- AND JUST AS EASY FOR YOU TO SLANDER A DEAD MAN'S NAME, BECAUSE HE CANNOT DEFEND HIMSELF! BATMAN, I ACCUSE YOU OF AIDING AND ABETTING BRUCE WAYNE TO ESCAPE JAIL--AND ATTEMPTING TO MURDER A COURT WITNESS-- AND OBSTRUCTING JUSTICE WITH YOUR INFERNAL MEDDLING AND YOUR ABSURD CRIME THEORIES! POLICE, ARREST THIS MAN!

WAIT!

COMMISSIONER GORDON APPEALS TO THE JURY-

I SPEAK FOR THE BATMAN-- THE FRIEND OF THE PEOPLE! YES--- HE WORKS "OUTSIDE THE LAW," AS YOU CALL IT, BUT THE LEGAL DEVICES THAT HAMPER US ARE HURDLED BY THIS CRIME-FIGHTER SO HE MAY BRING THESE MEN OF EVIL TO JUSTICE. THE EMINENT DISTRICT ATTORNEY CALLS HIM A MEDDLER WITH A THEORY---

WASHINGTON, THE WRIGHT BROTHERS, LINCOLN, EDISON AND OTHERS. THEY WERE "MEDDLERS," TOO--WHO PROVED THEIR THEORIES. THEY MADE SACRIFICES SO THAT WE MIGHT ENJOY THE SECURITY AND COMFORT WE DO. THE BATMAN HAS DONE THAT, TOO!

THIS MAN WHO HAS SAVED A NATION'S GOLD RESERVE, FOUGHT FIFTH COLUMNISTS AND SABOTEURS, BEATEN THE JOKER, THE PUPPET MASTER, AND OTHER CRIME GENIUSES.

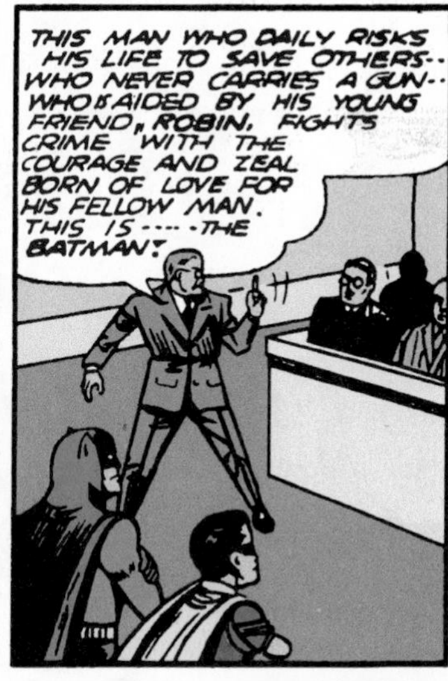
THIS MAN WHO DAILY RISKS HIS LIFE TO SAVE OTHERS-- WHO NEVER CARRIES A GUN-- WHO IS AIDED BY HIS YOUNG FRIEND, ROBIN, FIGHTS CRIME WITH THE COURAGE AND ZEAL BORN OF LOVE FOR HIS FELLOW MAN. THIS IS-----THE BATMAN!

PERHAPS THIS COMES A LITTLE LATE, BUT I, THE POLICE COMMISSIONER OF GOTHAM CITY, APPOINT YOU AN HONORARY MEMBER OF THE POLICE DEPARTMENT! FROM NOW ON, YOU WORK HAND IN HAND WITH THE POLICE!
THANK YOU, SIR! I WISH NOW THAT I COULD FIND THE PROOF THAT WILL PROVE BRUCE WAYNE'S INNOCENCE!

THEN A VOICE CUTS IN--
SURE HE'S INNOCENT! I KILLED DELMAR! UNDER ORDERS FROM HILL!

WHY, YOU SQUEALING RAT---I'LL KILL YA!
YOU'RE TOO LATE--HILL----- I'M DYING NOW, BUT AT LEAST I'M EVEN--- YOU----
13

LATER---
THE BATMAN HELPED ME ESCAPE-HE KEPT ME IN A HIDEOUT UNTIL I WAS CLEARED!
YES, I KNOW. HE TOLD ME ABOUT IT JUST BEFORE HE AND ROBIN LEFT!

YOU'RE RIGHT! I GUESS THE LIFE OF BRUCE WAYNE DOES DEPEND QUITE A BIT ON THE EXISTENCE OF THE BATMAN!

JUSTICE LEAGUE OF AMERICA: THE SILVER AGE VOL. 1

JUSTICE LEAGUE OF AMERICA: THE SILVER AGE VOL. 2

GREEN LANTERN: THE SILVER AGE VOL. 1

THE GOLDEN AGE

BATMAN

VOLUME TWO